HEALTH FOR HUMAN EFFECTIVENESS

Albert E. Bedworth

Bureau of School Health Education and Services
The University of the State of New York
The State Education Department
Emeritus

David A. Bedworth

State University College, Plattsburgh, New York

PRENTICE-HALL, INC., ENGLEWOOD CLIFFS, NEW JERSEY 07632

Library of Congress Cataloging in Publication Data

BEDWORTH, ALBERT E.
  Health for human effectiveness.

  Includes bibliographical references and index.
  1. Health. I. Bedworth, David A. II. Title.
RA776.B4   613   81-17736
ISBN 0-13-385500-7   AACR2

Printed in the United States of America

10 9 8 7 6 5 4 3 2 1

ISBN 0-13-385500-7

Prentice-Hall International, Inc., *London*
Prentice-Hall of Australia Pty. Limited, *Sydney*
Prentice-Hall of Canada, Ltd., *Toronto*
Prentice-Hall of India Private Limited, *New Delhi*
Prentice-Hall of Japan, Inc., *Tokyo*
Prentice-Hall of Southeast Asia Pte. Ltd., *Singapore*
Whitehall Books Limited, *Wellington, New Zealand*

This book is dedicated to those
who wish to know themselves rather than
dwell on themselves,
and who wish to be a part of eternity
rather than merely an observer of eternity.

contents

preface

Health for Human Effectiveness is a college text that describes pertinent health issues confronting each of us and our society. The book is designed to provide college students with accurate and timely health information for making appropriate personal health decisions and for becoming active in improving the health of society. Emphasis is placed upon the promotion and maintenance of personal and societal health and the prevention of disease, disability, and premature death.

The rapidly rising cost of health care necessitates that we find ways to avoid health hazards and unhealthful behavior, and that we become able to make use of our health care system efficiently. To achieve these ends, **Health for Human Effectiveness** treats health affairs in a holistic manner. By holistic we mean that health has three interdependent and interactional dimensions: psychological, physical, and social.

Health for Human Effectiveness is organized into four parts. Part I, Your Health Potentials, discusses the meaning of health in today's society, the factors that influence health, and the relationship of health to human effectiveness. The discussions that constitute Part I provide a sound conceptual base from which to explore the health issues presented in subsequent chapters.

Part II, Our Psychological Health, encompasses those health areas that are concerned with our intellectual and emotional development, and the principles of human behavior. Part II discusses the factors that influence personality development, our self-concept, mental and emotional health, family living and sexuality, and the significance of these topics to health behavior and interpersonal effectiveness.

Part III, Personal and Social Health Issues, includes those health areas that generally affect our biological well-being. Although each chapter emphasizes the promotion and maintenance of health, consideration is given to the role we must play in the prevention and alleviation of many health problems. Personal responsibilities relative to smoking, drinking, the use of drugs, and consumer products and services are given special consideration. The social, economic and political impact of several major health areas is discussed in detail.

Part IV, Personal Health Decisions, recognizes the vital role that each of us must take in dealing with personal health affairs, and places emphasis upon the personal and social responsibilities for solving health problems related to nutrition, infectious and noncommunicable diseases, fitness, genetic health, and safety and first aid.

   In summary, **Health for Human Effectiveness** discusses many of the traditional health problems and issues. It also includes detailed disussions of many controversial health issues, such as drug abuse, alcoholism, human sexuality, suicide, health quackery, death and dying, and genetic engineering. In addition, new areas of health concern are introduced and thoroughly discussed. These include health and politics, child abuse and neglect, criminal behavior, and adolescent pregnancy. In general, health issues that are emphasized are those in which each of us can do something about through improved personal health behavior, and by becoming active in improving social health actions.

   Finally, we would be remiss if we did not express our gratitude and appreciation to the numerous people who critiqued various aspects of the manuscript and provided constructive suggestions for its improvement. We especially want to thank the college students who read parts of the manuscript and provided us with their insight into the relevance of many sections. And a special recognition is necessary for Margaret (Jackie) Stafford who typed the manuscript for this important book.

   Graphic illustrations were created by Bruce and Rebecca Babbit.

PART

I

your health
potentials

PROLOGUE
THE MEANING AND
SIGNIFICANCE OF HEALTH

Health is human effectiveness; it is the qualifying factor for living. The healthier we are, the greater our potential for effectiveness. However, with a state of health, our effectiveness is not automatic—only possible.

Ill health is a significant factor that reduces our effectiveness. We will from time to time contract mild or severe illnesses that interfere with our functioning abilities, and each of us will eventually die as a result of disease or from some form of dysfunctioning of the body or a part of the body. However, what is vitally important for us to be concerned about is the *unnecessary* suffering and *premature* deaths resulting from *preventable* health problems.

Many of our health problems result from our failure to develop our full health potentials. These failures are due to a lack of adequate health knowledge, the acquisition of misinformation about health matters, the development of hazardous lifestyles, inadequate health care facilities or their unavailability, and misdirected health efforts by governments or other social institutions. Therefore, it is the unnecessary health problems and diseases with which we must be concerned; and it is these that we need to become knowledgeable about if we are to significantly reduce their incidences.

As Ward and Dubos have stated, humanity inherits two worlds: "One is the natural world of plants and animals, of soils and airs and waters . . ." The other is the created world of social institutions and artifacts used . . . "to fashion an environment obedient to human purposes and direction."*

Ironically, the world that we have created for ourselves is not always "obedient," and it is not always directed toward achieving human purposes within the society. Too frequently this created world has resulted in the development of numerous health hazards that threaten human functioning and human life.

The discovery or development of new and more powerful drugs, expanded industrialization, the inauguration of motorized transportation, the development of numerous household appliances and products, to name a few, have all made life easier. However, these, and others, have also presented us with new and more complex health hazards, and this in turn has made it vital that we become more informed about health matters so that we can behave more intelligently to avoid these hazards and to live more fully.

Each year, nearly 2 million people die in the United States from a variety of causes. All too many of these deaths are premature since they frequently result from a lack of accurate health knowledge, personal decisions based upon health misconceptions, and environmental hazards created by society. The tragedy is that these conditions could be improved with present technology and better health education. For example, in 1900, the leading causes of death among the American people were influenza and pneumonia, and tuberculosis—diseases over which medicine, at the time, had little control. Today, influenza and pneumonia have been reduced to the fifth leading cause of death, accounting for slightly

*Ward, Barbara and Rene Dubos, *Only One Earth*, W. W. Norton and Co., Inc. New York, 1972, p. 1.

under 3 percent of the deaths for all causes. Tuberculosis does not appear at all among the fifteen leading causes of death. In 1900, cardiovascular diseases ranked fourth as a cause of death while today it ranks first, accounting for more than 38 percent of the total annual deaths in America for all causes. In 1900, cancer ranked eighth as a cause of death while today it ranks second, accounting for more than 19 percent of all annual deaths. During this same period of time, deaths due to accidents moved from seventh to fourth place as a cause of death. Today, only one group of communicable diseases, influenza and pneumonia, remains within the fifteen leading causes of death. The four leading causes of death—cardiovascular diseases, cancer, stroke, and accidents—account for more than 72 percent of our annual deaths.

These shifts in the cause of death indicate that our current major health problems are created by us through the way we live. Any significant reductions in the incidence of current health problems will come about mainly through (1) a reduction of unhealthful behavior and (2) improved environments in which to live. Both of these measures take relatively long periods of time to achieve, and our health care system continues to be contented chiefly with treating people who become afflicted with diseases, rather than directing its efforts toward the development of effective preventive measures. Governments also have been slow to recognize the need to improve the environment. Although some important legislation have been enacted over the past two decades, federal agencies have often been reluctant or unable to effectively enforce these laws.

School officials have been equally slow in recognizing the urgent need to provide people with the health knowledge necessary for improving their health behavior. This is especially important because when our society fails to remove or reduce a health hazard, we must know how to avoid it or to reduce our personal level of risk from it. In addition, we need to know what to do if we fail in this endeavor.

We all have a health responsibility—a responsibility for our own health as well as that of others. Furthermore, each of us has a responsibility to see that government preserves and protects the health of its citizens and that the medical profession provides adequate services to all, regardless of profit incentives. We need to know that we don't have to get sick as often—that good health is an achievable goal for most of us most of the time; that it is more efficient to stay well than to become well; that we don't have to tolerate exorbitant medical, hospital, and drug prices; and, above all, that we can do something to change our nation's priorities and attitudes towards health care.

All of us inherit physical and psychological potentials for a degree and quality of health that is uniquely ours. Our physical potentials provide us with unique abilities to perform simple to complex physical tasks, while our psychological potentials enable us to think, learn, create, initiate, respond, express feelings and emotions, and control the expressions of our physical potentials. We are not a simple composite of individual parts functioning autonomously. Living is characterized not by a heart-beat, a breath, or a muscular movement, but by what results from these in terms of our effectiveness.

The development of the concept of health probably began with the first humans, although they may not have been able to verbalize it or to describe it. It is likely that if they did not feel sick or if they had no pain or if they were able to do the things necessary for them to survive, such as gather food, they thought they were healthy. But the modern view of health is different. In 1947, the World Health Organization (WHO) introduced a new concept of health: the idea that health is complete physical, mental, and social *well-being,* not merely the absence of disease or infirmity. By 1953, a President's Committee introduced the idea of *wellness.* The emphasis was placed on achieving the highest level of wellness possible. In 1964, the School Health Education Study emphasized that health is a *quality* of life. All of these concepts imply a *potential* rather than an *achievement.* It is now time for us to think of health in terms of *effectiveness,* of the dynamism of the individual, of what we are accomplishing within the scope of our inherited potentials and the environmental constraints that exist.

1

perspectives
on your health

HISTORICAL BASES OF HEALTH

Introduction

Concepts about health and how to achieve it evolved over the centuries within the cultures that were developing. However, it was not until travel and intercultural communications came into being that knowledge about health, disease, and medicine were interchanged. Probably the initial impetus for this interchange was the development of written language, approximately 3000 B.C. However, for nearly 2000 years very little exchange of information took place.

A turning point in early health care occurred about 1300 B.C. during the time of Asclepius.* Legendary accounts indicate that he was born a human but was the son of the god Apollo and the goddess Coronis. Asclepius is said to have had two daughters, Hygeia and Panakeia. Hygeia was the goddess of health who, "taught the Greeks that they could be healthy if they lived according to reason with moderation in all forms of behavior."[1] Thus was born the concept of *preventive medicine.* On the other hand, Panakeia (Panacea), the goddess of healing, exemplifies the search for a universal cure-all, representing the *restorative* aspects of medical practice. This search for a medical *panacea* has continued relentlessly throughout the history of humanity.

Many early civilizations made contributions to the health of their people. Noteworthy were the Romans, in sanitary engineering; the Arabs in medicines and surgery; the Egyptians in sanitation, pharmacy and surgery; and the Hebrews in sanitation.

The physician's symbol, the *caduceus,* signifies the association of current medicine with its ancient beginnings. The caduceus contains two snakes coiled around a staff that is crowned by two outstretched wings. The caduceus is the staff of Hermes, (Figure 1-1) or Mercury, the god of science and the conductor of the dead to Hades. Hermes' swiftness is symbolized by the winged sandals and winged hat he wears, while the caduceus he carries is his symbol of magical healing power.

Health in the Middle Ages

The Dark Ages, as they are sometimes called, extended from about the sixth to the fourteenth century. This period in history was marked by wars, famines, pestilence, disease, and early death. It has been estimated that the average life expectancy at birth could not have been more than eight years.[2]

Historians now generally agree that the Middle Ages were not as "dark" as previously thought. There was, at this time, the founding of great universities and the establishment of Christianity as one of the chief religions of the Western World.[3] But from a health point of view, much of what had been learned from the Romans, Greeks, Hebrews, and Arabs about sanitation and disease control was forgotten, ignored, or ineffective. Nevertheless, one of the most famous of the medical schools of the times, the University of Salerno, was established in 1150. This university was founded in honor of Roger of Salerno who composed

*Some accounts use the spelling as Esculapius or Asclepios.

Figure 1-1:
Caduceus or Physician's Herald

What Do the Snakes Symbolize?

the famous book of rules for healthful living *(Regimen Sanitatis)*. Historians view Roger of Salerno as the "Father of Hygiene."

During these early times, the concept developed that disease was caused and spread by visible filth; a concept that persists to some extent today. For example, the bubonic plague ravaged Europe for centuries, coming to a peak in the middle 1300s, but continuing with cyclic severity until the late 1600s. The physicians of the times thought that the black death was caused by a "corruption of the atmosphere."[4] For the most part, all of the efforts used to halt the spread of the bubonic plague were ineffective since the cause of the disease was unknown. It is estimated that more than one-half of the known world's population died of the plague. Numerically, it is thought that more than 60 million people died of the black death during this period in history.

The interest in trade, the religious pilgrimages and the lack of cleanliness and sanitation were significant contributors to the rapid spread of the plague and other diseases—cholera, leprosy, diphtheria, dysentery, and typhoid and typhus fevers.

Advances in the health sciences took place rather sporadically, being influenced chiefly by health crises. Noteworthy examples were the revival of isolation of the ill, improvements in sanitation, and the use of quarantine for the first time in 1348. However, it was not until 1383 that Marseilles passed the first

7

quarantine law and erected the first quarantine station.[5] Today, health crises still influence advances in the health sciences chiefly because they tend to bring to the general public the importance of health problems, and the people in turn, tend to demand action to curb them.

Health During the Renaissance

Historians have given the name Renaissance to the period between the middle of the fourteenth century and the early part of the seventeenth century because it literally was a time of rebirth for humanity. In western civilization the Renaissance was characterized by explorations of other continents and by developments in all aspects of human living: political, religious, and medical sciences. It was a time of Copernicus' discovery that the sun was the center of the universe around which the planets revolved (1543); Galileo's discovery of sun spots (1611); and Newton's law of gravitation (1684). Progress in medical science was exemplified by such discoveries as the clinical thermometer (1611), and the circulation of blood (1616). The microscope was also developed, which led to the discovery of microscopic organisms and minute structures of the body, such as the blood corpuscles. Finally, for the first time, scientific societies were formed for the primary purpose of finding the truth through advancement of scientific thought and investigation.

It was recognized that disease was caused by organisms rather than being a punishment for sin. By the end of the fourteenth century, many diseases were recognized as communicable, including leprosy, bubonic plague, smallpox, measles, influenza, typhus fever, typhoid fever, erysipelas, tuberculosis, diphtheria, trachoma, scabies, and impetigo.[6]

DISEASE

Definition

A *disease* is "any condition of the body or mind, acute or chronic, which interferes with the individual's ability to function effectively under ordinary environmental circumstances."[7] Both health and disease are associated with our ability to adapt to adverse environmental conditions. The greater our ability to adapt, the more likely we are to resist developing a disease state. This explains in part why some of us exposed to the same environmental factors are able to continue functioning effectively and are able to resist a disease-causing agent better than others.

Classification of Diseases

For convenience, diseases have been classified as follows:

- The *time* the disease is likely to originate in people. This also implies a causative factor. These diseases are classified as genetic, congenital, or acquired.

- The *course* that a disease generally takes: acute, subacute, or chronic. An *acute* disease is one that manifests itself relatively rapidly and possesses a relatively short duration or course. A *subacute* disease is one that has characteristics somewhere between acute and chronic. The *chronic* diseases are those characterized by a manifestation of symptoms over a long period of time.
- The *cause* of the disease. A disease caused by a microorganism is called *infectious,* while one caused by a chemical imbalance may be called *metabolic.*
- The presence or absence of symptoms or signs of lesions. If lesions (some change in a tissue or organ) are present, the disease is said to be *organic;* if there are no apparent lesions present, the disease is said to be *functional.*

Theories of Disease

Demoniac theory   According to the records that have been uncovered by archeologists, Stone Age people believed that diseases were caused by evil spirits. This belief in spirits or demons is called the *theory of animism,* or *the demoniac theory.* Essentially, primitive people thought that all things, inanimate and living, possessed a spirit. These spirits could be favorable or unfavorable. The favorable ones were worshipped while the unfavorable ones were exorcised or appeased. Health and disease were inseparably intertwined with religious beliefs for centuries.

Much of what we know about health today has been learned from our study of diseases, and ways of maintaining health are inferred from our knowledge of the cause and prevention of disease. This is not unlike the methods used by primitive people of ancient times and by those primitive societies that exist today, in that some attention was paid to ways in which diseases could be prevented.

The methods used by primitive peoples—and still used to some extent in remote areas of the world—were to wear charms and talismans and to offer sacrifices to the spirits. Treatment consisted of driving out the invading demons or allowing them to escape. If the elaborate rituals—which included dances and incantations—failed to effect a cure, the skull was occasionally perforated by rather crude surgical techniques to provide an escape route for the demons. This is called *trephining.* Archeological discoveries indicate that some of the patients miraculously survived this surgery.

Challenges to demoniac theory   It was not until after the beginning of civilization, about 3000 B.C., that people began to question the demoniac theory. Although progress was slow for many centuries, new philosophies about the cause and control of disease began to develop. For centuries, people tended to rely solely upon the writings of Aristotle. There existed throughout these early periods of our history the fear to explore new avenues, especially if they should contradict the teachings of the "masters." But the introduction of the inductive method of thinking and discovering by Francis Bacon in the 1600s stressed the need to study all of nature: plants, animals, and chemicals.

Besides Bacon, René Descartes, Galileo Galilei, William Harvey, and Isaac Newton were in the forefront of the scientific revolution during the 17th century. The Renaissance was well underway and many of the health misconceptions that dominated the thinking of people were to be gradually dispelled. However, because of the lack of rapid means of transportation and communications, significant advances in the health sciences took centuries to achieve. And, most importantly, many of these misconceptions continue to dominate the thinking of many people today, and remain important influencers of much of our current unhealthful behavior. Let us look at some of these theories beginning with a theory from ancient Greece.

Humoral theory   Hippocrates was born in 460 B.C. and has been honored as the "Father of Medicine." He is also designated as the originator of the humoral theory of disease, which is based upon the concept that the human body is composed of the four humors (liquids): blood, yellow bile, black bile, and phlegm. He advanced the theory that if these humors should become imbalanced, disease is the result. The obvious treatment was to put the humors back into balance. This was "accomplished" through bleeding the patient, a practice that was continued until the early 1900s in the United States and is still practiced in some parts of the world.

We do need to recognize, however, the close *theoretical* parallel between the humoral theory and the homeostatic concept that is generally recognized today. *Homeostasis* is essentially the tendency of an organism to maintain a physiological (chemical) equilibrium.

Miasmatic theory   The *miasmatic* concept of disease evolved during the Middle Ages. It was thought that mysterious poisons from decaying matter were carried in the atmosphere to people susceptible to them, causing illness. The miasmatic theory was finally dispelled with the development of the germ theory of disease during the nineteenth century. However, Benjamin Rush (1745–1813), a physician who was one of the signers of the Declaration of Independence, perpetuated the miasmatic concept even though he was unable to explain away the obvious communicability of such diseases as smallpox. As late as 1850, "the leading physicians still believed that environmental factors were all-important, and that a clean city meant a healthy city; they were still under the influence of Benjamin Rush and did not understand the contagious nature of disease."[8] Noah Webster wrote that there was "irrefutable proof that epidemics are a direct result of atmospheric disturbances."[9]

Germ theory   It was in 1683 that Anton van Leeuwenhoek announced his discovery of tiny "animalcules" in human secretions and excretions. His discovery of microorganisms was published by the Royal Society in England. This discovery opened a whole new world regarding the cause of disease and laid the groundwork for the beginnings of the science of bacteriology.

During the nineteenth century, the discoveries by Louis Pasteur and Robert Koch of the bacterial cause of several diseases and of putrefaction spelled the true beginnings of the sciences of immunology and bacteriology. From their work evolved the germ theory of disease, and "there is no more spectacular phenomenon in the history of medicine than the rapidity with which the germ theory of disease became accepted by the medical profession."[10]

The *germ theory* of disease established the doctrine of a specific cause (etiology). According to germ theory, "there is a single cause or pathological agent for each specific disease . . ."[11] However, as time passed and as new discoveries were made, it became apparent that a disease did not always follow an exposure to the organism and that symptoms of the same diseases in more than one person were not always identical. Furthermore, it was recognized that identical symptoms may result from a variety of causes. Thus, according to germ theory, "the characters of a disease are determined more by response of the organism as a whole than by the characteristics of the causative agent."[12]

Multifactorial theory   The *multifactorial theory* of disease emphasizes that a single factor—and only that factor—is seldom capable of causing a diseased state. This theory takes into account (1) the ability of the individual to resist the *pathologic* (disease) effects of the organism and (2) the nature of the environmental forces that exist at the moment. Essentially, disease can be explained best by recognizing the interrelationships between the total nature of the individual and the impact of the past and present environments.

The multifactorial cause of disease is explained by two hypotheses. First, a disease may result from several possible causes acting singly. That is, there may be several individual environmental factors that can cause the same diseased condition. Second, a disease may result only when several factors are present; they have a cumulative effect. Unless all causal factors are present, the disease will not result.

RESPONSIBILITIES FOR HEALTH

Personal

We all have a *fundamental* responsibility for our health. We have the primary obligation to do all that is possible to assure the attainment and maintenance of our health through appropriate behavior. In addition, we must insist that social agencies are responsive to our health needs and that they function within their capabilities and within the limitations established by law. No social institution should be allowed to be negligent, irresponsible, or incompetent when it comes to matters concerned with health. By the same token, each of us needs to become informed about health matters to be able to behave healthfully. Therefore, we need to do the following:

- become health conscious but not to the point of being obsessed with health or becoming hypochondriacs;
- become informed about health matters and apply this knowledge to our styles of living;
- become knowledgeable about health issues at the political level and become involved in influencing health legislation;
- support recognized health agencies;

- support important health education programs at both the community and school levels;
- become critical about health advertisements and learn to analyze their messages objectively;
- develop appropriate behaviors that can act as models for children.

Health Education

Through *effective* health education our life styles can be improved resulting in a decrease in the incidence of those health problems caused primarily by the way we live. It has been estimated that approximately 40 percent of the cost of medical care in the United States could be eliminated if all people acquired appropriate and timely health information and *applied this knowledge to their daily living.*

Societal

No one person or social institution is totally responsible for health since health is dependent upon a variety of interrelated and interactional forces. People give the responsibility for health, in part, to social institutions.

Governmental

The promotion and maintenance of our health is generally of little concern unless it is threatened, preventing us from achieving personal goals or pleasurable endeavors. It has only been in very recent years, as a result of the awareness that the control and treatment of disease has reached a cost level that is beyond the resources available to most people, that governments have given significant attention to promoting health and preventing diseases.

In 1969, a report from the Secretary of Health, Education, and Welfare made this urgent statement: "This nation is faced with a breakdown in the delivery of health care unless immediate concerted action is taken by Government and the private sector."[13] Thus, at least, one responsibility for health care has been indicated.

In the 1980s, we are facing severe economic crises. But this is not a reason for government to decrease its expenditure on health care. The increased costs of health care create an even greater need for government responsibility.

Costs of Health

It is important to note that our health care system continues to be more concerned with disease than with health.

More than 95 percent of our health resources are directed toward the treatment of disease and less than 5 percent toward the prevention of disease and the promotion and maintenance of health. Of the approximate $140 billion per year spent for health care during the latter part of the 1970s, more than $55 billion were spent for hospital care, more than $27 billion for physicians' fees, and about $9 billion for dentists' fees. This is compared with 1950 annual expenditures of $6.5 billion, $8.0 billion, and $3.2 billion respectively. This represents an annual increase of more than 14 percent for all health care expenditures. In the categories of expenditures, hospital costs and physicians' fees have risen at about the same rate as the total annual health care expenditures, while dentists' fees have risen more than 10 percent. In the 1980s, health costs continue to spiral with an estimated annual expenditure of over $200 billion. However, these figures are computed on actual dollars spent for health care; they do not take into account the rate of inflation.[14] Figure 1-2 illustrates these changes for a 30-year period. Figure 1-3 compares the annual health expenditures in the United States for a 50-year period, while Figure 1-4 illustrates what this means to each of us in terms of personal expenditures for health care.

THE HEALTH OF PEOPLE

Introduction

Health is the quality of our physical, psychological, and sociological functioning that enables us to deal adequately with self and others in a variety of situations.[15] Health is dynamic and functional and is a facilitator of our effectiveness. Health is never static. Generally, our health can be improved by altering our environment so that optimal promotion of inherent potentials can take place.

Figure 1-2:

Changes in Health Care Expenditures from 1950 to 1980

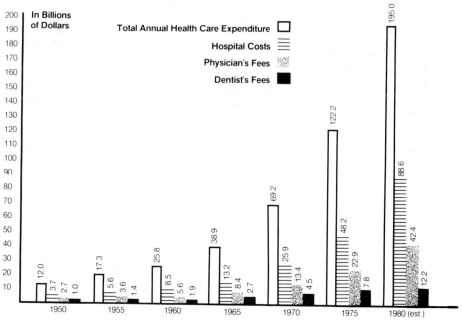

Source of Data: **Health: United States: 1976-1977,** U.S. Department of Health, Education, and Welfare.

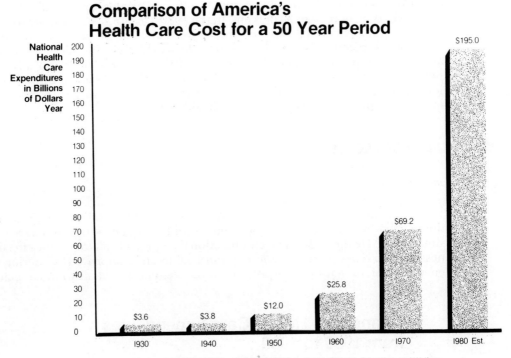

Figure 1-3:

Comparison of America's Health Care Cost for a 50 Year Period

National Health Care Expenditures in Billions of Dollars Year

Source of Data: **Health: United States, 1976-1977**, U.S. Department of Health. Education. and Welfare.

Of equal importance is the need to maintain health and the need to restore it when it fails.

Although some genetic potentials will develop automatically regardless of the quality of the environment, our ability to function effectively on the psychological and social levels requires an adequate environment and effort on our part. Each of us must be provided, from conception throughout life, with the essential ingredients for self-development. All major aspects of society must be improved in a variety of ways if health is to be promoted, and disease, disability, and premature death prevented.

Dimensions of Health

The physical dimension of health is related to our biological structures and functions. It is this dimension of health that is more likely to be observed whenever it fails to function as intended.

The psychological dimension of health manifests itself chiefly through our ability to function adequately within the complexities of our social environment. This implies that a positive self-image must be established before adequate *interpersonal* relationships can exist. This is generally expressed in terms of our mental and emotional health.

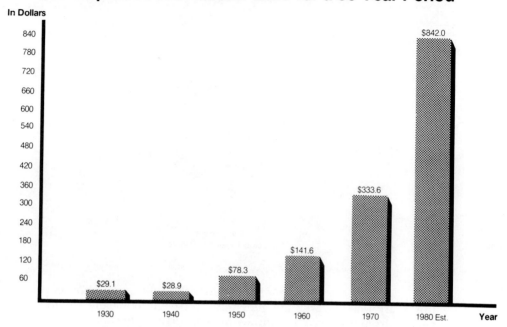

Figure 1-4:

Per Capita Cost of Health Care for a 50 Year Period

In Dollars

Source of Data: **Health: United States: 1976-1977,** U.S. Department of Health, Education and Welfare.

Mental health is our intellectual ability to function efficiently in relation to personal and social aspirations and expectations. The *mental aspect* is primarily concerned with ability to perform rationally. The *emotional aspect* lies within our ability to direct emotional responses in constructive and meaningful channels.

The sociological dimension of health manifests itself in the ability for us to deal effectively with our social environment. It is essentially our interpersonal relations.

It is obvious that when we speak of health, we are referring to the complex interactional forces among the physical, psychological, and sociological dimensions. Malfunctioning in one dimension lowers our effectiveness in the other two dimensions and, conversely, effective functioning in one dimension improves the potential effectiveness of the other two. Briefly, health *is* human effectiveness, but it is also the vehicle *for* human effectiveness. (Figure 1-5 illustrates this relationship of the dimensions of health.)

The Levels of Health

For our purposes, we can view people as falling within three broad levels of health status: (1) the primary level; (2) the intermediate level; and (3) the secondary level.

Figure 1-5:
The Dimensions of Health

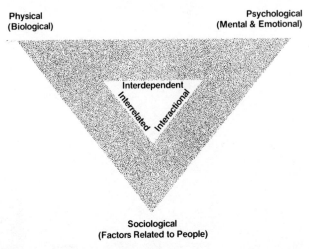

The three dimensions of health are interrelated, interactional and interdependent.

The *primary level of health* includes those of us who, for all practical purposes, are well and who are generally effective in our daily activities. However, we may from time to time contract minor, correctable conditions and be ineffective for short periods of time as a result of acute illnesses or injuries; but we generally regain our normal health spontaneously or with little medical assistance.

The *intermediate level of health* includes those of us who have contracted or developed a disease condition that interferes with our functioning ability. With proper treatment, however, we can return to a productive and effective life.[16]

The *secondary level of health* includes those of us who have developed progressive or permanent diseases or disabilities. Our effectiveness is significantly hampered because of the existence of the condition. Treatment is necessary to reduce the progress of the disease. Extensive rehabilitation procedures are usually indicated along with continuous treatment of the condition. However, if the condition is left untreated, severe inability to function or death will result.

It is important to recognize that the levels of health are intended to provide you with a convenience scale for health. Such categorizations are seldom pure for any given disease under the varieties of situations in which they can take place. Therefore, it is not possible to categorize diseases as such within these areas; but the categories can provide you with a rather general perception of the health levels that can exist.

Criteria for Health

Our health is so complex that no one index can be effectively isolated as an indicator of our overall health. This is especially true of those factors generally thought to be negative. It is, therefore, necessary to establish criteria that, in their totality, measure health in positive terms.

The standards for these criteria need to be developed. However, your answers to the following questions can be used to begin to determine your degree of health in terms of your degree of effectiveness.

- How well do you function in a variety of normal situations?
- Can you function better in a particular situation?
- Do you have significant handicaps?
- Are you expending energy needlessly to accomplish tasks?
- Are you accomplishing tasks efficiently?
- Do you possess a sense of self-worth?
- Do you have a sense of social sensitivity?
- Are you free from diseases that interfere with your functioning ability?
- Do you make judgments and choices based upon knowledge rather than feelings or emotions?
- Do you avoid self-destructive forms of behavior?
- Is your overall lifestyle both health-related and health-directed as conditions dictate?

With health viewed and measured in positive terms we may then move on to dealing with health issues effectively, dealing with their causes rather than only their symptoms, and dealing with life in its totality rather than dwelling upon the negative aspects of life that are generally far outweighed by its positive adventures.

Models of Health

Medical/clinical   When one considers the health of individuals or society, it is necessary to compare the degree of health to an established set of criteria. These criteria are often referred to as models. In Western societies, the prevailing model is the *medical model*. Essentially, proponents of the medical model advocate that health be measured and illness or disability diagnosed based upon the symptoms that are present. Treatment of the symptoms then follows. When the symptoms are reduced, the treatment is considered successful. Sometimes little or no attempt is made to eliminate the original cause of the disorder.

Traditonally, the medical model views health merely in terms of favorable reactions to medical examinations and screenings and favorable results from laboratory or other tests. Generally, little attention is given to whether or not persons are capable of reacting effectively to the environment and whether or not constructive contributions to life and to society are being made. Using the medical model, we could wrongly conclude that if a disease is not present, a state of health is.

Statistical model   *Morbidity* rates measure the level of illness in the population; *mortality* rates measure the number of deaths from various causes in the population. These rates are calculated in the following manner.

Morbidity rate = *the number of cases of a specific disease* x 100,000 divided by the total population

Mortality rate = *the number of deaths from a specific disease* x 100,000 divided by the total population

Vital statistics such as morbidity and mortality rates are relatively concrete measures of the causes of death and illness in a given population. They can be of particular value in measuring the effectiveness of a variety of treatment and/or prevention programs. For example, if the morbidity rate for a particular illness goes down, it may be assumed that a preventive program was successful. In like manner, if the morality rate goes down, a treatment program can be assumed successful.

However, the use of such measures has caused the terms "health" and "illness" to become synonymous—which they are not. According to William H. Carlyon, "Referring to health care, health personnel, and health insurance, when we mean illness care, personnel and insurance is one of the more widely embraced absurdities of our time."[17] This phenomenon has caused us to dwell upon the treatment and rehabilitation of the sick rather than emphasizing the promotion of health and the prevention of disease and disability.

Figure 1-6:

Changes in Life Expectancy in the United States for an 80 Year Period

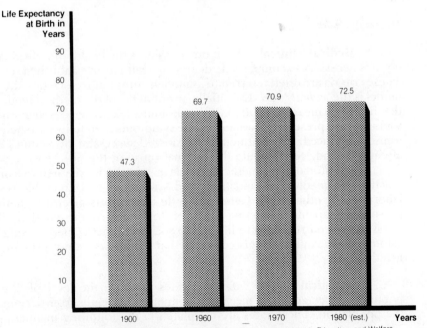

Source of Data: **Health: United States: 1976-1977,** U.S. Department of Health, Education, and Welfare.

The important concept is that vital statistics should be used with discretion and definitely not used to infer the overall health of the people. For example, if disease rates are low or nonexistent within a group of people, one might conclude that they are healthy. But the question arises: how healthy? This can be answered only by ascertaining what these people are accomplishing—how well they achieve personal and societal goals. Statistics can measure how many lives are lost, but not how many functional life-years are lost. (See Figures 1-6, 1-7, and 1-8 for the changes that have taken place in life expectancy, birth rate, and death rate in the United States in recent decades.)

Holistic.   The *holistic* view of health is predicated upon the concept that all individuals are an integrated whole, with their biological, psychological, and sociological dimensions being in constant interaction. As we have seen, any internal or external force that affects the functioning of one dimension also affects the functioning of the other two to some extent. Essentially, the holistic view of health recognizes our psychobiological integration and unity.

HUMAN EFFECTIVENESS

Influences

The following chief factors influence how effective we will be on a day to day basis:

- Our hereditary makeup
- Personal qualities that we develop
- The quality of our social and physical environments
- The quality of our health care system

Human effectiveness is variable, since we may be quite effective in one environmental setting, but ineffective when certain other environmental forces present themselves. For example, it was only during the last decade that federal legislation was enacted that required states, industries, and social institutions to identify environmental obstacles to the handicapped and to improve the environment accordingly. A result of this, for instance, is that city streets are being built with ramps at curbs for wheelchair access. These measures (the removal of obstacles) make the handicapped more effective (healthy) in spite of their handicapping condition.

Health Promotion

The promotion of health for an individual begins with the prospective parents. Before a new life is conceived, prospective parents should first evaluate the home and community environments to which the new life will be exposed

Figure 1-7:

Changes in the Birth Rate in the United States for a 70 Year Period

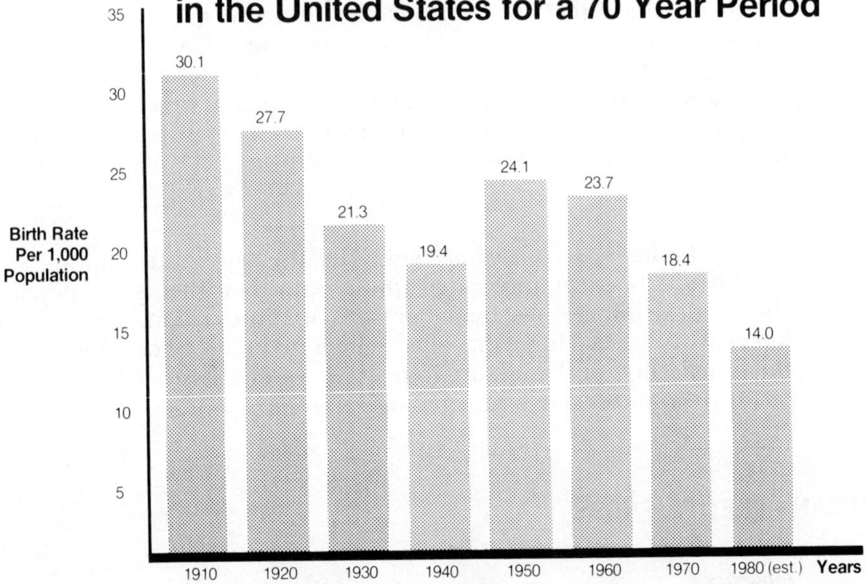

Birth Rate
Per 1,000
Population

Year	Birth Rate
1910	30.1
1920	27.7
1930	21.3
1940	19.4
1950	24.1
1960	23.7
1970	18.4
1980 (est.)	14.0

Years

Source of Data: **Health: United States: 1976-1977**, U.S. Department of Health, Education, and Welfare.

during its growing and developing years. Below are some questions that prospective parents should ask themselves:

- Will the infant and child be exposed to a healthful physical and psychological environment?
- Will the infant be provided with the basic physical, social, and psychological needs?
- Will the infant be provided with opportunities to develop innate potentials?
- How well will the prospective parents deal with the numerous crises the infant will face? The child? The adolescent?

The second responsibility of prospective parents is to evaluate their genetic endowments and to ascertain the genetic probabilities of their offspring.

- Are there genetic defects that could be transmitted to the child?
- What are the probabilities of transmitting genetic defects?
- How important are these defects to the health of the child?
- Will the home and community environments contribute to the development of *desirable* genetic potentials?

Figure 1-8:

Changes in the Death Rate in the United States for a 70 Year Period

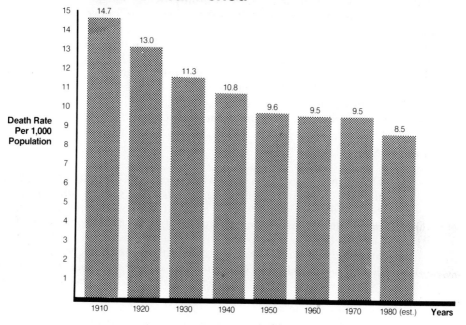

Source of Data: **Health: United States: 1976-1977,** U.S. Department of Health, Education, and Welfare.

Figure 1-9:

Controllers of the Quality of Health Promotion

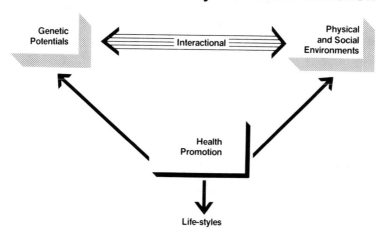

   Promotion of health is also related to the nature of the physical and social environments in which we grow, develop, and live. This means the elimination of health hazards, the provision of health care that is accessible to all of us, and that each of us takes an active part in in improving our lifestyles.

   As children grow toward maturity, they should develop a greater sense of responsibility toward self-health and toward social-health. This implies the acquisition of accurate health knowledge, the development of appropriate health attitudes and the expression of healthful behaviors. This is necessary since each child is potentially the next parent of future children and the cycle begins all over again. The quality of health of the next generation is dependent upon what we are doing during the lifetime of this generation. This is the chief determining factor of the quality of evolution of future societies.

Health Status

   The term *health status* is used when speaking about the level of health of individuals and of societies. However, health is not a static condition as we have seen, rather it fluctuates continually in quality from conception to birth to death. If health status were measured in terms of functioning abilities, we would find that it would extend from near zero (death) to maximum output.

   Among the *societal determinants* of health are environmental pollutants and unsafe consumer products. The chief pollutants in the atmosphere are particulate matter and noxious gases that are emitted mainly from all forms of transportation

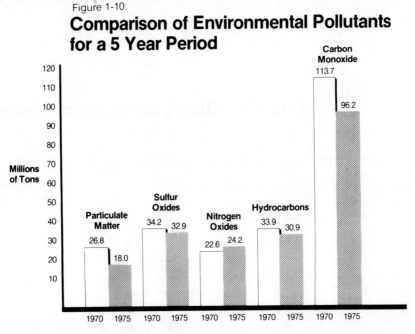

Figure 1-10:

Comparison of Environmental Pollutants for a 5 Year Period

Source of Data: **Health: United States: 1976-1977,** U.S. Department of Health, Education, and Welfare.

and industrial processes. (See Figure 1-10.) Examples of determinants of health status associated with *individual behavior* are the adverse effects of cigarette smoking, alcohol abuse, and overweight and other nutritional abuses. On the positive side, individual determinants include regular exercise regimens, prenatal care of expectant mothers, immunizations, and appropriate use of the health care system.

Optimal Health

As with other health concepts, the traditional definitions of optimal health have been stated in terms of a total absence of disease or disability, that is, stated in negative terms and made unattainable. To think of optimal health in this manner would be to consider a person unhealthy to a degree if she/he were suffering from a hangnail. Obviously, this isn't logical. Probably no person can think of a time when absolutely nothing was wrong with the body. To say that very minor disorders preclude our ability to attain optimal health is to deny the adaptibility of humankind. For our purposes, optimal health is "the highest level of functioning the individual is capable of under the existing environmental constraints."[18]

Therefore, optimal health implies effective functioning. However, it can also imply merely the *potential* to function effectively. Since we have equated health to achievement, having the potential but not achieving is a manifestation of ill-health. This is consistent with basic learning theory which states that we will always do the only thing possible within the limits of our physical inheritance, background of learning, and the forces that are acting upon us at the time.[19] This is not to say that our health behavior is predetermined, but rather, that all of our behavior is influenced by past experiences, genetic potentials, and environmental circumstances. These three factors, in other words, set limits upon our capabilities and, thus, define optimal health differently for each of us. For example, the optimal health criteria for a long distance runner is different from the criteria for a paraplegic. But both are able, under our definition, to achieve optimal health. However, the person's capabilities and environmental constraints necessitate the use of different health criteria.

Health Maintenance

Actions that direct us to adapt to changes in the environment operate on two levels: (1) the *biological level,* which is characterized by our ability to resist disease, maintain body temperature, and our total biological chemistry; and (2) the *interpretive level,* which is characterized by our need to establish feelings of self-worth, to interact socially, and to behave in ways that result in personal satisfaction, growth and actualization.[20] These two levels of action are in constant interaction, one affecting the other. When a balance does not exist, health is threatened.

Health maintenance is a sub-category of health promotion. Once optimal health is achieved through promotional activities, maintenance is necessary for the continuance of effective functioning. We should consider *health maintenance* as those measures that are taken to ensure that an optimal level of health continues.

These health maintenance measures are manifested in two forms of human behavior: (1) health-related behavior; and (2) health-directed behavior.

Health-related behavior may take the form of ensuring an adequate diet,
physical activity, rest, freedom from emotional stress—in short, those behaviors that are thought to be health maintenance activities, those normal activities of everyday life. *Health-directed behavior,* on the other hand, includes those
activities specifically designed to maintain health through the use of health
technologies—that is receiving the necessary immunizations, periodic check-
ups, and so forth. Health-directed behavior is essentially a conscious effort
on our part to do those things that will preserve, maintain, and promote our
health. For example, "watching" our diet for health reasons is engaging
in health-directed behavior. The person who stops smoking cigarettes, or
the alcoholic who receives help with his or her drinking problem, is practicing
health-directed behaviors. In the case of health-related and health-directed
behaviors our actions are influenced and motivated by our present state of
health.

The Relativity of Health

As we have seen, health is an ever-changing, dynamic condition that is
associated with a variety of established criteria. These criteria are also based upon
comparisons with other factors. None of these criteria alone can explain health;
but they do point up the fact that health is a relative phenomenon. This adds to
the complexities of understanding precisely what health is or is not. However, it
is generally agreed that health is relative to the following:

- *Biomedical standards* (the presence or absence of illness). If there is an
  absence of diagnosable disease, a state of health exists. This is chiefly an
  anatomy and physiology approach to health.
- *Statistical standards* (comparison with others). This criterion tends to
  stress norms and averages rather than individual differences. This is especially exemplified, for example, in regard to height and weight
  charts.
- *One's self,* in terms of what the individual expects and interprets as positive
  or negative health. One's effectiveness may be an important factor when
  using this criterion.
- *Environmental circumstances,* which affect one's ability to function.
- *A combination* of the above factors. Obviously, the use of any one criterion
  alone is inadequate, but when more than one is used, a more accurate
  picture of health emerges.

It is clear that our effectiveness varies from situation to situation. Indeed,
if we were to evaluate our health using the various criteria outlined above, it is
possible for us to be very healthy using one standard and very unhealthy using
another.

Table 1–1: Leading Causes of Death in the United States for All Ages

Cause of Death	Percent of Total Deaths
1. Cardiovascular diseases	37.9
2. Malignancies (cancer)	19.8
3. Stroke (cerebrovascular)	9.9
4. Accidents	5.3
5. Influenza and pneumonia	3.2
6. Diabetes mellitus	1.8
7. Cirrhosis of the liver	1.6
8. Arteriosclerosis	1.5
9. Suicide	1.4
10. Diseases of infancy	1.3
11. Homicide	1.0
12. Emphysema	0.9
13. Congenital anomalies	0.7
14. Nephritis and nephrosis	0.4
15. Septicemia and pyemia	0.3
All others	12.9

Source of Data: Vital Statistics of the United States, 1976.

OUR CHIEF HEALTH PROBLEMS

There are many criteria that may be used to identify major health problems in our society. Included in these are the number of people who die each year from specific causes. Tables 1-1 and 1-2 illustrate how the leading causes of death in the United States have changed since 1900. However, for our purposes, many other criteria should be used when identifying serious health problems. These criteria include:

- How many people die *prematurely* each year from the health problem?
- To what extent is the family unit disrupted or destroyed by the health problem?
- How much does the health problem interfere with human functioning?
- What are the economic implications of the health problem to the individual and to society?
- At what age does the onset of the health problem generally manifest itself and what is its incidence?
- What is the extent of threat of the health problem to large populations?
- To what extent is the health problem related to the cause or perpetuation of other health problems?
- To what extent can the health problem be prevented with existing resources?

Table 1–2: The Leading Causes of Death in the United States in 1900

Cause of Death	Percent of Total Deaths
1. Influenza and pneumonia	11.8
2. Tuberculosis	11.3
3. Gastritis and related conditions	8.3
4. Cardiovascular diseases	8.0
5. Stroke (cerebrovascular)	6.2
6. Chronic nephritis	5.2
7. Accidents	4.2
8. Malignancies (cancer)	3.7
9. Diseases of infancy	3.6
10. Diphtheria	2.3
11. Simple meningitis	2.0
12. Typhoid and paratyphoid	2.0
13. All other causes	31.7

Source of Data: *Facts of Life and Death*, U.S. Dep't. of Health, Education, and Welfare, DHEW Publication No. (PHS) 79–1222, p. 31.

Society's Attitudes

As alluded to earlier, there has been a significant shift in what society perceives as our major health problems. This shift is essentially from the communicable diseases that resulted in death to the chronic and degenerative diseases, and to health problems related to social disruption (such as alcohol abuse and criminal behavior). Generally, the number of people who die from the chronic and degenerative diseases is the basic criterion used in designating these as major health problems. However, many authorities consider criteria such as social disruption, incapacitation, and economic drain, as well as death rates for identifying a major health problem. For example, a little more than a decade ago, the 37th American Health Assembly met to consider "The Health of Americans." They cited as "urgent health problems" poverty, overpopulation, the aged, destructive behavior, accidents, obesity, indolence, smoking, and alcoholism and drug abuse.[21]

Regardless of the criteria that are used to determine what constitutes a major health problem, we know that many that exist today need not be as extensive as they are. We possess the technology and the knowledge to make significant reductions in their incidence and prevalence. However, since most of these health problems are "self-induced," that is, they result from improper living patterns of individuals, there is a need to provide the masses of people with the health knowledge necessary to change their lifestyles accordingly.

Availability of Health Care

Our health-directed behavior is significantly influenced by the availability and accessibility of health personnel and facilities. Although some effort has been made by the federal government over the past three decades to ensure an adequate distribution of health care facilities and personnel, large gaps remain within the health care system. Physicians, dentists, nurses, and other health workers are generally concentrated in metropolitan areas.[22] There has been no significant change in this situation since the beginning of civilization. More importantly, there have been no effective efforts by governments to bring adequate health care to the sparsely populated areas of the nation. The revered country doctor is essentially a myth, while rural health clinics are, for all practical purposes, nonexistent.

Moreover, those health personnel who deal in education and prevention make up a disproportionately low number of health professionals, reflecting the treatment and rehabilitation preoccupation of the health care system. As Milio points out, of the more than 4 million health workers in the United States, "those personnel whose task emphasis is counseling and education of ill or healthy consumers comprise the smallest proportion, less than 5 percent. . . . these include social workers, health educators, and dieticians."[23]

Human suffering and the needless loss of lives could be reduced significantly if the health care system were improved and health facilities and personnel were more accessible to the people who need them most. Senator Edward Kennedy, as chairman of the Senate Sub-committee on Health expressed great concern in this regard when he stated:

> I am shocked to find that we in America have created a health care system that can be so callous to human suffering, so intent on high salaries and profits, and so unconcerned for the needs of our people. . . . Our system especially victimizes Americans whose age, health, or low income leaves them less able to fight their way into the health care system.[24]

Certain segments of the health care system persist in protecting their veil of mysticism and insist that individuals, especially the general public, are incapable of learning or understanding the intricacies of health. Historically, it *was* possible and palatable for people to accept this philosophy, and most did. This was the time of the family physician or country doctor; it was a time when medical fees were in line with the general standard of living of the masses of people—and even a time when the physician was willing to make house calls and to wait some time before receiving payment for services. People were instructed by the family physician about what to do for their ills and were allowed to stay at home to recover. The physician even returned on a daily or less frequent basis to look in on the patient. True, the recovery rate under these circumstances may not have been as high as it is today for similar illnesses but, at least, it was possible to meet medical expenses.

Today, it is virtually impossible to obtain a house call from a physician or an office appointment in an emergency. The patient is nearly always referred to the emergency room of a hospital to be treated by whomever happens to be on duty that day. Physicians are reluctant to allow patients to recover at home and almost never provide the patient with clear explanations of his or her condition, the nature of the treatment prescribed, or other information pertinent to the illness. As a result, people must carry adequate health insurance, be prepared to learn little about any illness, be ready to spend some time in a hospital if their illness is at all serious, and be prepared to pay exorbitant prices for hospital care, drugs, and other therapeutic measures.

All of this has added to the enormous increases in our health care costs —an increase that is now out of reach of most of us and will soon be out of reach of insurance companies that cover the bulk of the people. For example, physicians' fees have gone from an annual average of $2.7 billion in 1950 to an estimated $42.4 billion in 1980. Health care costs in the United States are nearly 10 percent of the gross national product (GNP). Historically, medical care prices have increased at a greater rate than the registered total Consumer Price Index: medical costs have increased approximately 3.5 times as compared with the Consumer Price Index of approximately 2.5 times.

Patient/Physician Relationships

As the American public has become increasingly conscious of their rights as health consumers in recent years, there has been a corresponding increase in their demands for quality medical care. No longer do many people accept without question what their physician says or does as gospel. Now we *should* expect adequate explanations about our health and high quality care from our physicians and, indeed, demand an increased role in the maintenance of our health. As Milio has stated, "Efforts have been made to make explicit the rights of patients, including the right to know the alternatives available and their likely consequences; to give or refuse consent; to have access to information about themselves and their treatment, and control over the disclosure of that information to outsiders."[25] The demands of patients as consumers extend from seeking a second opinion to the demand for generic rather than brand named drugs to the choice of whether to be kept alive or being allowed to die.

We have been caught up in a tradition of waiting until something goes wrong before seeking the advice of a physician or of making use of other resources in the health care system. If this practice continues, we are likely to see only insignificant reductions in our health problems, since most major health issues are caused by or associated with inappropriate individual life styles. The medical community must begin to take a closer look at its own practices and begin to incorporate an expanded educational and preventive component into its programs.

Health Problems Created By People

As communicable diseases have been conquered by medical science, the major health problems now are such noncommunicable conditions as lung cancer, emphysema, skin cancer, cervical cancer, accidents, heart diseases, hypertension, and others. All of these could be prevented or significantly reduced in numbers if people would moderate their unhealthful behavior.

With the advancement of technology and an ever-demanding population has come the development of products and industry that benefit humankind on the one hand, but adversely affect the quality of life on the other hand. The by-products of industrialization are air and water pollution in chemical form, thermal pollution from nuclear powered generators, the exposure of the worker to hazardous substances and noise on the job, and overpopulation in our urban areas. Although laws have been enacted to minimize these conditions, we will be faced with some very difficult choices in the future—choices involving our willing-

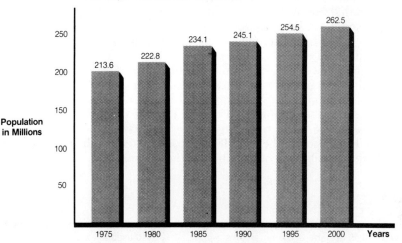

Figure 1-11

Expected Changes in the Population of the United States

Population in Millions

Year	Population
1975	213.6
1980	222.8
1985	234.1
1990	245.1
1995	254.5
2000	262.5

Years

Source of Data: **Health: United States: 1976-1977**, U.S. Department of Health, Education, and Welfare

ness to endure hardship, to defer wealth and comfort so that the next generation will be able to live effectively with a minimum amount of adversity. (Figure 1-11 illustrates the changes in the population of the United States since 1975.)

The growth in America's population alone will present problems vital to survival including those related to the food supply, increased industrialization with all of its related hazards, housing, and the like. Important health-related questions arise: Should farm land be used for industry or for growing food? What are the consequences of either choice on the economy, the health of the people, the standard of living, comfort, and convenience? To adequately answer these questions, there must be careful planning and determination of the affects over a short- and long-term period of time. It is conceivable that people are quite capable of their own annihilation as well as the development of a way of life free of unnecessary suffering with each individual provided with the opportunity to achieve the highest level of health possible.

Unnecessary Illness and Death

The incidence of lung cancer, the leading cause of death from cancer in men, is approximately 117,000 new cases in the United States and 101,000 deaths from it each year. The chief cause of lung cancer is cigarette smoking. It is estimated that 80 to 90 percent of lung cancers could be prevented if we simply convince youth not to start smoking. If cigarette smoking were eliminated, lung cancer would become a relatively rare disease. Incidentally, as a result of more girls and women smoking in recent years, the incidence of lung cancer for women is following the same pattern as for men.

Obesity is one of America's major nutritional problems and is associated with cardiovascular diseases, America's leading cause of death. Millions of dollars are spent each year on a variety of fad diets, none of which has been shown to be effective in overcoming obesity over a long period of time. We need to understand that obesity is caused from over-eating, and that crash diets are ineffective and some can be dangerous.

Another example of a health area that needs to be mentioned, one that is still haunted with stigmas, is the whole area of genetic defects. Enormous advances have been made in molecular biology in the past 20 or so years. As a result, many of the genetic disorders can be prevented through genetic screening and counseling of high risk populations. Through genetic screening, carriers can be detected and counselled on the risks of their children being born with the disease. Also, it is possible to monitor the development of the fetus to determine whether or not it is healthy. If a disease is detected, the parents can be counselled on the possibilities of terminating the pregnancy.

GLOSSARY

Acute: Sudden onset and usually of short duration.

Caduceus: Staff of Hermes; the physician's symbol.

Chronic: Of long duration, usually progressive.

Communicable: A disease that can be transmitted from person to person (or organism to organism).

Disease: Any interference with the ability to function effectively; usually used in conjunction with specific pathological conditions.

Ecological: Pertaining to the interaction of people with their environment.

Epidemiology: The science that is concerned with the nature of disease among groups of people.

Etiology: The causation of disease.

Extrinsic: Outside the body; chiefly, environmental.

Functional: A dysfunction with no apparent alteration in tissues of the body.

Growth: The process whereby the body increases in size.

Health: The quality of the individual that makes it possible to function effectively.

Health directed: A conscious effort to behave more healthfully.

Health-related: Any behavior that can affect one's health.

Health status: The general level of one's health at a given time and under specific circumstances.

Holistic: The functional interrelationship of all parts of the person: physical, psychological, and social.

Homeostasis: The chemical equilibrium of the body; also used to indicate psychological balance.

Hypochondriac: A person who is preoccupied with illnesses and their symptoms and who applies them to self; a neurosis.

Infectious: A disease that is caused by a microorganism; it may be communicable.

Intrinsic: Within the individual.

Lesion: A break in the cellular integrity of a tissue.

Maturation: The process of development to full effectiveness of cells, tissues, organs, systems, or the person in general.

Mental Health: The quality of one's psychological dimension of health which makes it possible to function effectively with self and others.

Morbidity: Refers to illness.

Mortality: Refers to death.

Organic: A dysfunction caused by a change in tissues.

Panacea: A cure-all.

Pathologic: Refers to a diseased condition.

Subacute: A disease with characteristics of acute and chronic.

Trephine: A small crown saw used in surgery.

Trephining: To operate with a trephine for the purpose of cutting a small hole in the head.

SUMMARY

Our concepts of health and disease have their roots deep in the history of humanity. For thousands of years, there was little progress in people's understanding of disease (or health) until the development of written language, which made it possible for various cultures to begin to share knowledge. Our concepts of the promotion and maintenance of health probably began during the thirteenth century B.C. During these times, the practice of medicine was closely tied with religion.

The Middle Ages were characterized by epidemics, pestilence, famines, and wars. From a health point of view it was a period of darkness for humanity with many millions dying from diseases. It was also a time of advances in medicine and public health practices, at least in rudimentary form.

The Renaissance was characterized by new developments in all aspects of life. It was a time of discovery, explorations, and scientific advances never before experienced in the history of humanity. Discoveries were beginning to be made about the structure and function of the human body, the pathologic nature of disease, and the expansion of the use of drugs for therapeutic reasons.

Health has three dimensions: the physical dimension, the psychological dimension, and the social dimension. All dimensions of health are interactional, one depending upon the others for proper functioning.

The quality of one's health continually fluctuates from birth to death in terms of functioning abilities—from minimums necessary for survival to maximum output. Rather than measuring health in the traditional manner of using morbidity and mortality rates alone, we must begin to measure health in terms of an individual's functioning abilities.

Optimal health is an attainable goal when viewed as the highest level of functioning the individual is capable of under the existing environmental constraints. Optimal health is achieved through the process of health promotion and health maintenance. One's genetic potentials, past experiences, and environmental forces make optimal health different for each individual.

For each person, the forces of the internal and external environments are in constant interaction and tend to maintain a state of equilibrium. When the equilibrium is interrupted, illness is the result.

The promotion of health is a process of elevating the degree of health of an individual or of a group of people. Health promotion is influenced by two factors: the quality of the individual's genetic potentials and by the quality of the physical and social environments. The promotion and maintenance of health is primarily the responsibility of the individual. Secondarily, it is the responsibility of government and other social institutions. In this regard, the responsibility for the health of people is a cooperative endeavor between individuals and institutions.

The availability of health care facilities and personnel has improved greatly in the past three decades, but there are still deficiencies in the health care delivery system, chiefly in the form of the distribution of facilities and personnel.

The American public has begun to demand rights as patients in recent years. This is revolutionizing some aspects of patient-physician relationships. Not only must the physician become more accountable for his/her actions, but the patient is demanding an ever increasing role in the prevention and maintenance of health and the treatment of disease. The medical community must increase its functioning in the educational and preventive health spheres.

PROBLEMS FOR DISCUSSION

1. What do people need to do to improve their own health as well as the health of others?

2. List who is responsible for health, ranked in order of importance. In what ways is each responsible?

3. Why is the rising cost of health care a significant factor in turning our attention from restoring health to promoting and maintaining health?

4. Discuss how the three dimensions of health are interactional.

5. Describe what you consider health to be. List the characteristics of a healthy person. Is the presence or absence of disease important in this determination? Why or why not?

6. In what ways does a knowledge of the history of health and disease contribute to our understanding of current health problems? Current health knowledge? Current health misconceptions?

7. State at least five things that each person can do to improve the general health of people.

8. Compare the various theories of disease and show the contribution each has made to our understanding of health and disease.

9. Why is the germ theory of disease an inadequate explanation of the causation of disease?

10. Define disease. How are diseases classified?

11. Explain how human effectiveness is associated with human health. What factors influence human effectiveness? How can they be controlled?

12. Why is it important for each person to attain the highest level of health in terms of economics, human effectiveness, and social improvements?

13. Distinguish between health promotion, health maintenance, and health restoration. What are the characteristics of each?

14. Discuss the causes of America's major health problems at the turn of this century and those that are most prevalent today.

15. What are some of the responsibilities of parents in ensuring the health of the next generation?

16. Define health status. What are the important characteristics of health status according to definition?

17. How is health status related to self-sufficiency?

18. What would changes in one's outlook, attitudes, and behavior do to the incidence of health problems related to lifestyles?

19. Why are morbidity and mortality rates inadequate indicators of the status of the nation's health?

20. Distinguish between health-related and health-directed behavior.

21. What is the significance of health-related and health-directed behavior for promoting and maintaining health?

22. What is homeostasis? How is it related to individual adaptiveness and effectiveness?

23. Should health be viewed in terms of the absence of disease and infirmity or in terms of human effectiveness? Explain.

REFERENCES

1. STONE, DONALD B., LAURENCE B., O'REILLY, and JAMES D. BROWN, *Elementary School Health Education: Ecological Perspectives.* Wm. C. Brown Company Publishers, Dubuque, 1976, p. 11.
2. MEREDITH, FLORENCE L., *Hygiene.* The Blakiston Company, Philadelphia, 1946, p. 146.
3. SMITH, EMMA P., DAVID S. MUZZEY, and MINNIE LLOYD, *World History.* Ginn and Company, New York, 1952, p. 112.
4. WINSLOW, C. E. A., and GRACE T. HALLOCK, *Health Through the Ages.* Metropolitan Life Insurance Company, New York, 1949, p. 16.
5. HANLON, JOHN J., *Public Health: Administration and Practice.* The C. V. Mosby Company, St. Louis, 1974, p. 16.
6. MEREDITH, *op. cit.,* p. 147.
7. BEDWORTH, DAVID A., and ALBERT E. BEDWORTH, *Health Education: A Process for Human Effectiveness.* Harper and Row, Publishers, New York, 1978, p. 346.
8. SMILLIE, WILSON G., *Preventive Medicine and Public Health.* The Macmillan Company, New York, 1958. p. 8.
9. *Ibid.,* p. 146.
10. DUBOS, RENE, *Man Adapting.* Yale University Press, New Haven, 1971, p. 324.
11. STONE, et al, *op. cit.,* p. 14.
12. DUBOS, *op. cit.,* p. 327.
13. JONES, BOISFEUILLET (ed.), *The Health of Americans.* Prentice-Hall, Inc., Englewood Cliffs, N.J., 1970, pp. 168–169.
14. United States Department of Health, Education, and Welfare, *Health: United States,* Washington, 1976–1977, p. 344.
15. BEDWORTH and BEDWORTH, *op. cit.,* p. 5.
16. *Ibid.,* p. 34.
17. CARLYON, WILLIAM H.,"The Seven Deadly Sins of Health Educators," Annual New York State Health Education Conference, Keynote Address, October, 1977.
18. BEDWORTH, *op. cit.,* p. 351.
19. BLAIR, GLENN MYERS, "Principles of Learning," unpublished paper, 1971.
20. BEDWORTH, *op. cit.,* p. 166.
21. JONES, *op. cit.,* pp. 98–101.

22. United States Department of Health, Education, and Welfare, *op. cit.,* p. 50.

23. MILIO, NANCY, *The Care of Health In Communities.* The Macmillan Publishing Company, New York, 1975, p. 143.

24. KENNEDY, EDWARD, *In Critical Condition: The Crisis in America's Health Care,* Simon and Schuster, New York, 1972, pp. 15–16.

25. MILIO, *op. cit.*, p. 248.

PART

II

our psychological health

2

your personality and mental health

WHAT IS PERSONALITY?

Variations and Unity of the Self

Longstreth defines personality as "all those behavior patterns that distinguish one individual from another."[1] Klausmeier and Goodwin's definition is somewhat more abstract: "a construct, or concept, that indicates the uniqueness and totality of an individual as a social being."[2] Kendler recognizes the environment in his definition, and defines personality as "those organized response systems (e.g., being aggressive) that occur in a variety of situations."[3] Ruch, on the other hand, defines personality in terms of three characteristics: "(1) the individual's external appearance and behavior, or social stimulus value; (2) his inner awareness of self as a permanent organizing force in life; and (3) his particular pattern or organization of measurable traits, both 'inner' and 'outer'."[4]

Although we vary in our rates of growth and development, such characteristics as physical health, psychomotor skills, knowledge and intellectual skills, the ability to adjust to changing circumstances, the ability to constructively react to social demands, and the development of an adequate self-concept, all play significant roles in the integration of our personalities. The variation in this integration process makes each of us different from everyone else.

Nomothetic Characteristics

Each of us possesses many characteristics, both physical and mental, that make us all more-or-less alike. Our gender; physical structure; our drives for food, air, water, and other basic needs; the desire for love, sex, and the like may be described as *nomothetic characteristics.* It is important for us to have many similar physical and psychological characteristics. These enable us to establish and maintain constructive interpersonal relationships, which facilitate adequate personality integration. However, it is equally important for us to be unique.

Idiographic Characteristics

Our genetic potentials and their development, the way we are reared by our parents, the quality of the education we have received, our interaction with our peers, and our physical development, interact resulting in each of us having unique qualities. The qualities that make each of us different from everyone else are known as *idiographic* characteristics.

Our physical, emotional, social, and intellectual development influence the way we view ourselves and influence the way others view us. This development of our self-concept significantly influences our ability to function effectively in society. Moreover, our differences enable and cause us to deal with everyday situations uniquely. The ways in which we deal with stress, overcome frustration, function within social restrictions, and deal with moral issues are different for each of us.

Genetic Factors in Development

Our hereditary characteristics are strongly manifested in our physical attributes and in our potential for growth and development. Because of the complex interaction of hereditary potentials with environmental factors, it is very difficult to identify which qualities of our personality are dependent upon genetics and which are controlled by and developed as a result of environmental forces. This question of "nature vs. nurture" has been studied by many researchers. It is hypothesized that many genetic potentials will never be manifested unless there is appropriate environmental stimuli. Skinner speculates that "genetic endowment is nothing until it has been exposed to the environment...."[5]

Heredity seems to provide personality potentials—guidelines as to how we will respond or are able to respond to environmental stimuli. To a large extent, hereditary potentials are the dependent variables falling prey to the many independent variables of the environment. On the other hand, our genetic endowments allow us to alter the environment so as to compliment the various attributes of our personalities.

Environmental Factors in Development

There seems to be little doubt that until we are able to identify those human traits that are purely genetic, the nature vs. nurture controversy will continue. But as we are confident that heredity plays a distinct role in setting guideposts for the development of our personality so too are we equally confident that environmental factors play at least an equally distinctive role in our development as social beings. In the final analysis, the development of the personality becomes meaningless when separated from the social context.

The impact of environment upon personality is extremely complex. Not only must the prenatal environment be considered (the health of the mother, as well as the exposure of the fetus to drugs, disease, and other potential hazards), but also such factors as the competence of the parents as parents, socioeconomic status, race, living conditions, climate, and cultural stimulation. All these factors and more, in combination with hereditary potentials, have an impact on the maturation process. It is when our ability to cope with the variety of environmental forces is interrupted that inappropriate personality characteristics result—which in turn hinder our future ability to function. When we are able to function effectively in the face of environmental challenges, our personality develops toward maturity and we approach actualization ... becoming truly a human being.

PERSONAL INSIGHTS

Behavioral Make-up

Our behavior is the manner in which we react to social stimuli, inner needs, or a combination of these. Behavior may be the result of innate determinants, such as reflex actions; this is *invariable behavior.* It may be a nonreflex but unconscious act; this is *automatic behavior.* Or it may be a conscious, calculated reaction that results from experience; this is *variable behavior.* Behavior may be internal (thinking, feeling) or external (action). External behavior can be observed by others, but the stimuli that make it happen may not be readily apparent. It is possible, however, to infer internal behavior or motivation from observable behavior.

Mental health behavior is related to the actions we take to promote our effectiveness as it is associated with psychosocial achievements. In terms of our mental health, we are concerned with behavior as a means of adjustment to life's activities. Adjustment may mean behavior necessary to change our environment to one more compatible with our goal-achievement. On the other hand, adjustment may mean a change in us to the extent that we are able to deal more effectively with our environment. This latter change is also referred to as adaptation, or *adaptive behavior*. For adaptive behavior to be successful, it is usually necessary for us to possess personal insights into our capabilities, values, and other factors related to our *self-concept*. The more accurate our self-concept is, the more likely we will be able to make effective adjustments to life's situations. Our *self-concept* is essentially what we believe we are. Some psychologists believe that the self-concept is important for determining one's immediate behavior and for guiding the person toward further personality development.

Self-understanding

Our self-concept is formed on the basis of our knowledge of ourselves. This knowledge may or may not be accurate. It may have been acquired from the false impressions or interpretations from past experiences, especially those related to other people and to perceived successes and failures. *Self-understanding* is characterized by an accurate knowledge of our capabilities, feelings, motivations, and total behavior. It can be acquired through personal self-analysis.

Self-analysis (also called *autognosis*) is a process used in the psychoanalytic method which consists of guiding a person to self-understanding by revealing to him/her the reasons for various behaviors as determined by self-confessions. This is usually applied to people who are seeking help for mental symptoms, but a person can also gain greater self-insight by applying self-analysis without the aid of others.

Introspection is a technique we all use from time to time to help us understand our feelings and actions. *Introspection* is simply a process of examining our own thoughts and feelings and acquiring an understanding of the reasons for them. The chief factor that we must consider when attempting to acquire a better self-understanding is that we are unaware of the unconscious processes that also impact upon our behavior. Therefore, self-understanding is limited to our ability to comprehend what we can consciously observe about ourselves. However, this can be an important factor in promoting and maintaining our mental health.

Values

According to Skinner there are two kinds of knowledge, one of fact and the other of value.[6] However, facts and values are not necessarily mutually exclusive, for facts influence our values. *Values* are the worth we place upon things that in turn affect our actions. Values provide us with a unifying philosophy of life. The more valuable we perceive something to be, the more important a place it takes in our lives. We learn values, or at least, the basis for them, very early in life.

Personal values are also established as a result of the presence of cultural values.[7] A *cultural value* is "a widely held belief or sentiment that some activities, relationships, feelings or goals are important to the community's identity or well being."[8] What our society expects of us is very often integrally related to the values we adopt. Not all cultural values; however, are universally applied resulting in personal and social conflict.

Social experiences have the greatest impact upon the establishment of our value system. These social experiences are related to the *significant others* with whom we are in frequent contact, but also those who enter our lives sporadically. These significant others influence us most during our growing and developing years; the time when we are establishing our self-concept, our total personality, which also includes our value system.

Values tend to be quite general, and we often act without ever having come to grips with them. By identifying our values and understanding the reasons for them we are able to grow as individuals and become more effective as a result. It is, therefore, desirable to develop techniques that will help us to identify and understand our moral, ethical and social relationships.

Simon and associates[9] pioneers in the field of *values clarification,* have identified what they call the values grid approach as an effective technique in helping people clarify their values. This technique requires a person to (1) choose a belief freely, (2) consider the various alternatives, (3) consider the possible consequences of the choice, (4) indicate whether or not the choice was prized or cherished, (5) affirm the choice to others, (6) act on the choice, and (7) repeat the choice to incorporate it into his/her life style. This and other techniques help us to clarify our beliefs in an atmosphere free of any attempts at imposition or indoctrination—an essential process for improving much of our health behavior.

By going through the process of values clarification, we will be able to identify our conceived values as well as our operative values. *Conceived values* are beliefs that reflect what we view as ideal, although our practices may not always reflect them. *Operative values* are those assumptions of right and wrong or good and bad that are used in making decisions. Thus, there may exist a discrepancy between our conceived values and our operative values. If the split is too great, we may have difficulty in coping with day-to-day stresses and making appropriate decisions.

Values provide a basis for our behavior and our beliefs. They are basic in helping us to interpret and cope with our environment. They are extremely difficult to change since our value structure, very often, affects not only *how* we see things, but also *what* we see.

The Ego

The *ego* is the rational, conscious aspect of our personality that regulates impulses so that we can meet the demands of reality and maintain social approval and self-esteem.[10] *Self-esteem* is the confidence and satisfaction we have for ourselves. It is a sense of self-respect that influences our competence in living effectively. Some authorities view self-esteem as a fundamental human emotional need.[11]

The protection of the ego status is involved in all of our daily activities. The more comfortable we feel about the self, and the more accurate and acceptable our knowledge of it is, the less likely the ego will be seriously threatened. Hence, the less likely our mental health will be threatened.

THEORIES OF PERSONALITY DEVELOPMENT

Many theories have been formulated in an attempt to explain the structure of personality and how it affects our functioning ability. These theories contribute, at least in part, to our understanding of the nature of personality and its role in our overall physical and psychological development.

Psychoanalytic Theory

One of the theories that has had great impact upon our understanding of personality is the *psychoanalytic theory* developed by Freud. This theory was the first major attempt to conceptualize the structure of personality and explain the reasons for behavior. Closely related to this theory is its counterpart, psychoanalysis, used in the treatment of some psychological problems.

Freud believed that people could be helped to overcome their problems by becoming aware of and understanding their unconscious desires and memories. Although refuted by some as not adequately explaining the psychological makeup of individuals, it nevertheless has had an impact upon psychological theory that still persists.

Freud's theory is based upon several premises.

1. All behavior is a result or function of prior stimulation.
2. Each individual has a conscious-unconscious dimension. The mind is made up of three parts: the conscious, preconscious, and unconscious. Those aspects of mental functioning of which the individual is aware is the *conscious.* Those thoughts that are easily brought to mind make up the *preconscious.* And those events that are brought to mind with great difficulty, if at all, make up the *unconscious.*
3. All behavior is ultimately determined by a set of unconscious drives or instincts. These drives comprise the individual's psychic energy and cause tension that a person seeks to reduce through behaving in a particular way.

Freud hypothesized that the personality is divided into three major segments, the id, ego, and superego. The id has been described as the primitive nature of humankind. All psychic energy runs through the *id* from which all instincts, or drives, emanate. In Freud's terminology, this psychic energy of the id is the *libido.* Freud viewed the libido as sexual in nature.

The *ego* is partly conscious and partly unconscious. It is, in essence, the controller of the personality. The ego allows for the expression of instincts in ways that are acceptable to society. It serves as the mediator between the id and the outside world.

The *superego* represents a person's moral code. It has two components: the *ego ideal,* which represents those things that are good and "rewards" the ego accordingly, and the *conscience,* which corresponds to what is wrong and "punishes" the ego.

Psychoanalytic theory may be described this way: In general, our personality can be viewed as a composite of biological aspects, represented by the id; psychological aspects, represented by the ego; and social aspects, represented by the superego. Our basic nature is irrational and selfish. Only social prohibitions and rules restrain our instinctive strivings.[12] Freud's theory emphasizes (1) the wholeness of people; (2) the interaction of heredity and experiences upon mental and emotional health; and (3) the factors related to learning and intelligence that play a key role in influencing human effectiveness.[13]

Analytic and Individual Theories

The *analytic theory* of personality was developed by Carl Jung after his philosophic break with Freud in 1912. Jung objected to the way Freudian theory placed emphasis on the sexual nature of the *libido.* In addition, Jung believed that Freud placed too much emphasis upon childhood experiences and their influences on adult behavior, leaving little room for adult growth.

Although analytic theory is extremely complex, it may be described as centering around four psychological functions:

1. *Thinking,* reflecting the ideational component of mental life;
2. *Feeling,* reflecting individual evaluation of life events;
3. *Sensing,* providing the individual with insight into the external environment; and,
4. *Intuition,* bringing the individual into contact with reality and extending beyond the meaning of external reality.[14]

Jung emphasized the importance of an individual's goals and strivings as well as a person's past experiences in the development of personality. According to Jung's theory, goals and strivings become the basis for motivation.

Individual theory, developed by Alfred Adler, focuses on the premise that a person is inherently social and that each of us has social urges, values, and interests. Adler felt that a person constantly strives to achieve self-actualization and personal fulfillment. The more a person fails to achieve his or her goals, the greater the likelihood that the person will develop an inferiority complex. Thus, the person seeks superiority.

Because of the social aspects of human nature, people continually strive to come to grips with the demands of society and, indeed, attempt to improve it. For Adler, social strivings are "a basic dimension of life."[15]

Self-actualization Theories

Many theorists who have centered their research into the structure of personality emphasize our inherent nature to actualize ourselves—to pass through "a sequential series of stages ... progressing toward higher levels of motivation and organization."[16]

The most prominent of these theories are: Carl Rogers' self-theory; Abraham Maslow's self-actualization theory; and the existential theories of Rollo May, Paul Tillich, and Erich Fromm. Rather than explaining each theory in detail, we will explore only the basic concepts that embody the self-actualization theories.

The stages that each of us pass through, according to the self-actualization theorists, range from the fulfillment of basic biologic needs (hunger, thirst, elimination, and the like) to the fulfillment of more complex needs that tend to be centered in the psychological and social aspects of our nature (esteem, the desire to know and understand, love, and so forth). It is when we are unable to satisfy a basic need that this need becomes paramount and progression toward self-actualization is interrupted. Therefore, when we are chiefly motivated to develop our fullest potentials, we are healthy. If other basic needs become active and chronic, however, we are unhealthy. This is true of both physical and emotional health.[17]

Abraham Maslow, most closely identified with self-actualization theory, emphasized a motivational tendency toward self-actualization among all individuals. Maslow describes the motivation toward self-actualization in terms of one's "inner nature" which is to a great extent natural or intrinsic. He emphasized that this inner nature is not intrinsically evil, but rather, it is either neutral or good. Evil tends to be a result of the frustration that the inner nature encounters. When it is allowed to guide our lives, we grow healthy, happy, and productive. If, however, the inner nature is suppressed, we tend to become sick in a variety of subtle ways. One of the important characteristics of our inner nature is that it is not strong and is easily overcome by habits and cultural influences. However, this inner nature never submits to total defeat and is always pressing for expression even in the face of overwhelming odds. Therefore, our motivation for self-actualization, one of our basic needs, continues throughout life, even to the moment of death as exemplified by our general denial of death even when death is inevitable.[18]

The *existentialists* feel that self-actualization is a function of a knowledge of self-identity; through self-actualization, we achieve a better understanding about our relationships with the world as well as a great insight into the self.[19] Great emphasis is thus placed upon our ability to find answers to the problems of life in our own unique way.

Trait Theory

The trait theory hypothesizes that our behavior is influenced by consistent behavioral characteristics (traits). Because of their enduring nature and because each of us possesses many traits, these, in turn, significantly influence our personality.

Researchers have attempted to identify and categorize the various traits that influence the development of personality. One of the most comprehensive efforts was undertaken by Raymond B. Cattell (1962) who developed the Sixteen Personality Factor Test.[20] This test identified trait norms as follows:

Low Score		*High Score*
Reserved	vs.	Outgoing
Less intelligent	vs.	More intelligent
Affected by feelings	vs.	Emotionally stable
Humble	vs.	Assertive
Sober	vs.	Happy-go-lucky
Expedient	vs.	Conscientious
Shy	vs.	Venturesome
Tough-minded	vs.	Tender-minded
Trusting	vs.	Suspicious
Practical	vs.	Imaginative
Forthright	vs.	Shrewd
Placid	vs.	Apprehensive
Conservative	vs.	Experimenting
Group-dependent	vs.	Self-sufficient
Undisciplined self-conflict	vs.	Controlled
Relaxed	vs.	Tense

According to those who support the trait theory, the traits that are identified in each person reflect the motives, beliefs, attitudes and values of the person and how these are interrelated.[21]

Body Type Theories

Body type theories hypothesize that a person's personality characteristics can be inferred by physical characteristics. Such theories date back to ancient times with the Hippocrates' humoral theory, which stated that a person's character could be determined through the identification of the balance of the four humors (blood, yellow bile, black bile, and phlegm). (See Chapter 1.) Thus, a person's personality could be determined as shown in Table 2-1.

An analysis of body structure and how it relates to a person's character has also been studied, most notably by W. H. Sheldon and his associates. Sheldon identified three major body types and rated people in each type on a scale of 1–7.

Table 2–1: Hippocrates' Body Humor Theory

Body Humor	Character or Temperment
Blood	Sanguine (hopeful, cheerful)
Black Bile	Melancholic (sad, depressed)
Yellow Bile	Choleric (irritable, irascible)
Phlegm	Phlegmatic (apathetic, lethargic)

From: Heidenreich, Charles A., *Personality and Social Adjustment*, Wm. C. Brown Company Publishers, Dubuque, 1967, p. 5. (By permission of Charles A. Heidenreich)

The body types identified were *endomorph,* characterized by a person being short and fat in the extreme form; *mesomorph,* characterized by a muscular body form; and *ectomorph,* characterized by a tall, thin frame.

Body type theories have not been shown to be valid through scientific investigation. They imply, however, a relationship between a person's genetic potential for development and the realization of these potentials through interaction with the environment that may have a significant influence upon personality development.

PERSONALITY OR CHARACTER DISORDERS

Personality or *character disorders* are terms used to describe behavioral patterns that may be considered to be social deviations. These disorders may be very mild or may be manifested in serious criminal acts. Such disorders occur in people whose personalities are not properly integrated. The disorders are different from other types of mental illness (such as psychosis) in that an individual may feel no sense of distress and in most cases exhibits no signs of organic disease or injury.

There are four basic classifications of personality or character disorders: (1) personality pattern disturbances; (2) personality trait disturbances; (3) sociopathic personality disturbances; and (4) special symptom reactions.

Personality Pattern Disturbances

Personality pattern disturbances are basically maladaptive personality types, characterized by responses to stress that are often inappropriate for the situation. In addition, physical abnormalities may accompany this type of disturbance. The person is often resistant to therapy. Under stress, people exhibiting this type of disorder are likely to experience decompensation (that is, ego or personality disorganization) resulting in psychosis.

The types of personality pattern disturbances are inadequate personality, schizoid personality, cyclothymic personality, and paranoid personality. An *inadequate personality* is generally a person who is unable to adapt to varying situations, possesses poor judgment, is generally inept, lacks physical and emotional stamina, is socially incompatible, and does not appropriately respond to intellectual, emotional, social, and physical demands.

A *schizoid personality* is characterized by coldness, aloofness, an avoidance of social contact or emotional closeness; the person is unable to express hostility and fearfulness, avoids competition, and has daydreams of being all-powerful. In addition, such people tend to be shy and withdrawn as children and become more introvertive, seclusive, and often eccentric at puberty.

People with *cyclothymic personalities* possess extrovertive tendencies with alternating elation and sadness. These people may also exhibit persistent euphoria or depression without an adequate external cause.

Paranoid personalities are characterized by an abortive paranoid reaction. This is manifested by projection (as a defense mechanism), suspiciousness, envy, extreme jealousy and stubbornness.

Personality Trait Disturbances

Personality trait disturbances are characterized by personality immaturity or maldevelopment that results in a person being unable to maintain emotional equilibrium and independence under stress. Such stress is likely to cause the individual to exhibit regression, that is, a return to an earlier stage of personality development. The major types of personality trait disturbances are emotionally unstable personality, passive-aggressive personality, and compulsive personality.

An *emotionally unstable personality* is characterized by excitability and ineffectiveness in the face of minor stress. A person with this condition exhibits fluctuating emotional attitudes that upset interpersonal relations and impair judgment, and the person has difficulty controlling hostility, guilt, and anxiety.

A *passive-aggressive personality* possesses a deep dependency, usually accompanied by deep resentment. This condition may take the form of (1) passive dependence with helplessness, undecisiveness, and a need to cling to others; (2) passive aggressiveness with an expression of aggression through pouting, stubbornness, procrastination, and passive obstructionism; or (3) active aggressiveness with irritability, tantrums, and destructiveness.

A *compulsive personality* is characterized by rigidity, overinhibition, and overconscientiousness. The person has an obsessive concern for conformity to standards and an inability to relax.

Sociopathic Personality Disturbances

Sociopathic personality disturbances are those conditions in which an individual is unable to cope or conform to prevailing social standards. There is a distinct lack of social responsibility. Subcategories include: (1) antisocial reaction; (2) dyssocial reaction; (3) sexual deviation; and (4) addiction to alcohol or other drugs. In this section, we will discuss antisocial and dyssocial reactions. For a detailed discussion of sexual deviations, see Chapter 6; for addictions, see Chapter 8.

Persons exhibiting an *antisocial reaction* are often said to be psychopathic personalities. These people seem to possess little ethical or moral development and have a great deal of difficulty adhering to established social mores. People with this condition include quack doctors and crooked politicians. According to Coleman, there are several distinct characteristics of antisocial reactions including inadequate conscience development, irresponsible behavior, establishment of unrealistic goals, lack of feelings of guilt, and defective social relationships.[22] These symptoms are general in nature and all need not be present for a person to be considered psychopathic.

A *dyssocial reaction* is distinguished from an antisocial reaction in that there is good ego strength and no personality disorganization. However, people with a dyssocial reaction are typically the product of an environment, the social codes of which differ from those of the society at large. They may, in fact, have a moral code that is very strong although it may go against that of society. Dyssocial reactions are usually exhibited by delinquents, racketeers, and others in organized crime.

Special symptom reactions are those conditions in which one symptom is identified; such symptoms include stuttering, nail biting, enuresis (involuntary discharge of urine after 3 years of age), tics, narcolepsy, and learning difficulties. From a social standpoint, special symptom reactions are the least serious of the various types of personality disorders, but can be an extreme burden to the individual sufferer, greatly interfering with the ability to function effectively. Fortunately, various types of treatment (psychotherapy, hypnosis, drug therapy, and so forth) seem to be effective in alleviating special symptom reactions, especially if they are treated early in their development.

DEFENSE MECHANISMS

Defense mechanisms are those reactions, common to us all, that occur when we are unable to deal effectively with a stressful or ego-threatening situation. Such reactions help us to maintain a sense of self-worth and adequacy despite our failure to deal successfully with a given situation. Defense mechanisms can be beneficial or can reflect a maladjustment if used to excess. This section will deal with the characteristics and ramifications of the use of ego defense mechanisms.

Relation to Stress, Anxiety, and Frustration

Many situations that we view as stressful result in anxiety or emotional tension that we may interpret as apprehension or fear. These situations are often difficult to cope with since it is relatively common for us to be unable to pinpoint the source of stress. In addition, such situations arouse anxiety because we fear for consequences of our actions. We thus develop and employ coping mechanisms to justify our actions to reduce this anxiety.

When we are unable to reach our goals, we often experience frustration. This occurs when obstacles—either physical, social, or psychological—interfere with our ability to satisfy our needs. As with anxiety we employ coping mechanisms to reduce this frustration. Our choice of coping mechanisms depends to a large degree not only on their effectiveness in reducing frustration, but also on their social acceptability.

Three types of conflict are possible:

1. *Conflicting attraction* (approach-approach) is when we must choose between two desired objects (goals) either by rejecting one entirely or by deciding which goal to achieve first.
2. *Attraction-repulsion* (approach-avoidance) is what occurs when a particular goal involves positive and negative characteristics. The closer we get to the attractive goal, the more we are repelled by the negative one. For example, a person who loves to eat but knows that dieting is more healthful will experience an approach-avoidance conflict. The closer he/she is to food, the more intense the conflict will become.

3. *Conflicting avoidance* (avoidance-avoidance) occurs when we seek to avoid two unpleasant situations, particularly when avoiding one may force confrontation with the second.

Ego Involvement

Some stressful situations are more serious than others from the point of view of being significant threats to our self-esteem. Unlike everyday annoyances, those situations that are threatening to our self-concept are said to be ego-involving. Such situations may involve a recognition of our inadequacies as well as those situations that may be imposed upon us and interfere with our ability to look at ourselves positively (loss of job, financial insecurity, failure in school, and so forth).

In such situations, we tend to employ mechanisms to defend against the harsh realities of life, since ego-involving frustrations can be highly painful. We must learn to handle these situations rather than simply covering for them through the use of defense mechanisms.

We gradually develop a repertoire of mechanisms that help us deal with stress and frustration. Whenever we are in situations that we view as threatening, we tend to employ defense mechanisms to maintain our integrity.

Basically, the use of defense mechanisms in an attempt to protect ourselves from stressful situations is normal and even healthy. It is only when we rely upon them to such a degree that they shelter us from reality and keep us from dealing effectively with stressful situations that they should be considered inhibitors to successful functioning. If this is the case, we function within a distorted reality and fail to make appropriate adjustments.

The problem with dealing appropriately with the use of defense mechanisms is that they are, for the most part, used unconsciously. When they are brought to the conscious level, they do not serve to defend us from stressful situations as well, because they then conflict with rational thought. If we consider defense mechanisms in the broadest sense, we find that they can be classified in three subdivisions: fight reactions, flight reactions, and compromise reactions.

Fight Reactions

When we encounter an obstacle that interferes with our ability to reach a goal, it is sometimes natural for us to attempt, through a variety of means, to eliminate the barrier. This may take the form of direct aggression, or of passive resistance.

Anger or hostility toward a given situation involves a great deal of emotional reinforcement. These emotions tend to reinforce the fight reaction, but may cause us to employ behavior that is socially unacceptable. This tends to increase anger and frustration, confounding our inability to deal with the situation.

It is often easier and more desirable, when we are frustrated, to take out our anger or hostility on a person or object other than the one that is actually the source of frustration. This reaction, a transfer of hostility, is called *displacement*.

Displacement of aggression is usually directed at a person or object less threatening than the true source of frustration. The source of frustration may be so abstract that anger and aggression is most easily directed at a person or object that is tangible.

Sometimes, rather than directing hostility at a particular person or object, we displace aggression more generally so that even neutral situations are interpreted as having hostile implications. In some instances, such *free-floating anger* may become so generalized that it results in a blind rage; in such a state, a person may inflict serious damage to another person or object.

Flight Reactions

Rather than fighting a particular situation, another basic form of defensive reaction is flight or withdrawal. Withdrawing from a threatening or potentially harmful situation can be a positive reaction because it allows us to continue functioning effectively. For example, if we discover that our superior in a job situation is corrupt, it may be most appropriate to seek employment elsewhere, rather than to risk becoming involved with or implicated in the corrupt activities. However, as we shall see, flight mechanisms may perpetuate or increase frustration resulting in a reduced capacity for effectiveness.

Flight reactions are basically a response to fear. Physical withdrawal may be as simple as seeking shelter because of adverse weather conditions or as complex as needing to physically escape a situation that threatens not only our physical well being, but our psychological well being as well.

Like other coping mechanisms, we *learn* to use flight reactions. As our life experiences grow, we learn that certain situations call for withdrawal rather than attack, and this withdrawal is reinforced by the fear generated by the threatening situation.

Physical withdrawal (escaping from a situation) is usually accompanied by emotional involvement. It is possible, however, for us to escape mentally without withdrawing physically. For instance, a fearful situation may cause us to fantasize about a return to past situations that were more secure, or dreaming about how life will become better in the future. This increases our security and may facilitate our ability to cope with the present.

When carried to an extreme, however, flight reactions can render us unable to face reality. This can result in a conflict between our abilities and our ego ideal which may cause feelings of guilt and a reduction in self-esteem.

Compromise Reactions

Throughout life we experience situations in which it is not feasible to use only attack or flight mechanisms as "solutions" to frustration. We find that we must use a combination of these, and possibly behave in conflict with our values structure to overcome problems and maintain our effectiveness. This requires compromise.

Compromise reactions include a change in our method of operations, altering our goals, and employing means of overcoming obstacles that we normally consider unacceptable. As with fight and flight mechanisms, we basically go through four steps when employing compromise reactions:

1. Identifying the problem
2. Deciding upon alternative solutions to the problem
3. Deciding upon the most appropriate action
4. Evaluating the results of the decision.[23]

Although compromise reactions may assist us in overcoming obstacles, they may cause further problems. In the compromise process, the various conflict mechanisms come into play. These can increase frustration and anger, lowering self-esteem.

If the decision to compromise is sufficient in helping us overcome the stressful situation, we can then move on to other activities relatively unhindered. Often, however, the act of compromise is only effective for the short term. We may not be able to fully accept the results of our decisions and may have to deal with them at a later time. Our inability to fully accept the results of our actions may generate further fear, guilt, and anxiety, affecting our overall effectiveness.

When compromise mechanisms are looked at in general, in comparison to fight and flight mechanisms, they are often the most appropriate. Effective living depends to a great extent on our ability to compromise with frustrating situations. (See Table 2-2 for a summary of the more common forms of coping mechanisms.)

CHARACTERISTICS OF MENTAL HEALTH

Foundations of Mental Health

Probably the most important determinant of a productive life is the quality of our mental health. Poor mental health interferes with our relationship with friends, family, and co-workers, as well as the self. Essentially it is these relationships that determine the extent to which life is worthwhile, pleasant, happy, or productive.

The quality of our mental health is determined by the quality of our hereditary traits, our social and physical environments, and the way we learn to react to the many and varied life's situations. Obviously, learning itself is dependent upon the quality of heredity and the environment; but in the end, mental health is evidenced by our reactions. These reactions provide us with the signs of mental health.

If our environment can be controlled to the extent that all of our basic biological and psychosocial needs are adequately met in infancy, childhood, and throughout life, we may expect that we will be mentally healthy. However, there is no guarantee. Our society is much too complex for it to be controlled completely to suit the variety of individuals who have a wide range of capabilities and needs. Nor is this absolutely necessary, for as we have learned, we are capable of coping with many of life's adverse situations; we possess a great ability for adaptation to rather extreme environmental conditions.

Table 2-2: A Summary of Defense Mechanisms

The Defense Mechanisms	Description
Repression	The unconscious preventing of threatening or painful thoughts from becoming conscious.
Fantasy	The process of adjusting to threatening situations by dreaming of imaginary achievements or by thinking of things that might have been.
Nomadism	A withdrawal reaction in which a person attempts to avoid frustration by continually moving from place to place or from job to job.
Regression	A mechanism in which a person retreats to an earlier level of maturity in an attempt to cope with frustrating situations.
Sublimation	A mechanism that involves the acceptance of a substitute goal that provides a socially acceptable outlet of expression; most typically associated with an undesirable sexual urge.
Substitution	The process of accepting substitute goals, but with no change in the quality of conscious desire.
Reaction Formation	A mechanism in which dangerous desires are repressed and in which the individual consciously advocates the opposed view or attitudes.
Projection	A situation in which the frustrated individual attributes to others the undesirable thoughts and attitudes which he/she has himself/herself.
Compensation	The attempt to disguise an undesirable trait by emphasizing a desirable one.
Intellectualization	A compromise reaction in which problems and frustrations are dealt with by the intellect through rationalization or other means of reality distortion.
Identification/Introjection	A mechanism in which an individual incorporates into his/her personality structure those characteristics of others who are threatening or, positively, those characteristics that are admired.
Amnesia	The repression of entire episodes of life as a reaction to extremely painful situations (usually considered a neurotic reaction).
Displacement	The transfer of hostility from the person or object causing the frustration to a less threatening object or person.
Negativism	A form of aggressive withdrawal in which a person exhibits a tendency to want forbidden things and has an aversion to those things for which one is praised; involves refusing to cooperate with commands or doing the opposite of what has been requested.
Fixation	An exaggerated attachment to some person or the arresting of emotional development at a childhood or adolescent level.
Egocentrism	A reaction in which a person becomes preoccupied with his/her own concerns while being insensitive to those of others.
Expiation/Atonement/Undoing	A form of intellectualization in which a person acts to atone for his/her misdeeds, thereby undoing them.
Hysteria	A reaction to stress in which psychological turmoil is converted into physical disturbances with no organic cause.

Definitions

Mental health is a relative, rather than an absolute, state of functioning. Generally, each of us develops and establishes a normal status of mental health which in itself has rather broad boundaries of functioning. We learn to deal with life's day-to-day situations. This pattern of behavior is our mental health; however, circumstances may change to alter—from time to time—how well we deal with a particular situation. If stresses, frustrations, and conflicts should persist, we may even react to a relatively normal situation with unexpected, even bizarre, behavior. Under most circumstances, once the stress is relieved, however, we will return to our usual mode of behavior. This is illustrated in Figure 2-1.

When we are behaving according to certain socially accepted standards, we are said to be mentally healthy. However, mental health is much more than conformity to standards; it is also creativity—nonconformity at the right time and under certain circumstances; it is individuality, responsible behavior, personal satisfaction from life; it is contributing to the betterment of society; it is within a concept of normalcy, making appropriate decisions; it is many things to many people. Obviously, to formulate a definition of mental health, we must take into account a variety of factors, both social and personal, and any definition will be controversial. Mental health professionals from different backgrounds and different philosophies will have different views on mental health and on our values— social and personal.

In brief, *mental health is the quality of a person's usual or integrated intrapersonal and interpersonal relationships.* From this definition, we can begin to identify the characteristics of a mentally healthy person.

Mental Health Is Functional

The signs of unhealthy mental conditions are evident, more readily observed and identified than those of a healthy condition. Mild and temporary inappropriate human behavior that may signal poor mental health may go unnoticed—at least for a while. However, when the inappropriate behavior becomes severe and more or less permanent, it is generally recognized quite readily as a

Figure 2-1:
Adjustment

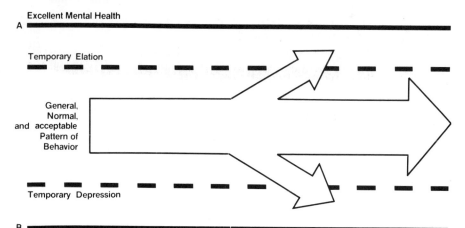

Excellent Mental Health

A

Temporary Elation

General,
Normal,
and acceptable
Pattern of
Behavior

Temporary Depression

B

Mental Illness—Inability to Deal With Even Simple Everyday Problems

We establish a General Lifestyle which Enables us to Adjust Adequately to Most Situations. Deviations Within the Extremes of A and B May Occur From Time to Time.

symptom of poor mental health. For example, unsocial, antisocial, and asocial behaviors that consistently interfere with the functioning of others can usually be recognized by other people. Characteristics of mental health will generally fall into one or more of three functional categories: (1) one's interpersonal relationships; (2) one's intrapersonal relationships; and (3) one's ability to realistically apply capabilities, feelings, and emotions to life.

In 1968, the National Association for Mental Health (NAMH) set forth a revised listing of some of the characteristics of people with good mental health. It was an attempt to identify chiefly those positive features that, when present in an individual, indicate their ability to function adequately in most of life's situations most of the time. The important contribution from our viewpoint is that these characteristics are functional and relate entirely to constructive human behavior. The National Association for Mental Health stated that "mentally healthy people are: good friends, good workers, good mates, good parents, and good citizens."[24] The NAMH recognized that mental health is far more than merely the absence of mental illness, but rather, it is inseparably associated with life and living, with functioning and effectiveness, with feelings, emotions, and rational, constructive behavior. It is more important to view people in terms of what they *do* than in terms of what they *are*.

Intrapersonal relationships have to do with:

- the ability for us to understand and deal with the feelings we have and how they relate to emotions, such as love, anger, fear, jealousy, guilt, anxiety.
- an understanding and acceptance of failures and successes, talents, and shortcomings—as well as life's happy moments and moments of disappointment.
- a sense of humor, especially as it is related to ourselves.
- a positive self-concept that results in self-esteem, self-respect, and a sense of dignity and worthwhileness.
- enjoying life from day to day, making appropriate plans and carrying through on them, and making the most of personal resources that we possess.

Interpersonal relationships have to do with:

- giving love to others and receiving it from them.
- trusting others and being trusted by them.
- making and keeping friends and working at satisfactory levels with them.
- projecting our self-respect to respecting others.
- possessing a sense of belonging to groups and contributing to these groups.
- accepting social responsibilities that result in constructive citizenship.

The *application of our capabilities,* feelings, and emotions has to do with:

- facing everyday problems, making appropriate decisions of action for solving them, but seeking help when necessary.
- adjusting to the existing environment when it cannot be changed, but working to improve it when appropriate.
- feeling excitement about future expectations, planning for them, and working to make them reality.
- accepting the challenges of life through responsibile and meaningful behavior.
- controlling behavior with rationality, intellect, and wisdom, rather than through impulse and emotion.
- making effective use of innate and developed talents, skills, and so forth.

It is important to point out that these characteristics are not in any way exclusive of each other, but tend to function holistically. The presence of an intrapersonal characteristic will influence interpersonal and application characteristics. For example, if we do not have a sense of self-respect we will find it difficult to respect others. In summary, mental health is functional; it is the quality of our psychological makeup that influences how well we can deal with life and the feelings or satisfactions and happiness that result from accomplishments for us, for others, and for humanity.

FACTORS AFFECTING MENTAL HEALTH

From a mental health viewpoint, we are really social beings, living in a world of others, but surrounded by inanimate objects. Although the inanimate objects affect our social selves, they are less important when we think of the changes in the physical environment that have taken place over the centuries—and when we think of people's ability to adapt to these changes. Certainly, adaptation is more difficult today, in some respects, than it was during the Stone Age, but people must have found it difficult to adapt at that time as well. The ever-present dangers, the lack of knowledge of very basic phenomena resulting in constant fears, must have played havoc with Stone Age people's mental health. Even though our environment is much more complex, we learn early how to deal with the things of modern living. The area that is less concrete—more difficult to learn about and to control—involves the psychosocial aspects of living. As a result, the more important factors affecting mental health today are not the physical elements of the environment, but rather the social environment. It is the social/personal aspects of life today that have the greatest impact upon our mental health.

The Social Environment

We are born into a world of people—parents, siblings (perhaps), other members of the family, strangers, peers—all of whom sooner or later will have a significant influence upon the kind of person we become: effective, ineffective, mentally healthy, mentally ill, social, unsocial, congenial, obstinant, whatever. In addition to these significant others are those aspects of the social environment that are less obvious—the social standards, mores, laws, and customs—that also play a significant role in sculpturing our personalities. As we mature, however, we acquire greater insight into the kind of person we are and the kind of person we hope to become. This insight, along with more profound knowledge of the significant people with whom we associate, make it less difficult for us to deal adequately with frustrations, stresses, anxieties, fears, and guilt feelings. These two general factors, the social environment and our knowledge, are the keys to the quality of our mental health and our ability to adjust or overcome the conflicts we must encounter from time to time.

The need to adjust should be viewed as a normal phenomenon of life. What we need to do is to find ways of making adjustment easier and less time consuming so that our energies can be used for more constructive endeavors than merely overcoming obstacles that stand in the way of our goal achievements.

Social Expectations

Social interactions are necessary facts of life. The kinds of interactions that we must consider are the result of (1) the nature of our social environment; (2) how we perceive our role as a social being; and (3) personal attributes, both innate and learned, that we possess. How well we interact socially has its foundations in the quality of our mental health.

The first aspect of mental health is exemplified in our consistent behavior on a day-to-day basis, while the second aspect deals with emotional stability, tolerance and resistance, and the wisdom necessary for finding the most appropriate reaction to the intense social changes taking place.

Societies establish certain expectations and each of us establishes our social expectations. The two may at times be identical and at other times they may be in conflict. When society's expectations are the same as ours and we perceive these as realistic and achievable, mental health status is usually high. However, when the two are contradictory or we do not perceive them as realistic and achievable, a conflict results that may adversely affect our mental health status. This may be severe or mild, very temporary or more or less permanent, depending upon the importance or severity of the social expectation conflict. This, for example, may help to explain at least in part, antisocial, unsocial, and asocial behaviors in some people some of the time. Success in achieving the goals established by society is important to our mental health development and status, but sometimes the goals of society need to be changed since they may be incompatible with our capabilities.

Personal Expectations

Personal expectations are essentially characterized by the goals each of us establishes. This goal-setting is influenced by what society expects, our personal desires, wants, and aspirations, and our innate and learned capabilities. Personal expectations may be appropriate to these factors or they may be inappropriate for one or more of them. For example, we may choose to pursue a career because it is glorified by society. However, we may not possess the intellectual or the emotional ability for achieving the goal. If the career requires a college education and we lack the qualifications for college admittance, for instance, we cannot achieve the goal.

It is probably not possible to completely separate social and personal expectations. The social group that usually has the greatest impact upon the establishment of personal expectations is the family. From the time a person is born, parents may have established their goals for the baby. These may be imposed upon the infant, either consciously or otherwise; these goals influence the infant's self-perception and aspirations. Depending upon other social reinforcers, parental expectations may be taken for granted as the child develops.

However, we need also to consider our personal contributions to the establishment of our expectations. If we have certain innate abilities or talents, there is a likelihood that these abilities will generate interest in their development. Society may also reinforce these interests. For example, one who has innate abilities for musical talent and who also lives at a time when being a musician is accepted or glorified may become a musician.

Personal Attributes

Usually, our personal attributes are identified as physical or mental. *Physical characteristics* are (1) physical abilities fundamental to normal functioning; and (2) physical abilities that are generally referred to as talents.

Mental attributes play an important role in our mental health quality. These can be viewed as fundamental to normal intellectual and emotional functioning, and as unusual talents. Mental attributes are most easily recognized in regard to intelligence since intelligence can be measured to some degree by various testing techniques. Some measurement of intelligence became possible with the development of intelligence tests by Albert Binet and Thomas Simon in 1905. Since this time, many revisions of the Simon-Binet Scale have taken place and new, more sophisticated techniques have been devised. In recent years, however, there has developed some controversy about the use of these tests and their validity.

Intelligence makes it possible for us to view life's circumstances realistically and to adequately solve problems that arise. Mental attributes are basically hereditary in nature, but disease or injury to the brain may alter this.

Intelligence

A person's level of intelligence can be a direct asset in the maintenance of mental health; and when mental health fails, it can be an important factor in the ease with which mental health is restored. This is because an intelligent person is better equipped to make appropriate decisions, to acquire accurate insight into life's problems, to find appropriate adaptations or to alter adverse conditions. Further, if mental illness should occur, an intelligent person is better equipped to understand the factors surrounding the cause and the course that must be taken to restore mental health. However, our rationality may at times be overcome by intense emotional experiences.

Our understanding of the mechanism of intelligence is incomplete. However, there are some agreements as to what constitutes intelligence and some of the mechanisms associated with it. Intelligence has to do with learning and with the functioning of the brain; it is associated with comprehension, reasoning, memory, and decision making; with space, verbal and numbering abilities, and with wisdom. *Intelligence* is a complex pattern of innate abilities that determine what we learn, how deeply we learn, how rapidly we learn, and how well we make use of this learning.

Dr. Paul D. MacLean and his colleagues at the National Institute of Mental Health have conducted research into the influence of the affective or emotional centers of the brain upon the rationality of human decisions. They have shown that human brains (actually, all primate brains) have evolved through three evolutionary developments identified as reptilian, paleomammalian, and neo-mammalian. MacLean refers to humans as having a triune brain made up of these three interrelated divisions. It has long been thought that the reptilian brain had only to do with motor activity, but MacLean's research indicates that it also controls innate, ritualistic behaviors, as well as some forms of learned behavior, especially those behaviors associated with a strong emotional component.[25] In other words, it is thought that the reptilian brain may be a repository for ancient, unlearned behavior as well as learned behavior that has become automatic.

The limbic system is generally recognized as the center of emotions and is the connecting link between the reptilian brain and the neocortex (the highest center of intelligence). The limbic system appears to be concerned with self-preservation by guiding emotional feelings and behavior toward satisfaction of basic biological needs and away from threats. According to MacLean, the neocortex responds to the external stimuli with trust while the limbic system responds to the reptilian (inner) stimuli. This may help to explain conflicts between what we *know* and what we *feel* and may provide us with clues to mental illness. Obviously, much more research is needed to draw any definitive conclusions and to corroborate MacLean's findings and hypotheses.

This new research seems to support in part Piaget's thoughts on human development. Piaget has asserted that human development is essentially the result of maturation of the intellect that comes about by the process of assimilation and accommodation. *Assimilation* is the intellectual process of transforming stimuli from the external environment as a part of the self. When complete, the stimuli become a part of one's cognitive structure. *Accommodation* takes place when assimilation is complete and the person has adapted to the external stimuli. If the external stimuli are incomprehensible, assimilation and accommodation are not possible and the person is unable to adapt appropriately. This may be manifested in frustration, conflict, or inappropriate responses, such as making immature decisions.

RESPONSIBILITIES FOR MENTAL HEALTH MAINTENANCE

Personal Responsibilities

It is difficult to separate our personal responsibilities for mental health maintenance from those of society, especially those aspects that are in direct contact with us. How well we can take responsibility for our own mental health is related to the strength of the foundations for mental health that have been established. The foundational elements of mental health include any attitudes toward the self—the self-concept—and our intellectual ability to understand the self and the environmental forces that impinge upon us; this includes the development of decision-making skills and the ability to act accordingly.

No matter what factors we identify as responsible for the quality of our mental health, either developmentally or disintegratively, the *primary* responsibility for the maintenance of mental health rests with each of us. However, when circumstances become too traumatic for us to accomplish this task alone, it is necessary to seek assistance from others. This assistance is available from community mental health related agencies and from individuals who are trained in various aspects of mental health.

Community Agencies

Nearly all of the programs that have been initiated at the community, state, or national levels are concerned chiefly with diagnosis and treatment of mental illness rather than with its prevention and the promotion of mental health. The chief goal of community mental health programs is to *prevent* mental illness and to establish procedures for early diagnosis and treatment of mental and emotional disorders. Ideally, community mental health centers should be multidimensional, providing promotive and preventive services, mental health education, inpatient and outpatient care, emergency services, consultation and coordination of other mental health services, diagnostic, treatment, and rehabilitation services, follow-up, and research.

The community agencies that are concerned with mental health and that devote, at least, some of their time, personnel, and facilities to it include the home, school, church, public health departments, business and industry, general hospitals and nursing homes, mental health clinics, family and child services, mental hospitals, and a variety of voluntary health agencies, such as the National Association for Mental Health, and the Association for Retarded Children. With a few exceptions these agencies have other responsibilities that frequently result in mental health promotion taking a low priority.

There appears to be developing a trend toward recognizing the importance of preventing mental illness.[26] However, a major deterrent to preventive mental health programs is the lack of knowledge of mental health by the general public. Another is the general lack of interest in prevention by the mental health professionals and legislators.

Mental Health Specialists

The use of the term "mental health specialist" is probably a misnomer; the term should be "mental illness specialist," since those who work in this broad, complex area are generally more concerned with mental illness than mental health. As a matter of fact, there is no specialty called "preventive mental health" (as there is preventive medicine in the general medical area). Throughout the literature, when the term "mental health" is used, there is usually a discussion of mental illness, and the specialists concerned with mental health (mental illness) are trained chiefly in some form of therapy for people with mental and emotional problems.

The *psychiatrist* is a medical doctor (physician) who specializes in the diagnosis and treatment of mental and emotional disorders. A psychiatrist may have completed the required training and experience to become Board Eligible or may have completed all the requirements to be Board Certified (by the American Board of Psychiatry and Neurology). Within the psychiatry and neurology specialty there are also several subspecialties, such as child psychiatry.

The *clinical psychologist* is trained in the administration of a variety of psychological tests that aid in the diagnosis and evaluation of the patient. The clinical psychologist generally practices psychotherapy. Clinical psychology is a specialty concerned with the treatment of mental and emotional disorders by nonmedical and nonsurgical techniques; group therapy is an example.

The *psychiatric social worker* is a person who deals with the interpersonal relationships of the patient. The psychiatric social worker is usually concerned with the rehabilitative process of the patient and attempts to identify and rectify adverse relationships between the patient and his/her significant others (family, employer, and so forth) that may be contributing to the mental or emotional problem.

The *psychiatric nurse* is a trained nurse (registered nurse, R.N.) who has specialized in nursing services related to psychiatric patients. Psychiatric nurses are generally employed by psychiatric hospitals, outpatient facilities, nursing homes, and mental health clinics. Much of their time is devoted to after-care of patients who have been discharged from mental hospitals, but many are also engaged in psychiatric nursing of patients while the patient is in a hospital or nursing home.

According to the United States Department of Health, Education, and Welfare[27] there are approximately 30,000 psychiatrists in the United States. Of these, approximately 2,500 are devoted to child psychiatry, 3,900 are devoted to neurology, and 23,600 are involved in general psychiatry. There are nearly 860,000 registered nurses with only a small percentage involved in psychiatric nursing. For all hospitals and nursing homes, there are nearly 940,000 nursing aides, 35,000 psychologists, and nearly 39,000 social workers. In addition to these specialists, the area of mental health also includes trained persons in such rehabilitation programs as occupational therapy (nearly 15,000); physical therapy (over 26,000); and vocational therapy (about 18,000).

FUTURE DECISIONS

It has taken humanity centuries to evolve from incarceration of the mentally ill, frequently characterized by inhumane, cruel care to a gradual understanding of the need for humane treatment and optimism toward cure. At one time in our history, it was unthinkable to believe that a person afflicted with a mental disease could ever become a contributing member of society. Today, it is unthinkable to believe that a person cannot be cured. This dramatic shift of attitude of the psychiatric, psychological, and sociological professions—along with the attitude of the general population—has made it possible for tens of thousands of individuals afflicted with a mental or emotional disorder to be returned to a productive life.

We have learned a great deal in the past 100 or so years about mental illness, and much of this knowledge has been applied to ways in which each individual can achieve optimal mental and emotional functioning. However, the task is not complete, we still have all too many instances of mental illnesses that are essentially preventable with present knowledge, and as William James stated three quarters of a century ago, " . . . to cure the disease by preventing it, is the only effective cure known."*

The promotion of mental health in our society is still far removed from the kind of world that was envisioned more than a half century ago. What is needed, as Albert Deutsch said only one-third of the way through the twentieth century is

> a world of peace and freedom, *from which the twin* spectors of war and insecurity will be banished, a world of equal opportunity, where people will be freed from stunting inhibitions and guilt feelings arising from outworn prejudices and taboos, a world where children may lead healthy, happy lives and grow into useful, well adjusted citizens, where the personality is permitted to develop naturally and freely, where the individual is given a sense of personal worth and dignity, and where his activities and ambitions are integrated with the development of group life—such is the goal for which mental hygiene must strive.[28]

We wonder if this goal can or ever will be achieved, but it is one worth all the effort and energy that each of us can muster and sustain throughout our lives for the lives that will follow.

GLOSSARY

Accommodation: Complete adaptation to external stimuli.

Adaptive behavior: Adjustments one makes to deal effectively with the environment.

Adjustment: The ability to adapt.

Assimilation: The cognitive transforming of an external stimulus into a part of one's personality.

Autognosis: A process used in psychoanalysis that results in self-understanding using self-confessions.

Conceived values: Beliefs that reflect what we view as ideal.

Ego: The rational, conscious aspect of our personality that regulates impulses enabling us to maintain self-esteem.

Id: The primitive aspects of the psyche.

Idiographic: The qualities that make each person different from everyone else.

Introspection: The process of examining one's own thoughts and feelings.

Neurosis: A form of compulsive, ineffective behavior of which the person is aware but unable to control.

Nomothetic: The qualities that make all people more or less alike.

Operative values: Our feeling of right and wrong that influence our decisions.

Psychosis: Mental illness characterized by a loss of touch with reality.

Self-concept: The idea, understanding, and feeling one has about him/herself.

Self-esteem: The confidence and satisfaction one has for him/herself.

Superego: One's moral code.

Values: One's beliefs about moral, ethical, and social relationships.

*William James (1908) as quoted by Clifford Beers in *A Mind That Found Itself,* New York: Doubleday, 1948, p. 393.

SUMMARY

Many definitions of personality have been formulated. Putting the definitions together, we see that personality encompasses all of an individual's characteristics. Variations in the development of these characteristics are what make us unique. These uniquenesses are called idiographic characteristics, while those that are common to all or most of us are called nomothetic characteristics.

The manner in which a person reacts to social stimuli and inner needs is called behavior. Behavior may result from innate determiners, unconscious motives, or from experiences.

To maintain mental health, it is necessary for us to adjust to varying situations. A positive self-concept makes adequate adjustments easier.

Self-understanding is characterized by an accurate knowledge of our capabilities, feelings, motivations, and total behavior. It may be acquired through self-confession.

Many theories of personality development have been formulated, including: the psychoanalytic theory, developed by Freud, the analytic theory of Jung, Adler's individual theory, self-actualization theories, the trait theory and body-type theories.

Our ability to function effectively is largely governed by our hereditary characteristics. The interaction of these potentials with the environment greatly influence the development of personality. When we are able to function effectively in the face of environmental challenges, our personality develops toward maturity and we approach actualization.

Functioning ability is significantly influenced by our value structure. Values are learned both from our significant others and as a result of existing cultural values.

When an individual's personality is not properly integrated, personality or character disorders may result. There are four types of personality disorders: (1) personality pattern disturbances; (2) personality trait disturbances; (3) sociopathic personality disturbances; and (4) special symptom reactions.

Defense mechanisms are used when we are unable to deal effectively with a stressful or ego-threatening situation. Such reactions help us to maintain a sense of self-worth despite our inability to deal successfully with a situation.

The quality of one's mental health is an important determinant of the extent to which one can live a happy, productive life. The factors that affect the quality of mental health are the social environment, social expectations, personal expectations, attributes, and intelligence.

The primary responsibility for the maintenance of mental health rests with each of us. Therefore, we need to understand the factors responsible for the promotion or erosion of mental health and know where to seek help when necessary. We can get assistance from a variety of community agencies and mental health specialists.

PROBLEMS FOR DISCUSSION

1. Describe the difference between nomothetic and idiographic. How are they related to personality?
2. Distinguish between invariable, automatic, and variable behavior.
3. Relate introspection to self-understanding.
4. Differentiate between Freudian and analytic theories of personality development.
5. Distinguish between Roger's self theory, Maslow's self-actualization theory, and existential theories.
6. How do heredity and environment affect personality development?
7. How do values contribute to functioning ability? How are values established? Can values be changed? Explain.
8. Relate defense mechanisms to stress, anxiety, and frustration.
9. How can the use of defense mechanisms interfere with functioning ability? In what ways are their use helpful?
10. What are the three categories in which the characteristics of mental health may be placed? Explain how they are related.
11. List the important factors that affect the quality of mental health. Describe how each plays a role in determining one's mental health.
12. What can people do to improve their mental health and that of others?
13. Distinguish between the various mental specialties; include training, functions, settings, and limitations.
14. Identify areas in American society that are in critical need of attention that will result in improving people's mental health.
15. What kinds of mental and emotional health problems are important in the United States? What kinds of programs do you feel will help to alleviate these problems?

REFERENCES

1. LONGSTRETH, LANGDON E., *Psychological Development of the Child.* Ronald Press Company, New York, 1968, p. 56.
2. KLAUSMEIER, HERBERT J., and WILLIAM GOODWIN, *Learning and Human Abilities,* 2nd ed. Harper & Row, Publishers, Inc., New York, 1966, p. 379.
3. KENDLER, HOWARD H., *Basic Psychology.* Appleton-Century, Crofts, New York, 1963, p. 437.
4. RUCH, FLOYD L., *Psychology and Life,* 5th ed. Scott, Foresman and Company, Glenview, Ill., 1959, p. 65.
5. SKINNER, B. F., *About Behaviorism.* Alfred A. Knopf, Inc., New York, 1974, p. 154.

6. SKINNER, B. F., *Science and Human Behavior.* The MacMillan Company, New York, 1953, p. 428.
7. BROOM, LEONARD, and PHILIP SELZNICK, *Sociology,* 4th ed. Harper & Row, Publishers, Inc., New York, 1968, p. 236.
8. *Ibid.,* p. 54.
9. SIMON, SIDNEY B., LELAND HOW and HOWARD KIRSCHENBAUM, *Values Clarification: A Handbook of Practical Strategies for Teachers and Students.* Hart Publishing Company, New York, 1972.
10. RUCH, FLOYD L., *op. cit.,* 1964 ed., p. 120.
11. *Essentials of Life and Health,* 2nd ed. CRM, Random House, New York, 1977, p. 9.
12. COLEMAN, JAMES C., *Abnormal Psychology and Modern Life,* 3rd ed. Scott, Foresman and Company, U.S., 1964, p. 639.
13. BEDWORTH, DAVID A. and ALBERT E. BEDWORTH, *Health Education: A Process for Human Effectiveness.* Harper & Row, Publishers, Inc., New York, 1978, p. 133.
14. SARASON, IRWIN G., *Personality: An Objective Approach,* 2nd ed. John Wiley & Sons, Inc., New York, 1972, p. 51.
15. *Ibid.,* p. 55.
16. HEIDENREICH, CHARLES A., *Personality and Social Adjustment.* Wm. C. Brown Book Company, Dubuque, Iowa, 1967, p. 77.
17. BEDWORTH, *op. cit.,* p. 106.
19. MASLOW, ABRAHAM H., "Personality Problems and Personality Growth," from C. G. Moustakes, ed., *The Self: Explorations in Personal Growth.* Harper & Row, Publishers, Inc., New York, 1956, pp. 232–233.
19. SARASON, *op. cit.,* p. 104.
20. CATTELL, RAYMOND B., *The Sixteen Personality Factors Test Profile.* Institute for Personality and Ability Testing, Champaign, Ill., 1962.
21. HEIDENREICH, *op. cit.,* p. 11.
22. COLEMAN, *op. cit.,* pp. 362–363.
23. *Ibid.,* p. 95.
24. NATIONAL ASSOCIATION FOR MENTAL HEALTH, *Mental Health Is 1, 2, 3.* The Association, Washington, D.C., 1968.
25. ROSENFELD, ANNE H., *The Archeology of Affect.* U.S. Department of Health, Education, and Welfare; Public Health Service; Alcohol, Drug Abuse, and Mental Health Administration; National Institute of Mental Health, DHEW Publication No. (ADM) 76–395, 1976, p. 12.
26. WILNER, DAVID M., ROSABELLE PRICE WALKER, and LENORE S. GOERKE, *Introduction to Public Health,* 6th ed. Macmillan Publishing Co., Inc., New York, 1973, pp. 157–158.
27. *Health: United States, 1976–1977,* U.S. Department of Health, Education, and Welfare; Public Health Service; U.S. Government Printing Office, Washington, D.C., 1977, p. 307.
28. DEUTSCH, ALBERT, *The Mentally Ill In America: A History of Their Care and Treatment From Colonial Times.* Doubleday, Doran & Company, Garden City (N.Y.), 1937, p. 463.

3

restoring mental health

INTRODUCTION

Our attitudes about mental and emotional illness have progressed through a variety of stages. We see uncertainties and inconsistencies of attitudes during various periods of history. There may have been one kind of attitude toward a person who was mentally ill (sympathy, for example), and quite another attitude toward how a mentally ill person should be treated to restore mental health (punishment, for example). As late as the 1800s, well-equipped mental hospitals (often called lunatic asylums) used bizarre treatments, such as the circulating swing chair. This device was operated by an attendant who, using a lever, was able to spin the patient who was strapped in the chair until he/she was dizzy. This apparatus was supposed to cure depression. Other cruel treatments were used, such as plunging patients who were strapped in a chair device into cold water to "shock them back to their senses" or pulling a chair out from under a patient to prove that he/she was not made of glass.

With the development of large state mental hospitals, even these kinds of treatment were abandoned because the hospitals became overcrowded and understaffed. Patients were ignored and provided with only minimal custodial care. Cure during those days was almost unknown, even though hospital records frequently showed high "discharged-as-cured" rates.

Attitudes about mental illness fluctuated through many phases which can be described as periods of awe and even worship of the mentally ill during prehistoric times, to fear of the afflicted during the 1600s into the 1700s. The sequence of attitudes and treatment began with cruelty and moved through imprisonment, apathy, tolerance, and finally, understanding and empathy. These, and many other attitudes, did not necessarily follow a pattern, and there were even periods of regression to former attitudes.

With new insights into the plight of the mentally ill and new theories of cause and treatment, however, came the development of more humane attitudes about the mentally ill. Much of the success in bringing about more humane attitudes resulted from the exposés published in newspapers, magazines, and books; the production of films portraying the plight of the mentally ill; political awareness and action; and public education campaigns conducted by governmental and voluntary mental health agencies. However, even today, one of the greatest obstacles confronting the recovered psychotic is overcoming the attitudes of society.

It is important to keep alive our courageous (sometimes) as well as our disgraceful (sometimes) history that is associated with mental health and mental illnesses. We need to continue to compare the attitudes, practices, and achievements of the eighteenth and nineteenth centuries with those of the twentieth century. We need to do this to make certain that what we do in the twenty-first century is not a repeat of the conditions of the past so that they remain as embarrassing historical memories.

THE MENTAL HEALTH
MOVEMENT

Let us explore some of the significant events that have led us to where we are today in our understanding of mental health, for these events have provided us with the basis for our present mental health practices.

Historical Perspectives

For all practical purposes, the mental health movement had its beginning on May 6, 1908 when Clifford Beers called a meeting of a small group of people to organize the Connecticut Society for Mental Hygiene.[1] Prior to this meeting, mental health was thought of only in terms of insanity and lunacy. There were no significant efforts to promote mental health or to prevent mental illness. Physicians, during the nineteenth century, had no training whatsoever in psychiatry and very little was known about the diagnosis and treatment of mental illnesses. There was no common nomenclature, no exchange of ideas, nor was there any thought for the need for these things; further, there were no textbooks. The mental hygiene movement, which was fully launched by the establishment of the National Committee for Mental Hygiene in 1909, began overcoming this lack of knowledge.

However, we need to return for a moment to 1792 when Philippe Pinel, a courageous French physician, was appointed to a position at the Bicêtre, an asylum for male lunatics in Paris. The mentally ill during this period were considered "dangerous animals"; they were treated much worse than criminals of the time, completely stripped of all of their human dignity, chained, beaten, starved, frozen.[2] Shocked by what he saw, Pinel ordered the chains and shackles removed from the inmates. Under great pressure of ridicule and opposition, he advocated the humane treatment of the mentally ill and ordered their transfer from prisons to hospitals. (It must be remembered that at this time and through most of the eighteenth century it was thought that the mentally ill possessed no sense or feeling, either physically or mentally.)

Three years later, Pinel proceeded to the Salpêtriere, an asylum for female lunatics, and removed the chains and shackles from these patients as well. These institutions were considered at the time the worst asylums in the entire world. This was the beginning of what became known as the moral treatment movement.

But the *moral treatment movement* was chiefly only one-step removed from gross, brutal treatment of the mentally ill. Moral treatment was characterized by treating the patients more humanely; they were given sufficient food (but not too much), chains were removed (but some mechanical restraints were kept—the straight jacket and leather belts), and the patients gradually were habilitated so that each could take care of himself/herself. The retreat concept was introduced and finally became reality by the efforts of William Tuke who began his crusade in 1792. One of the institutions, "The Retreat," built in 1796 in England, exemplified most clearly the moral treatment of patients. It was founded upon the principles of providing a family environment; there was emphasis on employment and exercise, and "the treatment of patients as guests rather than inmates."[3]

Similar actions were also introduced by Vincenzo Chiarugi at the Hospital of St. Boniface in Florence. Besides the removal of chains and shackles, Chiarugi also encouraged the use of occupational therapy, sanitation in the hospital, and humane treatment of the patients. Chiarugi was indeed a humanitarian at a time when such behavior was almost unheard of.

The Nineteenth Century

Nearly fifty years after Pinel's moral treatment movement began, Dorothea Lynde Dix crusaded for similar conditions in the United States. In 1844, the American Medico-Psychological Association was formed, the same year that Dix, a school teacher, began her crusade to improve the conditions in insane asylums in the United States. It was through her efforts, between 1844 and 1881, that large sums of money were raised to build better mental hospitals and to improve the care of mental patients. Dorothea Dix was instrumental in establishing 32 mental hospitals in the United States, Canada, and Europe, and it was through her untiring efforts that, in 1852, the first national mental hospital, St. Elizabeth's, was established in Washington, D.C. However great these achievements may have seemed at the time, it was only a matter of a few years before there was a return of the gross inhumane treatment of mentally ill patients; and, for all practical purposes, this was continued well into the twentieth century.

During the nineteenth century, psychiatrists were called "alienists" because they dealt with "alienated minds." This term survived into the first quarter of the twentieth century when they became known as psychiatrists. This was reflected in the name change of the American Medico-Psychological Association to the American Psychiatric Association in 1921.

Benjamin Rush was the first American physician to publish, in 1812, a comprehensive course of study on mental disease.* This book was the only text on the subject for over 70 years. Benjamin Rush is considered by many as the first American psychiatrist.

Although much of the treatment of the mentally ill degenerated to the pre-Dorothea Dix era, there were attempts by some to bring about reforms through exposés. One of the most well-known exposés was that of Nellie Bly, correspondent for the *New York World,* who in 1887, had herself committed to the New York City Lunatic Asylum. Later, she wrote a series of articles exposing the horrible conditions in the asylum. This was the beginning of a number of exposés that would follow in the next 50 years.

Between 1872 and 1888, the National Association for the Protection of the Insane and the Prevention of Insanity was in existence. For the *first* time, the word "prevention" was used in the title of a professional association. The State Charities Aid Association in New York State was founded in 1872 by Louisa Lee Schuyler, granddaughter of Alexander Hamilton. The Charities Aid was one of the most active organizations concerned with reform in the care of mental patients. This association is credited with developing the first formal training pro-

*The book was titled, *Medical Inquiries and Observations Upon the Diseases of the Mind.*

gram for psychiatric nursing (1885); the Charities Aid influenced the passage of laws establishing state care for all mentally ill patients in New York State. These were the forerunners of similar laws in other states.

In 1885, Sigmund Freud began his important work in psychiatry by applying hypnosis to the treatment of hysteria. This laid the foundation for his controversial approach to an understanding of personality and of psychoanalysis. His theories are responsible for much of the progress made in psychiatry during the early part of the twentieth century.

Although there were moments of enlightenment about the treatment and care of the mentally ill during the nineteenth century, these insights were restricted to a very small group of people. Society in general continued to view the mentally ill as lunatics, and attitudes, such as "once insane, always insane," persisted. Many of these stigmas remain to a large extent today, but much progress has been made in the treatment and care of the mentally ill.

And so, the foundations of mental health were laid from rudimentary understandings of mental illness—and much of this understanding evolved, not from science, but from the revulsion of cruelty of one human for another.

The Twentieth Century

We are still in our infancy when it comes to matters of mental health, even our understanding of what the term means. The term "mental hygiene" was first used in 1843 by William Sweetster, and continued in use until it was replaced in the 1940s by the term "mental health." Actually, mental hygiene is a more exact term than mental health. Mental hygiene means "a body of knowledge about the preservation and promotion of mental health."[4]

At any rate, it was not until after World War II that there were any real achievements and progress as a result of the mental health movement that began in Connecticut in 1908. Clifford W. Beers is the undisputed founder of the mental health movement. Beers' book *A Mind That Found Itself* vividly describes his struggle to regain sanity during his three years as a patient in mental institutions (1900–1902). The title of the book reflects the kind, or more accurately, the lack of treatment he received while a "patient" in several mental "hospitals." It was, indeed, through his own efforts that he was able to regain his sanity. During his struggle for sanity, he vowed to expend his energies in improving the plight of the mentally ill in America, and finally, throughout the world. His later goal was achieved in 1930 when the First International Congress on Mental Hygiene was convened in Washington, D.C.

This first Congress was attended by more than 3000 persons who represented 51 countries. The chief purposes of the Congress were (1) to exchange international information about the social problems associated with mental disease, mental defect, and mental and emotional maladjustments; and (2) to explore ways of world cooperation resulting in more effective means of promoting mental hygiene in the representative countries. It is important to note that this was one of the few references to the *promotion* of mental health; almost all other efforts were directed toward treatment and care of the mentally ill.

The National Institute for Mental Health In 1937, Albert Deutsch pointed out that "a well-planned, liberally financed program of research into causes and cure of mental disorders might well result in incalculable financial savings to society, not to mention the results in terms of the prevention of human suffering."[5] A turning point in this direction came in 1946 with the establishment of the National Institute for Mental Health (NIMH) with passage of landmark legislation, the National Mental Health Act. This act also provided for financial grants to state and private nonprofit agencies for mental health research, training and services. The primary functions of the NIMH were to assist states in developing community mental health services; to support research in the causes, prevention, and treatment of mental illness; and to provide grants for the training of psychiatrists, psychologists, psychiatric social workers, and psychiatric nurses.

After a history of being associated with various agencies and bureaus of the federal government, in 1973, the NIMH was reorganized as a branch of the newly created Alcoholism, Drug Abuse, and Mental Health Administration.

The Community Mental Health Centers Act It was not until 1963, with the passage of the Mental Retardation Facilities and Community Mental Health Centers Construction Act, that effective efforts for the promotion and maintenance of mental health were instituted. This came 100 years after Dorothea Dix began her crusade for the humane treatment of the mentally ill. The 1963 act provided for federal aid for construction of comprehensive community mental health centers, and authorized staffing, but funds were not appropriated. In 1965, the Community Mental Health Centers Act was amended and funds were authorized. Besides staffing and construction, the Community Mental Health Centers Act provided for grants to train teachers of mentally retarded and other handicapped children and for mental retardation education, research and demonstration projects.[6]

WHAT IS MENTAL ILLNESS?

Introduction

The term "mental health" and "mental illness" are frequently used interchangeably; this seems to be true among the general population as well as among mental health professionals. The meanings of these terms are vague because of the various contexts in which they are commonly used. Many authors who deal with the subject usually describe characteristics of mental health or mental illness rather than providing precise definitions. This seems justified to some extent because there really is no specific condition that is mental health or mental illness.

Mental illness and mental health are actually relative states of functioning with rather broad boundaries. (This is illustrated in Figure 3-1.) A mentally healthy person is one who is able to deal adequately with life's usual situations, but who may for short periods of time exhibit abnormal, bizarre behavior if the environmental circumstances are too severe to adjust to. A mentally ill person is one who is unable to deal adequately with *many* of life's usual situations and

Figure 3-1:

Mental Health and Mental Illness are Relative States of Functioning

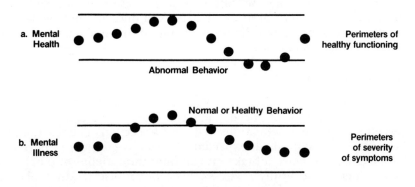

A mentally healthy person is one whose general mode of behavior is effective, but who may occasionally exhibit abnormal symptoms for a short period of time.

A mentally ill person is one whose general mode of behavior is ineffective, but who may occasionally exhibit normal behavior for a short period of time.

attempts to adjust through ineffective and bizarre behavior. From time to time, the environmental circumstances may vary so that the mentally ill person can deal adequately with them, but this is usually for a short period of time and only while the environment remains secure.

Many symptoms of mental illness are also characteristic of mental health. It is only when certain behaviors become extreme that one is mentally ill. Mental health and mental illness, therefore, are matters of *degree*s of behavior, rather than only the *type* of behavior. However, the type of behavior—when the degree is sufficient—will indicate whether the person is neurotic or psychotic.

Causes

Mental illness may be either organic or functional. This classification is based upon the *origin* of the illness. *Organic* mental illnesses are caused by damage to the brain which can result from disease, mechanical injury, chemicals, heredity, and metabolic or glandular dysfunctions. The causes of *functional* mental illnesses are still unclear; however, studies indicate that psychosocial factors, heredity, and body chemistry may be implicated. The functional mental illnesses are characterized by abnormal behavior resulting from no known or observable structural changes in the brain.

The *psychosocial factors* responsible for some forms of mental and emotional disorders probably have their basis in early childhood. These stem from faulty child-parent relationships, inadequate satisfaction of basic needs, and the development of poor intrapersonal insights. It is thought that these, and perhaps other factors, predispose the individual to maladjustments. There is evidence that faulty *heredity* may also predispose one to the inability to deal adequately with adverse environmental factors. Studies indicate, for example, that an identical twin of a schizophrenic sibling is eight times more likely to develop symptoms of schizophrenia than a step-sibling in the same environment.[7] Psychologists are cautious in interpreting the difference in *body chemistry* of normal persons and those with certain mental disorders. It is still unclear whether these differences are the cause of the mental illness or whether the mental illness causes the change in body chemistry.

What Is Normal Behavior?

Normal human behavior is usually measured in terms of psychological, psychiatric (clinical), or social standards. These standards are associated with certain environmental situations that elicit a reaction. The reaction, if within the boundaries of established, expected behavior is considered normal. However, such a definition does not take into account the varieties of other variables that may influence and justify *unexpected* behavior. It also tends to place limitations upon creativity and other motivations that influence human effectiveness. Therefore, *normal human behavior should be perceived as any form of behavior that results in effectiveness in responding to internal or external stimuli—that is, any behavior that is constructive and does not interfere with other social activities.* A form of behavior that is different from the usual should not necessarily be labeled as abnormal. Behavior should be considered abnormal only when it is unrelated to the stimulus that activates it, when it is bizarre, out of touch with reality, destructive to self or society, and/or repeated over and over, but accomplishing nothing. Therefore, normal human behavior may be biological or psychological, but in both cases it is achieving a purpose. Normal human behaviors are reactions that expend human energy efficiently and effectively.

NEUROTIC BEHAVIOR*

General Characteristics

Generally, the normal person deals with frustrations effectively. The normal person has available a wide range of behaviors that can be used to adequately handle most of life's situations. When these situations become too difficult to deal with, these behaviors may take on patterns of disorganization and exaggeration. Instead of helping the person deal with the problem, they actually interfere with effectiveness. If the person continues this ineffectual behavior, frustration heightens and the behavior becomes self-defeating. This may increase frustration. (See Figure 3-2.) However, the behavior may temporarily reduce the anxiety or frustration that tends to perpetuate the behavior. This is called the *neurotic paradox,* which is characteristic of the neurotic personality.

*In 1978, the American Psychiatric Association enacted a resolution calling for future reference to the various neuroses as "mental disorders." We will use both terms in this book.

Figure 3-2:

The Neurotic Paradox

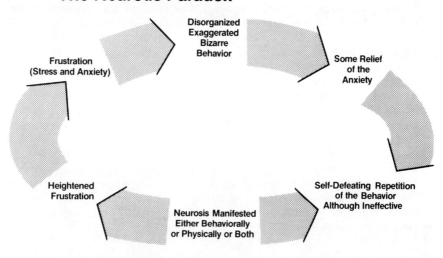

Neurosis is characterized by repetition of ineffective, sometimes exaggerated behavior that is self- defeating

Neurotic reactions do play some protective, but concealed, role in the psychological life of the neurotic. Neurotic symptoms are, for the most part, subjective, but some symptoms may be manifest in physical disturbances. All neurotic behavior has associated with it some level of anxiety. When anxiety is the dominating feature, it is called *anxiety reaction.* Other classifications of neuroses (psychoneuroses) are dissociative reaction, conversion reaction, phobic reaction, and asthenic reaction.

Causes

Neurotic reactions are *psychogenic,* that is, they arise from emotional or psychological factors. Generally these emotional or psychological factors are associated with earlier experiences and the degree of successes related to various childhood phases of development. The neurotic person tends to manifest characteristics of a child, feels inadequate or inferior, seeks attention, and displays other signs of personality inadequacy. Other types of psychogenic disorders are psychotic reactions and personality disorders. (Personality disorders were discussed in Chapter 2.) Neurotic and psychotic disorders are discussed in the following sections.

Anxiety Reaction

Anxiety reaction is a type of neurotic behavior that is characterized by continuous fear or apprehension resulting in heightened anxiety, tensions, sweating, and possibly fatigue. There are some differences of opinion among psychologists as to the specific nature and cause of anxiety reactions. Freudian psychologists explain it as a conflict in one's primitive organic and pleasure-seeking impulses (id) and the rational aspects of the personality or the self-concept (ego). Others explain anxiety reaction in terms of the inability for the individual to close the gap between his or her actual self and perception of the ideal self. Still others view it as a result of constraints that prevent one from attaining self-actualization.

Anxiety reaction interferes with a person's ability to function effectively in many situations; however, other normal everyday activities may be adequately accomplished, although frequently under great stress. Since neurotic anxiety is to some extent incapacitating and will not disappear by itself (although a reorganization of the personality may make it appear to have cured itself), it is imperative that the person seek competent professional therapy. If the symptoms of anxiety reaction disappear as a result of personality reorganization, it is likely to interfere with other future adjustments. Obviously, prevention of psychogenic disorders is what is needed, and this can occur chiefly through improved childhood experiences related to need gratification and other experiences affecting psychic development.

Dissociative Reactions

Overwhelming anxiety is the basis of dissociative reactions, a type of neurotic disorder characterized by a disorganization of the personality. Anxiety resulting in dissociative reactions stems from psychologically painful aspects of life. The three most common forms that dissociative reactions take are amnesia, fugue, and multiple personality, all of which result in some kind of mechanism to repress unacceptable or painful episodes of one's life. The extent to which these symptoms are manifested depends largely upon the severity of anxiety and the threat the experience has to the individual's security.

Amnesia, the loss of memory, is usually selective, involving only the anxiety-provoking situation. For example, the person may be able to recall everything except such identity factors as name, address, and occupation since these factors relate to the part of the self that is under stress. Since the amnesiac cannot identify with the painful experience, it no longer seems relevant.

Fugue is a memory loss characterized by an actual physical departure from the stress-producing situation. The person may wander aimlessly for short or long periods of time and may manifest symptoms of amnesia. When these people regain their memories, they are unable to recall the events that took place during the fugue, but do recall other past experiences prior to the fugue state.

Multiple personality is the most extreme form of dissociative reaction—but it is very rare. This disorder is characterized by the individual developing more than one distinct personality. These personalities are usually opposite, at least in some major character traits. For example, one personality may be kind, sympathetic, and patient, while the other is cruel and impatient. These are representative of conflicting motives of behavior and are perceived as two different people within the same physical or biological structure. Although there is more than one personality present within the individual and these may fluctuate from time to time, each personality that evolves is in complete contact with reality.

Conversion Reactions

When intense anxiety is changed (converted) into bodily functional symptoms the symptoms are called *conversion reactions.* This type of neurosis is relatively rare, but when it occurs, it is usually an effective means of relieving the anxiety that causes the conversion. Formerly referred to as *hysteria,* this neurosis is characterized by loss of sense, such as sight or smell, or paralysis of some part of the body. Upon examination and diagnosis, a physician will find no organic basis for the disturbance; however, the hysteria is real and incapacitating.

A conversion reaction provides the individual with secondary benefits. For example, a military person may develop blindness or paralysis upon seeing a buddy killed. The personal anxiety associated with this experience will make the hysterical soldier unfit for combat and thus remove him from the dangers of being killed. Conversion reactions are more common among military personnel than among civilians, probably because of the nature of the stress encountered during wartime. It is important, however, to distinguish between malingering, psycho-physiologic disorders, and conversion reactions. *Malingering* is merely a faked illness. The *psychophysiologic disorders* are associated with psychological stress resulting in bodily disturbances that are innervated by the autonomic nervous system whereas the *conversion reactions* are controlled by the sensorimotor nervous system.

Phobic Reactions

When anxiety is displaced upon an animal, object, or situation in the form of an irrational and intense fear, it is called a *phobic reaction.* Phobic reactions, also a type of neurosis, are formed by *displacement* or *symbolization. Displacement* is characterized by shifting of the fear-anxiety to an unrelated fear from that which precipitated the anxiety. *Symbolization* is characterized by a phobia that is related and that has specific, but unconscious, meaning to the person. This relationship may be illogical from an intellectual viewpoint, but quite meaningful from an emotional viewpoint. The phobic person is generally aware of the fear, recognizes the irrationality of it, but is powerless to control it. (See Table 3-1 for a summary of phobias).

Depressive Reactions

A neurotic depressive reaction is often characterized by the individual becoming much more depressed than could reasonably be expected, and the duration of the depression is often prolonged. A person may exhibit such symptoms as headache, constipation, anorexia (extreme loss of appetite), and fatigue. Because the neurotic person is in touch with reality, he/she often recognizes the source of frustration but overestimates its significance.

Obsessive-compulsive Reactions

The chief characteristics of the obsessive-compulsive types of neuroses are thought (obsessions) and actions (compulsions). Although the persons suffering from obsessive-compulsive reactions are aware of their existence and understand the irrationality of them, they are unable to control them. Obsessions may

Table 3–1: Phobic Reactions

Phobia	Characteristics —— Fear of:
Acarophobia	Skin-infestation
Acrophobia	Heights
Aerophobia	Fresh air
Agoraphobia	Open spaces
Aichmophobia	Pointed objects
Ailurophobia	Cats
Algophobia	Pain
Amaxophobia	Wagons
Amychophobia	Being scratched——Animal claws
Androphobia	The male sex
Anemophobia	Wind, drafts
Anthrophobia	Society
Aphephobia	Being touched
Apiphobia	Bees——buzzing insects
Astraphobia	Thunder
Ataxophobia	Motor incoordination
Autophobia	Being alone
Automysophobia	Personal uncleanliness
Bacillophobia	Bacteria
Ballistophobia	Missiles
Basiphobia	Walking
Bathophobia	High objects
Batophobia	Acrophobia
Belonephobia	Needles (See also Aichmophobia)
Bromidrosiphobia	Personal odors (See also Automysophobia)
Cainotophobia	Anything new
Carcinomatophobia	Tumors
Cardiophobia	Heart disease
Carnophobia	Meat
Catoptrophobia	Mirrors
Cenophobia	New ideas (See also Cainotophobia)
Cherophobia	Gaiety
Cholerophobia	Cholera
Claustrophobia	Closed places
Copraphobia	Filth
Doraphobia	Fur of animals
Eremophobia	Being alone (See also Autophobia)
Ereutophobia	Blushing (See also Erythrophobia)
Ergasiophobia	Responsibility
Ergophobia	Working
Erythrophobia	Blushing (See also Ereutophobia)
Gatophobia	Cats (See also Ailurophobia)
Gephyrophobia	Water——Boats——Bridges
Gymnophobia	Naked body
Gynephobia	Women
Haphephobia	Being touched (See also Aphephobia)
Hematophobia	Sight of blood
Kleptophobia	Stealing
Lyssophobia	Rabies
Maieusiophobia	Childbirth
Monophobia	Being alone (See also Autophobia)
Mysophobia	Dirt and germs

Table 3–1: (Continued)

Phobia	Characteristics——Fear of:
Mythophobia	Making a false statement
Necrophobia	Dead bodies
Neophobia	The unknown
Nosophobia	Illness
Nudophobia	Being naked
Nyctophobia	Darkness (See also Scotophobia)
Ochlophobia	Crowds
Odontophobia	Dentists
Ombrophobia	Storms——clouds
Ophidiophobia	Snakes
Panophobia	Evil——everything (Also Pantophobia)
Pantophobia	Panophobia
Pharmacophobia	Medicines
Photophobia	Light
Polyphobia	A number of things
Ponophobia	Pain
Psychrophobia	Cold
Pyrophobia	Fire
Rhabdophobia	Punishment (associated with a rod)
Rhypophobia	Feces——filth
Scotophobia	Darkness (Also Nyctophobia)
Sitophobia	Food
Symbolophobia	Symbolic expression
Syphilophobia	Syphilis
Thanatophobia	Death
Topophobia	A particular locality
Toxicophobia	Being poisoned
Trichophobia	Hair (See also Doraphobia)
Trichopathophobia	Hair on the face
Xenophobia	Strangers
Zoophobia	Animals

take the form of insignificant recurring thoughts or they may be associated with violent, antisocial, or immoral acts. Although these thoughts may be intense, the person seldom acts them out. However, they frequently result in extreme anxiety and apprehension that may lead to depression or suicide.

Three major sub-reactions are associated with obsessive-compulsive reactions: (1) ambivalence; (2) isolation; and (3) undoing. *Ambivalence* is characterized by the conflict to do versus the conflict not to do. Ambivalence reaches intense heights with this type of neurosis.

Isolation allows the person to avoid the conflicts by consciously placing them in logical, intellectual compartments of the mind. This allows the conflicting urges to function independently of each other, thus avoiding the conflict.

Undoing is a form of compulsive behavior that is symbolic of the emotional conflict that underlies it. By repeating the act, there results a form of relief from the tension created by the conflicts. Compulsive cleansing of the hands, for example, may be associated with a perceived "dirty" act that took place in childhood. The cleansing is a symbolic attempt to "wash" away the childhood conflict. It is thought that such acts as kleptomania (uncontrolled stealing), pyromania (uncontrolled setting of fires), and exhibitionism may have their roots in compulsive neurosis.

Asthenic Reactions

Asthenia may result from either physical or emotional exhaustion. If it is due to physical exhaustion, the treatment is rest, exercise, good food, and so forth. However, if it is due to emotional factors, it will be necessary for the person to identify the basis for the asthenia. Asthenic reactions are closely associated with conversion reactions; asthenic reactions also may be manifested by hypochondriacs, people who enjoy the symptoms of ill-health and achieve satisfaction in describing their illnesses to others at length. Asthenic reactions formerly were called neurasthenia, which literally means a loss of strength, weakness, and chronic fatigue resulting from nervousness or emotional stress. Treatment may involve taking steps toward achieving relevant satisfaction emotionally and socially.

PSYCHOTIC BEHAVIOR

General Characteristics

Psychotic disorders are a general group of mental illnesses that are characterized by the loss of ability to distinguish between what is real and what is fantasy. The symptoms of all psychoses are manifest as delusions, hallucinations, and distorted, exaggerated emotional behavior. These may appear either singly or in combinations.

Delusions are strong, unshakable *beliefs* that have no basis in reality. Delusions are of three types: (1) *grandeur,* in which the person believes he or she is a person of great renown; (2) *reference,* in which the person associates great meaning to insignificant events; and (3) *persecution,* in which the person believes other people are enemies who, in fact, are not. Delusions of persecution are accompanied by constant fear of bodily harm.

Hallucinations are sensory perceptions that have no environmental stimuli to bring them about. The most common of the hallucinations is auditory. The person hears voices or sounds that are not actually present. Less frequently, the psychotic may experience taste or smell hallucinations. Visual ones are very rare except in organic psychoses.

Emotional symptoms include catatonia, mania, and depression. *Catatonic* reaction is characterized by varying degrees of withdrawal wherein the psychotic becomes unresponsive to stimuli, sometimes to the point of being immobile. *Mania* is a highly emotional state characterized by excitement, elation, and restlessness that requires a high degree of energy expenditure. *Depression* is characterized by remorse, sadness, preoccupation with illness and death. It is during these deep depressive states that a psychotic may attempt suicide.

Causes

Psychotic symptoms may be caused by brain damage (organic psychoses) or by psychological factors (functional psychoses). Examples of organic psychoses are general paresis, caused by the syphilis organism; senile psychosis, caused by cerebral atherosclerosis or arteriosclerosis, a narrowing or hardening of the arteries supplying blood to the brain, and Korsakoff's psychosis, caused by excessive use of alcohol and possibly vitamin B deficiencies. The functional psychoses include schizophrenia, affective (manic-depressive) psychosis, paranoia, and involutional psychosis.

Schizophrenia

Schizophrenia has multidimensional symptoms including progressive withdrawal from environmental forces, personality regression, and deterioration of emotional responses. Approximately one-half of all admissions to hospitals are for patients with some form of mental illness, and of all patients admitted with a mental illness, approximately 50 percent are suffering from some form of schizophrenia. Most cases of schizophrenia are diagnosed in patients 15 to 35 years of age.

Formerly, for diagnostic purposes, schizophrenia was divided into seven distinct classic types. However, since schizophrenia tends to transit from one type to another during various phases of the psychosis, psychiatrists today are reluctant to use these diagnostic classes.

Some forms of schizophrenia manifest symptoms that are gradual, resulting in personality changes characterized by extreme emotionality, lack of interest, and withdrawal. Other forms may manifest symptoms of delusions, silliness, regression, and catatonia. When catatonia is present, the underlying cause of the schizophrenia is usually the result of an extreme emotional experience between the ages of 15 and 25 years. In all forms of schizophrenia, however, there is some degree of withdrawal, and frequently, periodic hallucinations.

Generally, with modern therapeutic techniques, the prognosis for schizophrenia is relatively good. However, depending on the type of symptoms a long-lasting remission may be difficult to achieve. Further, some symptoms tend to be progressive. Much of the success in restoration of mental health is dependent upon environmental circumstances (especially social attitudes and support), the type of schizophrenia present, and the effectiveness of therapy and follow-up treatment.

Affective Reaction: Manic-depressive Reaction

The manic-depressive manifests reactions of elation and deep depression without apparent reason. However, this psychosis can be initiated by either a manic or a depressive reaction. If it is initiated by a manic reaction, it usually occurs between 15 and 25 years of age. If it is initiated by a depressive reaction, it usually occurs between 25 and 35 years of age.

Since this psychosis seems to "run in families," some authorities believe that there may be a hereditary predisposition to it. Other authorities believe that since children tend to identify with their parents, those children of parents who are manic-depressive tend to acquire the symptoms.

If the first attack occurs before the age of 20 years, the prognosis is poor. However, between episodes, the individual functions quite normally. There does not appear to be any significant deterioration in the personality with manic-depressive psychosis as is the case with schizophrenia. However, some patients do show some impairment of judgment and lowered initiative. Chronic manic and depressive episodes are rare before the age of 40 years.

Involutional Psychotic Reaction

The symptoms of this psychosis usually appear in the late 40s for women and the late 50s for men. It is characterized by extreme anxiety, delusions, irritability, and depression. Paranoia may also be present. There is usually no history of mania or depression when the symptoms of involutional psychosis develop. The symptoms are frequently precipitated by conditions that usually take place in middle age, for example, death of a spouse (or other person one depends upon), loss of occupational position, impending retirement, health failure, and preoccupation with one's own death.

Convulsive therapy is the treatment used in some cases of involutional psychosis. It has been estimated that between 80 and 90 percent of the patients treated with electroconvulsive shock therapy are improved. The treatment is controversial, however, and is considered cruel and/or worthless by some opponents. Patients with predominantly paranoid symptoms do not respond as well to it as nonparanoid patients; however, insulin shock treatment following failure with electroconvulsive shock is sometimes helpful. Generally, the prognosis is good with adequate and timely treatment.

Paranoid Reaction

The paranoid psychotic possesses persistent delusions of persecution or grandeur, usually without hallucinations. Paranoid reaction can take one of two forms: (1) classic paranoia; or (2) paranoid state.

Classic paranoia is rarely seen. It is characterized by extreme projection and compensation defense mechanisms. The delusional states appear to exist without disintegration of basic drives or emotions. The delusions tend to be progressive, systematic and logical.

The *paranoid state* manifests symptoms somewhat between those of classic paranoia and paranoid schizophrenia. The paranoiac responds inadequately to situations; the responses include affective reactions and progressive disorganized associations. These responses are carried to extremes as attempts are made by the paranoiac to maintain self-esteem.

Generally, the persecution aspect of paranoia is manifested by blame being placed upon others, and by extreme suspicion and fear for personal safety. The grandiose aspect of paranoia is manifest in delusions that reflect the kind of person the paranoiac thinks she/he is. For example, the paranoiac may believe that he/she is God, or a disciple of God, and may take on the physical characteristics of God.[8]

Paranoia does not seem to affect deterioration of the intellect, but the prognosis for complete recovery is poor. However, hospital confinement may not be necessary in most cases. The paranoiac's chief problem is adjusting to the criticisms of a society that is likely to label the behavior as eccentric, crank, crazy, queer, and so forth.

SUICIDE

Incidence

The incidence of suicide, a self-destructive act, is on the rise. For example, in 1971, there were approximately 22,000 reported cases in the United States. By 1980, this figure had increased to approximately 27,000 reported cases. Suicide is the ninth leading cause of death for all ages in the United States. It is the third leading cause of death in the 15–34-year age group where nearly one-third of all suicides occur. There are nearly three times more suicides among males (19,500) than females (7,400) for all ages combined, and nearly six times more among males than females in the 15–34 year age group. Obviously, adolescence and early adulthood are critical years for establishing preventive measures.

It is important to note that the reported cases of suicide probably represent only about one-third of the actual cases. Many deaths that are actually suicides are reported as caused by some other factor—automobile accidents, for instance. According to the World Health Organization there are more than a half-million successful suicides in the world each year. If all cases of actual suicides were accurately reported in the United States, the incidence of successful suicides would be approximately 80,500 or nearly equivalent to deaths by accidents (about 101,000) each year. Accidents presently are the fourth leading cause of death for all ages in the United States. If those accidents that are actually suicides were reported as such, suicides would become the fourth leading cause of death for all ages in the United States, instead of the ninth leading cause of death.

Many attempts at suicide are planned, deliberate acts of aggression or hostility toward the self. However, it is difficult to determine which suicide attempts are deliberate and which ones the victims did not intend to be final. As Hanlon points out, "often the act is essentially a reaction to a crisis of despair or despondency and represents a dramatic appeal for help, an attempt to attract attention, a means of spiting others, or submitting one's self to trial by ordeal."[9]

The rate of suicides is extremely high among college students, ranking as the second leading cause of deaths among these people (accidents are first). According to some studies, there is approximately a 50 percent greater risk of death by suicide among college students than their noncollege counterparts. The reasons for this are unclear, but some authorities suggest that the demands that some students place upon themselves for academic achievement may be greater than necessary.

Means

Over 85 percent of suicides that are reported are achieved through the use of firearms and explosives, strangulation (hanging), drugs, and gases (natural and carbon monoxide). The ready access and availability of barbiturates has made this type of substance a frequent vehicle for drug-related suicides, accounting for more than 75 percent of all drug-related suicides. For example, it is estimated that upwards of 2000 people die each year as a result of an overdose of propoxyphene (Darvon), and that nearly all of these deaths are suicides. However, the use of firearms still outranks all other methods combined, with somewhere between 55 and 60 percent of all suicides resulting from firearms.

Causes

Who commits suicide? Numerous studies indicate that a variety of circumstances may precipitate or motivate attempts at suicide. Some victims are psychotic, usually of the manic-depressive type; some are alcoholic or addicted to drugs; some have personality disorders; many have no signs of pathology but are merely unhappy, despondent individuals.

Although there probably is not a suicidal type as such, certain circumstances or characteristics can act as warning signals. For example, the following persons should be taken seriously:

- those who exhibit depression, including the manic-depressive patient.
- those who have previously attempted suicide.
- those whose behavior has changed drastically, such as a sudden loss of interest in things that have been important to them, withdrawal from social activities, etc.
- those who threaten suicide.[10]

Suicide is an extremely complex phenomenon. The eminent sociologist, Emile Durkheim, theorized that there are three kinds of suicide:

1. *Egoistic suicide* in which a person is lacking in social group identity. The person has no feeling of belonging.
2. *Altruistic suicide* in which a person takes his/her own life for the benefit of society or family.
3. *Anomic suicide* resulting from a breakdown of social norms in which a person does not know or cannot identify his/her new role in society.[11]

Prevention

In recent years, numerous suicide prevention programs have been established in many large cities throughout the United States and the world. Probably the first recognition of the need for primary prevention measures came about with the establishment of the Anti-suicide Bureau of the Salvation Army in London in 1905. A significant step forward was taken in the United States with the establishment of the Center for Studies of Suicide Prevention as a part of the National Institute of Mental Health in 1966. This Center provides the following services: research support, pilot studies, training of personnel, consultation for suicide prevention agencies, dissemination of information, coordination of emergency services, case findings, treatment, and promotion of the application of research findings.

Bringing suicide into proper perspective and assisting the public to be more informed about its nature and prevention can do much for reducing the incidence of this unnecessary cause of death. It is thought by many authorities that if the social stigma associated with suicide were removed, those who contemplate it would seek help. Much still needs to be done, but as a result of the many positive actions that have been taking place in the past two decades, and the interest and enlightenment of governments, the future outlook for potential suicide victims is optimistic.

CHILD ABUSE AND NEGLECT

Extent of the Problem

One of the most widely neglected and ignored American disgraces is child abuse and neglect. It has only been since the very late 1970s that governments have been even willing to acknowledge the existence of child abuse and neglect, not only within families, but also within the institutions for children, many of which are government controlled and operated.

It is conservatively estimated that there are approximately 1 million instances of child abuse and neglect each year in the United States. Only about one-half of these are brought to the attention of authorities.[12] There are more than 2000 children reportedly killed each year by their parents, guardians, or custodians. There are another 60,000 children who are severely injured each year by these same people, with an additional 600,000 children who are permanently emotionally damaged.[13]

The problem of child abuse and neglect is even more serious than these figures indicate when we take into consideration the broad scope and long-term ramifications. For example, Helfer and Kempe state that

> child abuse and neglect is eroding every aspect of our society. The problem presents itself in a variety of ways, from the severely battered infant to the runaway adolescent who cannot tolerate the abuse any longer. It is ever with us. The end results are teenagers and young adults who are ill prepared to function with their peers, much less raise our next generation.[14]

Of the cases of child abuse and neglect that are reported to proper authorities, most of the children are returned to their parents by the courts. Of those that are returned, approximately 50 percent die within a few years. Hanlon estimates that fewer than 1 percent of battered children are brought to the attention of authorities.[15]

It was not until 1974 that the Child Abuse Prevention and Treatment Act was passed by the Congress. This act established a National Center for Child Abuse and Neglect within the Department of Health, Education, and Welfare. Its basic functions are to: compile and analyze child abuse research; establish a clearinghouse for information; develop and publish documents to be used to train personnel; provide technical assistance to states and agencies; and conduct research. However, as of 1979, the federal government had appropriated only $19 million per year for child abuse and neglect. This represents only a token effort by our federal government to deal with this national disgrace.

Homicide is the fifth leading cause of death among infants 1–4 years of age. Accidents are the leading cause of death for this age group, and some of these are probably associated with child abuse that resulted in the death but were reported as accidental. There is no significant difference between the homicide rate for boys or girls. Homicide is the fourth leading cause of death in the age group 5 to 14 years. How many of these homicides are the result of severe abuse by the children's caretakers is unknown.

Who Are Child Abusers?

Researchers have attempted to find answers to the numerous and complex questions that surround this confounding health problem: Who neglects their children? Why do they neglect them? Is there a pattern; a profile? Generally, parents who *neglect* their children, either moderately or severely, are themselves the victims of childhood neglect. They possess personalities characterized by:

- apathy
- inability to accept responsibility
- immaturity, both emotionally and in judgment development
- defensive reactions for their behavior, especially blaming others for their inability to provide for their children
- preoccupation with a fantasy world
- unwillingness to seek outside help (unless it satisfies their physical and emotional needs)
- resentment toward "interference" with raising their children
- indifference
- inability to set realistic goals and lack of determination to achieve goals
- withdrawal
- loneliness.

Neglect is not always of physical and biological needs—adequate clothing, cleanliness, and food; it may also be emotional neglect—neglect of "the soul, of life itself. It is neglect with menace."[16]

Child abuse follows a rather predictable, almost rigid pattern. Young describes child abuse in this way:

It [child abuse] is not the impetuous blow of the harassed parent nor even the transient brutality of an indifferent parent expressing with violence the immediate frustrations of his life. It is not the too severe discipline nor the physical roughness of ignorance. It is the perverse fascination with punishment as an entity in itself, divorced from discipline and even from the fury of revenge. It is the cold calculation of destruction which in itself requires neither provocation nor rationale.

Young goes on to emphasize it is important that we do not confuse the meaning and purpose of discipline and punishment, for "punishment divorced from discipline becomes a monstrosity. Yet it is precisely this separation that characterizes abusing parents."[17]

Characteristics of parents who abuse their children are generally quite different from those who neglect their children. Children who are abused are usually not neglected: the household is clean, well-kept; meals are served; and the house is warm. This is in contrast to the neglected child where these physical necessities are almost always lacking. In the child-neglect homes, usually all of the children are more or less equally neglected, while only one child of abusing parents is usually singled out for the infliction of abuse.

Abuse may take several forms including beatings, burnings, unusual and severe forms of "punishment," such as kicking and beatings with iron rods. These may go on for extended periods of time, eventually resulting in the need for hospitalization or in death. Occasionally, friends, neighbors, or relatives bring the abused child to the attention of the authorities. However, even though many are aware of the child abuse, they are too frequently reluctant to become involved. More often, when child abuse is detected it is in a setting such as school, usually by the school nurse, or from the observations of caseworkers, physicians, and hospital emergency room attendants.

Child abuse occurs in all socioeconomic groups. It is a symptom of a troubled society that results in a disintegration of the family. Prevention of child abuse and neglect must begin with the identification of these families. The earlier that these families are identified the greater the possibility that something can be done to halt the perpetuation of the problem from one generation to the next. Most children of neglecting and abusing parents can be helped to find a way of life much more productive than that which their own parents have forged for them. And this is where real prevention begins: preventing these children from becoming neglecting or abusing parents of their future children.

CRIMINAL BEHAVIOR

A *criminal* is a person who commits a serious act that violates some law. The act is called a crime, and may be either a felony or a misdemeanor. A *felony,* a serious crime such as robbery, usually results in confinement upon conviction of guilt. A misdemeanor is a less serious crime, for example, disorderly conduct.

A criminal may or may not have psychiatric conditions. If a psychiatric condition exists and it can be shown to fall within legal definitions of insanity, the person may not be convicted of the crime because the person was not legally responsible for the crime. Several court decisions define such lack of responsibility. For example, according to the *Currens* formula, if it is shown that a person committing a crime did not have the capacity to conform to the requirements of the law, he/she is not responsible for the crime. The *Durham decision* was a ruling that a person is not responsible for a crime if it resulted from a mental disease or defect. The famous *McNaghten decision* established that a person was not responsible for a crime committed while suffering from a defect of reason resulting from a mental illness that rendered him/her unable to know the nature of the act or, if he/she did, was unable to know that the act was wrong. Finally, a person is not responsible for a crime in *some* states if the act was precipitated by a psychotic condition resulting in an *irresistible impulse.*

Cause and Prevention

More crimes are committed in urban areas than in rural areas. It is in urban areas that we find more of the elements that may contribute to criminal acts: slums, crowded living conditions, poverty, competition, discrimination, parents with a lack of parenting knowledge, broken homes, and so forth. We have already seen that children brought up in neglect and abuse are more likely to treat their children in the same manner. Also, these children are less likely to receive the kind of attention, love, security, and the like that is essential for normal personality development. As a result, many resort to crimes in later life and many end up in our prisons or other "correctional" institutions.

The large numbers of chronic or repeat criminals and the continuous rise in the crime rate give evidence that our correctional system fails to rehabilitate the criminal and that punishment is not a deterrent. Punishment has for centuries been generally thought as the basic means for controlling undesirable behavior of people. However, there is no scientific evidence to show that punishment is a deterrent to crime or that it will, beyond some conditioned reflexes, elicit desirable behavior.

What is needed instead is a kind of discipline that is acceptable and realistic for the individuals during their developing years—a discipline that is associated with love, understanding, and security and that allows the person to grow, develop, make decisions, feel success, and accept failures.

Confinement may be necessary to remove a person from society so that the criminal behavior will no longer be a threat. However, when the punishment is meted out as a form of revenge upon the perpetrator of the crime, it is most likely to result in resentment and retaliation against society rather than to deter the person from further criminal conduct. Confinement should be accompanied by those other human ingredients that the person has been deprived of that precipitated the behavior in the first place. Otherwise, most criminals are caught up in the "revolving door" of crime itself. Many people who commit crimes can be helped; but we have the knowledge to be even more successful. However, the easiest, although the most expensive, way of dealing with crime is to punish and confine.

Most criminals grow up in a discordant environment, chiefly the home. The child feels threatened, develops hostile feelings and attempts to compensate or to relieve these tensions through criminal acts. Prevention of many crimes must take into consideration all of the basic factors that precipitate the behavior.

One of the most important measures that can be taken is expanding parenting programs for young adults who are contemplating a family and making these programs attractive and accessible to the people who need them most. Such programs have the potential for preventing criminal behavior, but of even greater importance, they have the potential for improving the mental health of all members of a family. This can result in greater productivity for each individual and a more harmonious society. As criminal behavior is bred in discordant families, so are productive behavior and mentally healthy people bred in harmonious and secure surroundings.

TREATMENT MODALITIES

Chemotherapy

The use of drugs in the treatment of mental and emotional disorders is called chemotherapy. Although drugs alone do not cure mental illnesses, they are important adjuncts to other forms of treatment. Depending upon the type of mental disorder, certain drugs can be used to alleviate symptoms, rendering the individual more amenable to other forms of treatment.

The kinds of drugs being used are tranquilizers sedatives, and antidepressants, and lithium. The use of these drugs has greatly reduced the time of hospitalization of many mental patients and has made it possible for them to control their behavior and function quite normally in society. The use of chemotherapy was significantly ushered in in the early to middle 1950s with the discovery of the value of tranquilizers in controlling the symptoms of some mental patients. (See Chapter 8 for a more detailed discussion of drugs.)

Tranquilizers The *tranquilizers* are a group of drugs that produce a calming effect without resulting in drowsiness or sleep. This group of drugs is further classified as minor tranquilizers and major tranquilizers.

The *minor tranquilizers* are used to treat anxiety, nervous tension, and some neuroses. These tranquilizers must be used with care since they are addicting and can produce withdrawal reactions as severe as those associated with barbiturates. The minor tranquilizers are meprobamate (Miltown and Equanil), chlordiazepoxide (Librium), and diazepam (Valium). Miltown was developed in 1952 and approved for marketing by the Food and Drug Administration as a muscle relaxant. Subsequent research determined that this drug was ineffective as a muscle relaxant, but effective in the treatment of anxiety and nervous tension. Librium is used for the treatment of presurgical anxiety and acute panic. Valium is an effective sedative used to treat tension and muscle spasms that recur or are prolonged. Some authorities question whether the minor tranquilizers are of any greater value than the barbiturates.[18]

The *major tranquilizers,* are not addicting and are useful in treating some psychoses, notably, schizophrenia. Beginning in 1955, with the widespread use of tranquilizers for the treatment of mental patients, hospitalized populations began to decrease dramatically. This is also due in part to the establishment of large numbers of community mental health centers.

The major tranquilizers are derived from phenothiazene, which was first synthesized in 1883. The commercial preparations of the phenothiazenes include Thorazine, Vesprin, Prolixin, Compazine, Mellaril, Dartal, Trilafon, Taractin, and Stelazine.

Thorazine, or chlorpromazine, is probably the most well-known of the phenothiazines. It was synthesized in 1950 and first used in the United States in 1954 for the treatment of psychomotor excitement and mania. As with all of the phenothiazine compounds, chlorpromazine reduces the symptoms of fear and hostility associated with a psychosis. This results in the patient becoming more manageable and amenable to psychotherapy. *Compazine,* or prochlorperazine, is effective in controlling the symptoms of emotionally disturbed children, including the nausea that frequently accompanies anxiety.

Sedatives   Sedatives are drugs that produce calm and help to alleviate anxiety. In smaller doses sedatives reduce anxiety, but do not cause drowsiness. Many sedatives are addictive.

Antidepressants   Antidepressants are drugs that serve to elevate the mood of depressed persons. Some types of antidepressants have potentially dangerous side effects.

Lithium   *Lithium* was approved in 1970 by the Food and Drug Administration for the treatment of mania. Lithium is an element that has been used for well over 100 years in the treatment of many conditions, for example, gout. However, because of its side effects, its use for this purpose was discontinued about 50 years ago. In 1949, it was discovered by Australian scientists to be effective for the treatment of mania. Much is still to be learned about this drug. However, it is possible that of all the drugs being used to treat mental and emotional disorders, lithium may be the only one that effects a cure.[19]

Electronic Therapy

Electroconvulsive shock therapy (ECT) is the successor to the use of insulin shock treatment and the use of other convulsion-inducing drugs. Electroconvulsive shock therapy is the most widely used convulsive therapy. It is accomplished by attaching electrodes to the head of a patient and applying from 70–130 volts of electricity for a fraction of a second; three or four shocks may be given in one treatment session. The shocks bring on a convulsion and loss of consciousness. Many believe ECT to be especially effective in treating severe depression. Since there are some adverse side effects associated with electroconvulsive shock therapy, such as a disintegration of functioning and possibly some loss of mental ability (learning and memory), some authorities believe this form of treatment should be reserved for only the most extreme cases or for emergency situations.

Psychosurgery

Psychosurgery is dramatic and complete. When it was first introduced as a means of treating psychosis, it was thought to be the panacea. The most renowned form of psychosurgery is *prefrontal lobotomy.* This is simply the severing of the nerves that connect the prefrontal lobe of the brain with the hypothalamus. When this is accomplished, symptoms of anxiety disappear because the sources of emotional disturbance cannot react with the person's thoughts and memories.

Persons experiencing this type of psychosurgery have had, as a result, profound personality changes characterized by childish behavior, shallowness of thought processes, apathy, and lack of enthusiasm. Since psychosurgery cannot be reversed and its long-range effects on the patient are unclear, it has all but been eliminated as a method of treatment in the United States, except with a few "hopeless" cases.

Social Interactions

The variety of treatment modalities that make use of social contact and communication are called *psychotherapy*. They all use the principle of *catharsis*, the release of emotional tension through *talking* out or *acting* out feelings.

Through these psychotherapeutic techniques the person gradually acquires insight into the self and an understanding of the feelings and emotions that contribute to or underlie the mental illness. Some forms of psychotherapy extend over long periods of time while others bring out the causes of the emotional stress quite rapidly. We will describe several of the many psychotherapies in this section.

Psychoanalytic therapy   Psychoanalysis may take many months or years. It focuses on unconscious motivations, conflicts, and repressions that may have their roots in early childhood. Techniques used are: (1) free association; (2) dream analysis; (3) analysis of resistance; and (4) analysis of transference. *Free association* consists of the patient relating to the therapist any thoughts that come into the mind. The therapist encourages the patient to reveal these thoughts and may provide the patient with interpretations of these thoughts. Through this, it is theorized that the patient will be able to reach deeper into the mind exposing repressed urges that have expressed themselves symbolically.

Dreams frequently provide the therapist with clues to unconscious motivation. The therapist attempts to interpret what the patient recalls of his or her dreams in such a way as to reveal its symbolic meaning. This whole process is referred to as *dream analysis.*

Analysis of resistance is necessary when a patient, during free association, becomes unable or unwilling to reveal certain painful thoughts. The analyst recognizes these moments and attempts to break down the resistances so that all of the elements associated with the patient's problem can be revealed and understood. If these resistances are not dealt with they prevent the patient from becoming conscious of the painful conflicts that underlie the emotional problems and preclude success in psychoanalysis.

As psychoanalysis proceeds, the patient often develops one of three kinds of emotional attachments to the therapist. These attachments are frequently associated with the person who created the original emotional conflict. If the attachment to the therapist is one of admiration or love, it is called *positive transference;* if hostile, it is called *negative* transference, or if both negative and positive attitudes are manifest, it is called *ambivalent transference.* Regardless of the path transference takes, the therapist must deal with the situation cautiously, helping the patient to understand what is taking place and why these feelings toward the therapist exist. This process is called *analysis transference.*

Group therapy   *Group therapy* exemplifies a true social interaction as a vehicle for understanding and dealing with emotional problems. The therapist uses both directive and nondirective techniques. Group therapy tends to help the individuals of the group clarify their values and establish new and more effective values systems. Not everyone can benefit from group therapy and it is common for several members of the group to drop out. Greatest success occurs among those people who are willing to become emotionally attached to others, who have the ability to express anger, and who have a flexible perception of authority.[20]

Hypnosis   The success of *hypnosis* is dependent upon the skill of the therapist *and* the willingness of the patient. Contrary to some popular notions, hypnosis is an induced state of suggestibility rather than a state of sleep. In the state of suggestibility it is possible for the therapist to make the patient perform a variety of acts the patient would ordinarily not perform or not feel were possible; the patient can also recall repressed events in life. In addition, the therapist can temporarily remove symptoms of anxiety, conversion reaction, or physical pain. The real value of hypnosis however, is as an aid in uncovering repressed experiences that may underlie the symptoms of the emotional problem.

There are two interesting aspects of hypnosis: (1) posthypnotic suggestion; and (2) hypnotic regression. While in the hypnotic state, the therapist can induce suggestions that the patient will respond to following a removal of the hypnotic state. This *posthypnotic suggestion* may remain for several days; however, unless it is reinforced, it will disappear. The value of posthypnotic suggestion is that physical or psychological symptoms can be removed for a short period of time allowing the therapist to deal with the patient using other therapeutic techniques. Hypnosis may be effective in removing symptoms, but it does not remove the cause of the illness, physical or emotional.

Through *hypnotic regression* the patient is "returned" to earlier years and "allowed" to relive some of the experiences that may have contributed to the emotional problem. This provides the therapist with greater insight into the patient's emotional life. The value of hypnotic regression is generally accepted by psychologists; however, much more research is needed. There remains, for example, the danger of removing the symptoms of the illness by hypnosis, possibly making the patient dependent upon hypnotic treatments, leaving the deep-rooted causes unresolved.[21] Certainly, the use of hypnosis has no place in the hands of amateurs and unskilled therapists.

Psychodrama   The use of *psychodrama* establishes a secure, non-threatening environment in which the patient can relive some of the painful experiences that are associated with his/her emotional problems. Generally, the therapist sets the scene with the patients, and assistants assume other roles related to the experience. The patients act out the situation, guided or directed by the realistic responses of the assistants. Psychodrama provides the patient with free association and catharsis; with the aid of the therapist, the patient acquires insight into why or how the experience contributes to the existing anxiety or other emotional state. Because of the reactions of the assistants, the patient frequently learns new and more effective adjustment skills that are related to the traumatic experience.

Existential therapy   *Existential therapy* is concerned with occurrences or happenings as they exist. The therapist helps the patient to take personal responsibility for what happens and seek success in self-actualization. The therapist deals with the person holistically and self-deterministically. The individual has control over the choices of behavior being made, and the therapist attempts to find the original choices the person had made that resulted in the maladjustment.

Behavior therapy   *Behavior therapy* is concerned with eliminating the symptoms of the maladjustment, that is, the unwanted behaviors, with little regard for the patient gaining insight into the basic causes. The behavior therapist is interested in having the patient "unlearn" certain maladaptive behaviors and, in their place, learn adaptive behaviors. The behavior therapist may use some rather harsh techniques, such as threats or possibly violence to eliminate the symptoms of maladjustment.

One treatment that has been used is called *systematic desensitization,* the step-by-step process of assisting a person to learn to reduce a fear reaction or negative response to an object or person. Another behavior therapy, *implosive therapy,* is based upon the assumption that extinction of an unwanted response will occur as the patient imagines the frightening stimuli that cause the fear or anxiety. *Operant conditioning* is used to achieve extinction of the undesirable behavior by rewarding desirable behavior and ignoring (sometimes punishing) undesirable behavior.

Other therapies   *Integrity therapy* is based upon the precept that maladjustment results from hidden antisocial actions that affect a person's moral structure. Integrity therapy attempts to persuade the person to take the consequences for his/her actions and not to place the blame on parents or others. As a result, the role of the unconscious mind is of little importance in overcoming the symptoms of maladjustment. Since this is a relatively new psychotherapeutic approach, it is still too early to make any definitive judgments as to its value as a treatment modality.

Play therapy provides an opportunity for venting pent up emotions without fear of punishment, and an opportunity to experiment with various ways of dealing with emotion-provoking situations. Play therapy is used almost exclusively with children. It consists, usually, of allowing a child to play in any way he/she may want to. A common technique is to provide a playroom with dolls, a dollhouse, and other things related to a family. The child is told to play with these as he/she wishes—even destroy them if the desire is present. Frequently, the child will give symbolic indications as to the needs that must be gratified by seeking love from the "mother doll," by "punishing" a "brother doll," and so forth.

GLOSSARY

Catharsis: A form of emotional release resulting from talking out problems with the aid of a therapist.

Chemotherapy: A form of treatment using drugs.

Child abuse: The cruel and unusually harsh treatment of a child by parents, guardians, or caretakers.

Child neglect: The failure of parents, guardians, or caretakers to provide a child with the basic necessities of life.

Electroconvulsive shock therapy: The passage of a controlled electrical current through the brain to promote a convulsion, as a means of treating depression.

Neurotic paradox: The use of temporary relief of tension and a tendency to repeat the ineffective behavior, which in turn may increase frustration.

Psychogenic illness: Illness resulting from emotional or psychological factors.

SUMMARY

Attitudes toward mental illness and the mentally ill have undergone marked changes over the centuries. Because of a lack of understanding about mental illness, people's attitudes were based upon superstition and misconceptions. Even today, one of the greatest obstacles confronting a recovered psychotic is the attitude of the society.

The history of the treatment and care of the mentally ill provides us with an understanding of present-day knowledge and practices. It has only been during the twentieth century that we have begun to focus our attention upon the promotion of mental health and the prevention of mental illness.

Probably the first attempt to treat the mentally ill as humans with feelings was in 1792 when Philippe Pinel ordered the chains and shackles removed from patients in two mental institutions in Europe. Dorothea Dix was successful in similar improvements in America. Benjamin Rush is considered the "Father of American Psychiatry" as a result of his work in this area. He published the first textbook on the subject, which remained the standard text for over 70 years. A turning point in the practice of psychiatry came about when Sigmund Freud announced his theories of psychoanalysis.

The beginning of the twentieth century saw the launching of the mental hygiene movement, known popularly today as the mental health movement. A significant advance to the movement came about in 1949 with the establishment of the National Institute for Mental Health. In 1963, the Mental Retardation Facilities and Community Mental Health Centers Act was passed.

The cause of mental illnesses may stem from damage to the brain or the cause may be psychogenic. Brain damage may result from injury, chemicals, infections, faulty heredity, and metabolic disturbances. The psychogenic mental illnesses may result from faulty child-parent relations, inadequate need gratification, or faulty self-insight.

All neuroses have anxiety associated with them. Although neurotic behavior is ineffectual, it does provide the person with some protective device in his/her total psychological life. The ineffectual behavior increases frustration, but may temporarily reduce anxiety, which results in a repetition of the behavior.

There are several explanations for anxiety reaction including a conflict between the id and ego, the inability for the individual to bring together actual and ideal self, and the inability for one to attain self-actualization. Phobic reactions are characterized by intense, irrational fears of places, people, or things.

In all forms of psychoses, the individual is incapacitated to some degree and has lost touch with reality. Some persons need extensive therapy and others may have to be hospitalized.

The incidence of suicide is on the increase; however, with the establishment of a variety of prevention programs, it is predicted that many suicides will be prevented. Persons most likely to attempt suicide are some psychotics, alcoholics, drug addicts, and those who have experienced tragedy with which they are unable to cope.

Child abuse and neglect is one of America's most widely ignored, but preventable, mental health problems. It disrupts, erodes, and destroys families, is perpetuated to succeeding generations, and contributes to violence and crime.

Criminal behavior is chiefly defined by law, rather than by psychological motivations. There is a significant gap between what science knows about criminal behavior and the way in which the law deals with it. The causes of criminal behavior are complex, involving a variety of personal, social, and legal circumstances.

The treatment modalities used for mental illnesses are the use of drugs, electroconvulsive shock, psychosurgery, and psychotherapy. Each has a place, but certain ones are more effective for particular psychoses than others.

PROBLEMS FOR DISCUSSION

1. Take a survey of class members to determine their attitudes about psychotic people including how they should be treated, and whether or not they should be returned to society. Analyze the results.
2. Make a list of some misconceptions that still exist about mental illness. Expose the misconceptions with scientific evidence.
3. What are the similarities of one who is mentally healthy and one who is maladjusted (psychotic or neurotic)? Associate the degrees and types of behavior with mental illness.
4. Discuss the significance of the causation of mental illnesses in terms of their prevention.
5. Distinguish between normal and abnormal human behavior. Compare this with your answer to question number 3. Should creative behavior that is different from expected social norms be considered abnormal? Explain.
6. Describe the characteristics of a neurotic personality.
7. What are the basic classes of neuroses? How are they similar?
8. List the causes of neuroses.
9. Define psychosis. What are the major forms psychoses may take? What is the prognosis for each?
10. Distinguish between "classic paranoia" and "paranoid state."
11. What is suicide? What are some of its causes? Who is most likely to commit suicide? Why?

12. Can child abuse and neglect be considered one of our most important preventable health problems? Explain.
13. Identify the usual causes of criminal behavior.
14. What kinds of new approaches should society consider in the prevention and alleviation of crimes?
15. What can society do to help the mental patient to complete recovery?
16. Why is the development of a historical perspective about mental illness and mental health important for understanding the factors associated with the promotion and maintenance of mental health?
17. What were three events that took place during the eighteenth century that were forerunners to the beginning of the mental health movement?
18. Describe why Clifford Beers is the undisputed founder of the mental health movement.
19. What provisions did the Mental Retardation Facilities and Community Mental Health Centers Construction Act of 1963 contain? Describe their importance to the advancement of mental health.

REFERENCES

1. RIDENOUR, NINA, *Mental Health In the United States: A Fifty-year History.* Harvard University Press, Cambridge, Mass., 1961, p. 1.
2. DEUTSCH, ALBERT, *The Mentally Ill In America: A History of Their Care and Treatment From Colonial Times.* Doubleday, Doran & Company, Inc., Garden City, N.Y., 1937, p. 90.
3. *Ibid.,* pp. 93–94.
4. RIDENOUR, *op. cit.,* p. 125.
5. DEUTSCH, *op. cit.,* p. 493.
6. *National Institutes of Health Almanac,* U.S. Department of Health, Education, and Welfare, DHEW Publication No. (NIH) 77–5, Washington, D.C., pp. 18–19.
7. KALLMAN, F. J., "The Use of Genetics in Psychiatry," *Journal of Mental Science,* 1958, pp. 542–549.
8. *The Merck Manual of Diagnosis and Therapy.* Merck & Co., Inc., Rahway, N.J., 1956, p. 1315.
9. HANLON, JOHN J., *Public Health: Administration and Practice,* 6th ed. The C.V. Mosby Company, Saint Louis, 1974, p. 448.
10. *Ibid.,* p. 455.
11. WARGA, RICHARD G., *Personal Awareness: A Psychology of Adjustment.* Houghton Mifflin Company, U.S., 1974, p. 447.
12. HELFER, RAY E. and C. HENRY KEMPE, *Child Abuse and Neglect.* Ballinger Publishing Company, Cambridge, Mass., 1976, pp. xvii–xx.
13. STEELE, BRANDT F., "Violence Within the Family," *Child Abuse and Neglect.* Ballinger Publishing Company, Cambridge, Mass., 1976, p. 6.
14. HELFER, *op. cit.,* p. xvii.
15. HANLON, *op. cit.,* p. 504.

16. YOUNG, LEONTINE, *Wednesday's Children: A Study of Child Neglect and Abuse.* McGraw-Hill Book Company, N.Y., 1964, p. 47.
17. *Ibid.,*   p. 45.
18. RAY, OAKLEY S., *Drugs, Society and Human Behavior.* The C.V. Mosby Company, Saint Louis, 1972, pp. 154–155.
19. *Ibid.,*   p. 150.
20. RUCH, FLOYD L., *Psychology and Life,* 7th ed. Scott, Foresman and Company, Glenview, Ill., 1967, p. 519.
21. *Ibid.,*   p. 523.

4

motivation of health behavior

HEALTH NEEDS AND DESIRES

Influence of Environment

Our environment and satisfaction of our health needs and desires are inseparably linked. Our environment is divided into the internal and external environments. Our *internal environment* consists of our body's processes that tend to maintain a state of homeostasis. Homeostasis must be maintained within very limited boundaries or illness results. We are capable of adjusting to rather wide variations in the external environment, but only slight variations in the internal environment. This is one important reason why healthful behavior related directly to possible changes in the internal environment is essential. For example, a person who smokes a cigarette for the first time may likely experience nausea and dizziness almost immediately resulting from a disruption of the internal environment. However, the body will adjust to this pollution and these symptoms may not be apparent after some time. If the smoking continues, the body's ability to adapt to the chemicals in the smoke may diminish, resulting in other, more serious symptoms, such as lung cancer or cardiovascular disease.

Our *external environment* consists of such factors as weather, temperature, mechanical devices, and all of the objects identified as plants, minerals, and animals. The *social environment* is composed of all factors related to people— history, cultures and so forth—and the everyday interactions we have with other people, as well as our intrapersonal relationships. Both the physical and social environments produce, besides direct and observable influences upon us, a psychological influence as well. Some authorities refer to this as the *psychological environment.* The psychological environment has an important impact upon our health behavior and is closely associated with our motivation.

The *total environment* is usually viewed as those factors in our surroundings. The environment consists of the effective (functional) and noneffective (nonfunctional) components. The *effective environment* is that part of our total environment that is stimulating us to respond in some way. The *noneffective environment* is that portion of the total environment that is *not* eliciting in any way a response from us. The effective environment may be in immediate proximity to us or it may be hundreds of miles away. Electronics, for example has broadened our effective environment. The noneffective environment may at any moment become effective, while the effective environment may at any moment become noneffective, but not until it has influenced us. It is the effective environment that acts to satisfy our needs, desires, and aspirations, or that acts to prevent their satisfaction.

The Nature of Perceiving the Environment

We begin our study of motivation and health by discussing perception, because if we do not perceive the environment, we cannot take action toward healthful behavior. *Perception* is receiving impulses through one or more of the sense organs, which results in an intellectual impression of the impulses and ultimately a reaction to them. The senses are the sense of *touch* (temperature, pressure, and pain), *smell, taste, sight,* and *hearing.* Most of these function as vehicles for communicating with the external environment. (See Figure 4-1.)

Healthy sense organs are essential for us to accurately receive and interpret the stimuli emitted from the environment. Through the senses, we interact with and respond to our environment, which makes it possible for us to grow, mature intellectually and emotionally, and to change our world. However, even with healthy sense organs, we sometimes misperceive stimuli for a number of reasons. This is exemplified, for example, in the case of a sensory illusion. An illusion is simply a false or misinterpreted sensory impression of a real stimulus. It can occur through any of the sense organs, but the most dramatic are visual illusions.

Illusions result when we organize erroneously, then misperceive and misinterpret stimuli from the physical environment as something contrary to reality.

All of the senses are vitally important to our functioning, each providing us with unique sensations, but also blending them for other perceptual experiences.

The quality of the perceptions are influenced by the strength of the stimuli, the health of receptors, and by the area of the brain that receives the impulse. Drugs may affect the area of the brain receiving impulses, resulting in an altered perception. Receptors are capable of generating limited impulses. For instance, if we are hit in the eye, besides pain from the touch receptor, a flash of light is received in the brain through the optic nerve. The optical center of the brain is not capable of perceiving the pain from the blow but is capable of perceiving light.

What we perceive is not so much dependent upon the sense organ that is stimulated as it is upon the area of the brain that is stimulated, although, normally, the two organs must work cooperatively. However, it is possible to bypass the sense organ and still experience all of the basic sensations. This may

Figure 4-1:

Perceptual Areas of the Brain

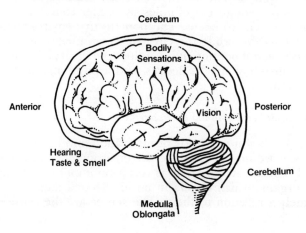

be achieved through direct stimulation of the brain using electrodes. It may also be achieved in a more modified, uncontrolled way through the ingestion of various types of drugs.

Perception is the intermediate level of contact with our internal or external environments. The perceptual area of the brain interprets the impulse as sight, sound, taste and so on, but other impulses may be generated and transmitted to other areas of the brain for significance, relationships and action. For example, when a mosquito bites us, the touch sense transmits the impulse to the brain for perception; the brain transmits impulses to the motor area, vision area, and others; these activate the appropriate muscles to swat the mosquito or to scratch the itch.

Psychological Factors in Perception

Frequently, perception is influenced, consciously or unconsciously, by what we *want* to perceive or by other factors in the environment suggesting what *should* be perceived. This is called *psychological selectivity* or *attention* and is characterized by a response to those stimuli that meet or help to meet an immediate need or interest.

WHAT IS A HUMAN NEED?

Human needs may be viewed in terms of those urgencies essential for biological life and those essential for mental, emotional, and social life. Our effectiveness is possible only when our basic needs are adequately satisfied. However, if satisfaction does not take place as the needs arise, our development may suffer, health may fail, and even death may result. These consequences will depend upon the urgency of the particular need, and how severe the deprivation is, as well as how well we are prepared for this deprivation. Learning how to satisfy needs is critical for the promotion and maintenance of our health.

The *basic needs* have traditionally been grouped as biological needs and as emotional or psychological needs. Our *biological needs* are essentially inherited drives, while our *psychological needs* are either inherited (there is still some question about this), the result of social stimuli, or both. Examples of our biological needs are the need for food, water, oxygen, elimination of wastes, relief from pain, and safety. If satisfaction of any one of these needs is sufficiently deprived over a period of time, ill-health results. Examples of psychological needs are a need for a sense of security, love, and self-esteem. Severe deprivation of any one of these needs may result in an emotional disturbance, a social disturbance, or both.

Our psychological and biological needs are in constant interaction. For example, if our biological needs are adquately met in appropriate ways, a portion of our psychological needs will also be met. Probably one of the most obvious is the satisfaction of the hunger drive in infancy, especially if the infant is held during feeding. Food satisfies the biological need, hunger, while being held tends to provide the infant with reassurance, a sense of security, and belongingness.

Characteristics of Needs

During prenatal development, the fetus must have oxygen and food, and must be able to eliminate waste products successfully. The necessity for satisfying these basic biological needs continues throughout life. However, following birth, new and more complex needs come into play; the psychological needs. The gratification of these needs is important for our psychological and social development, and mental, emotional, and social health. The biological needs, or drives, activate and direct much of our behavior and are powerful motivational forces. For example, the hunger drive activates us to seek food. This seeking process will continue until hunger is satisfied, unless other more powerful drives come into play to temporarily interrupt or overcome the hunger drive.

Our psychological needs also activate and direct our behavior. Behavior can infer the motivation, but motivation sometimes appears to be unassociated with the behavior. For example, one who eats too much may be doing so because of an emotional problem rather than because of hunger or the *need* for food.

The Effects of Unmet Needs

Generally, a preoccupation with need satisfaction is a symptom of illness. On the other hand, if needs are adequately and appropriately satisfied as the urgency presents itself, preoccupation with them is less likely to take place. We still may *want* greater satisfaction of certain needs, but most likely there will be no preoccupation with them. For example, as we leave childhood, the need for recognition from others decreases in intensity for most of us although the *desire* for recognition may continue. If we are recognized for certain achievements, it may result in pleasant emotional feelings; but if such recognition does not occur, there may be only temporary disappointment.

Motivators of Human Desires

Drives or needs tend to motivate us into actions necessary for survival and/or the attainment or maintenance of effectiveness. Our needs act as incentives that motivate behavior and are frequently the basis for more complex and learned personal desires and aspirations.

Our desires and aspirations are culturally influenced, but they are also the creations of our intellect and emotional mechanism. Desires and aspirations are our goals that seek achievement. These may be very limited and immediate or they may be complex and long-ranged. Goals may be clearly defined in our minds or they may be somewhat vague and obscure. Goals create a tension that is the basis for some form of action. Whenever there is a tension, biological or psychological, there is the tendency for us to seek relief from this tension. This is the basis for our motivation. It may take the form of a drive, feeling, emotion, desire, want, or aspiration; but the urge to act, to respond, to find relief from the tension is present and may persist until the tension is relieved. The more powerful the tension, the more powerful the motivation will be, and the more energy that will be summoned to deal with it.

PRIORITIES OF HEALTH NEEDS

Maslow's Hierarchy

Some needs, by their very nature, must be met immediately, while the satisfaction of others can be deferred to a later date. For example, the need for oxygen is immediate and continuous. For the most part, it is satisfied quite automatically and with little effort on our part. We seldom think about satisfying the need for oxygen unless something (such as emphysema) intervenes to prevent the automatic satisfaction from taking place.

Since some needs are more vital than others, attempts have been made to prioritize them according to their importance for survival, continuance and maintenance of life, and the enhancement of living. One of the most widely accepted grouping of needs in this respect is Maslow's hierarchy of needs. The hierarchy describes the biological needs as the most urgent, and the emotional as the more complex. Maslow's holistic-dynamic theory of motivation as reflected in his hierarchy of needs is summarized in Table 4-1.

Maslow stressed the importance of recognizing that there are two general categories of needs: one he refers to as the *basic needs,* and the other the *metaneeds.* Within the basic needs category are the physiological needs essential for biological survival and the psychological needs essential for emotional survival.

An analysis of Maslow's theory reveals insight into the necessity for people to be more than living organisms; they must also be able to function to their fullest extent.

Table 4–1: Maslow's Holistic-Dynamic Theory of Motivation

HIERARCHY	DESCRIPTION
Basic Needs	
The physiological drives	The need for oxygen, food (hunger), water (thirst), and elimination. These are influenced by physiological homeostasis and appetite.
Safety needs	These include the need for security; stability; dependency; protection; freedom from fear, anxiety, and chaos; and the need for structure, order, law, and limits.
The psychological and emotional needs	These include the need for love and belongingness, which are related to one's feelings toward others; and the need for self-esteem, which is manifested in self-respect and respect for others.
Metaneeds	
Self-actualization needs	These are described as each person actually behaving according to the ways in which he/she is fitted to behave.
Knowledge needs	These are related, basically, to cognitive development, such as the acquisition of knowledge, comprehension, and wisdom.
Aesthetic needs	These are associated with the beauty of life and the things of living.

Self-actualization occurs at various developmental levels and reaches its peak at full maturity, although there are alterations to it throughout life. Self-actualization is the stage of maturation when achievement of our full hereditary and developmental potentials are realized. It is the stage of fulfillment, of creative achievements, of self-insight, and activation of contributions to the self and to others. Self-actualization culminates in societal improvements and the achievement of personal goals.

Self-actualization does not take place until and unless we acquire a deep understanding of ourselves and are willing to accept both talents and shortcomings. This requires that we be motivated to seek satisfaction of our knowledge needs—the desire to learn, to understand, and to comprehend. This results in a more complete development of self-actualization. Satisfaction of self-actualization and knowledge needs is never complete, but rather is a continuous striving for more knowledge, greater creativity, and achievements. The quality of the satisfaction of these needs is influenced by and influences the quality of our psychosocial health. Self-actualization and knowledge need satisfaction is determined by our hereditary potentials and the motivating factors present in our environment.

It is clear that Maslow stressed the need to examine factors related to the development of healthy individuals rather than studying physiological and psychological weaknesses. He regarded all innate needs as basically good and that we do not inherit negative tendencies. Therefore, his hierarchy of needs and their satisfaction are associated with positive development, and only when the satisfaction of these needs is denied do they give rise to undesirable actions, such as unsocial or antisocial behavior.

Need Satisfaction and Maturation

We can consider basic needs themselves as incentives along with certain external stimuli. On the one hand, we have a primary stimulus, while on the other hand, we have a secondary stimulus. It is probable one stimulus, whether internal or external, can activate a whole series of stimuli before true action is evident. The complexities of our behavior would indicate that action related to need satisfaction is seldom energized by a single stimulus, although it may initiate the appropriate behavior. It is more likely that our behavior results from a kind of chain of events, and the behavior itself is simply the result of unconscious, even primitive, problem-solving that has taken place within us. These reactions to stimuli, and ultimately to motivation and action, change as we mature and develop more effective behaviors related to self and the environment.

Needs, drives, and desires are sometimes distinguished as being quite different and unique phenomena. In a sense this is true, but in other respects they take on very similar functional characteristics that relate to our overall health, especially when other health influences are taken into consideration. These other health factors, as we have seen, include adverse environmental conditions, such as air pollution or the invasion of pathogenic organisms into the body. Needs, drives, and desires relate to these in a variety of ways, especially in respect to when they are fulfilled and the way in which fulfillment occurs. For example, the hunger drive can be satisfied equally well with unhealthful foods as with healthful foods. If our diet is inadequate it may predispose us to certain kinds of diseases or retarded growth, for instance, but may still satisfy the hunger drive.

As we mature, preoccupation with need satisfaction should become less important, especially in terms of the biological needs. Maslow points out that a state of health can be directly associated with our preoccupation with need satisfaction. Unhealthy people, for example, are chronically seeking satisfaction of basic needs while a characteristic of healthy people is the tendency to develop and actualize their full potentials. What people can be, they must be. There is, at least initially, the strong desire for self-fulfillment; to become actualized is what we are potentially.[1] This is in essence what maturation is all about.

We must conclude, therefore, that maturation proceeds through a series of growth stages and through a series of developmental stages. Growth, which basically means changes in structure size, is associated with development, which is characterized by changes in functioning efficiency. Maturation of structure and function is further associated with our stages in life and is measured in terms of our growth and development as appropriate for the time periods in our lives. For example, studies indicate that at certain general periods of life, adolescence, for instance, one should have achieved certain levels of growth and development. Or to put it another way, at any given age one is mature or not mature.

We need to emphasize, however, that quality of hereditary potentials and the environmental conditions must also be considered since each of us is hereditarily unique and is exposed to unique environments, at least to some extent.

Stages of Maturation

Although many investigators have contributed significantly to our understanding of the maturation process, Havighurst, Erikson, and Freud stand out as having provided similar, but unique information about psychological maturation and how it takes place. Havighurst describes human development in terms of certain *developmental tasks;* Erikson categorizes development into eight *psychosocial stages;* while Freud initiated this concept in his *psychosexual stages* of development.

Havighurst's developmental tasks are characterized by important achievements during the various stages of growth and development. These stages are typified as infancy and early childhood, middle childhood, adolescence, early adulthood, middle age, and later maturity. Havighurst believed that as tasks arise, we must seek their accomplishment, and the degree to which the task is achieved determines the success of our achievement of subsequent tasks. If tasks are adequately achieved at each stage of development, we will reach appropriate levels of maturity for our particular stage of life.

Erikson's psychosocial crises are characterized by a series of eight encounters, one for each stage of development. These encounters contrast a positive success to a corresponding failure. For example, Erikson points out that the child's first emotional crisis occurs in infancy as the development of trust or mistrust. If the infant develops a sense of trust, certain emotional health foundations are established. If the basic needs of affection and belongingness are not satisfied, a sense of mistrust is likely to develop. Erikson's psychosocial stages of development are similar to, but more extensive than Freud's psychosexual stages. Erikson's psychosocial stages of development are summarized as follows:

- *Basic trust vs mistrust,* which is important during the first year of infancy.
- *Autonomy vs shame and doubt,* occurring chiefly from 1 to 3 years of age.
- *Initiative vs guilt,* arising about ages 4 to 5 years.
- *Industry vs inferiority,* extending from 6 to 11 years of age.
- *Ego identity vs self-diffusion,* occurring during puberty and adolescence, about ages 12 to 20 years.
- *Intimacy vs isolation,* which is characteristic of early adulthood.
- *Generativity vs self-absorption or stagnation,* which generally occurs during middle adulthood.
- *Integrity vs despair,* which characterizes late adulthood.

Freud's psychosexual stages of development consist of five major periods of life. Freud believed that children become preoccupied with different parts of the body at different stages and that these preoccupations provide a sense of "sexual" pleasure. Much of Freud's theory is not accepted by present-day psychologists, but it did lay the foundation for Erikson's psychosocial crisis theory. Freud's psychosexual stages are summarized as the *oral stage* (birth to one year), the *anal stage* (one to three years), the *phallic stage* (three to six years), the *latency stage* (six to eleven years), and the *genital stage,* (twelve years to adulthood). (See Chapter 2 for a more detailed discussion of the application of these and other theories to the development of a healthy personality.)

PRINCIPLES OF MOTIVATION

Motivation for action may be automatic, as in satisfying basic biological drives, or it may originate from environmental factors, or from our conscious desires and aspirations. However, regardless of the origin of motivation, the *way* our goals are achieved is the result of learning. We learn how to lessen the tension that accompanies all motivation, but the technique we use may or may not be desirable or effective.

What Is a Motive?

Some aspects of motivation theory are generally accepted while others remain controversial, awaiting further research. However, our knowledge of motivation is sufficient to help explain much of our behavior. Motivation of healthful or unhealthful behavior must be considered holistically. Something is responsible for the initiation of every action we take. The stimulus for action may be relatively simple or very complex. A series of stimuli may be necessary to bring about the action. Complex behavior may require only a simple stimulus while a simple form of behavior may require a complex of stimuli. Some behavior is controlled essentially by our genetic nature—heart action, for example—while other forms of behavior are the result of how well we learn to react to particular stimuli. (See

Figure 4-2.) These include complex motor skills, thinking, reasoning, and other matters requiring the use of the intellect. Some behavior occurs quite automatically, for example, simple reflex actions, or habitual behaviors that have become ingrained in our totality. Other behaviors may require careful deliberation as in the case of decision making. We can conclude that all behavior results from some kind of stimulus or stimuli referred to as the *motivational force.*

As a result of the complex nature of motives and our lack of complete knowledge of motivation, it is nearly impossible to formulate a concise definition. However, certain characteristics of motivation seem to generally hold true. For our purposes, we define *a motive as any internal force that compels us to behave in a particular manner under particular circumstances.* Characteristically, a motive is internal, conscious or unconscious, innate or learned. We learn not only how to react to a motive, but we also learn to "want" (be motivated) when certain situations or incentives are present in the environment. These situations are referred to as *environmental cues.*

The Genesis of Motives

Motives are generally thought to arise from the biological drives (referred to as biogenic motives), and those that emanate from the psychosocial needs (called sociogenic motives). The *biogenic* motives are manifested in terms of biological forces related to visceral needs: safety, sex, and sensorimotor. The *sociogenic* motives arise as a result of maturation and the influence of cultural mores. These are associated with our wants, desires, and aspirations that, in turn, arise as a result of the experiences we have during various phases of development. They are in essence what Maslow has identified as the metaneeds: self-actualization, knowledge needs, and aesthetic needs. They also include those associated with self-esteem, belonging, and love.

It is important to recognize, however, that motives are seldom either biogenic or sociogenic in a pure form. The satisfaction of any need, whether biogenic or sociogenic, tends to contribute to satisfaction of other needs.

Figure 4-2:
Needs, Motivation, Behavior and Health

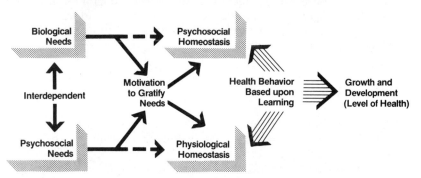

The Biological and Psychosocial Needs Are Interdependent and How Well They Are Satisfied Determines to a Great Extent the Level of Health of a Person

HOMEOSTASIS AND MOTIVATION

The Role of Homeostasis

The tension created by motivation is the result of a biological or psychosocial imbalance. When this occurs, homeostasis has been interrupted, and there is the necessity to take action to bring the body state back into balance. Once homeostasis is restored, the tension associated with it is reduced and the action ceases. This takes place because there is no longer a motivation to continue the action. When homeostasis is maintained, biological health is also maintained. However, complete and continuous psychosocial homeostasis results in a cessation of behavior. On the other hand, continuous interruption of psychosocial homeostasis can result in compulsive, unproductive behavior that is not appropriate for restoring homeostasis. Furthermore, prolonged or severe homeostatic interference, whether physical or psychosocial, will result in ill-health.

Homeostasis and Ill Health

When certain pathogenic organisms enter the body, bodily defense mechanisms are stimulated into action. The body tends to maintain homeostasis by destroying the pathogenic organisms. If the body's defenses fail to destroy or eliminate the pathogenic organisms, a disease results. Similarly, when we are confronted with a stressful situation, there is a tendency for us to solve the problem creating the stress—to restore psychosocial homeostasis. If we fail to reduce the stress, a mild or severe, temporary or perhaps permanent, mental or emotional illness results.

We have learned that failure to achieve optimal health and to maintain it is much more than merely the avoidance of pathogenic organisms, eating properly, getting plenty of exercise, rest, and recreation. Health is also related to our outlook on life and self. It is influenced by the positive genetic potentials, the way we learn to react to adverse environmental conditions, the body's ability to resist disease, and a variety of complex interactional factors associated with the maintenance of biological and psychosocial homeostasis.

Although we are concerned with the attainment and maintenance of health, it is necessary to become aware of those factors that can threaten health as well as those behaviors necessary for achieving and maintaining health. Each of us needs to learn how to live healthfully and to understand the mechanisms of motivation that can make healthful behavior possible.

INCENTIVES

When behavior *avoids* punishment or pain, we tend to continue this behavior under similar circumstances. When behavior results in reward (satisfaction of needs), we tend to repeat this behavior. It is important to recognize, however, that our perception of reward or punishment may not be accurate. For example, an adolescent who begins to smoke tobacco may have been motivated by the *false* notion that smoking is a stepping stone to maturity. After learning to smoke, other forms of gratification associated with addiction come into play. This is one of several reasons why changing this behavior is very difficult later in life.

Rewards and Punishment

Rewards and punishment are external incentives that are used to elicit certain kinds of behavior. Psychologists have long recognized that reward (success) is a more desirable incentive than punishment (failure). However, we must reiterate that one's technique for achieving a feeling of success may be less than desirable. For example, the hypochondriac may have a strong need for recognition from others and uses symptoms of ill health as the means for achieving this recognition. The preoccupation with need satisfaction is manifested in ill-health behavior in this situation. On the other hand, much of our behavior is directed toward a kind of reward. When we take care in eating the right kinds and amounts of food to maintain weight (and possibly health in general), exercise regularly, feel good about the self, reduce incidence of sickness, and so forth, we are rewarded. However, the presence of an incentive may or may not result in a reaction because it will motivate behavior only to the extent that it is associated with previous similar behavior. Incentives that have no meaning to us will not stimulate any significant action. Generally, incentives that are positive will result in positive behavior, while negative incentives usually result in an avoidance behavior. Avoidance behavior can be desirable or undesirable.

An incentive is primarily an object or feeling that we desire. It may be concrete, such as a bonus or trophy, or it may be quite abstract, as in the feeling of success. When an incentive is translated into some form of action, it has acted as a motivator. In this sense, motives may arise intrinsically, as a drive or urge, or extrinsically as an incentive or environmental stimulus.

Intrinsic and Extrinsic Motives

Intrinsically motivated health behavior is the most powerful, sustaining and meaningful. It is most often associated with health-related behavior. Extrinsically motivated health behavior is most often associated with short-term, health-directed behavior that ceases once the health goal is achieved. As pointed out by Knutson, "Health behavior seems so inseparably linked to motivation that logic impels one to orient any discussion of health practices to human needs and human motivation."[2]

In the broadest sense, healthful behavior is the ultimate achievement of each of us even though much of our behavior from day to day may be unhealthful. Ruch has observed that health behavior can be viewed in terms of human plasticity and human energetics. *Human plasticity* is a learned phenomenon that is associated with the ability to change, adapt, or modify oneself or one's environment. *Human energetics* is associated with motivation that influences the intensity of response to internal or external stimuli.[3] When an external motivator is related to some internal need, it activates the energy necessary for action to take place. The intensity of the motivation determines the amount of energy necessary for the endurance to achieve the goal.

Before conscious behavior results, an internalization of the motivation, and the factors surrounding it must take place. In essence, there is an intellectual and emotional interplay that finally results in the health behavior. This is explained by what is known as the P-I-S-A concept.*

Internalization of motives is the process of integrating stimuli (incentives) as a part of the total individual. The process of internalization proceeds along four sub-processes described as:

1. *Perception* of the stimulus (or stimuli). No action can result from a stimulus unless we perceive its presence. Perception is the process associated with becoming aware of the health (or health-threatening) situation; it is an understanding or comprehension within our intellectual capabilities. Once perception takes place, an interest is aroused.

2. *Interest* is a powerful motivational force. The more intense the interest in the health issue, the more powerful and sustaining the health behavior is likely to become.

3. *Significance* is related to both perception and interest. It results from an understanding of the health factor as it *applies* to the self. This in turn may intensify interest. If we do not view the stimulus and resultant behavior as personally significant, there will be little or no action taken.

4. *Application* results when we perceive the stimulus as meaningful. The reaction it elicits is the ultimate process associated with health-related or health-directed behavior. Success in this application to the self may result in greater interest, new understandings (perception), and greater significance, which begins the cycle anew.

It will be noted that the P-I-S-A concept exemplifies the holistics involved with motivation and health behavior. One sub-process can further reinforce another, which results in sustained motivation and the energy to continue to behave in a certain way. The energy resulting from motivation may be measured in terms of our determination to achieve a particular goal. Perceived success in achievement may be the motivational reinforcement (incentive or stimulus) that continues the P-I-S-A process.

THE EMOTIVE FORCE

Characteristics

All psychological processes are influenced by our emotional set. Nearly identical stimuli may elicit completely different responses depending upon our emotional condition at the time we are confronted by the stimuli. For example, a friend's sarcasm may be perceived as humorous if we are free of worry or anger, but may arouse hostility if these emotions exist.

*This concept was first introduced in 1978 by the authors in relation to the processes surrounding motivation as an integral part of effective health education methodologies, techniques, and strategies that can result in changed health behavior.

Although we are born with the potential for emotional development, most psychologists agree that the quality of emotional responses are learned as we are exposed to environmental stimuli. Emotions have three main characteristics: (1) they are conscious experiences; (2) they provoke physical responses; and (3) they motivate behavior. Some scientists believe that emotions may also be unconscious, and are expressed, for example, through the use of ego defense mechanisms. Emotions not only reflect our perception of the environment, but are affected by this perception.

The conscious aspect of emotions is very difficult to quantify. Although each of us may describe our emotional experiences similarly, we cannot be sure that we are experiencing identical feelings. Moreover, our emotions are continually changing from one extreme to another, for example, hate to love, and joy to sorrow.

Value of Emotions

Emotions and drives are closely intertwined. The basic drives (hunger, thirst, shelter, and so forth) give rise to emotions that assist in directing our behavior toward need satisfaction. Basically, emotions tend to direct our behavior toward or away from the object or symbol that gives rise to the emotions. Rather than being reflex or automatic responses, behavior that is directed by emotions is often unpredictable.

Most of our everyday emotional experiences are relatively mild. They do not enter the realm of the extreme. Such moderate changes in the quality of our emotions may be described as *moods.* Most changes in moods are relatively easy to deal with. It is when there are frequent, sudden, and violent changes in emotions that coping becomes difficult, and outside assistance is sometimes warranted.

Emotions elicit physical changes. Changes in facial expressions may influence the behavior of others. Emotions also cause internal or visceral reactions. Some of these internal reactions enable us to exert maximum strength, be less sensitive to pain, and maximize our endurance. We have all heard of people performing almost superhuman feats when emotionally aroused, such as lifting a car off a person pinned beneath it, or being unaware of a bullet or shrapnel wound during the heat of battle. Our visceral reactions produced by emotions always take the same form whether the emotion is viewed as positive or negative. This is a characteristic of the General Adaptation Syndrome (GAS) as described by Hans Selye.

In the early part of the 1950s, Selye wrote of the GAS as an explanation of the body's reaction to stress. He divided the total stress reaction into three distinguishable phases: (1) the alarm reaction; (2) the stage of resistance; and (3) the stage of exhaustion.

The alarm reaction is characterized by the physiological reactions resulting from a physical or psychological stressor. The stressor sets into motion a variety of biochemical changes that result in identifiable symptoms, including headache, fever, and fatigue. *The stage of resistance* is characterized by a disappearance of the symptoms present during the alarm reaction. This is explained by the body's secretion of the adrenocorticotropic hormone (ACTH) from the anterior pituitary and cortin from the adrenal cortex; these hormones establish a resistance to the stressor. Under prolonged stress the body's ability to continue to secrete these hormones (ACTH and cortin) and its ability to adapt to the stressor ceases. This is the beginning of *the stage of exhaustion;* it is characterized by the return of the original symptoms present during the alarm reaction phase.

If there is no relief from the severe stressor, death will result. However, the exact relationship between stress situations and debilitation resulting in death is still not entirely clear, but we do know that prolonged and severe stress can lead to a variety of physical illnesses (psychosomatic). Pathological conditions resulting from severe and prolonged stress are referred to by Selye as the "diseases of adaptation."[4]

THE BASIS OF EMOTIONS

Definitions

Because emotions are so closely related to our overall state of mental health, not only reflecting our perceptions but affecting them, definitions of emotions tend to be quite complex. For example, one medical dictionary defines emotion as "a state of mental excitement characterized by alteration of feeling tone."[5] The American Psychiatric Association (APA) defines emotion as "A feeling such as fear, anger, grief, joy, or love. As used in psychiatry, emotions may not always be conscious. (It is) Synonymous with *affect.*"[6] The latter definition is more complete, but does not reflect physiological changes that result from emotion.

One of the most complete definitions of emotion is ". . . a physiological departure from homeostasis that is subjectively experienced in strong feeling (as of love, hate, desire, or fear) and manifests itself in neuromuscular, respiratory, cardiovascular, hormonal, and other bodily changes preparatory to overt acts which may or may not be performed . . ."[7] This definition takes into account our physiological state and its effect on physiological functioning, and the motivational properties of emotions. *Emotions, then are feelings aroused by our perception of stimuli that energize certain physiological mechanisms and may improve rational behavior or intensify irrational behavior.*

Causes of Emotions

It was not until this century that the nature of emotions began to be understood. Historically, it was widely held that emotions were instinctual in nature. The work of J. B. Watson, however, largely dispelled this myth. Through his studies, Watson found that emotions are developed as a result of conditioning, that is learning. We learn, for example, that certain objects or sounds are pleasant or unpleasant. In addition, such things as physical support elicits a feeling of security. When this support is suddenly removed, an infant may express fear. The security resulting from cuddling and feeding, for example, is supportive of the emotion of love and the feeling of belongingness.

How we react emotionally to a variety of pleasurable and unpleasurable stimuli is based upon past experiences with similar situations. Because we learn to think abstractly, symbols also begin to be related to emotions. For instance, words, pictures, and other symbols that describe tangible objects or experiences often cause us to react with the same emotional intensity as that caused by exposure to those things that the symbols represent. Past experiences also cause us to react in similar ways to a variety of similar stimuli. This phenomenon is called *stimulus generalization.* For example, if a person develops a fear of snakes, that same fearful reaction may result from feeling or seeing a hose or rope unexpectedly.

Whether, or not we *expect* something to happen, or *expect* to see, feel, or hear something, strongly influences emotional reactions. We learn that, in certain situations, pleasurable or unpleasurable events may occur. This expectation may cause anxiety, worry, fear or pleasurable emotions. These expectations increase as we mature because we are continually exposed to a greater number of situations. Moreover, when something contrary to our expectations occurs, an emotional response is the result. For example, if a person studies thoroughly for an examination but discovers after he/she receives the test that questions are asked on topics totally foreign to those that were studied, the student may experience worry, anxiety, or possibly, panic.

The collective expectations of a group of people may also arouse emotion. A cumulative effect may occur in such instances as fear of a melt down of a nuclear reactor, the spiritual excitement caused by a charismatic evangelist, or as a result of massive displays of patriotism. This phenomenon has been labeled by sociologists as *emotional contagion.* Although the processes of emotional contagion are not fully understood, several characteristics have been identified. These are: (1) heightened suggestibility; (2) heightened stimulation; and (3) homogeniety of experience.[8] Emotional contagion may occur on a massive scale. It is most likely to occur among groups of people who are similar in age and socio-cultural status. It is less likely to occur among those of different education, age, or cultural backgrounds.

CONCEALING EMOTIONS

Why We Conceal Our Emotions

Not only do we learn how to *express* emotions, but how to *conceal* them. The concealment of emotions may be conscious or unconscious. A *conscious* attempt to conceal an emotion is called *suppression.* An emotion is *repressed* when the concealment is *unconscious.*

We learn very early in life that the overt expression of many emotions is not socially acceptable. When we become angry we may learn that a violent expression of this anger is not appropriate. We may also learn that sexual attraction to another person is not to be publicly exhibited in many instances in our society. We must learn to either completely suppress our emotions, or to find ways to express them that are socially acceptable.

The concealment of emotions becomes easier as we mature. As our ability to communicate verbally increases, we are able to express our emotions through language rather than only through physical acts, as is typical of a child. In addition, our experiences tend to temper our expectations allowing us to tolerate situations that once would have elicited powerful emotional reactions.

Very often the concealment of emotions is caused by conflict. If we are torn between two impulses, the result may be quite different than what would be expected when only one motive were directing our behavior. For example, it is quite common for us to be angry at someone we love. The anger, in this instance, may be suppressed so as not to hurt our loved one; or the anger may be *displaced* upon a relatively neutral object. Another example may be one in which we do not like our job, but the desire for a stable income results in our concealment of frustrations to remain employed.

The expression of emotion in our society is closely linked to sex roles that have grown out of custom and social expectations. In some cultures boys are taught that it is not manly to cry and to suppress any tendency to express sadness that may be interpreted as being within the realm of the "feminine." But sex roles vary from one culture to another. It is expected that men will embrace another man as a greeting in many European countries, but it may be looked upon with suspicion in the United States. In some cultures women are expected to show little, if any, passion; while in others, the reverse is true.

Although significant strides have been taken in recent years in the United States to eliminate some of the sexual stereotypes, many subcultures still hold strongly to tradition. On the one hand, clearly defined sex roles can provide emotional stability, while on the other hand, they can provide a significant degree of confusion and guilt for those individuals who find it difficult to conform with social expectations.

Effects of Emotional Concealment

Although frustrating at times, the concealment of emotions can enable us to relate to others productively, and to accomplish tasks efficiently. What we are talking about here is not total suppression of emotions, but *emotional control* —the harnessing of our emotions and using them to our benefit.

Unfortunately, we often become preoccupied with the emotion itself and not the underlying cause of the emotional experience. Parents, to avoid embarrassment, sometimes frown upon the expression of emotion in their children. This is sometimes done without considering the motives of the emotional expression in their children. This can cause conflict within the children resulting in an even more undesirable expression of emotion at a later time.

The degree to which emotions should be concealed, of course, depends upon the emotion pressing for expression and upon the environmental circumstances.

THE CHIEF EMOTIONS

Love and Affection

It is not clearly known how or why the emotions of love and affection develop. Some hold that they are inherent qualities of humans, that no learning is necessary for these emotions to develop. The belief that is more widely accepted, however, is that they are indeed learned and that they stem from the variety of pleasurable experiences most people have in infancy. These experiences include being cuddled, fed, and kept warm by our parents and other adults.

There is evidence that if love and security are withheld during infancy, normal development is retarded and one's capacity for expressing love later in life may be jeopardized. Two studies dynamically illustrate this. In his studies of monkeys, Harlow and his associates discovered that if surrogate mothers (made of cloth and wire) were used in rearing infant monkeys, the infants had difficulty establishing social relationships and adequate sexual responsiveness later in life. Moreover, when the infant monkeys were fed by the surrogates made of wire but were simultaneously in contact with the cloth surrogates, the infants sought comfort and security from the cloth "mother." This indicates the basic need for security.[9,10] Studies have also been conducted of children reared in institutions. These studies are largely inconclusive, although some indicate that children raised with a minimum of parenting are more likely to have difficulty in becoming socially mature.

The quality of love and affection of which we are capable varies considerably depending upon (1) whether that which is loved is a person or object; (2) the quality of our relationship to the person or object; and (3) whether or not any sexual feelings are present. The emotion of love can be relatively mild, affecting us only slightly; or it can be nearly totally debilitating. Our ability to control this emotion is also greatly influenced by our level of maturity. An adolescent is likely to experience almost violent shifts in mood, while an older person, because of past experience, is more likely to enter cautiously into feelings of love.

Sexual feelings compound the difficulties of expressing feelings of love. Since it is not always appropriate to show sexual attraction, it can result in frustration and conflict. Alternative means of expressing love must, therefore, by found.

Love affects us in many ways. It can provide security. It produces passion. It causes us to want to possess a person or object. And it can produce feelings of insecurity because we fear losing it.

Anger

When we are confronted with situations that block us from achieving what we desire, we may react with fear or anger. In general, if we feel we have the ability to overcome the obstacle, we tend to react with anger. If we perceive the obstacle to be beyond our power to control, our response is likely to be one of fear.

The expression of anger is influenced by a variety of personal and social restrictions. We learn not to cry, that it is not acceptable for a male to hit a female, that it is not acceptable to throw a tantrum in public, and so forth. We gradually incorporate these social restrictions into our own value system, which can cause conflict when we are confronted with a situation that arouses anger.

With anger, the typical reaction is to attack. We can attack our "victim" in a variety of ways. In most situations, physical violence is suppressed, so we resort to other, more acceptable means, such as raising our voice, thrusting out our chest and/or jaw, or taking action to emotionally hurt the object of our anger.

Moreover, if an overt display of anger is too threatening, we may resort to fantasizing—dreaming of getting revenge or conjuring up a death wish. These fantasies may bring emotional satisfaction, although we would not even consider carrying them out in reality.

When we are unable to achieve satisfaction by venting our anger in acceptable ways, we may direct our anger at ourselves. This may also occur when we see unacceptable traits in others that we attribute to ourselves. The most extreme form of self-directed hostility is suicide. Self-directed anger, however, can take other forms. Often this anger may be expressed as a psychosomatic illness, such as allergies, headaches, and peptic ulcers. We may also develop a tendency to frequently expose ourselves to various threatening situations that can result in "close calls" or accidents.

It is desirable to block certain manifestations of anger such as violence; but it is undesirable to block the emotion of anger itself. The key is to develop ways in which anger can be acceptably expressed that enable us to function more effectively when threatening situations arise.

Fear

When we feel that we are unable to cope with, or overcome, a threatening situation, it is quite normal to react with fear. Fear may be caused by simple stimuli, such as an unexpected loud noise, or by complex stimuli that may cause virtual incapacitation, such as fear of failure, fear of getting a job, or fear of being hurt in a dangerous situation.

Most of our fears are irrational. They result from our perception of situations that have not yet happened. We may seek shelter in our fears and use them as an excuse for not functioning effectively. Sometimes people fall into the "what if" syndrome—"What if I fail?", "What will the neighbors think?", "What if my boss finds out?", and so forth. When we allow ourselves to fall victim to our fears, our productivity decreases, and the chances that our fears will become self-fulfilling prophecies increase.

Because fear sometimes results from the unknown, it is best to learn to experience the unknown. Only then will we be able to harness our fears and increase our effectiveness.

Anxiety and Worry

Anxiety and worry are basically feelings of unsettledness, sometimes caused by sources that are difficult to pinpoint. Quite often, however, the sources of anxiety and worry can be identified and result from the anticipation of stressful events.

Long-term anxiety can result in serious complications. This was particularly evident as a result of the near tragic nuclear reactor malfunction at the Three Mile Island nuclear plant in Middletown, Pennsylvania in 1979. Physicians in and around Middletown reported a significant increase in complaints of diarrhea, nausea, and nightmares in the weeks immediately following the incident. In this case, the people knew the cause of their anxiety, but felt totally helpless and at the mercy of something they could not control.

Of course, most causes of anxiety do not affect as many lives nor are they as potentially serious as that which occurred at Three Mile Island. In most instances, we are able to deal with the source, either by directly confronting it or by changing the environment to avoid or neutralize the source. The mere act of dealing with the source can relieve anxiety since we are no longer in the position of anticipating the host of ways things can go wrong. Anxiety and worry should alert us to the potential for undesirable consequences, but should not rule our lives, causing us to be unable to react appropriately to the myriad of life's events that possess the potential for contributing to fulfillment.

Guilt

Unlike fear, anxiety, and worry that result from the threat of events that have not yet occurred, guilt results from remorse over events that are in our past. It may result from either acts of commission or omission; that is, we may be feeling guilty because of inappropriate actions or thoughts, or we may be feeling guilty as a result of not taking action when such action was required.

Guilt can be thrust upon us by others, often in an attempt to explain away their failings. It can also be used as a means of manipulating others to take action they may not have been taken in its absence. Parents are often faced with a variety of guilt-producing situations—being too lenient with their children, being too strict, not giving their children enough or, depriving them.

There is no adolescent foible or misfortune ranging from reckless driving to pregnancy out of wedlock, that has not been attributed to the fact that parents have been too lenient or too strict, too overprotecting or too neglecting, too solicitous or not solicitous enough, too aggressive or too passive in asserting their masculinity or femininity, too weak or too domineering.[11]

The fact that guilt-producing events are in the past must be realized. We can do nothing about them. We must move forward. Aside from causing us to learn from our mistakes, guilt does nothing that is productive. To dwell on guilt renders us unable to effectively address present situations that must be acted upon. We can never recapture the past, but we can create a better future.

GLOSSARY

Biogenic: Motives originating from biological needs or drives.

Coping: The ability to deal adequately with an environmental situation or with one's self.

Drive: A biological need.

Effective environment: The part of the external environment to which the person is responding.

Emotion: An intense feeling that results in characteristic physiological changes and the psychological need to act.

Emotional contagion: An emotion that spreads to others as in a mob.

Incentive: An external reward (or punishment) that brings about motivation.

Motive: An internal force that compels a person to behave in a particular way under particular circumstances.

Needs: Urgencies whose satisfaction is essential for continuance of health and life.

Noneffective environment: The part of the external environment to which the person is not responding.

Phobia: An intense, irrational fear of something or a situation; true phobias are neurotic.

Repression: An unconscious action of the psyche that prevents a painful experience from becoming conscious.

Sociogenic: Motives originating from social needs, expectations, and aspirations.

Stimulus generalization: A similar reaction to a variety of stimuli.

Suppression: A conscious effort to forget an event or experience.

Visceral: Refers to the internal organs, such as stomach, intestines.

SUMMARY

Our mental, emotional, and physical health is directly related to the influences of the total environment. The total environment consists of the effective and ineffective aspects. These can be further divided into the social and physical environments. Our mental and emotional health is greatly influenced by the quality of our social environment and how well we perceive our experiences.

Our needs are satisfied by factors in the environment that are the vehicle for need gratification. A need is an urgency that must be satisfied if life is to continue. Optimal human effectiveness is not possible unless needs are adequately satisfied.

Human needs may be classified as biological and psychosocial. Some needs are the result of heredity while others seem to arise as a result of maturation and stimuli present in the social and physical environments. Deprivation of needs can result in retarded development, ill-health, and possibly death. The satisfaction of one need may contribute to the satisfaction of other needs.

Maslow has developed a hierarchy of needs describing basic needs (the drives for biological survival) and metaneeds (the drives for self-actualization). Maslow believed that all innate needs are basically good and that a person does not inherit negative tendencies.

Havighurst describes maturation in terms of developmental tasks while Erikson describes psychosocial stages of development. Freud laid the foundation for these theories when he formulated the concept of psychosexual stages of development of the male.

A motive is an internal force that directs behavior and provides the energy to achieve a particular goal. Motives arise biogenically or sociogenically. The force created by motivation is generated by the need for all living things to maintain a biological and emotional homeostasis. When homeostasis is maintained, the individual is said to be healthy; a disruption of homeostasis, if severe enough, results in ill-health.

Incentives are internal or external objects or feelings that we desire. Before incentives can become motives, they must be internalized. Internalization of incentives follows the P-I-S-A principle: perception, interest, significance, and application.

All psychological processes are influenced by our emotional set. Emotions are basically conscious experiences that motivate behavior and provoke physical responses. Emotions cause changes in overt behavior as well as visceral changes.

Because of social norms, we are confronted with many pressures to conceal our normal reactions to emotions. This concealment can be either conscious (suppression) or unconscious (repression). The concealment of emotions is facilitated by maturity. We learn how to deal with emotion through the use of language, or we may conceal emotion because of conflicting motives, or because of sex roles imposed by society.

The emotions of love and affection stem from infancy as a result of the need for security and the experience of being cuddled, fed, and being given shelter.

When our goals are blocked, but we feel we have the power to overcome the obstacle, we tend to react with anger. If we feel we are unable to overcome an obstacle that blocks our goals, we may react with fear.

Mild fears are referred to as anxiety and worry. The key to reducing anxiety and worry is to confront the cause of them and deal with them.

Guilt results from past events that we feel have not been adequately addressed. In dealing with guilt, we should learn from past mistakes, but not dwell on past events since we can do nothing about them.

PROBLEMS FOR DISCUSSION

1. Distinguish between the internal and external environments. Discuss the importance of each in influencing health behavior.
2. List three things present in the effective environment. What makes these part of the effective environment? Were these a part of your effective environment a week ago? Explain.
3. Describe how our perception affects how we function.
4. Distinguish between a need, want, and desire.
5. How are needs classified? Are they separate entities? Explain.
6. How are needs associated with motivation? How is homeostasis associated with motivation? What is motivation?
7. Distinguish between a basic need and a metaneed. Which is more closely related to survival and which is more closely related to human effectiveness? Explain.
8. What is meant by self-actualization according to Maslow?
9. Describe the stages of maturation according to Havighurst, Erikson, and Freud. How is each theory similar? Different?
10. Describe how environmental cues tend to motivate behavior.
11. What is an incentive? How is an incentive related to motivation?
12. Identify the characteristics of emotions. How can emotions be conscious or unconscious?
13. How is the emotive force developed?
14. Define emotional contagion. Identify three characteristics of this phenomenon.

15. Why do we sometimes conceal our emotions? Discuss why emotional concealment may have both positive and negative effects.
16. Explain how the emotions of love and affection are established. How can the work of Harlow be related to the study of human emotion?
17. Describe ways in which anger may be beneficial. Why may anger be directed inwardly?
18. Why may most fears be described as irrational? How may fear be overcome?
19. Discuss why anxiety and worry adversely affect functioning ability. How can anxiety and worry be overcome?

REFERENCES

1. MASLOW, ABRAHAM H., *Motivation and Personality,* Harper & Row, Publishers, New York, 1970, p. 38.
2. KNUTSON, ANDIE L., *The Individual, Society and Health Behavior,* The Russell Sage Foundation, New York, 1965, p. 212.
3. RUCH, FLOYD L., *Psychology and Life,* 7th ed. Scott, Foresman and Company, Glenview, 1967, p. 375.
4. RUCH, FLOYD L., *Psychology and Life,* Scott, Foresman, and Company, Brief 5th ed., Glenview, 1959, pp. 145–146.
5. *Dorland's Illustrated Medical Dictionary,* 24th ed. E. B. Saunders Company, Philadelphia, 1965, p. 481.
6. *A Psychiatric Glossary,* 3rd ed. American Psychiatric Association, Washington, D.C., 1969, p. 35.
7. *Webster's Third New International Dictionary of the English Language,* G & C Merriam Company, Springfield, Mass., 1976, p. 742.
8. BROOM, LEONARD, and PHILIP SELZNIK, *Sociology,* 4th ed. Harper & Row, Publishers, Inc., N.Y., 1968, pp. 223–224.
9. HARLOW, H. F., "The Nature of Love," *American Psychologist,* Vol. 13, 1958, pp. 673–685.
10. HARLOW, H. F., "The Heterosexual Affectional System in Monkeys," *American Psychologist,* Vol. 17, 1962, pp. 1–9.
11. JERSILD, ARTHUR T., *The Psychology of Adolescence,* 2nd ed. The Macmillan Company, N.Y., 1963, p. 247.

5

grief, dying, and death

CAUSES OF GRIEF

Introduction

There is conception, then birth, then growing, learning, happiness, sorrow, joy, frustration, working, playing—all a part of living. Then there is death. Death is a part of living, but it comes easier if we have first lived to our fullest potential. Living a full life makes it easier to accept death—a loved one's, at first, and finally, our own.

Grief can be one of the most debilitating emotions, interfering with mental, emotional, and physiological functioning. Grief can be mild, severe, momentary, or prolonged; it can interrupt our ability to deal with simple everyday problems or it may result in behaviors that are positive and constructive, but which may appear to be inappropriate at the moment. Many factors can precipitate grief, but the one that is most commonly thought of is the death of a loved one. However, according to Elisabeth Kubler-Ross, death of a loved one which results in grief, can be the first step toward growth. Says Kubler-Ross:

> Death is the key to the door of life. It is through accepting the finiteness of our individual existence that we are enabled to find the strength and courage to reject those extrinsic roles and expectations and to devote each day of our lives—however long they may be—to growing as fully as we are able[1]

The causes of grief, the time it takes place, and its intensity are closely associated with our total psychological make-up, our ability to deal with *any* emotion, and the value we place on the particular grief-causing stimulus. For example, the more deeply that love is felt and expressed for the person, the more likely the grief-stricken person will react intensely in times of tragedy, all other factors remaining constant. However, says Nichols, "When grief is acute, when death is sudden, when the event is unwanted, grief knows no dignity; it is raw, naked and cruel, and it tears one's dignity to shreds."[2]

Tragedy

According to Clayton the stages of grief are characterized by numbness, depression, and recovery.[3] *Grief can not take place unless we consciously recognize and perceive a loss.* A typical characteristic of grief, as opposed to depression, from a psychological viewpoint, is that grief is almost always self-limiting and will gradually decrease in intensity with the passage of time. Depression may not, and may require professional attention. However, grief can be the forerunner to a state of depression that may require therapeutic measures.

Grief can result from many forms of tragedy. *Tragedy* is characterized as a severe event that excites the emotions of pity and terror in such a combination as to result in grief. The events leading to this are usually a calamity—a death or event that involves severe suffering, remorse, sadness, distress, and anguish.

What one person perceives as tragedy that leads to grief may have little or no influence upon another person. Much depends upon our previous experiences with the tragic situation, those involved, and how well we have learned to accept tragedy. These factors, therefore, also influence the intensity of grief and the time necessary for it to be overcome. This is called the *mourning process.* This process allows us to manage our grief until full functioning effectiveness is restored. For all practical purposes, mourning is a health-restoring reaction to grief.[4]

Personal Interpretations

We may love two (or more) people with equal intensity, although in different ways. If tragedy should strike one or the other, the grief reaction may be quite different since our interpretations of the tragedy may be quite different. For example, if death should occur to a loved one who is also a child, the grief reaction may be very intense because of the age of the child or other circumstances surrounding the death. If, on the other hand, an old person should die, we may interpret the death as a "blessing" or, at least, with less emotional involvement because this person may have already lived a "long and full life."

Our early experiences with tragedy, especially death, how successfully we have faced the situation, and how frequent these tragedies have occurred will have an impact on the intensity and time-span that grief will take. The more mature we are, our general state of psychological health, how well learning about tragedy and the establishment of objectivity have occurred, among other factors, will influence how well we can deal with any form of acute grief. These experiences may be in the form of death of pets, religious teachings, how our parents react to death in general, and cultural attitudes that prevail.

Some people, therefore, are more vulnerable to debilitating grief than others. This vulnerability may take the form of physical or emotional illness, or even a higher death rate than those not experiencing the tragedy. For example, studies indicate that the death rate among widows in the first year following the death of their husbands is more than 700 percent higher than among women in otherwise comparable age and socioeconomic groups.[5]

THE BIOPSYCHODYNAMICS OF GRIEF

Grief as an Emotion

In Chapter 4 we learned that all human emotions possess certain common characteristics, although the extent to which one emotion may influence behavior may differ greatly from another. Some emotions result in pleasant sensations while others are unpleasant, and some emotions may improve our performance while others may render us helpless. Grief, as with other emotions, is no exception; it has both intellectual and emotional levels of expression. Intellectually, we may be able to accept and understand the causes of grief, the feelings it creates, and even what we must do to overcome its debilitating effects. However, at the emotional level, it may be necessary for us to proceed through the natural stages it produces, hastening them and lessening their severity with assistance from others or through engaging in creative activities.

Grief is an extremely powerful emotion and as with any emotion it must be dealt with in some way. Being able to manage our emotions in a general sense is essential for preventing these emotions from finding expressions in physical or psychic channels. This is exemplified with psychosomatic illness, which is a manifestation of destructive expression of unmanaged emotions.

Psychological Reactions to Grief

Grief is the emotion that sets into motion the mourning process. Mourning reactions are influenced by our knowledge of how they should proceed, what we believe we should do, and how we believe others will react to our behavior. There has been a tendency in our society to view mourning as a sign of weakness. However, in recent years, attitudes toward expressing grief openly have been evolving. Educational programs have been established that focus attention on an understanding of the process of death and dying and the need to view this as one of life's more important experiences. Feeling grief is one thing; expressing it is quite another.

Kubler-Ross has identified five *theoretical* emotional stages that one passes through when faced with imminent death.[6] These are:

Stage one: Denial and isolation. This is characterized by disbelief, the inability to accept the termination of one's own life; it is usually followed by isolating oneself from facing the truth. This may be expressed in terms of refusing to discuss death, making plans for the future, and the like. Denial and isolation seem to be valuable because they tend to insulate, for a time, the person from the intense shock associated with facing death.

Stage two: Anger. Once denial and isolation can no longer be rationalized, anger usually follows. This anger may be displaced on a variety of people or circumstances—the family, physician, hospital, or other institution. The target for this anger is frequently those who have done the most for the person—a loved one who has been more or less constantly with the patient, and the nurses who are caring for him/her. At this point, the patient may become demanding and difficult to deal with. Those on whom the anger is displaced need to understand this and not provide the person with further reasons for being hostile, because the objects of the anger are generally irrelevant to the real issue, which is to avoid or delay death. One's sense of immortality is threatened and it seems necessary to blame death on someone or something other than accepting the fact that "I, too, am mortal."

Stage three: Bargaining. Hope is a powerful part of all of life's experiences and it comes into play most prominently when one is faced with death. Hope is evidenced by the bargaining the dying person exhibits: making promises, especially to God, in exchange for a prolonged life.

Stage four: Depression. Once all signs of hope have been eliminated, the dying person may enter a state of deep depression. This depression is characterized by grief for oneself; it is a kind of personal mourning of one's own sense of loss and awareness of the many things that are unfinished or yet to be pursued.

Stage five: Acceptance. This final stage is achieved when the person has had time and help in passing through the previous four stages. It is characterized by resignation to the fact that death is inevitable. The person may respond by making final arrangements, completing unfinished tasks, and so forth. Once acceptance occurs, death can usually be faced with dignity and finality.

Throughout the stages of facing death, hope seems to be a common denominator. While hope is in one sense, another form of denial, it also provides the dying person with the courage to endure the physical and emotional pain that often accompanies prolonged terminal illness. Hope is a stabilizing factor of living and an aid for facing the problems we confront throughout life and which we maintain to the very end.

Grief and Stress

Grief is a stress on the total person. As we saw in Chapter 4, these are physical responses to stress—labeled the General Adaptation Syndrome by Selye. The pituitary gland responds by secreting hormones that at first establish a resistance to stress. If grief-induced stress is severe enough, illness or ultimately death could result.*

GRIEF AND THANATOLOGY

What Is Thanathology?

Thanatology is the study of death, but it is not a simple, single discipline that is concerned only with the advent of death. The issues raised by death, and prolonging life are related to "philosophy, law, theology, the social sciences, literature, and history."[7] So important are these considerations to society that in 1969 the Institute of Society, Ethics, and the Life Sciences was founded. This institute consists of leading authorities in biology, medicine, philosophy, law, and the social and behavioral sciences. Thanatology is more concerned with life than death itself, with the societal impact advanced technology has on the prolongation of life, organ transplant technology, medicolegal and ethical issues related to death and birth, to genetic engineering, and all of the issues associated with who shall live and who shall die.

Attitudes About Death

An understanding of what we know about dying and the events that terminate in death can help to reduce and perhaps eliminate some of the fears and superstitions associated with death and dying. This can further result in more positive and constructive attitudes that will influence the quality of life for each of us.

*For a more complete discussion of this stress theory see Weider, A. (ed.). *Contributions Toward Medical Psychology,* Vol. 1. New York: Ronald Press, 1953, and Selye, Hans, *The Stress of Life.* New York: McGraw-Hill, 1956.

We cannot eradicate death as such. The best that we can do is to come to terms with it, to understand it, and to use this understanding to improve our living quality. Through medical technology we have been able to eliminate some of the earlier causes of death and to postpone the onset of death in many cases; but we have not been able to eliminate death as an imminent and universal experience. One of the problems with which we grapple is the inability to describe the experience of death; how does it feel to be dead?

Our fears of death are probably unfounded because no matter how we individually perceive death, religiously or otherwise, it must be an experience unequalled in our lifetime except, perhaps, the experience of being born, which none of us can recall. Rather, our concern should be upon the time we are alive and able to function within the environment. Preoccupation with preventing the occurrence of death and prolonging life indefinitely is inherently unhealthy. Such, however, is the obsession of some. The development of "cryonic suspension (deep freezing at death to preserve individuals until a later date when their diseases would be curable) provides a flamboyant example of the pursuit to avoid death without regard for the profound social consequences which would be raised by circumventing the usual limits of life."[8] Perhaps the real fascination of cryonics is to see if it can be done!

What Is Death?

Death terminates life and living as we generally perceive it. Death is the only "event" of living that *cannot* be truly experienced, for an experience is something that affects, in some way, how we live. Death terminates living and is therefore not an experience. However, *is* death an event or process? Death, as with all elements of life and living, is a process with identifiable characteristics. Death may occur abruptly or it may be the terminal process of dying—or it may be viewed as the end of one process (living) and the beginning of a new one. Death is our destination, while dying is the process of getting there.

Defining death is not as simple as might be thought on the surface. Kass points out that "there are two 'definitions' that should not be confused. There is the conceptual 'definition' or meaning and the operational 'definition' or meaning."[9] In the former Kass is speaking of defining a state of death while the latter refers to criteria to determine that death has occurred. These definitions become increasingly important in view of the legal, medical, and ethical issues that today surround what was taken for granted 50 years ago—at that time, a person was dead who was dead. But today, because of medical interventions, we cannot always determine simply if death has occurred. For example, is death merely the cessation of breathing?

In June, 1968, the Council for International Organization of Medical Science of the World Health Organization established five *criteria* for the presence of death: (1) loss of all responses to the environment; (2) complete lack of any reflexes and the loss of muscle tone; (3) cessation of spontaneous respiration; (4) abrupt drop in arterial blood pressure; and (5) a flat electroencephalogram (EEG), a measure of brain function. However, "Now it appears that, even before the guidelines have been fully circulated, a flat EEG is being found to be an inadequate index. Instead the consumption of oxygen by the brain appears to be the significant indicator."[10] Thus, determining death is complicated.

THE AGING PROCESS

Introduction

Although death can occur at any age, more than 65 percent of all deaths are among people over 45 years of age. The leading cause of death in the United States, cardiovascular disease, is frequently the result of deterioration associated with the aging process. This is also true of other leading causes of death, such as some kidney disorders.

Research Into Aging

Growing old, with all its consequences, has been pretty much an accepted part of life. In the past, little thought seems to have been given to answering the question, "What process or processes are responsible for the gradual degeneration of the body?" It was not until May, 1974 that the Congress of the United States authorized the establishment of the National Institute on Aging. Its purpose was to "conduct and support biomedical, social, and behavioral research and training related to the aging process and diseases and other special problems and needs of the aged.[11]

The National Institute on Aging conducts and supports research on a variety of levels. At the Gerontology Research Center in Baltimore research is being conducted on:

- the *behavioral changes* that take place with age. Its purpose is to develop techniques to eliminate or modify behavior changes related to learning, memory, cognition, and the personality.
- the *aging process.* A program has been established to study the effects of aging on the body; included in the study are: the monitoring of cardiac, renal, and pulmonary functions; body composition; exercise physiology; carbohydrate and lipid metabolism; drug pharmacokinetics; nutrition and endocrine factors; and behavioral and social variables.
- the nature of the *age-related deterioration* of certain cells of the immune and related systems, and the molecular mechanisms responsible for this deterioration.
- the inability of organisms to maintain their *physiological control system and genetic information transfer system.* Included are studies on the impact on the mechanisms of age-dependent changes in kidney function, muscle activity, heart function, and metabolism.

The Adult Development and Aging Branch of the National Institute on Aging is supporting research on other aspects of aging including: (1) *cellular aging;* (2) *endocrine change with age* (with emphasis on the menopause and post-menopausal states); (3) *immunologic aging;* (4) *cognitive change with age;* and (5) *societal aspects of aging.* [12]

As can be seen, very little is presently known about the aging process and its mechanisms. Much more research is necessary before we will be able to understand even the most basic principles underlying degeneration and deterioration associated with aging. However, other factors also need to be considered besides the biological mechanisms of aging. As stated by the National Institute on Aging, "the obvious need for tangible and immediate improvement in the quality of life for the aged has shifted research away from its exclusive disease orientation to a broader inquiry into normal physiological changes with age, the behavioral constitution of the aged, and the social, cultural, and economic environment in which we grow old."[13]

The results of these investigations should shed light upon improving the quality of life of the young as well. Perhaps in the future we will appreciate more fully the need to improve human effectiveness at a time when it is most important, during the preaged years.

Gerontology

Gerontology is that branch of medicine concerned with the scientific study of the aging process—clinical, biological, and social—and the problems that aging reveals. Although humanity has succeeded in extending its life expectancy, it has not been able to prevent old age and the medicosocial consequences of it.

Life expectancy at birth in the United States in 1900, was approximately 49 years. A person born today can expect to live to more than 72 years of age. The life expectancy at birth is greater for white females (77 years) than white males (69.7 years). Black females can also expect to live longer (72.6 years) than black males (64 years). The longer we live, the greater are the chances that we will encounter those health problems associated with aging. (See Table 5–1.)

Actually, the longer we live, the more likely we will live longer. The more we are able to eliminate the causes of death during the younger years, the greater the life expectancy becomes. Since youth has greater ability to overcome diseases, the more we can expect successes in the elimination of the diseases that result

Table 5–1: The Ten Leading Causes of Death in the United States According to Age and Sex*

Causes of Death 65 Years of Age and Older	Total	Male	Female
Diseases of the heart	549,000	272,000	277,000
Malignancies	225,000	124,000	101,000
Cerebrovascular disease	159,000	65,000	94,000
Influenza and pneumonia	48,000	24,000	24,000
Arteriosclerosis	28,000	11,000	17,000
Diabetes mellitus	25,000	9,000	16,000
Accidents	24,000	13,000	11,000
Bronchitis, emphysema, and asthma	18,000	13,000	5,000
Cirrhosis of the liver	8,000	5,000	3,000
Nephritis and nephrosis (kidney diseases)	6,000	(a)	3,000
All other causes	155,000		
Total	1,245,000		

*Source of Data: United States Department of Health, Education, and Welfare, National Center for Health Statistics, 1978.

(a) The tenth leading cause of death for males is suicide with 3,500 cases annually.

in death during youth. (Table 5–2 provides the remaining life expectancies at specific ages.) As this takes place, the more we will need to draw upon the science of geriatrics to maintain the quality of life for the aged.

Geriatrics

Geriatrics is that specialized branch of medicine concerned with *treating* the health conditions associated with senescence and senility. *Senescence* is the term used to describe aging and the deterioration of the body resulting from growing old. *Senility* is the term used to describe the deterioration of mental processes. The chief distinction between gerontology and geriatrics is that gerontology is concerned with the study of senescence while geriatrics is concerned with applying scientific findings to alleviating the diseases resulting from senescence.

In 1900, one person in 25 was over 65 years of age in the United States. It is estimated that approximately one person in 12 will be over 65 years of age during the early 1980s. In other words, we can expect our aged population to approximately double during the 1980s over what it was in 1900. In the year 2000, it is estimated that 11 percent of the population will be over 65 years of age.

Table 5–2:   Average Remaining Lifetime in Years for Specific Ages for Years 1900 and 1980

AGE IN YEARS	AVERAGE REMAINING LIFE-YEARS*		TOTAL LIFE EXPECTANCY	
	1900	*1980*	*1900*	*1980*
0	49	73	49	73
5	55	69	60	74
10	51	64	61	74
15	47	59	62	74
20	43	55	63	75
25	39	50	64	75
30	36	45	66	75
35	32	41	67	76
40	28	36	68	76
45	25	32	70	77
50	21	27	71	77
55	18	23	72	78
60	15	19	75	79
65	12	16	77	81
70	9	13	79	83
75	8	10	83	85
80	5	8	85	88
85	4	6	89	91

*Rounded to the nearest whole year.
Source of Data: *Facts of Life and Death*, U.S. Dep't. of Health, Education, and Welfare, DHEW Publication No. (PHS) 79–1222, p. 6.

There are vital social and medical ramifications that accompany the increase in the aged population. These include the need for health care that is accessible, both geographically and financially, to those who need it the most. In addition, we need to explore ways of decreasing the number of people who are receiving essentially custodial care because of the loss of ability to function effectively.

SHOULD LIFE BE PROLONGED?

Death With Dignity

Health is the right of each of us; death, also is the right of each of us. As with health and living, death has its own special kind of dignity that should not be denied. Death is an event in the lives of all humans in spite of the advances in medical technology to delay it. Historically, (and still in many primitive societies) death was considered inevitable and accepted as an honorable phase of life. However, according to Aries, today, "We do not believe that the sick person has a right to know he is dying; nor do we believe in the public and solemn character accorded the moment of death. What ought to be known is ignored; what ought to be a sacred moment is conjured away."[14] How can we die with dignity if the truth of our death is denied?

As with living, dying should possess a certain quality. Dying is a personal matter; it always has been. However, today, dying is also a matter of loneliness; too often it means dying alone in a strange surrounding, a technical environment —the hospital or nursing home. In previous generations one could be content in the belief that when the time came to die, he/she would be surrounded by members of the family, one's loved ones, in a familiar environment, the home. Modern technology and the changing family structure have made dying in this context not only obsolete, but impossible—even unthinkable.

Unfortunately, physicians tend to be more concerned with the *disease* of the dying person than with the *person* who is dying. The very nature of our health care system, its institutions and technical expectations, makes it difficult if not impossible to direct attention to anything but the gadgets that support life, rather than the life itself. Death today comes hard, unless it comes suddenly. Ramsey said it best when he stated that "there is nobility and dignity in caring for the dying, but not in dying itself."[15]

Morison put it even more explicitly when he stated that, "There is an implicit indignity in the conception of the meaning of human life revealed by overvigorous efforts to maintain its outward, visible, and entirely trivial signs. It is not breathing, urinating, and defecating that makes a human being important even when he can do these things by himself. How much greater is the indignity when all these things must be done for him, and he can do nothing else."[16] Finally, Kass summarizes the problem of dying with dignity by noting that it "can be diminished, undermined, or even eliminated by many things in many ways, for example, by coma or senility, unbearable pain, madness, sudden death, denial, depravity, ignorance, cowardice, isolation, destitution, as well as by excessive and impersonal medical and technological intervention . . ."[17] Morison clarifies this further by stating that "clearly, then, the omission of what are so oddly referred to as *heroic* means can spare us at least in part from death with indignity."[18]

Euthanasia

Euthanasia is essentially a question of who shall live and who shall die. It is a question with legal, medical, and ethical overtones; it is also a question whose answer can affect the future of the survival of humanity. Euthanasia is sometimes equated with mercy death (killing), with hastening death in one way or another, by removing life support technology or deliberately bringing about death. In any case, according to Smith there are two chief questions that must be considered: (1) who shall make the decision; and (2) what criteria should be used?[19]

Another critical issue arises related to the procedure for salvaging organs. May suggests four options for salvaging organs: (1) a system of routine salvaging that can be exempted only by the special initiative of the predeceased or his/her family; (2) a program of organized donations of organs by the donor or the family; (3) a system for selling organs by the predeceased or the family; or (4) provision for crediting a family account in anticipation of when it may require an organ.[20] There are arguments for and against each of these options. (See Figure 5–1.)

SHIFTING ROLES IN DEATH AND DYING

Before 1960, an estimated 40 percent of all deaths occurred at home, while today less than 20 percent do.[21] With this shift in place of death has also come a shift in the roles played by the physician, clergy, funeral director, and the family.

Figure 5-1:

Uniform Donor Card

of ....
                        Print or type name of donor

In the hope that I may help others, I hereby make this anatomical gift, if medically acceptable, to take effect upon my death. The words and marks below indicate my desires. I give:

(a) ___ any needed organs or parts

(b) ___ only the following organs or parts

Specify the organ(s) or part(s)
for the purposes of transplantation, therapy, medical research or education;

(c) ___ my body for anatomical study if needed.

Limitations or
special wishes, if any: ....

Signed by the donor and the following two witnesses in the presence of each other.

Signature of donor   Date of birth of donor

Date signed   City & State

Witness   Witness

This is a legal document under the Uniform Anatomical Gift Act or similar laws.

For further information consult your physician or

National Kidney   116 East 27th Street
Foundation   New York, N.Y. 10016

The Role of the Physician

Because traditional medical training revolves around preventing death through medical, surgical and other forms of treatment, death is almost always perceived by the physician as evidence of medical failure. This is a situation that most physicians find unacceptable. Centuries ago, Francis Bacon divided the practice of medicine into three basic parts: (1) the preservation of health; (2) the cure of disease; and (3) the prolongation of life.[22] It has only been within very recent years that some attention has been given to improving the physician's role in accepting death and the dying process as an integral component of the practice of medicine. This role revolves around responsibilities to the dying patient, members of the family, as well as to the ethics of the medical profession.

America's population is changing. Illich has written: "The old in the United States constitute 10 percent of the population and consume 20 percent of health services, overwhelmingly for the treatment of arthritis, loneliness, cancer, and other afflictions for which modern therapy cannot be shown to have either healing or soothing effects."[23] Therefore, it becomes imperative that the medical professions alter their role accordingly. Should we direct our resources to prolonging life that can no longer contribute to society even if death can be averted, or should these resources be directed toward reducing the suffering associated with old-age and imminent death? What effective new roles should the physician assume in the face of the pending and inevitable aging population? What role should the physician play in preventing untimely deaths of the young? Should the medical profession be involved in the area of death and dying at all, or should the medical profession continue in the traditional roles as outlined by Bacon? White suggests that it is clear "that if physicians cannot change their ideas about their roles as physicians, they are going to feel frustrated and on many levels a failure because of their inability to cure dying patients."[24]

Obviously, then, although the basic role of the physician is to *cure* the patient, when this is not possible, the role must be to *care* for the patient. Care implies attention to the psychological and social as well as the physical needs of the patient. Sometimes appropriate care of the patient results in dramatic improvement. The physician, therefore, possesses a sense of the patient's concerns and through care helps the patient to deal with his/her illness at realistic levels. This simply means that hope is ever-present; that there is always something that can be done for the patient.

The Role of the Clergy

In our society, death is almost always associated with religion and divine powers, rather than as a reality of life and living. As a result, the denial process is reinforced, with death as a real phenomenon being very difficult to accept. Some writers suggest that there is nothing in life more final than death. This concept is abruptly contradictory to what many people want to believe, that is, that death is the beginning of eternal life. Probably adding to the difficulties in accepting death, at least, as an earthly finality, are the numerous fictitious accounts of death, spirits, ghosts, haunted houses, angels, and so forth. These fantasies (if, indeed, they actually are) tend to amuse us when we are healthy, but also horrify us at times and intensify emotional reactions to death when it is imminent.

Our elaborate cemeteries, with their various monuments, are "reminders" that these people once lived, are now dead, and their bodily remains lie beneath the earth. From the beginning of our country, those who died and were buried were remembered by simple grave markers that were placed upon their "resting places." (See Figure 5–2.)

Figure 5-2:

From the beginning of recorded history, the role of the clergy has not changed very much. Regardless of the religious (or nonreligious) beliefs of the dying person and the close survivors, the chief role of the clergy remains one of providing hope, comfort, and union with God. Generally, the clergy views his/her role clearly at the time of tragedy and enters the grieving process to give comfort to the bereaved and to the dying in accordance with the scriptures. The clergy is in a position to provide meaningful comfort and to assist the bereaved to accept the "will of God," which can make the grief process less painful and allow it to take its natural course.

However, even the clergy do not always play their roles effectively. According to one study, 48 percent of widows interviewed stated their clergy were indifferent, while 45 percent found them to be helpful during their bereavement.[25] Perhaps the role of the clergy, from their own viewpoint, is unclear or perhaps the expectations of the bereaved are different from the way the clergy view themselves. However, one thing is clear, the clergy are central figures along with physicians and funeral directors at the time of most deaths and their roles extend beyond the point of commitment of the body.

The Role of the Funeral Director

It appears that the role of the funeral director will vary according to a variety of circumstances. These include how well the bereaved know the funeral director, the bereaved's experiences with funerals, the wishes of the decreased, and the suggestions made by the funeral director. For example, in one study, 41 percent of the bereaved asked their funeral directors to make all possible arrangements while 30 percent asked them to make many of the arrangements.[26] Arrangements may include the ordering of flowers, engaging pallbearers if there is to be burial, arranging cremation if this is to occur, and notifying friends and relatives.

Since the funeral director is contacted by the bereaved during the time of acute grief, the funeral director must assume the role of counselor. This is a critical period and the manner in which he/she handles the bereaved during these early hours following the death can be vital for the grieving process. The funeral director must provide comfort from the start, through the visiting periods, and finally, the funeral and commitment of the body. All of these roles are in addition to the professional services of preparing the body for the wake and the funeral services, if these occur. The selection of a funeral director is important, for some will be more helpful than will others. In one study, 61 percent of the bereaved felt that funeral directors went out of their way to offer help during the grieving period, while only 8 percent felt the funeral directors did not.[27]

New Approaches to Dying

Should one die at home, in the hospital, in the nursing home, or at some other institution? There is no doubt that a person can die more peacefully, with more acceptance, when surrounded by the familiar environment of the home. However, today our society has tended toward the opposite—more deaths occur in the hospital.

Fortunately, however, there are new alternatives evolving for the dying to supplement the hospital, nursing home, or home. In recent years, what is known as the hospice movement is providing some terminally ill patients with an opportunity to die with medical care, but also in the presence of relatives. The original hospice is St. Christopher's Hospice, founded in 1948. Hospice literally means an "inn for travelers." St. Christopher's Hospice, and others patterned after it, is designed to be a combination of a hospital/nursing home and the patient's own home. However, it was not until 1967 that St. Christopher's Hospice was built and readied for the admittance of the first patients. The hospice care combines medical technology with personal care. St. Christopher's Hospice is financed by gifts as well as funds made available from the National Health Service of Great Britain. Following the lead of St. Christopher's, there are now more than 100 hospices in operation or being established throughout the United States. Some are actual in-patient facilities, which combine medical services with a home-like atmosphere. Other hospices are organizations that provide care in the patient's own home.

American hospitals and nursing homes have been unable to keep pace with the health care needs that are evolving. There is a critical need for health care providers to begin to direct more attention to the psychological and social health needs of the terminally ill patients (as well as any sick person). This means that physicians, nurses, nursing aides, and others who come into direct contact with the patients should be trained with more emphasis on their personal qualities, their ability to relate to terminally ill patients and provide comfort, understanding, and opportunities for socializing and communicating. Nearly anyone can easily learn to make a bed, empty a bed-pan, and fill out a hospital report form; but not everyone naturally possesses the personal qualities of compassion, empathy, and understanding to raise the hope and spirits of the dying person and to provide for the critical psychological and social needs that are so vital during this period of life. Persons must be trained in these compassionate skills. What is needed is a shift from the almost purely medical model of caring for the terminally ill patient to a humanizing model.

For example, in the late 1970s Dr. H. James Wallace, Jr. recognized the importance of family interaction with adolescent cancer victims. He initiated the development of the first adolescent cancer unit at Roswell Park Memorial Institute in Buffalo, New York. The unit is designed to respond to the special needs of the adolescent cancer patient: physical, psychological, and social. To meet these needs, the unit provides for total adolescent care focusing on the growth process, social adjustments, and family counseling. The adolescent is encouraged to maintain identity as a person. To achieve these formidable goals, the unit is staffed with a specially trained medical team of physicians, nurses, psychosocial counselors, psychiatrists, psychologists, rehabilitation specialists, nutritionists, and oncologists (cancer specialists).

CHILDREN AND GRIEF

Preparing children for their own or for someone else's death is not a simple process. The age of the child appears to be less significant than the child's "experiences, temporal concerns, life circumstances, and self-concept at the time the question is posed."[28] Children tend to be aware of death at a very early age, but their perception of it will vary considerably from a kind of sleep to an understanding of its finality. There is some controversy as to what kinds of exposures a child should have, when these should take place, and the kinds of assistance they need to help them to deal adequately with death—their own or someone else's.

Exposure to Illness

As a general rule, children under 14 years of age are not permitted to visit sick relatives in a hospital. There are no valid reasons for this prohibition except that children may tend to disrupt hospital routine. Since children are shielded from this experience, they are frequently left to their own fantasies as to what has taken place when they do find out that the sick relative has died. However, most nursing homes do allow children to visit patients, the goals of a nursing home being quite different from those of a hospital. The hospital strives for the image of providing medical care, treatment, and rehabilitation to restore patients to health. It is a place to get well, not to die. The image of a nursing home for many people is more one of a place where people go to await death. Death in a hospital is perceived as a tragedy by the hospital and physicians, while death in the nursing home is expected.

We do children a disservice by shielding them from sickness and from death. They, too, need to know the truth about health, illness, hospitals, death, and other aspects of life. The important factor is how well they are prepared for these aspects as with any aspect of living.

Children and the Funeral

Our "reality world" is full of fantasy and pretense. We tend to teach children through this fantasy world rather than to teach them reality when it is associated with death and sickness. Children need to feel a part of the experience of dying and death. They need to feel needed during this critical period, and involved in preparations. They need to begin their mourning process to feel and express grief as much as adults. Through their involvement in the funeral, they can begin their grief with their family instead of being kept from it. It is an experience that can help them to reflect upon their lives and to profit from it by living more fully; to grow that much more.

AFTER DEATH—THEN WHAT?

The Funeral

The wake and finally the funeral provide opportunities for the bereaved to come to the realization that a loved one is dead. The wake and funeral tend to hasten the beginning of the grieving process. The very nature of the funeral seems to indicate that this is the time and the place to express the emotions that before now may have been repressed. Jackson states that "the funeral is the time to relate the grieving individual to the multiple resources of a larger community which serves as a resonant sounding board for talking out deep feelings at a time and place that are appropriate and meaningful."[29] At this time, the bereaved becomes both intellectually and emotionally aware of the loss and grieving takes place on both levels in the presence of others who too are concerned. This sharing with others the grief you feel helps to make the parting a little more tolerable, for as Pinette puts it, ". . . grief shared is grief diminished." No one should have to bear the burden of grieving in solitude because "there is nothing worse than going through a crisis alone."[30]

In this regard, the funeral is a process for the living, not the deceased. It provides for a social interaction that is important for the survivors to face reality, begin the mourning period, and adjust to a new life without the person who has died. Since the funeral tends to expedite, in most cases, the process of grief and the subsequent return to a state of normalcy, it is therapeutic. To deny death is to prolong the recovery period and to intensify the debilitating effects that result from the death of a loved one. Therefore, the funeral should direct its attention to the living rather than the dead.

New Adjustments for Survivors

No matter how much we may fear or deny death, we can not escape it in one form or another. It is one event of living that all of us will experience, although the specific way in which it occurs may vary somewhat from one person to another. In a sense, death may be perceived as one of the most effective activities that each of us undertakes. Death is always a successful venture.

There is a kind of contradiction, at least at the emotional level, in regards to dying. We are taught early in life that death is glorious in a religious sense, and yet we tend to be horrified of the thought of our own death and that of loved ones. We can intellectually accept death as an integral part of living, but we still tend to deny its personal occurrence. On the other side of the picture are those who become preoccupied with death, fearing its inevitability, but knowing it will some day occur.

The unknown qualities that surround death have also created rather bizarre (but possible) impressions about what it is like to be dead. Some of these impressions have evolved into pseudosciences, such as spiritualism, ghost studies, and so forth. How much truth we can glean from these is yet to be demonstrated. Probably one of the reasons why these beliefs continue is the powerful hope that death is not final to life, but rather, a transition into another and more beautiful form of existence.

Although death is the end of life for the person who had died, it can be the beginning of living for those who remain, for death of a loved one provides us with the opportunity to reflect upon our own lives and to live more fully as a result of this reflection. As Aeschylus (525–456 B.C.) so eloquently wrote: "He who learns must suffer. And even in our sleep pain that cannot forget, falls drop by drop upon the heart, and in our despair, against our will, comes wisdom to us by the awful grace of God."

The message is clear: life is somewhat like a kaleidoscope. Slight changes in the intermingling components can bring about drastic changes in what we perceive and feel. These changes that interrupt what is beautiful, peaceful, and exciting result in new feelings and experiences—at first, strange, unwanted, but finally, beautiful once again. Every event can have this result if we will allow it to happen. Death, one of the most traumatic of life's events, should be allowed to bring on new horizons of living, not stagnation in the pleasures of the past. This does not mean that these should be forgotten (as though they really could), but rather should be used as a means of going forward. Such is really the kaleidoscope of life. And the moment of death is the final adjustment to life.

GLOSSARY

Cryonic suspension: A theoretical process of freezing a person and bringing him/her back to life at a future time.

Euthanasia: A process of bringing about a painless death of a person.

Geriatrics: A specialized branch of medicine concerned with treating health conditions associated with senescence.

Gerontology: A specialized branch of medicine concerned with the scientific study of the aging process.

Grief: A powerful emotion associated with an important personal loss.

Mourning process: The period of time and the emotional stages of grief from the time of a tragedy through recovery and acceptance.

Senescence: Aging and deterioration of the body resulting from growing old.

Thanatology: The medicolegal study of death and the conditions surrounding the dead.

SUMMARY

Many experiences of life can result in feelings of grief, but the ones that are most traumatic are the death of a loved one and our own imminent death. When grief is intense and prolonged, it can result in varying degrees of debilitation. Grief-provoking stimuli are called tragedies. The resultant grief is a part of the mourning process.

Grief is a powerful emotion, and as with any emotion, it must be expressed in some satisfactory way. There are signs that open expression of grief resulting from death is becoming more acceptable in our society. Repression of grief delays its normal process. Mourning is important for decreasing the psychological reactions to grief.

Thanatology is the medicolegal study of all facets surrounding death. However, in recent years, it has been concerned with philosophy, law, theology, the social sciences, literature, and history. New technologies related to organ transplants, prolongation of life, and others, have brought into focus the need to be concerned with medical ethics, social ethics, and legal ethics. Even our definitions of death have had to undergo changes in view of these new technologies as well as establishing criteria to ascertain a state of death.

In the past two decades the number of people who die in hospitals rather than at home, has more than doubled. With this shift has come new roles for the physician, clergy, and funeral director since survivors are less likely to be involved in the dying process of loved ones. However, there is evidence of changes in attitudes taking place in where a person should be allowed to die and the way in which death arrives. There is evidence that a recognition of the human qualities of terminally ill need attention as well as the medical treatments for the illness.

The question of how to prepare children for death is a complex one. Some authorities advocate shielding children from death, while others feel they should experience it on a positive level. Death can be a form of growth and an understanding of it can bring about a richer life for those who are living.

The funeral is a process for the survivors. It can help to initiate the grieving process and bring about the realities surrounding the death of a loved one. New adjustments to a life without the deceased must be made. Death of a loved one should result in the survivors reflecting upon their own lives so that they can live more fully in the future.

PROBLEMS FOR DISCUSSION

1. Besides death, what are five other tragedies that may bring on grief? What characteristics do these tragedies have that are similar to death?
2. What factors assist us in dealing with grief as a result of the death of a loved one?
3. Explain grief as an emotion. How should grief be expressed? Why?
4. What is thanatology? Discuss the bioethical issues associated with death and dying.

5. How do you define death? Support your answer with objective evidence.

6. Analyze the five criteria for ascertaining the presence of death as established by the Council for International Organization of Medical Science. Are they adequate? Why or why not?

7. Should one be allowed to die with dignity? Discuss what you mean by dying with dignity. What issues does this concept bring to light?

8. Should life be prolonged? Support your answer. What are some reasons given for prolonging life? What social issues arise because of prolonging life? Legal issues? Medical issues? Ethical issues?

9. Discuss the issues surrounding organ transplant and organ salvaging technology.

10. Define euthanasia. Discuss the forms that euthanasia can take.

11. Compare the role of the physician, clergy, and funeral director in relation to death.

12. List some new approaches to care of the dying.

13. Should children be exposed to death? Explain. Compare and discuss the various sides of the controversy regarding children attending the funeral.

14. Discuss the purposes of the funeral. Why is a funeral important?

15. Distinguish between gerontology and geriatrics. Why are these two medical sciences important in regards to prolongation of life, dying, and death?

16. What are the basic functions of the National Institute on Aging?

REFERENCES

1. KUBLER-ROSS, ELISABETH, *Death: The Final Stage of Growth.* Prentice-Hall, Inc., Englewood Cliffs, New Jersey, 1975, p. 164.

2. NICHOLS, ROY VAUGHN, "Acute Grief, Disposal, Funerals and Consequences," *Grief and the Meaning of the Funeral,* Otto Margolis, et al (eds.), MSS Information Corporation, New York, 1975, p. 33.

3. CLAYTON, PAULA J., "The Funeral Director and Bereavement," *Grief and the Meaning of the Funeral,* Otto Margolis, et al (eds.), MSS Information Corporation, New York, 1975, p. 67.

4. JACKSON, EDGAR N., "The Wise Management of Grief," *Grief and the Meaning of the Funeral, op. cit.,* p. 3.

5. *Ibid.,* p. 2.

6. KUBLER-ROSS, ELISABETH, *On Death and Dying,* MacMillan Publishing Co., Inc., New York, 1969, Chapters 3–7.

7. CALLAHAN, DANIEL, "Preface," *Death Inside Out,* Peter Steinfels and Robert M. Veatch (eds.), Harper & Row, Publishers, New York, 1975, p. ix.

8. ENGELHARDT, H. TRISTRAM JR., "The Counsels of Finitude," *Death Inside Out, op. cit.,* p. 119.

9. KASS, LEON R., "Death As An Event," *Death Inside Out, op. cit.,* p. 73.

10. GILLON, HADASSAH, "Defining Death Anew," *The Individual, Society and*

Death: An Anthology of Readings, David W. Berg and George G. Daugherty (eds.), 1972, p. 9.

11. *National Institutes of Health Almanac,* U. S. Department of Health, Education, and Welfare, Public Health Service, National Institutes of Health, 1977, p. 98.

12. *Ibid.,* pp. 99–101.

13. *Ibid.,* p. 101.

14. ARIES, PHILIPPE, "Death Inside Out," *Death Inside Out, op. cit.,* p. 11.

15. RAMSEY, PAUL, "The Indignity of 'Death With Dignity' " *Death Inside Out, op. cit.,* p. 82.

16. MORISON, ROBERT S., "The Dignity of the Inevitable and Necessary," *Death Inside Out, op. cit.,* p. 98.

17. KASS, LEON R., "Averting One's Eyes, or Facing the Music—on Dignity and Death," *Death Inside Out,* p. 103.

18. MORISON, ROBERT S., "The Dignity of the Inevitable and Necessary," *loc. cit.*

19. SMITH, DAVID H., "On Letting Some Babies Die," *Death Inside Out, op. cit.,* p. 140.

20. MAY, WILLIAM, "Attitudes Toward the Newly Dead," *Death Inside Out, op. cit.,* p. 140.

21. MAY, WILLIAM, "The Metaphysical Plight of the Family," *Death Inside Out, op. cit.,* p. 55.

22. ILLICH, IVAN, "The Political Uses of Natural Death," *Death Inside Out, op. cit.,* p. 26.

23. *Ibid.*

24. WHITE, LAURENS P., "Death and the Physician: Nortuis Vivos Docent," *New Meanings of Death,* McGraw-Hill Book Company, New York, 1977, p. 94.

25. CLAYTON, PAULA J., "The Funeral Director and Bereavement," *Grief and the Meaning of the Funeral, op. cit.,* p. 68.

26. KHLEIF, BAHEEJ, "The Sociology of the Mortuary: Attitudes to the Funeral, Funeral Director, and Funeral Arrangements," *Grief and the Meaning of the Funeral, op. cit.,* p. 230.

27. *Ibid.,* p. 233.

28. LANGNER, MYRA BLUEBOND, "Meaning of Death to Children," *New Meanings of Death, op. cit.,* p. 52.

29. JACKSON, EDGAR N., "The Wise Management of Grief," *Grief and the Meaning of the Funeral, op. cit.,* p. 4.

30. PINETTE, RAOL L., "Acute Grief and The Funeral," *Grief and the Meaning of the Funeral, op. cit.,* p. 116.

6

sex, marriage, and lifestyles

TYPES OF FAMILY STRUCTURE

Introduction

The family today seems to be a troubled institution. The divorce rate is high, and the number of separations is large. In big cities in the United States about one in twelve persons under forty-five or fifty years of age is living away from his or her mate. Families without children are numerous. In large urban centers every other family, approximately, is without a child living at home, and perhaps a fifth of the married women who reach forty-five years of age have never borne a child. This situation is a source of anxiety to many persons, because the home is the place where the personal and social virtues are developed. The type of citizen one becomes is related closely to the type of mother, father, and home life one has.[1]

This statement could have been written today. It was published, however, in 1946. Our concern for the future of the family is not new. However, when social crises arise, it is the family that we turn to in hopes that the crises will be successfully weathered. So basic is the family as a social institution that we continue to cherish it in our society, although its structure and function evolves with advancements in other areas of society.

Cultural Influences on Family Structure

The family, regardless of its structure, is a primary means of sustaining a society. Throughout the world, family structure varies in line with the values of society. The United States Bureau of the Census defines the family as a group of two or more people related by blood, marriage, or adoption and who are living together. However, others prefer a broader definition that encompasses the concept that there is a relatively solid, long lasting relationship among a group of people regardless of blood or legal relationship.

The family may be considered as having "an established order . . . as an element of organized society . . ."[2] In other words, the family is a basic element of the social fabric. If it were eliminated, there is no doubt that the result would be a major social disruption.

Many aspects of society reflect our reverence for the family. Children, for instance, must be born into a family or they are called illegitimate. Some religions believe that living together out of wedlock is sinful. This is reflected in many of our laws that make it illegal in some states for unmarried people to engage in sexual intercourse. There is virtually no aspect of society in which the family is not respected.

The Changing Scene of Family Life

We have experienced a shift from an agrarian society to one that is largely industrialized, with a corresponding increase in mobility. This has changed the elemental structure of the family, at least in the view of some authorities. Prior to the industrial revolution, it seemed that the prevailing norm was the *extended family* in which children, parents, and grandparents lived under the same roof. However, as urbanization occurred and mobility increased, the extended family was no longer necessary or practical. What evolved was the *nuclear family,* characterized by children and parents living under one roof with only incidental contact with other relatives. Many have viewed this shift as evidence of a breakdown in family structure that threatens society as a whole. There are, however, other factors that must be considered.

Our changing economy, coupled with the women's movement, have resulted in more and more women entering the workforce—women who would not have entered it in the past. This puts a distinct strain on the household. Children must often be cared for by people who are not family members. Less time is also spent together as a family unit.

There are some groups in our society in which women are commonly the head of the family, primarily because of a high incidence of divorce and separation early in the marriage. It is thought by some that the lack of a male presence may have a profound negative impact upon the children. This issue, however, is highly debatable.

The discussion of family structure is closely entwined with the structure of marriage and other living arrangements. According to Goldberg and Deutsch,[3] there are five basic forms of marriage: monogamy (marriage to one person; discussed in detail later), polygamy, polygyny, polyandry, and group marriage.

Polygamy is having more than one husband or wife at one time. Although polygamy exists in the majority of societies throughout the world, monogamy is usually the dominant value. Polygamy, where it exists, is accepted by both men and women who participate in it and is closely related to the values of the society and to economic conditions.

The most frequently occurring form of polygamy is *polygyny,* in which one man is married to more than one woman. In general, only wealthy men are able to practice polygyny, even though others in the society may believe in its practice. Much less frequent in occurrence is *polyandry* in which women have more than one husband.

Group marriage may involve two couples, two couples and an additional person, one couple and an additional person, and the like. Group marriage is not practiced on a wide scale and it appears that its success rate is not high. The most famous experiment in group marriage in the United States was the founding of the Oneida Community in upstate New York in 1844 by John Humphrey Noyes. This experiment ended in the 1880s, when the community splintered and Noyes went to Canada.

A resurgence of group marriage occurred during the 1960s in conjunction with the development of *communes,* but they too have been largely unsuccessful. Communes can be group marriages or they can be economically based living arrangements in which income, property, and functions are shared, with each nuclear family being held intact. Communal living, therefore, may be thought of as a variation in living arrangements rather than a variation in marriage, per se.

Another variation in living arrangements that gained popularity during the 1970s was mate swapping or *swinging.* Although the traditional marriage remained intact, there was an overt attempt to have sexual relations with others outside of the marriage with both marriage partners knowing of it and consenting to it. Advocates of swinging claim that this increased sexual freedom and enhanced the marriage by reducing the possibility of sexual frustration.

Swinging may be a part of what has been termed an open marriage as opposed to the traditional, or closed marriage. According to O'Neill and O'Neill, an *open marriage* is "a relationship in which the partners are committed to their own and to each other's growth."[4] This growth occurs in every aspect of life, including the sexual, according to adherents of this philosophy. It is interesting that even the O'Neills have since found problems with such an arrangement and are not as enthusiastic about it since their original book about open marriage was published in 1972.

Another type of living arrangement that apparently has not yet peaked in popularity is living together without being married in the conventional sense. Such an arrangement is gaining acceptance in our society, the rationale being that it allows a couple to see if they are compatible before they get married. Also called *cohabitation,* "living together" may involve sexual relations, while in other instances the arrangement may be more one of convenience than of intimacy. Whatever the case, couples should not enter such a relationship believing that it will predict success in marriage. Cohabitation and marriage are two unique experiences and should not be evaluated using the same criteria.

MARRIAGE AND FAMILY ISSUES

Engagement

Traditional marriage has surrounding it a variety of ceremonies and practices that legitimize the process of marriage. When two people fall in love, there is usually a period of "going steady" during which the relationship is cultivated. Following this period the couple may become engaged, that is, they make a commitment to each other that marriage will occur sometime in the foreseeable future. There are no set rules, however, that dictate behavior during the engagement period.

Whatever the customs surrounding an engagement, it is generally held that it will help a couple know each other better, thus resulting in a better marriage. On a cross-cultural basis, engagement may serve a variety of other purposes as well: It may take the couple out of sexual circulation; serve as a trial marriage; serve to enforce a culturally imposed sexual abstinence; serve as a period in which property rights and property exchanges are settled; serve to orient the couple to their new relationships with other members of the community; and control the couple's mobility from one social class to another.[5]

More practically, however, engagement in our society is typically thought of as a time when the couple prepares for marriage. They often decide whether they want children and the size their family will ultimately be. They also identify their life's goals, determine whether or not they can get along with each other's family, and plan the wedding.

The psychological pressures put on a couple who are engaged are enormous. Sometimes these pressures result in terminating the engagement. In other instances, the couple may choose to elope to escape these pressures. Those who survive the pressures with the relationship still strong are exhibiting signs that the ensuing marriage has a good chance of being successful.

The Termination of the Engagement

When an engagement fails, there is a natural tendency to view the relationship as unsuccessful. Though this may be the case, the engagement may be viewed as successful, however, since its basic purpose is to determine if the couple should become legally bound to each other. In other words: "A truly successful engagement period leads either to a successful marriage or to a broken engagement."[6] Most broken engagements are based upon mutual agreement. However, problems can arise, especially if the breaking of the engagement is not agreeable to both parties. In fact, there may be legal issues involved.

Legal issues can arise especially when there is property to be divided. There have been cases, for instance, when a broken engagement has been ruled a breach of promise. Damages sought may be of two types: (1) compensatory, in which an award is granted by the court for what the party has suffered; and (2) punitive, in which the court rules that payment must be made as a punishment to the person who has violated the agreement.

Engagement is not something to be taken lightly. It should be entered into only after careful consideration and when it seems relatively certain that a marriage will follow.

Marriage

Most couples enter marriage hoping and believing that life will be better and more fulfilling than when they were single. Often this is the case. But almost never is life after marriage merely an extension of the good times people have during the courtship and engagement periods. A successful marriage is dependent upon love, sharing, sacrifice, compromise, and just plain work.

Marriage was historically a legal bond between two people in which the woman and her possessions essentially became the property of the man. This, of course, is in addition to the religious factors often involved in the marriage. These customs were incorporated into statute and are still explicit or implied in many that regulate marriage. However, many of these traditions are now open to challenge as women have pressed for equality under the law. Some of the legal issues being questioned are the requirement that the wife submit sexually to her husband, even against her will; the requirement that the wife move to another location, even against her will, or face being charged with desertion (grounds for divorce in some states); and the fact that the husband is legally entitled to his wife's services without having to compensate her for them.[7]

As women have sought marital equality, it has become increasingly popular for them to keep their maiden names. Though this has rarely been a legal issue, some still feel that in refusing to take her husband's name, a woman is somehow denying a permanent marital bond.

Another increasingly popular practice in the movement toward equality is the formulation of a marriage contract—an agreement prior to marriage outlining the rights and roles of each partner concerning issues of importance to them. Such issues as the surname the wife and children will assume, the types of birth control methods to be used, the desired frequency of sexual relations, ownership of property, and division of household chores, may be spelled out. Ironically, even if such a contract exists, it is not likely to be legally binding. Discussions about the agreements concerning such issues, however, may clarify marital expectations and lead to a more stable marriage than might otherwise exist.

Depending on the state in which you live, there are also legal requirements to be met before marriage can take place. These laws set standards as to age of consent, whether or not a blood test is required, how long a couple must wait until a marriage license is granted, and how long after a license is granted a couple must wait until the marriage ceremony can be performed.

None of the legal requirements described here, or those concerning marriage contracts, will ensure a successful marriage. Laws only serve to protect society. They do not serve to solidify a relationship.

Marital Communications

A successful marriage is dependent upon a couple's commitment to each other: an overt effort to make the relationship increasingly stable. The basis for such a stable relationship is positive communication. Cox[8] has identified three processes essential for positive marital communication: (1) *commitment,* in which the couple works together to enhance their relationship; (2) *growth orientation,* in which the couple recognizes that they will change as individuals and, therefore, their relationship must grow accordingly; and (3) *noncoercive atmosphere,* in which the couple must be honest and open with each other if communications are to be successful. It is marital communication that is the key to dealing with many of the family issues with which a couple will be faced throughout their marriage.

Family Issues

There is possibly no change in lifestyle as significant as that which occurs when two people get married and begin a family. No longer are we living just for ourselves but for our partners as well. We begin a new family with apprehension, for no one can foresee all the adjustments that must be made. Our decision to start a family creates stress because, for most of us, it is a decision that should last forever.

One of the major changes that we must face in marriage is our role as individuals. No longer is the wife viewed as a servant to the husband. The responsibilities of managing the household, raising children, handling finances, all must be shared. It is no longer sufficient for the husband to be the breadwinner (traditional male role) and the woman to be the housewife (traditional female role). Our economy—coupled with other social factors—now dictates that for many families the wife and husband together must share in all aspects of family maintenance. This changing view of the roles of husband and wife is the source of a great deal of anxiety for some people, and yet it provides an opportunity for increased personal fulfillment.

A major family issue that has taken on new proportions in recent years is the personal desire and social expectation for children. No longer are we living in an agrarian society in which large families are desirable. Ours is a society in which resources are at a premium. The world's population is increasing significantly. Food and other resources are insufficient for many. This is to say nothing of the ever increasing cost of rearing a child. For marriage, there is the engagement period in which a couple gets to know each other and to become prepared for the new challenges that lie ahead. There is no corresponding period, however, that prepares us for the challenges of raising children. And yet, society still expects children to be produced.

There are also personal reasons for wanting children. Childbearing and childrearing does provide personal fulfillment for many. It offers a chance to create and raise a new human being who will become a contributing member of society. Children also offer an avenue through which any accumulation of wealth may be passed. One's genetic potentials are kept alive resulting in a possible improvement of the human race. Finally, prospective parents view children as contributing to future pleasure and marital stability. Little affects the family more, in terms of its functions and future, than the choice of whether or not to have children.

Conversely, little affects a child's development more than the family. Within the family context, gender roles are established, and regardless of our intellectual efforts to the contrary, we tend to treat boys and girls differently as we raise them. Unfortunately girls tend to be treated as delicate, dependent, and feminine, whereas boys are given more independence, being encouraged at an earlier age to explore and to make outside contacts. We, therefore, tend to raise our children to reflect society's view of masculinity and feminity. This is changing, however.

After the first few years of life, peer influences become increasingly significant in their effect upon the development of the child. This can create conflict in parent/child relationships, particularly in the adolescent years. This quest for independence places a distinct strain on family relationships and can be minimized only by the recognition that it will occur.

In addition to open communication and the decision to have or not to have children, financial considerations are also extremely important in shaping the family. We in the United States have become accustomed to achieving material gratification immediately. The typical new family desires a car, a house, furniture, vacations, and a host of other material goods. Unfortunately, we have difficulty waiting until we can afford them. Why wait, when we can satisfy our desires through the use of credit cards and securing loans and charge accounts? Because the things we desire are so attractive, we become blind to the horror we can experience when the bills come rolling in, and we are not able to pay them all.

The result of this self-imposed financial insecurity is both marriage partners working at the possible expense of their children, new loans to pay off others that have come due, moonlighting, or possibly, bankruptcy. The strain this imposes on a young family is severe and can lead to the destruction of the family. Young couples should remember that there is always time to save for material goods. Why fall prey to the temptations of business and industry and risk your financial future and your marriage? Why be owned by others when you can control your financial destiny through the prudent use of your income?

When Marriage Fails

Although we hold to the philosophical concept that marriage should be permanent, in practice we are moving toward a belief in marriage for convenience. The degree of social stigma that was once attached to people who were divorced is lessening, particularly as the stigma was applied to divorced women.

A failure in marriage may be manifested in many ways: divorce, desertion, separation, or when a couple lives separate lives but still live together to legally maintain their marriage. Desertion once was generally confined to the poor. It was also primarily characterized by a man deserting his family. This is no longer the case. Although the total number of desertions seems to be decreasing, the number of middle class women deserting their families is on the rise. Separating may be temporary or permanent, often involving legal agreements outlining such things as child support payments and visiting rights. It is not known how many separations end in divorce.

Divorce, however, is the ultimate action a couple takes to disestablish a marriage. The grounds for divorce are many: incompatability, separation, alcohol or drug abuse, adultery, cruelty, desertion, or merely a breakdown of the marriage. Many of these grounds have been incorporated into the divorce laws of many states.

Divorce laws, as with other laws, tend to reflect the prevailing attitudes of society. When society frowned upon divorce, the laws allowing divorce tended to be restrictive. However, as more people began to seek divorce to free themselves from unhappy marriages, the laws were modified. The increasing lenience of divorce laws is reflected in the growing number of states in recent years that have enacted laws providing for no-fault divorce. Under such laws, neither party is found guilty of causing the other to have grounds for divorce (for example, adultery). In such cases, the marriage is judged irreconcilable, and property is divided equally. This has tremendously simplified divorce proceedings for many where both parties in question view divorce as the only alternative.

Underlying marital discontent, which may result in divorce are:

- the tendency to ask too much from marriage, such as, instant and continual bliss;
- changing sex roles, particularly on the part of the woman;
- varying beliefs in what the institution of marriage can provide; and
- basic social change.

We must decide if the increasing frequency of divorce in our society is undesirable. It is thought by many that divorce is more acceptable than an unhappy marriage or staying together for the sake of the children. But have we gone too far? What is needed to save the institution of marriage, if it should be saved? Is it, for instance, more desirable to get a divorce or to remain married and accept conflict as unavoidable? Should we believe that an improvement in life is not possible? Should a couple establish an "arrangement" in which each partner seeks satisfaction extramaritally? Or should we believe that if divorce is sought, it means there is something wrong with us? There is a growing feeling that we should not tolerate unhappy marriages, that marriage should not prevent one from seeking personal happiness.

Many authorities also believe that we should make it more difficult to marry and make it easier to get a divorce. Such people advocate mandatory premarriage counseling programs, a minimum time a couple must wait before marriage, and parenting education.

An issue that has always been an influencing factor in deciding whether or not a couple should seek a divorce is the effect it will have on children. It was long held that a divorce negatively affected children, resulting in such problems as emotional instability, an increase in delinquency, and other emotional or social problems. It appears, however, that such problems stem not so much from the divorce itself, as from the marital conflict which preceded the divorce.

In the event of a divorce, children are not automatically awarded to the mother as they were in the past. The father is increasingly looked upon as one who must share in the rearing of his children. Importantly, when older children are involved, there is an increasing tendency for the courts to consider their wishes before awarding custody.

We will continue to grapple with divorce for the foreseeable future. The issue, however, remains one of the increasing marital success. If we continue to hold to our belief in the value of the family as a basic social unit, it is then society's responsibility to improve the likelihood that when people decide to marry, it is for the right reasons. Sex and love and even children may no longer be sufficient reasons for marriage.

SEXUALITY

Sexuality includes our feelings, the way we look physically, our perceptions of how others see us, and how we behave on a psychosocial level with other people of the same and oppostie sex. Sexuality is being feminine or masculine; it is the way in which we accept our role as male or female as personally perceived and as culturally influenced. *Sexuality is being human!* All of these combined characteristics may be referred to as sexual behavior, although in the narrow sense, only the sex act itself is considered.

Sexuality, as opposed to sex, implies physical, psychological, and social actions and feelings related to our sex. Sexuality is dynamic. One who is born a boy has the *potential* to become a man, to be masculine. One who is born a girl has the *potential* to become a woman, to be feminine. How these potentials are ultimately developed and expressed are determined by: heredity, relationships with others (especially the parents in the early years), cultural influences, intellectual development, and self-perception. In the final analysis, however, members of both sexes are human with all the characteristics of humans.

Sexual behavior, because of its generally perceived narrow definition, is an aspect of American life that is controversial. It touches upon our religious beliefs, sexual preferences (both in the sexual object and the method of sexual expression), existing social mores and society's legal restrictions that are placed on various kinds of sexual expressions. Throughout history, people have been curious about who participates in sexual activities, when, and how often. People continue to wonder, for example, if penis size is important; if sexual activity should be planned or spontaneous; if orgasms should be simultaneous, single, or multiple. So basic is the drive for sexual activity that the very survival of the species depends upon it; and yet, it is so misunderstood that it has taken on a mystical quality that perpetuates its controversial nature.

Our perceptions of the basic elements of sex and sexuality vary greatly. It is quite likely that if a group of people were asked to define sex or sexuality, a variety of answers would be elicited, among them being genitals, sexual behavior, gender, and sexual intercourse (the interaction of two or more people for sexual gratification). However, for our purposes, our sexuality is "concerned with the totality of human beings functioning in a variety of social settings."[9] Sexual behavior that allows us to enhance our effectiveness without violating the rights of others should be considered healthy sexual behavior. Our sexual behavior is based in large part upon primary sexual development, people's view of population, choice of sexual partners, and sexual responsiveness. These are the aspects of human sexuality that need to be emphasized, rather than merely sexual intercourse.

BIOCHEMISTRY OF SEX

Sexual development results from the interplay of many influencing factors. The physical and social environments are important determiners of sexual expression.

Our sex is determined at the time of conception. The gonads and pituitary gland are the chief structures that control our sexual biochemistry, that, in turn, affects sexual development. For instance, the biochemistry of sex controls the kind of secondary sex characteristics that will appear at puberty and even the time of their appearance.

The Pituitary Gland

The chemical control of sexual development is initiated by the pituitary gland. Located at the base of the brain, the pituitary gland is part of the endocrine system. Like all other glands of the endocrine system, it is ductless, secreting its hormones directly into the bloodstream. The pituitary gland is composed of two lobes: the anterior pituitary and the posterior pituitary lobes. The anterior pituitary lobe is often referred to as the "master gland" because it plays a coordinative role for the entire endocrine system.

The anterior lobe of the pituitary gland secretes three major hormones directly associated with sexual development and functioning. These hormones are: follicle-stimulating hormone (FSH); luteinizing hormone (LH) in the female, interstitial cell-stimulating hormone (ICSH) in the male; and prolactin in the female. (See Figure 6–1.)

Figure 6-1:

The Influence of the Pituitary Gland on Sexual Development

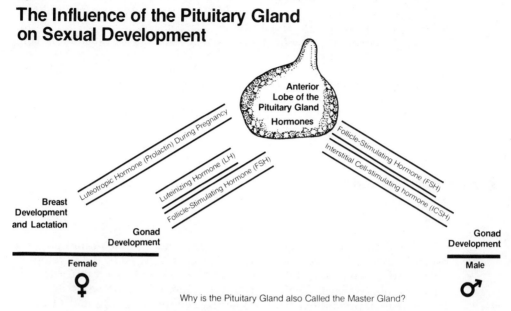

Why is the Pituitary Gland also Called the Master Gland?

In women, the *follicle-stimulating hormone* (FSH) stimulates the primary graafian follicles to develop to the point of ovulation. *Graafian follicles* are small sacs in the ovaries in which the egg (ovum) matures and from which it is discharged at the time of ovulation. FSH also stimulates follicle cells to secrete estrogen, another important sex hormone. In the male, FSH stimulates the development of the seminiferous tubules and maintains the process of spermatogenesis. The *seminiferous tubules* are a network of the tube-like structures in the testicles in which sperm development takes place. *Spermatogenesis* is the manufacture of sperm in the male, while *oogenesis* is the maturation of ova in the female.

The *luteinizing hormone* (LH) in women causes ovulation and is associated with the secretion of progesterone and estrogens. In the male, *interstitial cell-stimulating hormone* (ICSH) is associated with development of the testicles and the secretion of the hormone testosterone.

Prolactin or lactogenic hormone is secreted by the pituitary gland of women during pregnancy. It stimulates the breasts to develop and to produce milk.

Gonads

The gonads are the sex glands: the testicles in the male and the ovaries in the female. The gonads in both sexes affect the body biochemically through the secretion of sex hormones.

For example, the hormone ICSH causes the development of mature sperm as well as the production of testosterone. Testosterone circulates through

149

the body triggering the development of the secondary sex characteristics. These changes, such as the development of pubic hair, begin to appear at puberty and are signs that physical sexual maturity is taking place.

The hormonal influences upon female sexuality are much more complex than the corresponding influence in the male from the standpoint of their cyclical nature. Once FSH stimulates the ovaries, estrogen is secreted which not only influences the development of the external secondary sex characteristics—such as the development of the breasts—but several internal changes as well. Progesterone is also secreted on a cyclical basis to prepare the uterus for the implantation of a fertilized egg.

SEXUAL DEVELOPMENT

Puberty

Puberty, or pubescence, is the stage of life in which rapid physical and psychological changes take place. These are characterized by the development of reproductive potential and the development of secondary sex characteristics. In females, puberty usually begins between the ages of 9 and 12 years. *Menarche* (the first menstrual period) typically occurs between the ages of 11 and 14 years.[10] In contrast, male pubescence is initiated at about 12 years of age and continues to the age of 18 years. Thus, the male pubescent period begins later and lasts longer than that of the female.

The structural changes that occur in the female during puberty include development of the uterus and vagina. The wall of the uterus thickens as does the lining of the vagina. In addition, estrogen stimulates the enlargement of the pelvis, the development of the breasts and fatty pads in the hips and buttocks, and the growth of the labia and clitoris. Estrogen, in combination with hormones secreted by the adrenal glands, is also responsible for the growth of pubic and axillary hair.

In the male, testosterone is primarily responsible for the physical changes during puberty.[11] These changes include enlargement of the penis and testicles; the development of skeletal muscles; a broadening of the shoulders; growth of pubic, axillary, and facial hair; a deepened voice; and a receding of the hairline of the head. In addition, the development of the testicles and the hormonal influence upon the prostate gland makes it possible for the emission of seminal fluid during orgasm. Often, pubescent boys experience nocturnal emissions, or wet dreams, as a result of the rapid development of the sex organs; they may also experience spontaneous erections, not necessarily associated with sexual stimulation.

There is considerable debate about the role of heredity, environment, and hormonal influence on our sex drive. Moreover, there are a number of criteria by which to measure the sex drive so that coming to consistent and widely accepted conclusions is difficult. Some believe that our sexual motivation is learned, while others believe that it is primarily due to our hereditary potentials and the resultant influence of hormonal activity. Whatever the primary influence is on our sex drive, it is generally accepted that our capability for sexual arousal is influenced by our genotype, hormonal levels (primarily androgen), activity of our central nervous system, sensory perception, prior experiences, age, environmental factors, cultural influences, and stress.[12]

The male sex hormone, androgen, is most closely linked to the sex drive in both sexes. Research has shown that men who have been castrated (gonads removed) show a decided reduction in sex drive. In the male, the gonads are the primary source of androgens. In the female, however, removal of the ovaries (the primary source of estrogen) results in little alteration of the sex drive. Removal of the adrenal glands, the source of most of the androgen in females, results in a considerable loss of sexual motivation.[13]

Reproductive Potential

Of all the pubescent functions, certainly the most significant is the development of the ability to reproduce. This involves the maturation of sperm in males and ova in females. Upon maturation of the testicles during puberty, spermatogenesis commences and continues throughout a male's reproductive life. During this time, literally billions of sperm are produced. Unlike the cyclical nature of oogenesis in the female, sperm production is continuous and proceeds uninterrupted unless the male is exposed to excessive environmental hazards, such as radiation, or contracts a disease that may inhibit the maturation of the sperm.

The *testicles* are housed in a sax-like structure called the *scrotum,* which allows for optimal sperm production at a temperature slightly lower than that of the body. High temperatures tend to destroy the sperm. An undescended testicle, for example, may become sterile if allowed to remain in the abdominal cavity. Supporting muscles control the distance the testicles are held from the body, maintaining a relatively constant temperature. For instance, in cold weather, the testicles are drawn close to the body; in warm temperatures, they are lowered away from the body.

After spermatogenesis, the sperm move out of the seminiferous tubes by peristaltic action into the *epididymis.* Here, the sperm are nurtured and mature. Ciliary actions move the sperm into the *vas deferens,* a tube that passes from the epididymis into the abdominal cavity. The sperm mix with fluids secreted from the seminal vesicles and the prostate gland, which together make up the bulk of the seminal fluid.

The development of ova in the female begins during the last half of fetal life with the development of approximately 2 million primary oocytes in the ovaries. The *primary oocytes* are cells that have the potential of developing into mature ova during a woman's reproductive life. However, through a process known as *atresia,* these cells are reduced in number to about 20,000–60,000 at puberty and to a few hundred at menopause.[14] *Menopause* is basically the period in life when the menstrual cycle ceases. This number of ova, however, is quite substantial considering that a woman's reproductive life is 30 to 40 years in length and that she releases, generally, one mature ovum per month. Thus, she will only release 300 to 500 mature ova during her life time.

PREGNANCY

Menstrual Cycle

Maturation of the ova begins at puberty with the onset of the cyclical process called the *menstrual cycle.* Typically, this cycle is about 28 days in length, although a wide variance is possible among women. It is not uncommon for the cycle of a woman to vary considerably from month to month. FSH stimulates estrogen production which, in turn, prepares the ovum for ovulation. *Ovulation* is the expulsion of the mature ovum from the ovary into the *fimbria* of the *fallopian tube.* Progesterone helps to carry the woman through pregnancy, should the ovum become fertilized. If fertilization does not occur, the lining of the uterus, which has thickened in preparation for pregnancy, is discharged (menstrual flow), and the cycle begins again. Phases of the menstrual cycle are illustrated in Figure 6–2.

Conception

Pregnancy begins with the fertilization of an ovum by a sperm cell. This process involves the joining of the nucleus of the sperm cell with that of the egg cell. Once fertilization, or conception occurs, the entire process of prenatal development begins.

It is sometimes said that it takes only one sperm cell to cause pregnancy. This is true when viewing only the fertilization process itself. However, it is estimated that a male's ejaculation must contain at least 25 million sperm in order for him to be considered fertile. The average ejaculation contains between 150–600 million sperm. Because of environmental hazards and the relatively long journey that the sperm must make to reach the ovum, it is estimated that only about 2000 of the original several hundred million sperm reach the vicinity of the egg. Many die along the way; many go to the Fallopian tube that does not contain the egg; and many remain in the vagina and uterus and eventually die.

Figure 6-2:

The Menstrual Cycle

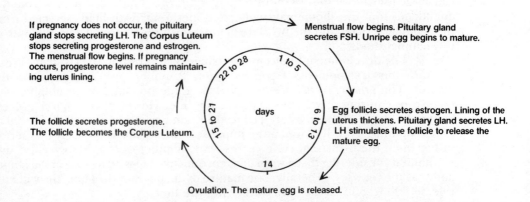

If pregnancy does not occur, the pituitary gland stops secreting LH. The Corpus Luteum stops secreting progesterone and estrogen. The menstrual flow begins. If pregnancy occurs, progesterone level remains maintaining uterus lining.

Menstrual flow begins. Pituitary gland secretes FSH. Unripe egg begins to mature.

22 to 28

1 to 5

15 to 21

days

6 to 13

The follicle secretes progesterone. The follicle becomes the Corpus Luteum.

Egg follicle secretes estrogen. Lining of the uterus thickens. Pituitary gland secretes LH. LH stimulates the follicle to release the mature egg.

14

Ovulation. The mature egg is released.

Upon ovulation, the ovum moves into the fallopian tube where, if intercourse is timed correctly, fertilization takes place. The fertilized egg, or *zygote,* moves down the fallopian tube into the uterus where it becomes implanted in the uterine wall. This process takes from five to seven days. The embryo, later the fetus, develops within the uterus throughout the duration of the pregnancy, which is approximately 280 days. The developing child is referred to as an embryo through the first eight weeks of gestation and a fetus for the remaining prenatal period.

Signs of Pregnancy

There are a variety of behavioral and physical changes that take place during the early part of pregnancy that may indicate a woman is pregnant. These changes have been classified as presumptive signs, probably signs, and positive signs.[15] The *presumptive* signs are:

- lack of menstrual flow (amenorrhea);
- breast changes—increased fullness; tenderness around the nipples; deeply pigmented areolae;
- morning sickness;
- increase in urinary frequency;
- unusual food cravings.

All of these characteristics are considered to be presumptive signs because, although they are associated with early pregnancy, they also may occur as a result of a variety of other conditions not associated with pregnancy.

The *probable signs* are more likely to be reliable indicators of pregnancy. These signs are usually documented by a physician as follows:

- softening of the uterus, first at the site of implantation and then between the cervix and uterine body;
- changes in uterine shape;
- uterine contractions;
- fetal movement.

Positive signs of pregnancy include those indicators, detected by a physician, that leave no doubt that a woman is pregnant. These include:

- feeling fetal movement through the abdominal wall;
- detecting the fetal skeleton through the use of x-ray;
- or ultrasonic techniques *Note: the use of radiation in the early stages of pregnancy can result in congenital defects; a pregnant woman should not allow x-ray to be used indiscriminately.*
- identification of fetal heart beat;
- detection of chorionic gonadotropin hormone (HCG) in the urine.

A relatively recent development is the availability of over-the-counter pregnancy tests that can be used in the home. Costing about the same as a test performed by a physician, they are significantly less reliable and should not be considered as a substitute for a test performed by a physician. Table 6–1 compares the stages of pregnancy with the corresponding development of the embryo and fetus

Embryonic and Fetal Development

Embryonic development is characterized by a rapid development of the head (brain, eyes, and ears) and by the development of a rudimentary heart and liver. All of these structures are developed by the end of the fourth week of pregnancy. From the fourth to the eighth week, the eyes, ears, nose, and mouth become clearly distinguishable. The fingers and toes develop between the sixth and eighth weeks, as well as the intestines and the gonads; bone ossification begins to occur.

Development of the fetus from the eighth to twelfth weeks is characterized by the development of the skin and the differentiation of male and female internal genitalia. Throughout the *first 12 weeks or trimester,* the embryo/fetus is most susceptible to adverse environmental conditions, such as drugs (including alcohol) or the presence of microorganisms, such as rubella (german measles).

By the beginning of the *second trimester* of gestation, the fetus is clearly recognizable as human. The head is fully developed as are the limbs. In the fifth or sixth month, hair begins to develop on the head. Throughout this period, there is a rapid maturation of the systems of the body and a significant increase in the overall size of the fetus. By the end of the sixth month, the average fetus is 14 inches long and weighs approximately 2 pounds.

During the *third trimester,* the fetus assumes a head-down position in preparation for birth. The fetus gains more than 2 pounds during the ninth month of gestation. Hair and fingernails mature and grow, and the fetus is able to breathe on its own upon birth. At the end of the third trimester the average fetus weighs 7.5 pounds and is 20 inches long. The fetus is typically delivered from a head-down position. If the fetus is delivered in any other position, such

Table 6–1: Stages of Pregnancy

Gestation	Stage of Development	Physical Characteristics
First trimester (0 to 12 weeks)	Embryo (0 to 8 weeks)	Development of head, heart, liver, fingers, toes; bone ossification; development of gonads.
	Fetus (8 weeks to birth)	Development of skin; differentiation of male and female internal genitalia.
Second trimester (12 to 24 weeks)		Development of hair; maturation of organ systems; rapid growth.
Third trimester (24 to 36 weeks)		Maturation and growth; positioning for birth.

as, feet-first or buttocks-first, it is called a *breech birth.* The physician usually can determine the position of the fetus prior to the onset of labor and may be able to manipulate the fetus if there is a potential for a breech birth. If this is not possible, a caesarian section may be necessary. A *caesarian section* is accomplished by surgically removing the fetus through a transverse incision in the lower abdominal wall and uterus.

Childbirth

The normal birth process is divided into three stages of labor: dilation, expulsion, and placental.[16] *Dilation* of the cervix occurs as a result of contractions of the uterine walls. These contractions usually begin at intervals of 25–30 minutes and each lasts approximately 30 seconds. The dilation of the cervix results in the mucus plug being expelled and, often, the rupturing of the amnionic sac (bag of waters). The cervix is considered fully dilated when the opening measures 10–11 centimeters.

The *expulsion phase* of labor begins when the contractions are 1–2 minutes apart and when the head of the fetus (or other parts of the body) gains access to the opening of the cervix. At this time, each contraction typically lasts 45–95 seconds. It is during this stage of labor that the birth occurs. As the head of the baby reaches the opening of the vagina (or birth canal), an incision is usually made at the entrance to the vagina extending toward the anal opening to prevent undue stretching and tearing of the tissues. This procedure is called an *episiotomy.*

The *placental stage* of labor is the final stage and occurs after the delivery of the baby and results in the expulsion of the placenta from the uterus. This is the shortest stage of labor, usually lasting 1–15 minutes.

ADOLESCENT PREGNANCY

Introduction

We are using the term adolescent to mean the developmental age at which pregnancy can occur through age 20. This is necessary because chronological ages can be deceiving. For example, there are instances of girls becoming pregnant long before they reach their teen years; some records show pregnancy occurring in girls as young as nine and ten years of age. The other end of the scale is also somewhat misleading, but not nearly as much because almost all girls (unless there is some abnormality in growth) have reached reproductive age by the time they are in their middle to late teens. Adolescent pregnancy, therefore, is the period of life that a girl becomes pregnant before becoming an adult—a time when she is still growing and developing.

Incidence

Adolescent pregnancies have reached epidemic proportions in the United States in the past two decades and the incidence continues to rise. During the 1970s, the adolescent birth rate for girls 15–19 years of age was 58 per 1000 girls. It has been estimated that each year about 10 percent of teenagers get pregnant and 6 percent give birth.[17] Of the approximately 21 million boys and girls between the ages of 15 and 19 years in the United States, it is estimated that about one-half have experienced sexual intercourse. In addition, it is estimated that approximately 1.3 million boys and nearly 0.5 million girls under age 15 years are sexually active.

Consequences

Babies born to adolescent mothers are much more likely to die during the first year of life than babies born to mothers in their early to mid-twenties. We also find that babies of adolescent mothers are of low birth weight and that there is a much higher maternal death rate. When a girl becomes pregnant during her adolescent years, she and her unborn baby compete for nutrients that they both need for their own growth. This results in the adolescent becoming more susceptible to illnesses.

There are, in addition, the economic, familial, and educational consequences of early pregnancy. For example, adolescent mothers are much more likely to drop out of school, they lack employment skills, and are at a disadvantage for developing them; and young marriages, if they take place, are less likely to remain stable. Marriages that take place before the girl reaches 18 years of age are three times more likely to end in divorce, annulment or other forms of breakup. Since most pregnancies of adolescents are unintended and occur out of wedlock, the adolescent girl is likely to attempt to conceal the fact that she is pregnant. As a result, at least 70 percent of these girls do not receive any prenatal care during the first trimester of pregnancy—a period most crucial for the health of the child and the mother. Finally, about one-third of all legal abortions in the United States are obtained by pregnant adolescents.

CONTRACEPTION AND BIRTH CONTROL

Throughout history, people have attempted to control the incidence of pregnancy. These attempts have included the insertion of objects into the vagina and uterus, the covering of the penis, the use of mystical ceremonies, the interruption of coitus, surgical procedures, and the interruption of pregnancy itself. Only recently have methods been employed with a high degree of reliability resulting, in Western cultures, in a significant reduction in the birth rate.

People's views of birth control techniques (or family planning) take on political, social, legal, and moral ramifications in terms of their potential to influence the course of humanity. These issues must be resolved on a personal as well as institutional level if effective population control procedures are to be universally accepted. Questions that must be answered include:

- Should birth control techniques be used to control the birth rate among those who have genetic defects?
- Should birth control techniques be used to control the birth rate among those who have committed sexually related crimes?

- Should each family be limited in the number of children it can produce?
- Who should decide upon the most appropriate method of birth control to be used for each individual?
- What should be the influence of religion in restricting or condoning various types of birth control procedures?

Not all of these questions, of course, apply to every culture or country. Many have not yet become issues. But each of us must be prepared to deal with such issues should they manifest themselves some time in the future.

For the purposes of this discussion the available contraception and birth control methods are divided into the following categories: mechanical, chemical, hormonal, surgical, and natural. The effectiveness of each method is determined by calculating the number of pregnancies that occur per 100 woman-years. In other words, if 100 women and their partners used a particular method exclusively for one year, the resulting number of pregnancies would reflect the effectiveness of the method.*

Mechanical Methods

Mechanical methods of contraception and birth control include the use of devices that prevent the sperm from reaching the egg or prevent the implantation of a fertilized egg in the uterine wall. These methods include the use of an intrauterine device, a diaphragm, or a condom. These may be used singly or in combination.

The *intrauterine device* (IUD) is usually made of plastic and comes in a variety of shapes. Considered to be nearly as effective as the "pill," it is inserted directly into the uterus by a physician. IUDs may be divided into two categories, inert and active. *Inert IUDs* are simply plastic devices that inhibit implantation of the fertilized egg as a result of their presence in the uterus. *Active IUDs* are wound with a copper wire that releases ions that add an implantation inhibiting factor. It is not totally clear how IUDs work. However, only 3–4 pregnancies occur per 100 woman-years if the IUD is used correctly.

Upon insertion of an IUD, it is quite common for a woman to experience cramps and irregular bleeding. In addition, expulsion may occur in the body's normal attempt to rid itself of any foreign material. For this reason it is advisable for a woman to check the position of the IUD often. If any part of the IUD can be felt extending into the vagina, it will not be effective, and a physician must be consulted as soon as possible to make the necessary adjustments.

The most serious side effect of the IUD is the potential for perforation of the uterine wall. This may result in hemorrhaging and possible death. Several such deaths have been recorded. This danger, combined with cramps, spotting (the discharge of blood at times other than the menstrual period) and possible expulsion have contributed to a marked decline in the use of what was once considered to be the answer to the problem of birth control.

*The effectiveness of various contraceptive measures can also be judged by comparing the pregnancy rate with that if no measures were employed. Between 70 and 100 pregnancies normally result per 100 couples using no means of contraception over a period of one year.

The *diaphragm* fits over the entrance of the cervix and serves as a barrier to sperm. It is most effectively used in conjunction with a spermacidal cream or jelly that is placed on the rim of the diaphragm and on the inside of its cup before insertion. The diaphragm must be put in place not longer than 2 hours prior to intercourse and should be left in for at least 6 hours after intercourse. If a couple using this method has intercourse a second time within this 6-hour period, a second application of the spermacidal cream or jelly should be applied *without removing the diaphragm.*

A diaphragm must be fitted by a physician, since a variety of sizes are available. In addition, it is recommended that if the woman has more than a 10-pound change of weight, the fit of the diaphragm should be rechecked. The side effects of the use of a diaphragm include possible irritation of the vagina or penis by the cream or jelly used. In addition, many couples complain that the spontaneity of their love-making is reduced because of the necessity of inserting the diaphragm prior to intercourse. The pregnancy rate from the use of the diaphragm is 10 to 12 per 100 woman-years.

A relatively recent entry into the contraceptive market is the *cervical cap,* essentially a diaphragm that is fitted over the cervix. This type of diaphragm is much more convenient because it can remain in place for several days, thus not interrupting sexual spontaneity. A variation of the cervical cap is currently being tested that can remain in place for several months. A valve in the cap allows passage of the menstrual flow, while not allowing entrance of seminal fluid into the uterus. It is thought by some that cervical caps have not been widely advertised because of the low profit margin to its producers.

The *condom,* also called a rubber or prophylactic, is one of the few contraceptive methods available for which the male is responsible. Made from a variety of materials and available in a variety of colors, the condom fits over the penis and prevents sperm from entering the vagina. Some varieties of condoms are lubricated to facilitate penetration; some are ribbed or studded to increase stimulation.

The major objection to the use of the condom is a possible loss of sensation. In addition, a reduction in spontaneity may occur since the condom must be put on after erection has occurred. After ejaculation, the condom should be held on the penis when it is withdrawn from the vagina to prevent the possibility of spilling the semen. The pregnancy rate when couples use the condom as the primary means of contraception is 15 per 100 woman-years.

Chemical Methods

The use of chemicals as a contraceptive measure is subdivided into three varieties: foams, creams, and jellies; douches; and vaginal suppositories. *Foams, creams, and jellies* are spermicidal in nature, containing chemicals that kill sperm on contact. Use of these substances in combination with other methods can be highly effective; but used alone they are less effective than most other methods available. They may cause irritation to the vagina and/or penis and are associated with a pregnancy rate of 20–22 per 100 woman-years.

Douching is based upon the principle that sperm can effectively be rinsed from the vagina immediately after intercourse. However, it often serves to force the sperm into the cervix, thereby *increasing* the likelihood of pregnancy. Moreover, by the time douching is done, sperm may already have entered the uterus. If used alone, douching results in a pregnancy rate of 36–40 per 100 woman-years.

Most recently, the *vaginal suppository* has been introduced into the contraceptive market. The suppository is inserted into the vagina prior to intercourse, where it effervesces and serves as a spermicidal agent. It may also serve as a barrier to the sperm. The promoters of vaginal suppositories claim that they are nearly as effective as the pill. However, the Food and Drug Administration has directed that no such claims shall be made; they are no more effective than the other spermicidal agents.

Hormonal Methods

Hormonal methods of contraception refer to oral contraceptives, commonly known as the "pill." The four basic varieties available are the combination pill, sequential pill, minipill, and postcoital or morning after pill.

The *combination pill* contains both synthetic estrogens and progestogens that are similar to progesterone. Taken for 20 or 21 days, beginning with the fifth day of the menstrual cycle, the combination pill inhibits ovulation and may have a secondary effect of making the endometrial lining of the uterus inhospitable for the implantation of a fertilized egg. In addition, the cervical mucus may be altered, becoming a hostile environment for the sperm.

The *sequential pill* was developed in an attempt to mimic the normal menstrual physiology of the woman. The first 15 pills taken in any given cycle contain synthetic estrogen; the remaining five or six contain both estrogen and progestogen. The estrogen inhibits ovulation, while the progestogen prepares the uterus for a menstrual flow.

In 1973, the *minipill* was introduced to the American public as still another alternative in oral contraceptives. Minipills contain only synthetic progestogen at about one-third the dose level found in combination pills. Because estrogen is not present, most of the adverse side effects characteristic of the combination and sequential pills have been eliminated. The primary effect of the minipill is to inhibit implantation rather than to inhibit ovulation. It is not quite as effective as the combination or sequential pills in preventing pregnancies and has been associated with a higher incidence of breakthrough bleeding and irregular menstrual cycles. Taken together, the pregnancy rate associated with the use of combination, sequential, and minipills is 1–3 per 100 woman-years.

The pill has been associated with such adverse side effects as thrombophlebitis, pulmonary embolism, cerebral thrombosis, and an increase in blood pressure. Most physicians advise that women with a history of blood clots, hypertension, varicose veins, or migraine headaches should refrain from using the pill. It has recently been shown that women who smoke and use oral contraceptives have a significantly higher rate of cardiovascular disease than women who do not smoke.

The use of the *postcoital,* or *"morning after"* pill is surrounded by controversy. Its active ingredient, diethylstilbestrol (DES) has been used for many years to treat a variety of ailments, among them being menopausal symptoms in women and cancer of the prostate gland in men. In addition, women who are prone to miscarry have been treated with DES to maintain their pregnancies. Recently, studies have indicated that the female offspring of these women have a greater likelihood of developing cervical and vaginal cancer. A paradox exists in that DES can be used to maintain pregnancies or to inhibit implantation of the fertilized ovum. (See Figure 6–3.) It was recommended by the Food and Drug Administration in 1973 that DES be used in postcoital pills only in emergency situations, that is, in cases of rape, incest, or other similar severe emergencies. The postcoital pill also results in severe nausea and vomiting. It is for these reasons that the postcoital pill should never be used routinely as a contraceptive technique.

Surgical Methods

Surgical methods of contraception result in sterilization of either the male or female. The procedures used are intended to prevent or block the passage of the egg through the fallopian tube in the female or the passage of the sperm through the vas deferens in the male.

Figure 6-3:

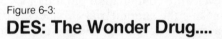

DES: The Wonder Drug....

A *vasectomy* in the male is a relatively simple procedure, usually taking from 10–20 minutes and not requiring hospitalization. A local anesthetic is administered to the scrotum where the vas deferens is located, and an incision is made. A small section of each sperm duct (vas deferens) is then removed and the ends are sealed by clipping, tying, or cauterizing with an electrode. Few complications have been reported from this surgical procedure, with a relatively small incidence of such after effects as minor scrotal bleeding and some discomfort. Other methods of contraception should be continued for a period of time since there may be some sperm still present beyond the point of the vasectomy that could impregnate one's partner.

Although sperm production continues after a vasectomy is performed, the sperm are absorbed into the body through the action of phagocytes in the blood. Even though the surgery itself can often be reversed, a vasectomy should be considered permanent since only a small percentage of men are able to impregnate a woman after the reversal procedure has been performed.

When compared with a vasectomy, a *tubal ligation* in women is much more complex. Whatever technique is used, the ultimate purpose is to tie off the fallopian tubes so that sperm and egg cannot meet. Tubal ligation is also called a partial salpingectomy.

The traditional method of performing a tubal ligation involves making an incision through the abdominal or vaginal wall. The middle third of the fallopian tube is tied off, and a section removed. If the incision is made through the abdominal wall, a general anesthetic is typically used, whereas, if the incision is made through the vaginal wall, a local anesthetic is administered. These methods require at least a two-day hospital stay.

More recently, however, procedures have been developed allowing a tubal ligation to be performed on an outpatient basis. One method called a *culdoscopy sterilization* technique is an unproven method of the cauterization of the fallopian tubes where they join the uterus. Scar tissue develops, closing the entry into the tubes, rendering the woman sterile. This procedure takes only about 15 minutes to perform and approximately 2–4 hours for recovery of the patient.

One of the most popular methods of female sterilization is called *laparoscopy sterilization*. It takes about 20 minutes and requires only 24 hours in the hospital for recovery. Also referred to as the "bandaid operation," this procedure involves making two incisions through the abdominal wall, one just below the umbilicus and a second about 8 centimeters below the umbilicus. The abdomen is distended with an inert gas through the first incision, giving the surgeon a clear view of the fallopian tubes. They are then tied off through the second incision. The incisions are closed using surgical clips and covered with a bandage.

The surgical methods for sterilization of the female as with the male should be considered irreversible. Their effectiveness in preventing conception is evidenced by the low pregnancy rate of 0.003 per 100 woman-years.

Natural Methods

"Natural" methods of contraception include abstinence from sexual intercourse, the rhythm method (which is associated with ovulation), and withdrawal of the penis prior to ejaculation.

Total abstinence from sexual intercourse is 100 percent effective in preventing pregnancy since there is practically no possibility for the sperm and egg to come together. From a heterosexual viewpoint, however, it is not practical since it eliminates a primary expression of affection between the man and woman. Therefore, unless abstinence is adopted for religious or medical reasons, it should not be considered a viable alternative for most couples. It may be used as a temporary measure, however, until other contraceptive methods can be employed.

The *rhythm method* involves careful observation of a woman's menstrual cycle with abstinence practiced when ovulation is most likely to occur. The cycles of many women, however, are not regular and ovulation is difficult to predict. Moreover, ovulation may occur at any time during a cycle and is influenced by emotional stress, illness, and changes in environmental conditions. The male sperm is capable of remaining alive and active within the vagina or uterus for several days, and even though ovulation has not taken place at the time of intercourse, it may take place within a few days and fertilization can occur from the sperm remaining from the previous intercourse. To increase the reliability of the rhythm method, many women use a variety of indicators to determine when ovulation has occurred or is about to occur. The following are some of the more popular indicators:

- *Mittleschmerz*—this refers to an abdominal pain experienced by some women at the time of ovulation.
- *Changes in body temperature*—there is usally a slight drop in body temperature of about 0.2 degree immediately prior to ovulation and an increase in body temperature of about 0.6 degree immediately following ovulation.
- *Changes in the consistency of cervical mucus at the time of ovulation*—because of the changes in the estrogen levels at the time of ovulation, the cervical mucus becomes stringy. This can be detected by use of the spinnbarkheit test which is essentially accomplished by blowing a sample of cervical mucus on a slide and stretching it out with a cover glass. The time at which it can be drawn out to its maximum length usually coincides with the time of ovulation.
- *Spotting at the time of ovulation*—sometimes intermenstrual bleeding will occur which is an indication that ovulation has occurred.

No indicator used in conjunction with the rhythm method is totally reliable. Many advocates of this method urge that as many indicators as possible be observed. The pregnancy rate for the rhythm method is 14–16 per 100 woman-years.

Withdrawal is the practice of removing the penis from the vagina just prior to ejaculation. It is called *coitus interruptus*. The major drawback of this method is that sperm are often contained in the preejaculatory fluid in sufficient quantities to impregnate a woman. In addition, the physical and emotional involvement of the coital experience often results in withdrawal not being accomplished in time. The result is a pregnancy rate of about 16 per 100 woman-years when this method is used. Another, closely related method is *coitus reservatus,* which is simply an attempt to suppress ejaculation.

Any of the contraceptive and birth control techniques are more effective than using none at all. The important issue is that the least effective method mentioned may be the only acceptable one for some women and men because of religious, medical, psychological, or other reasons. However, the use of contraception has far-reaching ramifications related to population growth whether or not a couple wants to have a child or is capable of rearing children. The use of contraceptives has, in some instances, created political and other social debates. For example, the dissemination of contraceptive information to the people of developing nations, where the greatest increases in population growth are taking place, and where their technological development is not adequate to take care of the basic physical needs of the people, has created sociopolitical controversies.

ABORTION

Introduction

Abortion is the termination of any pregnancy which results in the death of a fetus prior to the 20th week of gestation.[18] An abortion may be spontaneous or induced. An *induced abortion* may be for therapeutic reasons. It is important to recognize that abortion is a method for terminating a pregnancy. It should *not* be considered a contraceptive method since contraception means preventing conception from taking place.

A *spontaneous abortion* (miscarriage) occurs without deliberate efforts. It has been estimated that as many as 27 percent of all pregnancies are aborted spontaneously.[19] As pregnancy progresses, however, the likelihood of a spontaneous abortion decreases. It is hypothesized that reasons for spontaneous abortions include:

- A lack of one of the sex chromosomes
- Other genetic defects present in the embryo
- Abnormal placental development
- Poor implantation
- Congenital defects present.[20]

Spontaneous abortions are more frequent as women increase in age and generally occur about two weeks after the embryo has died.

Therapeutic Abortions

Abortion as a birth control technique is probably more common than any other method employed on a world-wide basis. For example, according to Goldstein[21] the annual number of abortions in the Soviet Union is approximately 2 ½ times the number of babies born. In the United States there are approximately 271 abortions per 1000 live births each year.

Therapeutic abortion includes techniques designed to terminate a pregnancy because of a diagnosed genetic or congenital defect in the developing fetus, to avoid medical complications to the mother, or to prevent the birth of an unwanted child through legally accepted procedures. This latter reason is an indication of the failure of society to adequately educate its people about the more appropriate methods of birth control.

The method of abortion that is chosen is largely dependent upon the age of the fetus, the health of the mother, and the preference of the attending physician. Therapeutic abortion techniques include menstrual extraction, vacuum aspiration, dilation and curettage, saline induction, and hysterotomy.

A relatively new method for therapeutic abortions is *menstrual extraction,* performed within two weeks after the first missed menstrual period. It is often done before a reliable pregnancy test can be performed. It makes use of a suction technique by inserting a fine flexible plastic tube into the uterus. Dilation of the cervix is not necessary. This technique requires little medication and can be performed on an outpatient basis. One of its chief advantages over other techniques is that the woman may never know whether or not she was pregnant, which eliminates the stigma associated with the controversy of destroying a life. Long-term effects from frequent menstrual extractions are unknown.

A *vacuum aspiration* (suction curettage) involves the use of a suction pump in which the embryo and the other products of pregnancy are sucked out of the uterus. Blood loss is kept to a minimum. Physicians recommend that this procedure be used only through the eleventh week of gestation. As with the menstrual extraction, it is usually done on an outpatient basis.

A more traditional method for performing an early abortion is through the use of *dilation and curettage* (D&C). The cervix is dilated using graduated instruments, and the contents of the uterus are scraped away with a curette. As with the suction curettage, it is recommended that this method be performed prior to the twelfth week of gestation.

Two methods are used when performing an abortion between the thirteenth and nineteenth weeks of gestation. *Saline induction* involves the removal of about 200 cc of amniotic fluid and replacing it with a saline solution. Within 24 hours, labor is induced and the fetus is expelled. A *hysterotomy* resembles a ceasarian section. An incision is made through the abdominal wall and the fetus and other products of pregnancy are removed.

Illegal Methods

Prior to the 1973 Supreme Court ruling that many of the traditional restrictions on abortion were unconstitutional, all of the methods described above were considered to be illegal in most states, except in such cases as pregnancy resulting from rape or incest, or to save the life of the mother. Now, illegal methods are: those abortions performed after the twentieth week of gestation, those *not* performed by a licensed physician, or those induced by the mother. Such illegal methods are dangerous. They frequently result in death of the mother, or are often unsuccessful in accomplishing the desired abortion.

The ingestion of drugs or other compounds will *not* bring about an abortion without also endangering the life of the mother. Some of the substances that have been *unsuccessfully* used for this purpose include quinine sulfate, ergot compounds, and castor oil.

Other attempts at bringing about an abortion have included inserting various things into the uterus including solid objects, liquids, and air. The insertion of such objects as knitting needles, pens, curtain rods, wire, and coat hangers have been used usually with disastrous results. For example, these objects can perforate the uterine wall resulting in hemorrhage or infection. Liquids that have been tried include soapy water, lye, and alcohol. These can result in damage to the delicate lining of the uterus. Lye, for example, is extremely caustic and can cause extensive burning to the tissues lining the uterus. Frequently, infection results causing hemorrhage and finally death. Air is sometimes pumped into the uterus to cause a dilation and abortion. The danger here lies in the possibility of the formation of an air embolus that can result in sudden death of the mother.

The desperation to prevent the birth of a baby has led some mothers to attempt to abort by falling down stairs or by lifting heavy objects. Such methods are most likely to injure the mother, but probably will not cause an abortion. In any event, the use of illegal abortions cause a significantly higher death rate among women than do therapeutic abortions performed under surgical conditions.

HUMAN SEXUAL RESPONSE

Introduction

Much of our sexual behavior is centered around our ability to respond to a variety of sexual stimuli. Contrary to some myths that have prevailed for centuries, it has become clear that the sexual response of men and women is more similar than dissimilar, and women's sexual capacity is at least equal to that of men.

Sexual responsiveness is determined and controlled by our genetic potentials and learned experiences. The learned experiences are associated with our entire psychosocial capacity, which involves our total emotional make-up. This emotional factor helps to explain the variations in people and their abilities to respond sexually on a variety of levels. These levels may be thought of in terms of which stimuli bring about the need or desire to seek sexual satisfaction and the methods to be used in achieving it.

Early exploratory experiences with sex provide us with some indications of what will bring us both pleasure and satisfaction in sexual activities. Obviously, this is related to the so-called normal responses as well as the abnormal ones.

The sexual act can have four purposes, either singularly or in combination: (1) to reproduce; (2) to demonstrate affection for another person; (3) to provide sexual pleasure and satisfaction for one's partner; and (4) to provide sexual pleasure and satisfaction for oneself. Sexual intercourse is much more meaningful when it is a mutual activity motivated by the strong desire to bring pleasure to one's partner rather than for only one's own gratification. Sexual relations should possess social, psychological, and physical dimensions as well as sensual stimulation.

Erogenous Zones

Areas of the body that are particularly sensitive to sexual stimulation are called *erogenous zones*. It is through the stimulation of these areas that sexual arousal takes place, often to the point of orgasm. This is in addition to the emotional factors related to sexual activity that are extremely important for complete sexual arousal and satisfaction.

There are a number of erogenous zones, the most sensitive being the genitals and the areas immediately surrounding them in most individuals. In the male, the penis is the most sensitive erogenous zone, especially the glans penis. The corresponding structure in the female, the clitoris, is the most sexually sensitive part of the woman's body. Other erogenous zones include the breasts (especially the nipples), armpits, small of the back, shoulders, neck, earlobes, scalp, eyelids, mouth, tongue, eyes, nose, and anus.

Sexual arousal from the stimulation of many of these areas of the body is a learned response, resulting in part from cultural expectations. Moreover, it is possible for areas of the body to be stimulated and elicit no sexual response on one occasion, but elicit extreme arousal on another occasion.

Characteristics of Sexual Arousal

In both males and females, sexual arousal results in a variety of physiological changes as well as psychological reactions. It has been only recently that these changes have been documented through careful scientific observations.

In the female, sexual arousal is characterized by the vagina becoming lubricated within 10–30 seconds after the onset of stimulation. The barrel of the vagina darkens in color, and as stimulation progresses, the inner two-thirds of the vagina increases in both length and width. Women experience nipple erection and swelling of the areola, as well as an enlargement of the breasts themselves. In addition, the clitoris becomes erect and increases in diameter during sexual excitement, and as orgasm approaches, recedes under the hood formed by the inner labia.

Most women also experience a sex flush—a rash that develops as a result of vasocongestion of the blood vessels near the surface of the skin. The sex flush begins at the stomach, throat, and neck, and spreads to the breasts. Myotonia (muscle tension) develops in the abdominal region and as orgasm approaches becomes involuntary resulting in a trembling of the muscles as well as the characteristic pelvic thrusts. Internally, fibrillations begin in the body of the uterus. It increases in size, and at the peak of excitement, is pulled upward into the lower abdomen.

The most apparent sign of sexual arousal in the male is penile erection. In addition, many men experience nipple erection and a small percentage experience a sex flush. There is vasocongestion of the scrotum, with the testicles generally drawn close to the body.

Both males and females experience an increase in pulse and blood pressure, and more rapid and deeper breathing. All of the characteristics cited above lead to orgasm. *Orgasm* is a series of involuntary muscular contractions lasting from 3–10 seconds, usually accompanied by ejaculation in men. Women are generally more capable of experiencing multiple orgasms while only a small percentage of men are capable of more than one orgasm during a single sexual experience.

Masters and Johnson identified four basic phases of sexual arousal that are experienced by both men and women. The *excitement phase* is characterized by vasocongestion of the genitals and breast, vaginal lubrication, rapid breathing, increased pulse rate, and other physiological signs of sexual arousal. The *plateau phase* is characterized by the maintenance of sexual arousal and the building of excitement toward orgasm. The *orgasmic phase* is characterized by orgasm, muscle spasms (accompanied by ejaculation in the male), a significant increase in the rate of breathing, and a rise in blood pressure. The *resolution phase* is characterized by a gradual return to the pre-excitement stage. A *refractory period* in males occurs immediately after orgasm. It is a period when further sexual stimulation is difficult and which usually renders a man incapable of experiencing a second orgasm in rapid succession.

Sexual Preference

Heterosexuality

Heterosexuality is a sexual attraction to members of the opposite sex. In Western cultures, including the United States, it is considered the norm, and until recently, was considered almost without question the only acceptable form of sexual behavior.

While heterosexual contact is necessary for procreation (in the absence of artificial insemination) and while most people seem to prefer heterosexuality to other forms of sexual relationships, there appears to be an increasing tolerance to those whose sexual preferences do not fall into the heterosexual category.

Homosexuality

Historically, *homosexuality* was considered to be a mental disorder in the United States. However, with changing public attitudes and objective research, the American Psychiatric Association, in 1973, removed homosexuality from its list of mental disorders.

Homosexuality, the sexual attraction toward members of the same sex, was once thought to be a higher level of love and affection than heterosexual love. Over the centuries, however, linked to religious views and the value of procreation, heterosexuality became the dominant value, with homosexuality being condemned as sinful or as an illness.

Only recently, have homosexuals begun to assert their sexual preference as a legitimate alternative to heterosexuality. It is estimated that the number of homosexuals in the United States may range from 5 million (a conservative estimate) to about 20 million as the gay activists claim. Whatever the case, homosexuals are more numerous than previously thought, resulting in a potential for political and economic influence.

Gay rights organizations exist on over 200 college campuses in the United States.[22] However, even with this new-found assertiveness it appears that the majority of homosexuals still prefer to remain anonymous.

Many theories exist that attempt to explain the cause of homosexuality. The *hereditary theorists* believe that since homosexuals grow up in a heterosexual environment, homosexuality cannot be learned and is, thus, inborn. *Environmental theorists* hold to the view that homosexuals are conditioned through learning and other environmental factors to adopt homosexual behavior patterns. A third theory claims that male homosexuality results from a *hormonal imbalance* characterized by low testosterone levels and diminished sperm production. In 1979, Masters and Johnson released their findings claiming that homosexuality is, indeed, a learned phenomenon.

Since an overt showing of affection between females is more readily accepted in our culture than affection between males, it is difficult to determine if gay men outnumber gay women as statistics indicate. For instance, in 1948 Kinsey indicated that female homosexuality was about half that of male homosexuality.[23] It is probably more valid to rely on one's "pureness" of sexual preference. Kinsey identified six categories describing one's sexuality as follows:

> 0—exclusively heterosexual
> 1—primarily heterosexual, but incidentally homosexual
> 2—primarily heterosexual, but more incidentally homosexual
> 3—equally heterosexual and homosexual
> 4—primarily homosexual, but significantly heterosexual
> 5—primarily homosexual, but incidentally heterosexual
> 6—exclusively homosexual

It is interesting to note that as age increases for males, the incidence of homosexual tendencies (categories 1–6) decreases, while there is an increase in homosexual tendencies for females. Still, a sizable majority of both sexes rate themselves as exclusively heterosexual.

Bisexuality

Bisexuality applies to those who engage in sexual relationships with members of both sexes. People who fall into this category are in the middle range of Kinsey's sexual preference ratings. Bisexuals tend to desire relationships with both sexes, although they may exhibit greater anxiety about their sexual preferences than those who are committed to homosexuality.

Although the exact nature of bisexuality is not completely understood, several hypotheses have been promoted as to its cause. It is possible, for example, that some people experiment with both sexes; some people may be moving from one sexual preference to another and experience bisexuality during this transition; others may merely desire sexual stimulation regardless of its source; while others may have a positive attraction to both men and women.[24] Although one may be bisexual, most often there is a dominating preference for one sex over the other; it is rarely an equal preference.

Sex in Today's Society

It has often been said that we are experiencing a sexual revolution in our society with a free flow of sexual information, open discussions about sex in the media, an ease of accessibility to pornographic materials, and increasingly effective contraceptive measures.

Products are promoted by appealing to our sexual responsiveness. Some techniques are subliminal. The promoter attempts to influence us as consumers by appealing to our attraction to sexual messages. We have seen a liberalization in our attitudes about sex in recent years, especially as these attitudes relate to the sexual behavior of others. However, when personal attitudes are investigated—those that relate to our own behavior—we find little change. We still tend to be monogamous. We tend not to be highly promiscuous. We still value the family. And we tend to seek affection and love to enhance our sexual activities.

Still, we have changed gradually. This change is most marked in our view of female sexuality. While we now accept and recognize that women desire and respond to sexual stimulation as much as men, *this was not always the case, as was described in 1915:*

> **Passion in Women**—There are many females who never feel any sexual excitement whatever; others, again, to a limited degree, are capable of experiencing it. The best mothers, wives and managers of households know little or nothing of the sexual pleasure. Love of home, children and domestic duties are the only passions they feel. As a rule, the modest woman submits to her husband, but only to please him; and, but for the desire of maternity, would far rather be relieved from his attentions. This is doubly true of women during the periods when they are with child, and when they are nursing.[25]

If any major changes in our view of sex have been made in recent years, none is more significant than our heightened state of sexual consciousness. We demand to know more about sex—our own as well as that of others.

SEXUAL VARIANCES

Definition

Labeling sexual behavior is a very difficult task, and probably little good comes of it. For this discussion, however, sexual variances are those sex acts engaged in by adults that vary from penile-vaginal intercourse. (The major exception to this definition is that of homosexuality.)

Why Sexual Variance?

There are many theories that have been developed as explanations of variant sexual behavior. Some feel that such acts reflect a regression to our ancestral past—that what was once acceptable behavior recurs inappropriately in the present. Another, more Freudian theory, is that these acts result when a person gets "stuck" at an early stage of development, for example oral or anal, and never progresses to the genital stage. Neither of these theories is widely accepted because they cannot be tested. The most widely held belief is that variant sexual behavior results primarily from environmental stimuli to which a person is conditioned. What might be considered to be variant sexual acts are rewarded, either through pleasure or through social approval, and as a result, they are incorporated into a person's sexual repertoire.

It must be emphasized that many so-called sexual variances are widely practiced and it is only when a person becomes totally fixated on one or more of these that it may be considered abnormal. Table 6–2 is a summary of the more common sexual variations.

Table 6–2: Sexual Variances

Sadism——Act(s) in which sexual pleasure and fulfillment are derived from inflicting physical and/or psychological pain on another person. Very closely linked to masochism. Such acts as whipping, biting, cutting, slapping, and punching are common. A lust murder is sadism in its most extreme form.

Masochism——Acts in which sexual pleasure and gratification are derived from being the object of physical or psychological punishment. This punishment is usually planned with the sadistic partner. It may be that for both sadism and masochism there is an attempt to punish or be punished for feeling sexual pleasure, which may be perceived as "dirty."

Exhibitionism——Gaining sexual gratification from exposing one's genitals to others. More common in males than in females from a legal point of view. Sexual arousal caused during the act of exhibitionism may be followed by masturbation.

Voyeurism and Scoptophilia——The term voyeurism is used to describe gaining pleasure from viewing nudes, while scoptophilia is gaining sexual gratification from viewing sexual acts and genitalia. The "Peeping Tom" most typically describes this syndrome.

Saliromania——A disorder found primarily in men in which sexual gratification is gained through damaging or soiling the clothes and/or body of a woman or a representation of a woman. Such an act is usually accompanied by erection and sometimes by ejaculation.

Gerontosexuality——A variance in which a young person gains sexual gratification from having sexual relations with a person who is much older.

Incest——Sexual intercourse between two people who are close relatives.

Mate-swapping——Also called swinging, involves the sexual exchange of partners of two or more married couples. In most instances, all of those involved are aware of the swapping activities.

Klismaphilia——Gaining sexual gratification from receiving enemas.

Nymphomania——A rare phenomenon involving the uncontrollable desire of a woman for sexual fulfillment. A true nymphomaniac will seek sexual gratification no matter what the consequences.

Pedophilia——Gaining sexual gratification by having sexual relations with children.

Bestiality——Obtaining sexual gratification by engaging in sexual relations with animals. The term *zoophilia* is often used interchangeably with bestiality.

Necrophilia——A rare sexual variance in which sexual gratification is achieved by looking at or having intercourse with a corpse. The necrophiliac may kill to provide himself with a corpse. This is usually considered the most deviant of all sexual variances.

Fetishism——A condition in which sexual impulses become fixated on a symbol. They may be used in conjunction with masturbation or heterosexual activity. Such objects as hair, feet, fur, leather, and so forth may symbolize the fetish.

Frottage——The act of obtaining sexual gratification from rubbing against or pressing against the desired person, often in crowded places.

Troilism——Gaining sexual gratification while a third person looks on, or in the company of another couple who also engage in the sex act.

Transvestism——Emotional and/or sexual gratification derived from dressing in clothes of the opposite sex. It is usually not accompanied by a homosexual preference.

Transsexualism——A condition in which a person is severely uncomfortable with his/her physiological gender. In some instances, it is possible to make one's physiological gender compatible with one's psychological gender through surgical procedures.

Analism——Also called *sodomy*. This condition refers to gaining sexual gratification through anal intercourse. It appears that liberalization of sexual attitudes is related to an increase in the number of people at least occasionally engaging in anal intercourse.

Satyriasis——The male counterpart of nymphomania, it is characterized by an uncontrollable urge on the part of the man for sexual gratification

---

GLOSSARY

Abortion: Terminating a pregnancy.

Birth control: Means used to control conception.

Bisexual: A person whose sexual preference is for persons of the same and the opposite sex.

Cohabition: An arrangement in which two or more people live together outside the bonds of marriage.

Coitus: Sexual intercourse.

Contraception: Means used to prevent the union of a sperm with an egg.

Extended family: A family in which children, parents, and grandparents live under the same roof.

Family: A group of two or more people related by blood, marriage, or adoption who live together.

Gonad: The testes in the male and the ovaries in the female.

Heterosexual: A person whose sexual preference is for persons of the opposite sex.

Homosexual: A person whose sexual preference is for persons of the same sex.

Nuclear family: A family in which children and parents live together with only incidental contact with other relatives.

Polyandry: A condition in which one woman has more than one husband at one time.

Polygamy: A condition of having more than one husband or wife at one time.

Polygyny: A condition in which one man is married to several women at one time.

Secondary sex characteristics: The appearance of traits during adolescence that are typical for the mature sex of the person as male or female.

Sex: Male or female. Also used to mean coitus.

Sexuality: One's personality traits related to being masculine or feminine.

SUMMARY

The family is a basic social unit that the society has depended upon for its perpetuation. As society has changed throughout history, corresponding changes in the structure and function of the family have also occurred. Two major types of family structures exist in our society: extended and nuclear.

Engagement is a time when the couple's marital expectations are defined and agreed upon and when the various preparations for marriage occur.

The traditional marriage is now being questioned by many. This is particularly the case as it applies to a woman's role in marriage. A successful marriage is dependent upon many factors. These include commitment, a growth orientation, and a noncoercive atmosphere, all contributing to a general state of open communication.

Once a family is established, our role as individuals changes. This role change is never more evident than when children become part of the family.

The termination of marriage may be manifested as divorce, desertion, separation, or merely living separate lives under the same roof. As divorce becomes more accepted as a viable alternative to marriage, it is affecting more people.

Sexual behavior, and people's view of it, is controversial by its very nature. Sexuality is concerned with the totality of human beings functioning in a variety of social settings.

The development of our sexual nature and reproductive potential is significantly influenced by hormones, which are responsible for the development of the secondary sex characteristics, the development of the genitalia, and the maintenance of pregnancy.

Pregnancy may be determined using three sets of criteria: presumptive signs, probable signs and positive signs. The most crucial stage of prenatal development is during the first trimester, when the embryo and fetus is most susceptible to infections and other adverse environmental conditions. The birth process can be divided into three states of labor: dilation, expulsion, and placental. The birth of the baby is complete at the end of the expulsion phase.

Adolescent pregnancy refers to any pregnancy occurring through the age of twenty. Such pregnancies result in the birth of babies who are much more likely to die during the first year of life.

Birth control and contraceptive techniques include: mechanical, chemical, hormonal, surgical and natural. Each method varies according to its effectiveness, number of possible side effects, cost, and ease of use. For some, a seemingly ineffective technique may be the only alternative available considering religious sanctions, medical history, and cost. Abortions are classified as spontaneous (miscarriages), therepeutic, and illegal.

Basically males and females experience a similar sexual response cycle characterized by four stages: excitement, plateau, orgasm, and resolution.

Homosexuality refers to the preference of engaging in sexual encounters with members of the same sex. Theories as to the cause of homosexuality focus on genetic factors, environmental factors and hormonal factors.

Our sexual awareness has become more conscious in recent years with the public demanding to know more about sex. Although there appears to have been a liberalization in people's attitudes about what others do, there has been less of a change in actual sexual behavior.

Although many theories exist as to the cause of sexual variances, the most widely held belief is that such behavior results primarily from environmental stimuli to which a person is conditioned. Only when a person becomes totally fixated on one or more of the variances can a person be considered abnormal.

PROBLEMS FOR DISCUSSION

1. Discuss how advancements in society as a whole have influenced the family.
2. Analyze existing marriage laws in your state. Are they antiquated? What revisions in them would you recommend?
3. Why do some social scientists believe that an abandonment of the extended family has been harmful to society?
4. Discuss the alternatives to traditional marriage. Do you feel that any are viable alternatives in our society? Why? Why not?
5. Why should cohabitation not be considered a valid preparation for marriage?
6. Describe the purpose of engagement. Why should a breaking of an engagement be viewed positively? What are the legal consequences of breaking an engagement?
7. What can a couple do to ensure that a marriage has the best chance of success? Should personal marriage contracts be written prior to marriage? Why? Why not?
8. Describe the role of positive communication in marriage.
9. What issues should be considered when deciding whether or not to have children?
10. Should divorce laws continue to be made more lenient? Why? Why not?
11. What strategies should be employed, if any, to make marriage more difficult?
12. Describe the positive and negative effects of divorce on children.
13. What is the primary function of the pituitary gland and gonads in terms of their effects on sexual development?
14. Why is it important for women to receive prenatal care from a physician? When should the care be sought?
15. Which type of birth control method is most effective? Why is it not possible for some people to use this and other highly effective methods?
16. Should abortion remain legal as an elective procedure to control unwanted pregnancies?
17. If a ban on abortion were imposed upon the American public, should the IUD also be illegal? Explain.
18. Should sterilization procedures be used to control births from parents with genetic defects?
19. Should homosexuality be legalized and accepted as an alternative to heterosexuality in our society?
20. Should people with less than average intelligence be allowed to have children? Explain.
21. Is it ethical for manufacturers to promote their products by appealing to one's sexuality? Explain.

22. Are people's potential for sexual arousal primarily learned or innate? Give examples.
23. Who should be more responsible for the use of contraceptives, the male or female? Why?
24. Distinguish between sexual variance and sexual variety.
25. Discuss the economic and social implications of adolescent pregnancy.

REFERENCES

1. OGBURN, WILLIAM F. and MEYER F. NEMKOFF, *Sociology*, Houghton Mifflen Company, Boston, 1946, p. 698.
2. *Standard Dictionary of the English Language*, Int. Ed. Vol. 1, Funk & Wagnalls, New York, 1974, p. 658.
3. GOLDBERG, STELLA R. and FRANCINE DEUTSCH, *Life-Span Individual and Family Development*, Brooks/Cole Publishing Co., Inc., Monterey, Cal., 1977, p. 87.
4. O'NEILL, NENA and GEORGE O'NEILL, *Open Marriage: A New Life Style for Couples*. Evans Publishing Co., New York, 1972, p. 406.
5. *Ibid.*, pp. 280–81.
6. COX, FRANK D., *Human Intimacy: Marriage, The Family and Its Meaning*, West Publishing Company, St. Paul, Minnesota, 1978, p. 103.
7. GAGNON, JOHN J., and CATHY S. GREENBLAT, *Life Designs: Individuals, Marriages, and Families*, Scott, Foresman and Company, Glenview, 1978, pp. 231–232.
8. COX, FRANK D., *op. cit.*, p. 148.
9. BEDWORTH, DAVID A., and ALBERT E. BEDWORTH, *Health Education: A Process for Human Effectiveness*. Harper & Row, Publishers, Inc., New York, 1978, p. 80.
10. KATCHADOURIAN, HERANT A., and DONALD T. LUNDE, *Fundamentals of Human Sexuality*, Holt, Rinehart and Winston, Inc., 1972, p. 83.
11. *Ibid.*, p. 91.
12. GOLDSTEIN, BERNARD, *Human Sexuality*, McGraw-Hill Book Company, New York, 1976, p. 97.
13. *Ibid.*, pp. 98–99.
14. *Ibid.*, p. 43.
15. *Ibid.*, pp. 170–173.
16. *Ibid.*, p. 175.
17. *11 Million Teenagers*, The Alan Guttmacker Institute, The Research and Development Division of Planned Parenthood Federation of America, New York, 1976, p. 7.
18. *Manual of Standards in Obstetrics and Gynecology*, 2nd ed. American College of Obstetricians and Gynecologists, 1965.
19. GOLDSTEIN, *op. cit.*, p. 205.
20. *Ibid.*, p. 206
21. GOLDSTEIN, *op. cit.*, p. 21.

22. HECHINGER, GRACE, and FRED M. HECHINGER, *"Homosexuality on Campus"*, *The New York Times Magazine*, March 12, 1978, p. 15.

23. KINSEY, A. C., et al., *Sexual Behavior in the Human Male*, Saunders Publishing Co., Philadelphia, 1948.

24. GAGNON, JOHN H., *Human Sexuality*, Scott, Foresman, and Company, Glenview, Ill., p. 259.

25. TRUITT, W. J., *The Science of Human Life*, S. A. Mulliken Company, Marietta, Ohio, 1915, p. 162.

PART
III

personal and social health issues

7

smoking or health?

IS SMOKING REALLY HARMFUL?

The First Scientific Report

During the 1950s a number of reports from Canada, England, Denmark, Norway, Sweden, Finland, and the Netherlands announced that "Smoking is an important health hazard, particularly with respect to lung cancer and cardiovascular disease."[1]

Concerned about the impact of such revelations, the Tobacco Industry Research Committee was established to study the relationship of tobacco smoking and health. This, among other factors, stimulated the U.S. Public Health Service to become engaged in an evaluation of the available information about smoking and health. In 1956, a scientific study group, under the initiative of the Surgeon General was established. The group's findings led them to conclude that "there is a causal relationship between excessive smoking of cigarettes and lung cancer."[2]

In the 1960s, groups such as the American Heart Association and the American Cancer Society called for an official government study of the relationship of smoking to human health. An expert scientific advisory committee was selected by the Surgeon General and consisted of ten persons from a number of scientific backgrounds. In January, 1964, the committee issued its first report on the smoking issue: *Smoking and Health: Report of the Advisory Committee to the Surgeon General of the Public Health Service.* The impact of this report has significantly influenced the tobacco industry, the advertising of tobacco products, and the smoking behavior of millions of Americans. In addition, it had, and continues to have, significant political ramifications.

What Is the Evidence?

The report, *Smoking and Health,* presented such overwhelming evidence of the association between cigarette smoking and ill health that the expert advisory committee made the following sweeping statement: "Cigarette smoking is a health hazard of sufficient importance in the United States to warrant appropriate remedial action."[3] Investigation by the expert advisory committee revealed evidence of the health hazards resulting from cigarette smoking. The following is a list of *some* of the findings:

- Cigarette smoking is causally related to lung cancer in men and the risk increases with duration of smoking and the number of cigarettes smoked each day.
- There is a causal relationship between cancer of the lip and pipe smoking.
- Cigarette smoking is a significant factor in the causation of laryngeal cancer in men.
- An association exists between smoking and cancer of the esophagus, emphysema, and peptic ulcer.
- Cigarette smoking is the most important cause of chronic bronchitis in the United States.

- Cigarette smoking is associated with a reduction in ventilatory function.
- Women who smoke during pregnancy have babies of lower birth weight than nonsmoking women. The relationship is unclear.
- Smoking is associated with accidental death from fires in the home.
- There is some evidence of a morphological difference between smokers and nonsmokers.

Subsequent reports have strengthened the evidence of the health hazard of cigarette smoking and more evidence is being compiled relative to the hazards of cigar and pipe smoking and the use of snuff. For example, since pipe and cigar smokers usually do not inhale the smoke, the risk of developing lung cancer is significantly lower than for cigarette smokers, but it is still much greater than for nonsmokers. This is also true for the development of chronic bronchopulmonary diseases.[4]

The 1979 report of the Surgeon General supports the evidence gathered over more than two decades of scientific investigation of the health hazards with tobacco smoke. There is no other single factor in American society that causes and contributes to more premature deaths and disabilities than tobacco smoke. Tobacco is a lethal substance that has only token control over its use by government. The fact that over 54 million Americans smoke makes this a societal health issue that must not be ignored. The facts are clear as presented in Tables 7–1 and 7–2. (See also Figure 7–1.)

It is estimated, for example, that the following are directly related to cigarette smoking: 70 percent of all cases of lung cancer; 30 percent of all cases of arteriosclerosis; 75 percent of all cases of bronchitis; and 80 percent of all cases

Table 7–1: Association Between Smoking and Excess Mortality

Cause of Death	Mortality Ratio	% of Excess Deaths Among Smokers
Aortic aneurysm (nonsyphilitic)	6.0 (average)	500
Bladder cancer	2.0	100
Cardiovascular diseases	1.6	60
Chronic obstructive lung disease	1.5	50
Coronary heart disease	1.7 (average)	70
Emphysema and bronchitis	7.5	650
Esophageal cancer	5.3 (average)	430
Kidney cancer	2.0	100
Laryngeal cancer	9.0	800
Lung cancer	10.0	900
Oral cancer	6.5	550
Pancreatic cancer	2.0	100
Stomach cancer	1.6	60
Sudden cardiac death	2.6	160

Source of Data: *Smoking and Health: A Report of the Surgeon General*, U.S. Department of Health, Education, and Welfare, Public Health Service, DHEW Publication No. (PHS) 79–50066, 1979.

Figure 7-1
Hazards of Smoking

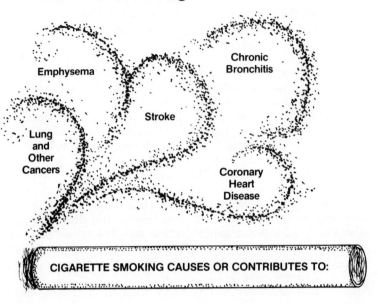

Emphysema

Chronic Bronchitis

Stroke

Lung and Other Cancers

Coronary Heart Disease

CIGARETTE SMOKING CAUSES OR CONTRIBUTES TO:

Table 7–2: Kinds of Relationship of Smoking to Disease

Disease	Relation of Smoking to Incidence and Mortality
Cardiovascular diseases	One of several independent risk factors. Acts synergistically with other risk factors.
Lung cancer	Causally related.
Laryngeal cancer	Causally related.
Oral cancers	Causally related.
Esophageal cancer	Causally related.
Urinary bladder cancer	Associated. Acts synergistically with other risk factors.
Kidney cancer	Associated (men). Insufficient data on women.
Pancreatic cancer	Dose-relationship.
Chronic bronchitis	Causally related.
Emphysema	Significant association.
Chronic obstructive lung disease	Causally related.
Peptic ulcer	Significant association.

Source of Data: *Smoking and Health: A Report of the Surgeon General*, 1979.

of emphysema. There are approximately 175,000 cardiovascular disease deaths among people under 65 years of age annually. Twenty-five percent of these, or 43,750 deaths each year, are unnecessary—they are caused by cigarette smoking, a behavior entirely under the control of each person. (See Figure 7–2.)

The following is a selected summary of the conclusions of the 1979 Surgeon General's report on smoking:

Mortality

- The overall mortality rate for male smokers is 70 percent in excess compared to nonsmokers.
- Mortality ratios increase with the amount of cigarettes smoked.
- The longer one smokes, the greater the risk of dying.

Figure 7-2:

Comparison of Death Rates for Smokers and Non-smokers for Specific Ages

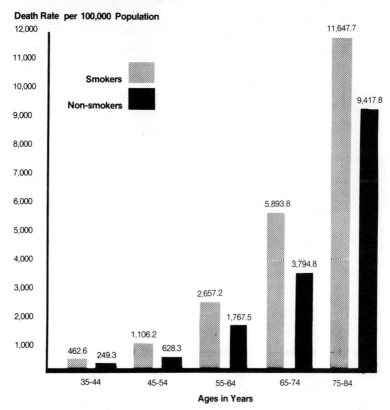

Source of Data: **Health: United States: 1976-1977,** U.S. Department of Health, Education, and Welfare.

- The younger the age of initiating cigarette smoking, the higher the mortality ratio.
- Mortality ratios are higher for those who inhale cigarette smoke than for those who do not inhale.
- The mortality ratios are higher at younger ages and decline with increasing age. However, the actual number of excess deaths attributable to cigarette smoking increases with age.
- Those who stop smoking cigarettes experience overall declining mortality ratios. After 15 years of abstinence, mortality ratios are nearly equal to those who have never smoked.
- The overall mortality ratios for cigar smokers are higher than for nonsmokers and are directly proportional to the number of cigars smoked.
- The overall mortality ratios for pipe smokers is slightly higher than for nonsmokers.
- Life expectancy is significantly shorter for cigarette smokers than for nonsmokers—up to 9 years for two pack-a-day smokers.
- Overall mortality ratios increase with the tar and nicotine content of the cigarette.
- Overall mortality ratios for female cigarette smokers show a similar, although lower, pattern as for men smokers.
- Excess mortality is greatest for men and women in the age group of 45 to 54 years.
- The excess in mortality is found chiefly as a result of coronary heart disease, lung cancer, and chronic obstructive lung disease in that order.
- Pipe and cigar smoking are associated with increased mortality ratios for cancers of the oral cavity, larynx, and esophagus.

Morbidity

- Male and female cigarette smokers suffer from more chronic bronchitis, sinusitis, emphysema, peptic ulcer, and arteriosclerotic heart disease than nonsmokers.
- The incidence of acute conditions for male smokers is 14 percent higher and 21 percent higher for female smokers than for those who have never smoked.
- Male smokers have 33 percent excess days lost from work while females have 45 percent excess lost work days as compared with nonsmokers.
- Male smokers have 14 percent excess days of bed disability while females have 17 percent of excess bed disability as compared to nonsmokers.[5]

The Kinds of Studies That Have Been Made

For many obvious reasons, it is not possible to study the relationship of cigarette smoking to disease and death by experimenting on humans. However, scientists do have several other approaches available including animal experimentation and use of various epidemiological methods. These include clinical and autopsy studies, and population studies, both retrospective and prospective.

Animal experimentation consists chiefly of exposing experimental animals to the tars and smoke from tobacco and observing the effects on the exposed tissues. *Clinical and autopsy studies* consist of observing patients clinically over a period of time, both smokers and nonsmokers, and, through autopsies, examining cellular and tissue changes and characteristics. *Retrospective studies* consist of studying the smoking histories of persons with specific diseases and comparing them with comparable control groups. Generally, the data and evidence gathered through these techniques support each other in respect to the health hazard of cigarette smoking. Further evidence has also been obtained through *prospective studies.* The eight original prospective studies that were analyzed represent 16 million person years and over 300,000 deaths.

WHAT INFLUENCES SMOKING BEHAVIOR?

Biochemical Factors

There are a number of factors associated with the initiation and continuance of the smoking habit. These may be placed into categories such as biochemical, psychological, and social factors. In addition, some authorities believe that the motor activities associated with smoking, such as holding the cigarette and lighting it, are important factors that perpetuate the smoking habit. It is likely that all factors are important and interact with each other as reinforcers and that none of the factors taken singly is, in and of itself, the major one that sustains the false pleasures from smoking.

Certainly, the chemical composition of tobacco has a profound effect upon the smoker's desire and craving for the tobacco smoke. This is supported by a statement of the Surgeon General: "Cigarette smoke contains a number of compounds that may act as pharmacological reinforcers and facilitate establishment of the smoking habit."[6]

Tobacco smoke contains a number of chemicals in gas and particulate form. It is thought that nicotine, carbon monoxide, and tar are the chief substances associated with smoking habituation. Actually, *tar* is an accumulation and condensate of a number of particulate components found in tobacco smoke. *Nicotine* is the most powerful pharmacological agent in tobacco smoke. It is an oily alkaloid poison which is metabolized in the liver, taking between 20 and 30 minutes.

Studies indicate that smokers develop a tolerance for the chemicals found in tobacco smoke and chiefly for nicotine. Since smokers develop a tolerance, we can expect that a dependency for the chemicals in tobacco smoke is also established. This, in turn, results in a withdrawal syndrome when tobacco smoke is denied. Although the development of dependence on tobacco smoke is generally accepted, the exact mechanism and nature of withdrawal is still unclear. Studies to ascertain the length of the withdrawal syndrome have resulted in a variety of time-lines from a few weeks to several years, varying with individual smokers and their smoking behavior.

Psychological Factors

A person must learn to become a smoker. The painful experiences one encounters initially must be overcome and other more satisfying social or personal needs must be reinforced. As a person continues to smoke, a psychological tolerance and dependence develops that makes smoking "enjoyable" in its own right and the social and personal reinforcers take on less significance. Certain environmental stimuli also play an important role, at least, in the continuation of smoking. These may be referred to as environmental cues. For example, smokers usually enjoy smoking at certain times or under certain circumstances, such as with a cup of coffee or a cocktail.

Not only does the pharmacological components of tobacco smoke provide the smoker with certain chemical pleasures related to release of tension and the like, smoking prevents the onset of the withdrawal syndrome. These two factors, along with a host of other psychological, environmental, and social stimuli, tend to perpetuate the smoking habit and to interfere with efforts at stopping. It is estimated, for example, that an average one pack a day smoker takes about ten puffs per cigarette, or more than "70,000 nicotine 'shots' in a year—a frequency which is unmatched by any other form of drug taking."[7]

It can readily be seen that the psychological factors (satisfaction of some emotional need) cannot be dissociated from the social factors that may contribute to the satisfaction of an emotional need. This is exemplified, for example, in peer pressure to start the smoking habit and peer approval of it. Quitting smoking, once it is established, requires the smoker to establish a determination to deal effectively with the pharmacology of cigarette smoke, gain emotional need satisfaction in more realistic ways, and to acquire social approval and acceptance without the use of tobacco.

WHAT DOES TOBACCO CONTAIN?

Gases and Particulate Matter

Tobacco *smoke* contains about 60 percent gases and about 40 percent particulate matter. The particulate matter consists of tar and nicotine and 27 percent water. Nearly 99 percent of the gas phase of cigarette smoke consists of seven gases: nitrogen, oxygen, carbon dioxide, carbon monoxide, hydrogen, argon, and methane. The remaining 1 percent consists of more than 45 other compounds in trace amounts. Table 7–3 lists the chief chemical components of the gas phase and particulate phase of cigarette smoke.

Of the chemicals found in the gas phase of cigarette smoke, nine are known carcinogens (cancer-producing), four are ciliatoxic (harmful to cilia, tiny hair-like outgrowths of certain cells that protect various body parts), one is a tumor initiator, and four are toxic. In all, more than 3000 chemicals in tobacco smoke have been identified.

Table 7–3: Chemical Composition of Cigarette Smoke

Gas Phase	Particulate Phase
1. Nitrogen⎱ comprises 2. Oxygen ⎰ more than 70%	1. Nicotine (major factor in tobacco habituation)
3. Carbon dioxide	2. Nonvolatile N-Nitrosamines
4. Carbon monoxide	3. Aromatic amines (associated with bladder cancer)

5. Nitrogen oxides
  • nitric oxide
  • nitrogen dioxide
  • nitrous oxide
	4. Alkanes and alkenes (minor role if any in carcinogenesis)
	5. Isoprenoids (several hundred have been isolated)

6. Ammonia	6. Benzenes and Naphthalenes
7. Volatile N-Nitrosamines (8 have been identified; some are known carcinogens)	7. Polynuclear Aromatic Hydrocarbons (co-carcinogenic)
8. Hydrogen cyanide (major ciliatoxic agent in cigarette smoke)	8. N-Heterocyclic Hychocarbons (cocarcinogenic)
9. Cyanogen	9. Phenols (cocarcinogenic)
10. Volatile sulfur compounds	10. Carboxylic acids (more than 50 have been identified, accounting for 4—7 percent of the particulate matter)
11. Volatile nitriles (33 have been identified in tobacco smoke; one is suspected of being carcinogenic)	11. Metallic constituents (76 have been identified; some are carcinogenic)
12. N-Containing volatile compounds (more than 600 have been identified; some are reported as being tumorigenic)	12. Radioactive compounds.
13. Volatile hydrocarbons	13. Agricultural chemicals
14. Volatile alcohols	
15. Volatile aldehydes and ketones (inhibitors of ciliary action)	

Source of Data: *Smoking and Health: A Report of the Surgeon General*, 1979.

Chemical Composition of Tobacco

The tobacco used for cigarettes, cigars, and pipes has the botanical name *Nicotania tabacum,* named after the French explorer, Jean Nicot. Nicot, in 1560, promoted tobacco for what he thought was its curative value. For more than 400 years, tobacco has been used by nearly every nation throughout the world and the quantity consumed has steadily increased with only sporadic periods of decreased consumption. For example, total tobacco consumption in the United States in 1964 was 1.41 billion pounds. By 1975, this consumption had decreased to 1.35 billion pounds. Ironically, the number of cigarettes manufactured during this same period had shown a steady increase.

Obviously, the chemical components of tobacco smoke are related to the chemical components of the tobacco leaf. The chemicals found in the tobacco leaf consist of cellulose, starches, proteins, sugars, alkaloids, pectics, hydrocarbons, phenols, fatty acids, isoprenoids, sterols, and a number of inorganic minerals. These chemicals are also found in other plants; however, alkaloid nicotine, nornicotine, myosmine and anabasine are specific to tobacco. The concentration of the various chemicals in tobacco will vary depending upon how the tobacco is grown and the growing conditions, as well as processing practices such as curing and the location of the leaf on the tobacco plant. The United States Department of Agriculture has established certain standards of classes, grades, and types for tobaccos.

How Safe Is Safe?

Filter cigarettes have been on the market for many decades; however, it wasn't until the latter part of the 1950s that cigarette manufacturers made concentrated efforts to develop more brands of cigarettes containing filters. This trend was in response to some of the early research findings that cigarette smoking was harmful to health. There were considerable efforts following the release of the first Surgeon General's report in 1964 to counter some of the adverse publicity about the hazards of smoking. As a result, a wide range and variety of new filter-tipped cigarettes were created including a variety of filters. It is interesting to note that the tobacco industry rejects the scientific evidence that cigarette smoking is harmful to health; nevertheless, the industry did put filters on cigarettes.

A number of efforts have been made to reduce the toxicity, tar, nicotine, and carbon monoxide content of cigarette smoke. These efforts include improved agricultural methods, tobacco processing, selection of the tobacco leaf, and improved quality of the cigarette paper, as well as the development of filters. Below is a summary of the success of these efforts.

- *Carbon monoxide:* Better selection of the tobacco and the use of charcoal filters results in a slight reduction of carbon monoxide.
- *Ciliatoxic gases:* The use of charcoal filters reduces the content of some ciliatoxic gases up to 97 percent. However, some are completely ineffective.
- *Volatile phenols:* Some types of cellulose acetate filters have been demonstrated selectively to remove volatile phenols from cigarette smoke.
- *Volatile N-Nitrosamines:* Improved tobacco selection for use in cigarettes and the use of cellulose filters will reduce the concentration of volatile N-Nitrosamines. However, there is no evidence that the degree of reduction is sufficient to reduce the tumor causing potential of the smoke.
- *Tar:* Careful selection of the type and quality of the tobacco leaf for use in cigarettes can reduce the tar content of the smoke. Tar content of cigarettes is listed on the packages of cigarettes.
- *Nicotine:* Selective breeding and other agricultural methods, along with special curing techniques, can reduce the amount of nicotine that will be present in the cigarette smoke. Cigarette manufacturers list the nicotine content of their cigarettes on the package.

According to recent investigations on the effect of nicotine and tar levels of cigarette smoke and the consumption of cigarettes, "nicotine dependency plays a minor role in determining the smoking habits of those who continue to smoke on a long-term basis."[8] The conclusion was based on evidence that indicated that smokers who smoked one or more packs of cigarettes per day did not tend to increase their consumption of cigarettes when they changed to low tar and nicotine cigarettes. However, more than half of the less than one pack a day smokers did increase their consumption when they changed to a low tar and nicotine cigarette.

In conclusion, *there is no safe cigarette.* As a matter of fact, it is still unknown what constitutes a safe cigarette. Although many cigarettes have reduced the tar and nicotine content of the smoke and some filters are effective to some extent in reducing harmful gases, the chemical composition of cigarette smoke remains toxic.

THE ECONOMICS OF TOBACCO

Tobacco Consumption

The per capita consumption for persons 18 years of age and older was less than 50 cigarettes in 1900. By 1930, this had increased to nearly 1400; by 1960 it was over 4000, reaching a peak in 1963 of 4336. During 1953 and 1954, there was a decline attributed to reports appearing in the press that linked cigarette smoking to lung cancer. There was also a decline in consumption in 1964 following the issuance of the first Surgeon General's report, but consumption returned to 1963 levels during 1965 until 1968 when there was once again a significant decline in consumption. By 1978, per capita consumption reached approximately 4000 cigarettes.

The economic impact of the tobacco industry is staggering. It is estimated that more than $15 billion is spent on cigarettes alone. In addition, hundreds of millions of dollars are spent for cigars, pipe tobacco, smoking accessories, medical and hospital costs from health problems related to smoking, and government subsidy to tobacco farmers. The tobacco industry spends approximately $300 million annually for advertising. In a 5-year period, 1971–1976, over 105 new brands of cigarettes were introduced at a total cost of about $600 million for development, advertising, and promotion. Only 13 of the new brands were successfully marketed.[9]

Revenues from Tobacco

The United States government has imposed a federal excise tax on tobacco for approximately a century. The tax revenue from tobacco products constitute nearly 2 percent of all federal receipts, which is more than 15 percent of all excise taxes. In addition, all states impose a tax on cigarettes, some have taxes on other tobacco products, and many municipal governments impose a tax on cigarettes. The tax on cigarettes constitutes more than 98 percent of the federal tobacco tax revenues, yielding more than $2.3 billion annually. Federal, state, and municipal tobacco taxes together yield more than $6.2 billion annually. Tobacco tax revenues have shown a steady increase over the past 30 years as shown in Table 7–4.

Tobacco Advertising

The amount of tobacco consumed each year is directly related to the promotional efforts of the tobacco industry. Six manufacturers of cigarettes dominate 99.9 percent of the sales of cigarettes in the United States. Twenty brands of cigarettes account for about 93 percent of all annual sales, and companies spend approximately $260 million dollars each year in their promotion and advertising.

Prior to 1971, when the Public Health Cigarette Smoking Act (P.L. 91–222) went into effect, cigarette manufacturers spent about $300 million on advertising, with nearly $200 million of this for television. The Public Health Cigarette Smoking Act strengthened the warning appearing on each pack of cigarettes and banned all radio and television commercials. (The first federal legislation requiring a warning on the packages was authorized by passage of the Federal Cigarette Labeling and Advertising Act (P.L. 89–92) which became effective in 1966.)

More than 150 bills have been introduced into the Congress between 1966 and 1980, but since 1970, none has been passed. Their defeat is directly related to the powerful tobacco industry lobby and the members of Congress from tobacco producing states. The influence of the economics associated with tobacco production and sales, far outweighs the influence of the millions of Americans incapacitated and killed each year as a direct or indirect result of tobacco smoke. Even though tobacco smoke is a hazardous substance of greater magnitude than any other, the Consumer Product Safety Commission has decided not to exercise its legal authority under the Federal Hazardous Substances Act of 1960 in respect to high tar and nicotine content cigarettes.[10]

It is necessary to note here that government support for the growing, manufacture and marketing of tobacco is incongruent with its efforts to protect the American people from known health hazards from tobacco smoke. The Fed-

Table 7–4: Federal and State Tobacco Tax Revenues 1950–1980*

Year	Federal (In billions)	State (In billions)	Total
1950	$1.5	$0.5	$2.0
1955	1.6	0.5	2.1
1960	2.0	1.0	3.0
1965	2.2	1.3	3.5
1970	2.1	2.0	4.1
1975	2.3	2.2	4.5
1980	2.9 (est.)	2.6 (est.)	5.5 (est.)

*Figures are rounded to the nearest $0.1 billion. These figures are computed on per capita consumption of tobacco (chiefly cigarettes) at $0.08 federal tax and an average state tax of $0.13 per cigarette.

eral government spends in excess of $70 million annually to merely administer
its price support program and related tobacco production activities. This is in
contrast to the U.S. Department of Health, Education, and Welfare (now the
Department of Health and Human Services) budget of about $5 million a year
to combat the health hazards resulting from smoking.

Most states have introduced bills to control smoking, especially in public
places. Nearly one-third of the states have passed some legislation related to
smoking. Some states also have placed smoking restrictions in such places as
public meetings at the state level, public schools, department stores, and restau-
rants. (See Figure 7–3.)

WHO SMOKES?

Trends

Approximately 37 percent of America's population are smokers. From
1955 to 1964, adult male smokers showed a slight decline, while for females there
was a significant increase in the number of smokers. Beginning in 1966, there has

Figure 7-3:

Nonsmokers Bill of Rights

$\mathfrak{Non\text{-}Smoker's}$ $\mathfrak{Bill}$ $\mathfrak{of}$ $\mathfrak{Rights}$

*NON-SMOKERS HELP PROTECT THE HEALTH, COMFORT AND SAFETY OF
EVERYONE BY INSISTING ON THE FOLLOWING RIGHTS:*

THE RIGHT TO BREATHE CLEAN AIR

NON-SMOKERS HAVE THE RIGHT TO BREATHE CLEAN AIR, FREE FROM HARMFUL AND IRRITAT-
ING TOBACCO SMOKE. THIS RIGHT SUPERSEDES THE RIGHT TO SMOKE WHEN THE TWO CONFLICT.

THE RIGHT TO SPEAK OUT

NON-SMOKERS HAVE THE RIGHT TO EXPRESS — FIRMLY BUT POLITELY — THEIR DISCOMFORT
AND ADVERSE REACTIONS TO TOBACCO SMOKE. THEY HAVE THE RIGHT TO VOICE THEIR OB-
JECTIONS WHEN SMOKERS LIGHT UP WITHOUT ASKING PERMISSION.

THE RIGHT TO ACT

NON-SMOKERS HAVE THE RIGHT TO TAKE ACTION THROUGH LEGISLATIVE CHANNELS, SOCIAL
PRESSURES OR ANY OTHER LEGITIMATE MEANS — AS INDIVIDUALS OR IN GROUPS — TO PRE-
VENT OR DISCOURAGE SMOKERS FROM POLLUTING THE ATMOSPHERE AND TO SEEK THE RE-
STRICTION OF SMOKING IN PUBLIC PLACES.

National Interagency Council on Smoking and Health, 419 Park Ave. So., Room 1301, New York, N.Y. 10016 been a steady decrease in the number of male and female smokers although the decrease has been greater for men than women. Prior to 1964, nearly 53 percent of men were smokers as compared to nearly 32 percent of women. By 1980, less than 39 percent of men and less than 28 percent of women were smokers. Fortunately, there has been an increase in the number of adult men and women who have stopped smoking. For example, in 1955 about 11 percent of men and only 4 percent of women had stopped smoking. By 1980, these figures increased to over 30 percent for men and over 15 percent for women. (These trends are illustrated in Figure 7–4.)

The trends in the percentage of teenage smokers shows quite a different pattern from adult smokers since 1968. Boys have shown a fluctuating pattern reaching a peak in 1970 among 17- and 18-year-olds, while girls have shown a steady increase in the percentage of smokers until, at present, there is no significant difference between the two sexes. Of importance is the relative steady decrease in the number of boys who smoke. This is significant since the tobacco industry has for years attempted to project the masculine image as one who smokes. Perhaps boys no longer consider smoking as an indication of achieving manhood. The pattern is different for girls, however, since there has been a concerted effort by the tobacco industry to associate smoking with femininity, charm, and sex appeal. Perhaps the girls have accepted this image, which may be an important factor for the increase in girls who smoke. However, there is recent evidence that the number of girls who smoke is declining faster than for boys. Figure 7–5 shows the trends in smoking among teenage boys and girls. (See also Figure 7–6 for smoking patterns for 12–18 year olds.)

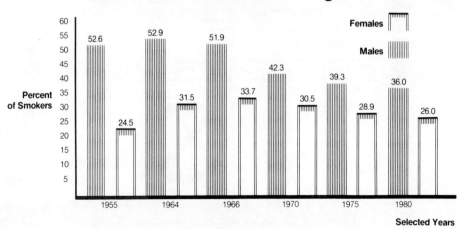

Figure 7-4:

Trends in Percent of Male and Female Smokers, Ages 21-65 + Years

Source of Data: **Smoking and Health,** Public Health Service. 1979. p. A-10.

Figure 7-5:

Trends in the Percent of Boys and Girls
Who Smoke For Selected Ages In 1975

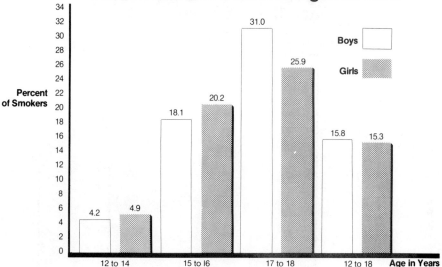

Source of Data: **Smoking and Health,** Public Health Service, 1979, p. A-14.

Factors Associated With Smoking

The relationship of cigarette smoking and demographic factors have also been studied. The noteworthy factors are race, educational achievement, family income, occupation, and marital status. In 1965, more than 51 percent of white men smoked cigarettes regularly as compared with nearly 61 percent of black men. By 1975, these figures had decreased to about 41 and 51 percent respectively. The trends for white and black women are not as clear. In 1965, more than 34 percent of white and black women smoked cigarettes. By 1975, there was a slight decrease for white women (to about 32 percent), and a slight increase for black women (about 35 percent). Generally, however, the percentage of blacks who smoke is greater than for whites.

Although smoking patterns for adults within various educational categories has shown a steady decline, the percentage of male college graduates who smoke is significantly lower than for those who have not completed college. This trend, however, is somewhat different for females. The percentage of females who have only a grade school education or less is about 18 percent as compared with about 21 percent who have completed college. It is interesting to note, however, that the greatest percentage of females who smoke are those who have some high school education (about 33 percent) followed closely with those who have some college education (about 32 percent). Figure 7–7 shows the relationship of educational achievement among men and women and the percentage who smoke.

Figure 7-6:

Comparison of Cigarette Smoking Among Teenagers Ages 12 to 18 Years

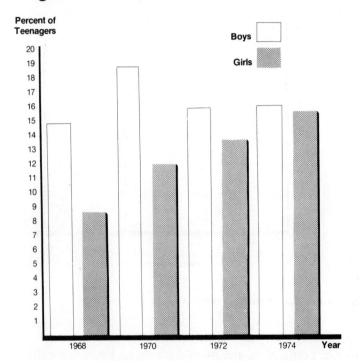

Source of Data: **Health: United States: 1976-1977,** U.S. Department of Health, Education, and Welfare.

Certain family characteristics appear to affect smoking behavior. For example, the percentage of males who smoke whose family income exceeds $25,000 annually is less than for those whose family income is less than this amount, about 35 and 45 percent respectively. However, for females the trend is quite different. For those whose family income exceeds $25,000 annually, there are about 35 percent smokers compared with 33 percent of females whose family income is between $5,000 and $24,000 per year.

The percentage of smokers within several occupational groups also varies. Among professional and technical male workers the percentage of smokers is lowest with about 30 percent. This is similar for females with about 29 percent of smokers. For males, the highest percentage of smokers is among those who are unemployed (about 57 percent) followed closely by blue collar workers with about 50 percent. For females, the occupations with the highest percentage of smokers are managerial and administrative workers with about 42 percent. This is followed by unemployed females with about 40 percent.

Figure 7-7:

Percentage of Regular Cigarette Smokers According to Educational Achievement*

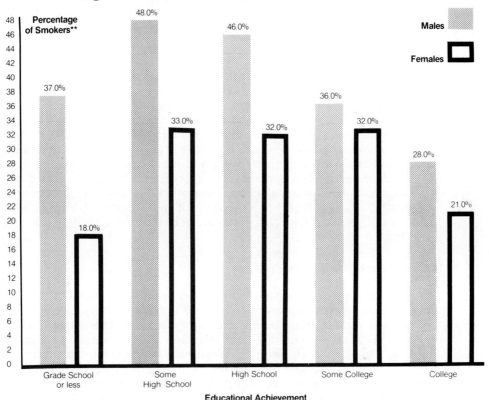

*Source of Data: **Smoking and Health,** Public Health Service. 1979. p. A-15
**Percentages are rounded to the nearest whole percent.

Finally, marital status shows a rather interesting pattern. Both men and women whose spouses have died have the lowest percentage of smokers with about 33 and 20 percent respectively. The highest percentage of male smokers is among those who are separated (about 63 percent) while it is highest for females who are divorced (about 55 percent).[11]

Even with the results of valid nationwide surveys that reveal certain trends in cigarette smoking and differing patterns among demographic groups, it has not been possible to establish a valid smoker's profile. More research and analyses of data are necessary to determine whether or not certain personality or demographic factors are associated with those who are at risk of becoming a smoker. We do know, however, that for adolescents, if one or both parents smoke, they are more likely to smoke. In addition, if a parent and older sibling smoke, the younger child is more likely to smoke. From these results, we might conclude

195

that parent or older sibling models may have a significant bearing upon the future smoking behavior of children in a family.

STOP SMOKING PROGRAMS

Some General Comments

The success of the numerous methods for stopping the smoking habit vary with the age of the smoker, how much he/she smokes, how long smoking has taken place, age at which smoking began, and motivation for stopping. Of the nearly 30 million Americans who have been successful in stopping smoking, it is estimated that about 95 percent did it on their own. This would suggest that personal reasons and determination to stop are very important determiners of success rather than the methods used by formal quit smoking programs. It is suspected that even when persons seek assistance through one of the quit smoking programs, their personal effort, determination, and satisfaction are more important to success than the techniques of the program. However, many ex-smokers indicate that the reinforcement received through a quit smoking program can be very helpful.

A Look at Some Stop Smoking Programs

Stop smoking programs employ a wide variety of methods such as withdrawal clinics; the use of nicotine substitutes (lobeline); tranquilizers, stimulants, and other medications; counseling; group therapy; and hypnosis. Studies indicate that as many as 80 percent of smokers enrolled in some cessation programs stop smoking temporarily. However, follow-up studies indicate that fewer than 20 percent are able to sustain tobacco abstinence for any extended period of time. Most smokers who have been successful in stopping have tried to stop several times before they were able to abstain. For many, the chief motivating factor is personal health. Smoking cessation programs have been established by voluntary health agencies, governmental health agencies, religious groups, and commercial enterprises. Below is a brief summary of some of the more popular smoking cessation programs.

- The Seventh Day Adventists' Five-Day Plan consists of five consecutive 2-hour sessions with follow-up meetings. The sessions include films, lectures, discussions, and a buddy system. This program claims up to 33 percent success one year following exposure to the program.
- Voluntary health agencies such as the American Cancer Society, American Heart Association, and the American Lung Association have similar stop smoking programs that consist chiefly of a trained volunteer working with smokers. Usually, the volunteer is an ex-smoker. The major emphasis is placed on educational experiences related to learning why one smokes and the advantages in stopping. These programs claim an abstinence success rate of from 18–48 percent after one year.

- Three commercial enterprises, Smoke Watchers, SmokEnders, and Schick claim a one year abstinence success rate of up to 37 percent, 27 percent, and 53 percent respectively. These programs are usually highly structured using gradual withdrawal and positive reinforcement. The Schick Smoking Control Centers also employ aversive conditioning techniques.

Since smokers who participate in these smoking cessation programs are highly motivated to stop smoking, it is difficult to evaluate whether the program or personal desire to stop smoking is the chief factor in success. Probably both of these factors play important roles, but the strong determination of the smoker is most likely the chief factor. Some commercial cessation programs screen applicants before they are allowed to participate. This may be another factor in their success rate since those who enter the program are already highly motivated and susceptible to any form of assistance.

GLOSSARY

Abstinence: Completely avoiding the use of tobacco or other substance.

Causal: The factor, either alone or in combination with others, that is responsible for the onset of the disease.

Cessation: The process of stopping the smoking habit.

Ciliatoxic: Affecting the action of the cilia, the hair-like structures found in the bronchii.

Particulate matter: The solid substances found in a gas.

Tar: The condensate of tobacco smoke composed of a variety of chemicals.

SUMMARY

In 1964, the first scientific report, *Smoking and Health,* on the health hazards of smoking was released. Among other things, the Surgeon General's Report of 1964 concluded that cigarette smoking is causally related to lung cancer; is a significant factor in laryngeal and esophageal cancers; is a cause of chronic bronchitis; and is related to emphysema and coronary heart disease among others. Subsequent reports over the next 15 years supported earlier findings and revealed new associations between cigarette smoking and diseases.

Further studies have been made to ascertain the factors that influence smoking behavior. Generally, these factors are associated with the biochemical nature of tobacco smoke, the personality of the individual, and certain social influencers. It is thought that these may function interactionally rather than singly.

Tobacco smoke contains a number of chemical substances that affect health. Many attempts have been made over the past 30 years to reduce the hazard effects of tobacco smoke. These include the development of a variety of filters for cigarettes, improved agricultural techniques, and improved curing and processing of the tobacco. Although many cigarettes today are less harmful than two or three decades ago, there is no agreement on what constitutes a safe cigarette.

The economic impact of the tobacco industry is great. The enormous revenues received by governments makes this a product of political influence. The federal government has passed several measures to control advertising and some other activities of the tobacco industry.

Since 1955 there has been a steady decline in the number of male smokers and an increase in the number of female smokers since 1966. There has been a trend toward greater numbers of adult men and women who have stopped smoking. However, this pattern is not the same for teenage smokers. Although the percentage of teenage boys has leveled off, the percentage of teenage girls who smoke has increased steadily.

Generally, the percentage of blacks who smoke is greater than for whites; fewer college graduates smoke than those who have not completed college; persons in higher income groups are less likely to smoke; and the percentage of smokers is greatest among blue collar workers than among professionals.

A number and variety of cessation programs have been established in the past two decades. Studies indicate, however, that success in permanently stopping smoking appears to be more associated with the motivation of the person than on the type of cessation program. The greatest motivational force seems to be concern for one's personal health.

PROBLEMS FOR DISCUSSION

1. Why was the first Surgeon General's report, *Smoking and Health,* an important document?

2. Compare the conclusion of the 1964 Surgeon General's report with the 1979 report. What new evidence was presented in the 1979 report? From the evidence presented in both reports, what can you conclude about smoking and health? Support your premise.

3. Trace the history of the research conducted on the health hazards of smoking from 1950 to 1979. What do all these findings have in common?

4. List three diseases that have smoking as a *causal* factor. List five diseases that are associated with smoking? What can you conclude?

5. What is meant by excess mortality? Excess morbidity?

6. Describe the kinds of scientific studies that have been analyzed. Are the results valid? Explain.

7. Describe the biochemical, psychological, and social factors that influence smoking behavior.

8. Distinguish between the gas phase and the particulate phase of tobacco smoke. Select five chemicals found in each phase and state how each is an associated health hazard.

9. Describe how governments and the tobacco industry have attempted to make smoking safer. Describe the effects of various methods on the reduction of gases and particulate matter of cigarette smoke.

10. What is the significance to governments of the tobacco tax revenues?

11. Is there a smoker's personality or profile? Explain.

12. Describe the demographic factors associated with smoking. What are the smoking rates of each factor? What can you conclude?
13. What is generally thought to be the chief factor in stopping smoking?
14. Describe the nature of most smoking cessation programs. What are the success rates of these programs? How can you stop smoking?

REFERENCES

1. *Smoking and Health: Report of the Advisory Committee to the Surgeon General of the Public Health Service,* U.S. Department of Health, Education, and Welfare; Public Health Service; PHS Publication No. 1103, Superintendent of Documents, U.S. Government Printing Office, Washington, 1964, p. 6.
2. *Ibid.,* p. 7.
3. *Ibid.,* p. 33.
4. *The Smoking Digest: Progress Report on a Nation Kicking the Habit,* U.S. Department of Health, Education, and Welfare; Public Health Service; National Institutes of Health; National Cancer Institute, Bethesda, Md., 1977, pp. 21–22.
5. *Smoking and Health: A Report of the Surgeon General,* U.S. Department of Health, Education, and Welfare; Public Health Service; DHEW Publication No. (PHS) 79–50066, 1979, pp. 1–10 to 1–13.
6. *Ibid.,* p. 15–5.
7. *Smoking and Health: A Report of the Surgeon General, op. cit.,* p. 16–6.
8. GARFINKEL, LAURENCE, "Changes In The Cigarette Consumption of Smokers In Relation to Changes in Tar/Nicotine Content of Cigarettes Smoked." *American Journal of Public Health,* Vol. 69, Dec., 1979, page 1274.
9. *The Smoking Digest, op. cit.,* p. 95.
10. *Ibid.,* p. 79.
11. *Smoking and Health: A Report of the Surgeon General, op. cit.,* 1979, pp. A–14 to A–17.

8

drugs and your health

PERSPECTIVES ABOUT DRUGS

The human body is the most magnificent chemical factory known. It produces many of its own chemicals, controls their quality and level of production, and the way they interact with each other—all for the purpose of maintaining life, health, and creativity of the body. Occasionally, however, this chemical factory needs assistance when things go wrong, and drugs from the environment may help. To use these drugs in other ways may interrupt the intricacies of the body, interfering with creativity, health, or life itself.

What Is a Drug?

How would you distinguish between a drug and a medicine? If you heard that a person was taking a drug, what would your reactions be? If, however, you heard that a person needs to take medication, what would your reaction be? Actually, according to the Food and Drug Administration, there is no difference between a drug and a medicine.[1] *A drug is any medicinal substance possessing qualities that will aid in diagnosing, treating, curing, or preventing disease, or maintaining health.*

Drugs may be used singly or in combinations depending upon the effects needed or desired to achieve a particular purpose. For example, there are drugs that can stimulate or depress the activity of certain organs or tissues; there are drugs that can improve blood circulation and coagulation, as well as to lessen coagulation; and there are drugs that can be used to stabilize chemical homeostasis and diagnose diseases.

There is evidence that people used drugs in prehistoric times. There are ancient records describing drugs; the most famous of these is the *Papyrus Ebers* (1550 B.C.), which describes over 700 different drugs that were used in ancient Egypt. Although most of these were of botanical origin, some were also of animal and mineral sources.

The Sciences of Drugs

The science that is concerned with the study of the composition, use, and history of drugs derived from plants and animals is called *pharmacognosy.* The science that is concerned with the nature and action of drugs on biological functions is called *pharmacology.* Several other sciences compose pharmacology including materia medica, toxicology, and therapeutics. *Materia medica* is that branch of medical science that deals with the sources, preparation, properties and uses of the drugs used in preventing, diagnosing, treating and controlling diseases. This is in contrast to *therapeutics,* which is concerned with medicinal substances that have curative potentials. *Toxicology* is the science that is concerned with the way in which chemical substances interact within the body resulting in tissue damage or malfunctioning. It is the study of poisons.

Sources of Drugs

There are four primary sources of drugs: (1) those derived from plants, such as cocaine; (2) those derived from animals, such as hormones; (3) those that are partially synthesized, (semisynthetic), such as morphine; and (4) those that are totally synthesized, such as the barbiturates.

Marketing and Marketing Controls

Pharmaceutical companies conduct continuous research in attempts to discover new drugs and to improve the effectiveness of existing ones. However, before a new drug can be marketed, it must be approved by the Food and Drug Administration (FDA) as being safe *and* effective. Approval for marketing also includes the correctness and completeness of the drug's labels and any descriptive materials. The burden of proving to the FDA that a drug is safe and effective lies with the manufacturer. The process of development, testing, and manufacturing of a drug may take years. Throughout this period and following marketing approval, the manufacturer must maintain high levels of *quality control.* This is to ensure that every dose of the drug is exactly the same.

Once scientists have discovered a new drug, the first test it undergoes must determine its effectiveness. This requires involvement of the pharmacologist. The second test is to determine whether the drug is safe. To ascertain its degree of safety and possible side effects, the toxicologist and pathologist are called upon. All of the pertinent research data related to safety and effectiveness must be submitted to the FDA for its review, accompanied by a new drug application (NDA). Safety data include results of tests on animals and humans, lists of all ingredients and amounts, quality control procedures, among others.

The 1962 Kefauver-Harris Amendment to the Food, Drug, and Cosmetic Act requires that all drugs be effective for their intended uses. Following the marketing of a new drug, the FDA requires the manufacturer to report periodically any adverse effects of the drug or other experiences not revealed in premarketing testing. The FDA has the authority to suspend further marketing of any drug that is found to be hazardous to health.

Labeling of Drugs

All drugs, whether over-the-counter or prescription, must contain a label and certain basic information. The chief purpose of label information is to ensure safe use of the drug by the consumer. For example, *over-the-counter drug labels* must provide directions for safe use, such as quantity and frequency of dose, time and duration of use, and procedures for preparing the drug for use. In addition, it must contain any warnings related to whether it is habit forming and conditions when the drug must not be used. A *prescription drug label* must include the name and address of the pharmacy, the name of the physician, prescription number and date the prescription was filled. Usually, however, other information is included such as directions for use, refill directions, and the name of the patient.

Generic vs Brand Name Drugs

"All drugs, whether they are sold under their brand names or their generic names, must meet the same FDA standards for safety, strength, purity and effectiveness. And all drug manufacturers, big or small, are subject to FDA inspection and must follow the Agency's Current Good Manufacturing Practice Regulations.''[2] However, the pharmaceutical industry contends that there is more to a drug than merely its chemical composition. Companies are concerned with the quality control that can make a difference in such factors as rate of absorption and disintegration of the drug in the stomach. In this regard, both chemical and quality equivalents need to be considered by the physician when prescribing drugs, since therapeutic action is dependent upon the chemical composition *and* its therapeutic level in the body.

The New York State Legislature enacted Chapter 776 of the Laws of 1977, commonly referred to as "Generic Drug Substitution Law," the first of its kind in the United States. This law became effective in 1978. The New York State Department of Health developed a model prescription form to be used by physicians where drug substitutions are appropriate. (See Figure 8–1.)

A chief purpose of allowing generic substitutions is to provide the consumer with the same therapeutically effective drug at much less than the price of brand name drugs. For example, the price for chlordiazepoxide HCL (generic) is approximately $10.00 for 100 pills of 10 mg each when sold as Librium (brand name), compared to approximately $2.50 when sold under its generic name. Terramycin (brand name) is approximately $30.00 for 100 pills of 250 mg each, but costs only about $5.50 under its generic name, oxytetracycline.[3] Of course,

Figure 8-1:

New York State's Model
Drug Substitution Prescription Form

Name of Physician _____

Address _____
Street _____

City and State _____

DEA # _____

Name _____ Age _____
Address _____ Date _____

Rx:

_____   _____
Dispense As Written   Substitution Permissible

This prescription will be filled generically unless the physician signs on the line stating "Dispense As Written."

these prices will vary from time to time because of inflation and other reasons, but the price relationship has remained quite steady. Since the price of drugs vary considerably from one pharmacist to another and one region to another, it may be worthwhile to comparison-shop before buying.

Concluding Remarks

The use of drugs in therapeutics has become a necessity. Can you imagine physicians practicing medicine without the array of drugs available to them? Prior to the 1930s, this was essentially the case. Physicians had only a few drugs they could prescribe, chiefly the opiates for pain, a few tonics, laxatives, salves, and ointments. The development of new drugs accelerated during World War II. A turning point was the accidental discovery of penicillin by Sir Alexander Fleming in 1928. However, it was not until 1944 that penicillin became commercially available, which began a new wave of excitement in pharmaceutical research and resulted in the discovery of a number of other antibiotic drugs. Most of the drugs used in therapeutics have been discovered or developed in the past 40 years.[4]

Each year many new drugs are discovered and some are approved for marketing, all of which are intended to improve the health of people, assist in the restoration of health, and alleviate pain. Drugs meeting certain specified standards are eventually listed in the *United States Pharmacopeia, The National Formulary,* and perhaps, the *Homeopathic Pharmacopeia of the United States,* and the *International Pharmacopeia.* Drugs listed in the *United States Pharmacopeia* must be manufactured, regardless of the manufacturer, according to the standards listed. This means, for instance, that the quality of all aspirins is the same in respect to chemical formula regardless of the brand name. (Look for the initials USP or NF on the label.)

There is no question about the role drugs play in preventing, diagnosing, and treating diseases. Their benefit to humanity cannot be measured. However, as with so many other technological developments over the centuries, drugs can also be harmful if not properly used and controlled. We have seen this in the recognition of the widespread abuse of psychoactive drugs during the 1960's and continuing to the present.

WHAT IS YOUR DRUG BEHAVIOR?

What Is Drug Abuse?

We have seen that drugs are used for the benefit of people. They can also be used in ways that interfere with human effectiveness. It is difficult to specifically characterize drug abuse; however, certain factors are generally agreed upon. These factors are the kind and amount of a drug used and reasons for using it. *Drug abuse* is "the use of legal drugs in a manner or amount contrary to their intended dosage or purpose, and the use of illegal drugs for the purpose of bringing about a change in feelings, mood, and behavior."[5] In other words you are abusing drugs if you use a drug in any of the following ways:

- to change your self-perception or perception of your environment outside the scope of materia medica and therapeutics;
- in quantities exceeding those listed on the label or prescription;
- in ways that interfere with your effectiveness or society's, or for the purposes of creating unusual or abnormal behavior, or destroying life;
- when the effects, safety, or dosage are unknown.

Proper Use of Drugs

Many people are not aware that it is important to follow the directions on the label of over-the-counter drugs (sometimes called proprietary drugs) or to follow the directions of the physician in the case of prescription drug use. Even fewer people are aware that taking drugs in combinations can result in serious side effects or may even lower the effectiveness of a drug. A *side effect* is an action of the drug that is not needed or intended. (Some people may be more susceptible to a side effect than others.) Side effects are more likely to occur with prescription drugs than with over-the-counter drugs. This is one reason why a prescription is required and professional supervision is important. Some drugs may be beneficial in one part of the body while they may be harmful in another part of the body. A drug taken at the wrong time or in the wrong way could be dangerous.

The dosage of a drug and its means of administration, orally or by injection, for example, are scientifically determined. The dosage prescribed is intended to safely reach the *therapeutic level* and to maintain this level until the desired effects are achieved. Hypothetically speaking, suppose a physician prescribed a drug to be taken as follows: four tablets every 6 hours for the first day and two tablets every 8 hours for 1 week. This could mean that the higher dosage for the first day is necessary for reaching the therapeutic level in the body as quickly, but safely as possible. The reduced dosage is all that is necessary to maintain the proper therapeutic level, and the length of time will usually result in recovery.

Taking drugs in various combinations can also result in dangerous side effects or reduce the effectiveness of some drugs. For example, if your physician has prescribed an anticoagulant and you take an antacid drug, the antacid may slow down the rate at which the anticoagulant is absorbed. Since the anticoagulant is absorbed too slowly, it may not reach the desired therapeutic level to be effective. Aspirin, on the other hand, increases the blood-thinning effect of anticoagulants and could result in hemorrhage. Drinking alcohol (which is a drug) interferes with the rate at which an anticoagulant is metabolized. For the heavy drinker this may result in a reduced effect of the anticoagulant, but drinking an excessive amount of alcohol in a very short period of time may slow down metabolism resulting in blood that is too thin.[6]

When your physician prescribes a drug, be sure to let him/her know what other drugs you are taking including alcohol and proprietary drugs. Be cautious about the drug combinations you take since this is a relatively new area of pharmacology and much is still to be learned about how drugs interact in the human body.

Three other side effects from mixing drugs need to be mentioned because they are relatively pertinent to the drugs that are commonly abused for psychological effects. When, for example, alcohol and barbiturates are taken together, the combined effect is greater than the sum total effects of the two drugs if taken separately. This is known as a *synergistic effect.* This is in contrast to the effects of two drugs taken together that produce reactions equal to the two when taken separately. This is called an *additive effect.* Finally, *potentiation* occurs when the action of one drug induces or enhances the action of another. The use of alcohol with various drugs which affect the central nervous system can produce any one of these three effects depending upon the specific second drug used. It is important to note that generally, either the term *potentiate* or *synergist* is used to describe any increased effects of drug combinations. The important point is that *combining drugs can be very dangerous and the use of alcohol in combination with other drugs has the potential for disastrous results.*

Drug Dependence

In 1964, the World Health Organization's Expert Committee on Addiction-producing Drugs recommended that the term "drug dependence" be substituted for the terms "habituation" and "addiction." *Drug habituation* is characterized chiefly by a psychological craving for a drug, a general absence of the development of physiological tolerance, and an absence of a withdrawal syndrome when the drug is denied. *Drug addiction,* however, is characterized by a general state of continuous intoxication produced by chronic use of a drug, the development of physiological tolerance necessitating increased amounts of the drug, accompanied by psychological craving, and the appearance of the classical withdrawal syndrome when the drug is denied.

Drug dependence is a more general term that does not make this distinction between habituation and addiction. Also, the characteristics of the dependency vary according to the drug or drugs being used. This is clarified by indicating the specific drug causing the dependency, such as heroin dependence, alcohol dependence, barbiturate dependence, and so forth.

A *withdrawal syndrome* consists of the combination of symptoms resulting from the denial of the drug one has become dependent upon (addicted to). The general pattern of the *withdrawal syndrome* varies according to the drug-specific dependency. In any case, withdrawal is characterized by the appearance of unpleasant physical and/or psychological symptoms upon the sudden and prolonged abstinence from the drug. For example, the symptoms that can be expected for *heroin dependency* when heroin is denied include: (1) drowsiness within 8–16 hours following the last dose; (2) during the next 12–24 hours, restlessness, yawning, profuse sweating, running of the nose and eyes, feelings of anxiety, insomnia, and muscular aches; and (3) after 24 hours and up to about 72 hours, gooseflesh, insomnia, uncontrolled muscle twitching, vomiting, diarrhea, muscular aches, a rise in body temperature, dehydration, and increased systolic blood pressure.

In the case of *barbiturate dependence,* some of the physiological symptoms found in heroin dependence will also be present: anxiety, muscle twitching, nausea, vomiting, and so forth, during the 16 to 24th hours after the last dose.

However, of significant importance with barbiturate dependence are the appearance of bizarre psychological symptoms. These include delerium tremens, psychotic episodes, paranoic reactions, delusions, and hallucinations. These symptoms usually reach their peak during the second or third days of withdrawal. With barbiturate dependence, death from exhaustion, or respiratory or heart failure is possible. *Medical attention is vital for those withdrawing from barbiturate dependency.*

THE EXTENT OF AMERICA'S DRUG PROBLEM

Historical Perspectives

Prior to the societal recognition of a serious drug problem in the United States during the decades of the 1960s and 1970s (and continuing into the 1980s), drug abuse was generally considered a form of criminal behavior. It still is to a great extent, but with the passage of the Comprehensive Drug Abuse Prevention and Control Act of 1970 and subsequent amendments, we see some efforts to deal with drug abuse as a preventable health problem. However, the bulk of funds allocated were channeled into law enforcement and treatment rather than into prevention-oriented programs.

Societal attitudes about drug abuse have undergone marked changes since the beginning of the twentieth century. Prior to 1900, there were virtually no controls over the use of the opiates and marijuana. Opium and heroin addiction were widespread chiefly among the over 30-year age group with the greatest concentration of addicts on the West Coast. Opiates were widely used in patent medicines and physicians freely prescribed heroin as a cure for opium and morphine addiction. This finally led to the passage of the Federal Pure Food and Drugs Act in 1906. This Act regulated the use of patent medicines that contained opiates, and was followed by the Opium Exclusion Act in 1909 and the Harrison Narcotics Act in 1914.

Several other pieces of legislation were enacted until, in 1937, the Marijuana Tax Act was passed by the Congress. However, all of these acts were directed toward control of imports, exports, manufacture, and so forth, which essentially brought in revenue for the government rather than controlling the individual use of the narcotics and marijuana.

One exception to this was the enactment of the Narcotics Control Act of 1929 which authorized the construction of two U.S. Public Health Service Hospitals for the treatment of drug addition. Treatment in these hospitals consisted chiefly of detoxification and correction of any physical conditions that may have existed. Not until 40 years later was some emphasis placed on rehabilitation and follow-up services of detoxified addicts.

The Lexington (Kentucky) Hospital, which began admitting patients in 1935, was, for all practical purposes, a prison. The patients consisted of more than 65 percent prisoners. It was not until 1967, when the hospital was placed under the control of administration of the National Institute of Mental Health, that the treatment program included emphasis on rehabilitation in addition to detoxification. Today it is a major drug research center and its name has been changed to the Clinical Research Center.[7]

One other significant historical note needs to be mentioned because of the criminal attitude that was established and persists to the present. In 1930, the Bureau of Narcotics was created within the Treasury Department. Its first commissioner, who remained as such until 1962 when he retired, was Harry J. Anslinger. The passage of the Marijuana Tax Act in 1937 was essentially the result of his efforts, along with the passage of the Narcotic Drug Control Act of 1956. He initiated and perpetuated the misconception that marijuana caused crime, and later (in 1951) the misconception that marijuana use led directly to heroin addiction. This was in contrast to his early belief when (in 1937) he stated that marijuana users and heroin addicts were quite different. Many of the misconceptions he promulgated persist today among the general public in spite of scientific evidence to the contrary.

Current Perspectives

Despite the near hysteria in recent years among certain segments of America's population, the highest percentage of opiate addicts in the United States occurred during the latter part of the nineteenth century. At that time, it is estimated that approximately 1 percent of the total population was addicted to opiates—chiefly Chinese laborers on the West Coast, and middle-aged "housewives." However, with the development of a number of new drugs over the past 40 years, the incidence of drug abuse has increased. Much of this increase is in the 18–25 year age group, although no age group or socioeconomic strata has been immune. For example, recent studies indicate that more than 50 percent of young adults (18–25 years) have at least experimented with marijuana and more than 15 percent are regular users.

It is difficult to obtain accurate information about who uses drugs, the kinds being used, and the extent of use. We do know that during the 1970s, there was an increase in the numbers of people using various drugs, especially marijuana, and that the kinds being used changed from time to time. These changes seem to result from such factors as availability, new research evidence, and the introduction of new fads. To the false relief of some adults, there was evidence during the late 1970s that many young people were returning to the use of alcohol. However, alcohol abuse is America's number one drug problem, adversely affecting, either directly or indirectly, more than 15 percent of our population.

Conclusion

We have traveled the road of drugs as a source of revenue, to an initiator of crime, to drug addiction as a treatable disease. Beginning in about 1978, drug abuse was starting to be viewed as a preventable social health problem. In the middle and late 1960s, our society was horrified, disgusted, and angry when it learned that many high school and college students were using drugs. Society reacted to these emotions, initiating a number of programs, such as educational, half-way houses, counseling and treatment centers, and harsh laws. There was an intense 10 or more years of bungling, some successes, many failures, until society became accustomed to the problem, and apathy among many set in.

Now we have entered the 1980s, armed with new insights from past successes and failures, and you are the people who will be directing new efforts to deal with the drug problems. What role will you play in solving one of our most serious health problems? Before you can answer this, you will need to learn about what we know about drugs of abuse.

COMMON DRUGS THAT ARE ABUSED

Introduction

Nearly any drug can be abused, whether it is legal or illegal, prescription or over-the-counter. Taking aspirin in excess is a form of drug abuse; sniffing volatile substances for a "high" is drug abuse; taking illegal chemicals, such as LSD is drug abuse; getting drunk on alcohol is drug abuse. However, the drugs we are concerned with here are those that are psychoactive. A *psychoactive* (also called psychotropic) drug is one that affects the functioning of the central nervous system in such a way as to distort perception of reality. There are three general classes of psychoactive drugs: (1) stimulants; (2) depressants; and (3) hallucinogens (also called psychedelics, psychomimetics, or psychotogenics). Let us explore each of these.

The Stimulants

A *stimulant* is a drug that increases the activity of the central nervous system characterized by excitation, restlessness, wakefulness, and extraordinary alertness. Obviously, the degree to which these symptoms are manifest depend upon the pharmaceutical properties of the drug, the dosage taken, the rate of absorption, mode of administration, blood level, and rate at which the drug is metabolized. Examples of stimulants are caffeine, cocaine, and the amphetamines. (See Table 8–1 for a summary of stimulants.)

Caffeine is the most commonly used stimulant in America. It is found in coffee, tea, and cola drinks among others. The use of caffeine has a long and sometimes interesting history, being related to the establishment of coffeehouses first in England, then France, and being related to early trade: For example, competition between the Dutch East India Company and the British East India Company was implicated politically when a tax was imposed on imported tea to be used medically.

Caffeine is a mild central nervous system stimulant and when combined with sodium benzoate is used as an emergency treatment for cardiac and respiratory failure. However, its chief use is as a beverage. Caffeine dependence develops in some people who consume large quantities of coffee, and the major withdrawal symptom associated with abstinence is headache. Generally speaking, the use of caffeine in the popular American beverages appears to be harmless to most healthy adults.

Table 8–1: Summary of the Stimulants

Name of Drug	Commercial Preparation	Medical Use	Effects	Dependence Potential	Historical Note and Comments
Caffeine	Coffee Tea Chocolate Cola drinks	Mild stimulant	Stimulates central nervous system and skeletal muscles.	Habituation	The use of coffee dates back to about the 8th century, chocolate about the 15th century and cola drink the 19th century, chocolate also contains theobromine.
Cocaine	Synthetic agent with similar anesthetic properties is procaine or, commercially, novocaine discovered in 1905.	Formerly used as a local anesthetic; rare today. Sometimes used in eye and throat surgery.	Depresses hunger; exhilaration. Can cause convulsions and paranoia.	Habituation	Earliest recorded use of coca leaves is about the 6th century. Source is the *Erythroxylon coca* plant. A class A narcotic.
Amphetamine group • Dextroamphetamine • Methamphetamine • Salts of racemic amphetamine	Ritalin Benzedrine Dexedrine Methedrine Desbutal Desoxyn Dexamyl Preludin	Treatment of narcolepsy and minor brain dysfunction in children, and hyperkinesis.	Brain stimulation, change in blood pressure, tremors, and increased heart action.	Addiction	Hazardous to anyone with high blood pressure in any amount. First developed in 1927 by Gordon A. Alles after he isolated epinephrine in the 1800s.
Ephedrine	Ephedrine	Used to treat asthma.	Longer lasting effects than epinephrine. Dilates the bronchi and depresses smooth and cardiac muscles.		Obtained from a herb, found chiefly in China and used there for more than 5,000 years. First used in U.S. in 1923.

Cocaine is derived from the coca plant, and there is evidence of its use in Peru about 500 A.D. Cocaine is *legally* classed as a narcotic although pharmacologically it is not. Its anesthetic potentials were discovered in 1860, and between 1885 and 1905 (when it was replaced by the development of Novocaine), it was used extensively in eye surgery and dentistry. In 1885, Sigmund Freud recommended injections of cocaine as a treatment for withdrawal symptoms from morphine addiction. He also suggested its value in psychiatric practice.

Cocaine, it was discovered, would numb an area and remain localized when injected, making it possible to perform painless, localized surgery. When injected systemically, however, small amounts stimulate heart action as well as the central nervous system. Larger amounts can result in cardiac arrest.

The leaves of the coca plant are commonly chewed, especially by Peruvians, resulting in psychological and physical stimulation and a dulling of the appetite. In America, as a drug of abuse, cocaine is sniffed or injected and sometimes mixed with other drugs. The use of cocaine results in a psychological dependence. The stimulating effects of cocaine are short-lived, lasting less than one-half hour. To maintain the exhilarating effects, one must repeat the dosage about every 20 minutes or so, which results in dangers of overdose (and infection if it is injected). When sniffed, cocaine can have devastating, deteriorating effects on the nasal mucus membranes.

Amphetamines are the most powerful and dangerous of the stimulants. Because of the widespread abuse of amphetamines, both legally (by prescription) and illegally, in 1970, the Drug Enforcement Administration limited the production to 6000 pounds per year. Prior to this action, more than 100,000 pounds were manufactured in the United States. However, even with these limitations, amphetamines continued to be abused—mostly prescribed for weight control. Since the potential for abuse is so great, in 1979, the Food and Drug Administration withdrew approval of amphetamines for weight control purposes. At this time, nearly 3.5 million prescriptions were being written each year with upwards of 90 percent for weight control. This means that the production of amphetamines can be reduced by 80–90 percent and still maintain supplies needed for the treatment of narcolepsy (a rare condition of uncontrollable sleepiness) and minimal brain dysfunction (hyperactivity) in children.[8]

First introduced in tablet form in 1937, amphetamine is a colorless, volatile liquid with three basic chemical forms: salts of racemic amphetamine, dextroamphetamine, and methamphetamine. Although the specific pharmacology of amphetamine is still unclear, it is thought to potentiate the effects of norepinephrine, which is a neurohormone that activates nervous impulses in the sympathetic nervous system. Amphetamine releases norepinephrine normally stored in the nerve endings, which concentrates in the higher centers of the brain resulting in increased heart action and metabolism. High doses of *methamphetamine* results in decrease in salivation, tremors, increased heart action, diarrhea, and others. *Dextroamphetamine* produces fewer side effects than methamphetamine while it continues to stimulate the higher centers of the brain.

When methamphetamine is injected into a vein, it is called *"speed."* The body rapidly builds a tolerance and the amount injected may increase from about 30 milligrams to over 500 milligrams for those on a prolonged "speed trip."

One of the serious side effects from the use of speed is the frequent development of a paranoid psychosis syndrome. It is still not clear whether this syndrome results from the chemical action of the drug on the brain, excessive fatigue resulting from prolonged stimulation, or both. Even though the syndrome was described as early as 1938, serious efforts to study it did not begin until the middle 1950s. Other possible dangers resulting from intravenous injections of amphetamine are the development of serum hepatitis and abscess from the use of unsterile equipment; abnormal heart action; and, with an overdose, death.

The Depressants

A drug that slows down the activity of the central nervous system is called a *depressant.* Some depressants, depending upon their intended use and dosage, merely relax a person while others result in sleep, and still others render a person insensitive to pain. The depressants include the narcotics, sedatives, hypnotics, barbiturates, and anesthetics. Table 8–2 summarizes the important depressants.

A *sedative* is prescribed to relieve feelings of anxiety. *Hypnotics* are drugs that induce sleep, but since they are generally slowly eliminated from the body, they make poor anesthetics. The *narcotics* are the most effective analgesics since they can relieve pain without inducing sleep. *Anesthetics* induce sleep and render a person insensitive to pain. Anesthetics may be used locally without inducing sleep or they may be administered generally to induce sleep. The *barbiturates* are a group of drugs drived from barbituric acid, that, when taken in small dosage, act as sedatives, and in a larger dosage induce natural-like sleep.

Paraldehyde and chloral hydrate are two nonbarbiturate hypnotic drugs whose actions on the central nervous system resemble that of alcohol. Chloral hydrate was sometimes used prior to 1900 as "knockout drops" (Mickey Finn) to shanghai sailors to the Orient. When chloral hydrate is used over an extended period of time, physical dependence develops and a withdrawal syndrome will appear when the drug is denied. Paraldehyde has been replaced by the barbiturates. Both chloral hydrate and paraldehyde come under the regulations of the Drug Abuse Control Amendment of 1965.

Methaqualone came into popular use chiefly on the West Coast as a substitute for barbiturates in the early 1970s. It was referred to as "intellectual heroin" because drug abusers thought that it was not addicting as is heroin. Methaqualone was introduced in 1966 (Qualude) by the William H. Rorer Company as a substitute for barbiturates for people who could not tolerate the chemical actions of barbiturates. It is generally prescribed by physicians as a sleeping aid. Although authorities do not agree on the addicting nature of methaqualone, there is general agreement as to a tolerance being developed in some people, especially heavy users. The withdrawal syndrome includes convulsions, gastrointestinal hemorrhaging, and without medical supervision, death is possible.

Barbiturates are chemically composed of barbituric acid, which was synthesized in 1846 by Adolph von Baeyer. The first commercial preparation, Veronal, was developed in 1903 by Emil Fischer and Joseph von Mering which began a flood of barbituric acid preparations over the next few decades: Luminal in 1912, Amytal in 1923, and Nembutal and Seconal in 1930. Although more than 1500

Table 8–2: Summary of Depressants

Name of Drug	Commercial Preparation	Medical Use	Effects	Dependence Potential	Historical Note and Comments
Ethanol	Alcohol	Medicinal Solvent Relaxant	Depresses the central nervous system.	Habituation; alcoholism in some people.	See Chapter 9 for a detailed discussion.
Paraldehyde	Paraldehyde	Substitute for barbiturates for persons allergic to them. Treatment of delirium tremens in alcoholics.	Depressant. Can cause respiratory depression and cardiovascular collapse.	Habituation	Discovered in 1829; first used in medicine in 1882.
Chloral hydrate (trichloroacetaldehyde)	Chloral hydrate, "Mickey Finn" when combined with alcohol.	Sedation and as a hypnotic.	Combined with alcohol results in acute intoxication.	Addiction	Synthesized in 1832 and used in medicine in 1870.
Barbituric Acid (Barbiturates) 1. Aprobarbital 2. Amobarbital 3. Barbital 4. Butabarbital 5. Cyclobarbital 6. Diallybarbituric Acid 7. Heptabarbital 8. Hexethal 9. Pentobarbital 10. Phenobarbital 11. Probarbital 12. Secobarbital 13. Talbutal 14. Thiopental 15. Vinbarbital	1. Alurate 2. Amytal 3. Veronal 4. Butisol 5. Phanodorn 6. Dial 7. Medomin 8. Ortal 9. Nembutal 10. Luminal 11. Ipral 12. Seconal 13. Lotusate 14. Penthothal 15. Delvinol	Sedation and hypnotic 1. long-acting 2. short-acting 3. long-acting 4. short-acting 5. short-acting 6. long-acting 7. short-acting 8. short-acting 9. short-acting 10. long-acting 11. short-acting 12. short-acting 13. short-acting 14. very short-acting 15. short-acting	Produces stupor or sleep. Some act as anticonvulsants.	Addiction	The American Medical Association has asserted that only five or six of the barbiturates are necessary for medical use, although there are more than 50 brands available.

barbiturate preparations have been developed, only about 50 are in general use by the medical profession.

Barbiturates are prescribed for anxiety (sedation), for epilepsy (as an anticonvulsant), to reduce pain, to induce sleep, and as a presurgical anesthetic. Some barbiturate preparations are prescribed for their short-acting and fast-starting pharmocological properties (Nembutal, Seconal, and Delvinal), while others are prescribed for their long-acting and slow-starting properties (Luminal, Veronal and Amytal). Generally, the short-acting barbiturates reach their therapeutic level in about 15 minutes and last for 2–3 hours, while the long-acting reach their therapeutic level in about 1 hour and last from 6–10 hours.

When barbiturates are used excessively and over a prolonged period of time, they produce a tolerance and dependence. The withdrawal syndrome associated with barbiturate dependence is severe and death can result if proper medical attention is absent. Many "suicides" attributed to barbiturate overdose are thought to be the result of *drug automatism,* rather than an attempt at suicide. Drug automatism results from a state of confusion characteristic of barbituric acid. During this period, a person may not be aware of having taken the barbiturate (sleeping pills), or may have lost track of how many pills were taken, resulting in an overdose. Because drug automatism cannot be clinically measured, some medical authorities question its existence, and use it only as a construct to describe the phenomenon of distorted perception.

Tranquilizers

Tranquilizers are a group of depressant drugs that usually do not produce sleep or drowsiness except when taken in large dosage. These drugs are classified as major tranquilizers and minor tranquilizers. The major tranquilizers are sometimes used as an antidepressant. For a more detailed discussion of tranquilizers, see Chapter 3.

The Narcotics

With one exception (cocaine), the narcotics are depressant drugs but because of their specific nature, relatively widespread abuse, and legal restrictions, we are discussing these drugs separate from the other depressants. There are four classes of narcotics: (1) Class A narcotics, which include opium and its derivatives; coca leaves, their alkaloids and derivatives; meperidine, methadone, and other synthetic opiates as established by the Commissioner of Narcotics; (2) Class B narcotics, which includes drugs having relatively little addicting potential including Papaverine, codeine, and others as determined by the Commissioner of Narcotics, (3) Class M narcotics, which includes those drugs that are especially exempt and may be prescribed by a physician without filling out a narcotics order —drugs in this class are considered nonaddicting; (4) Class X narcotics, which includes drugs containing a prescribed minimum amount of narcotic and are nonaddicting as prepared.

The group of drugs that produces sedation in small amounts and coma and death in large amount, causes insensitivity to pain, and results in feelings of euphoria is called narcotics. (See Table 8–3 for a summary of the narcotics: natural, derivatives, and synthetic substitutes.)

Table 8–3: Summary of the Narcotic Drugs

Source	Name of Drug	Medical Use
Opium alkaloids (Natural derivatives)	Morphine sulfate	Analgesic
	Codeine (methylmorphine)	Minor pain, antitussive
Synthetic derivatives	Heroin (diacetylmorphine)	No use in medicine in the United States
	Dihydromorphinone (Dilaudid)	Analgesic, antitussive
	Oxycodone	Analgesic
	Dihydrocodeinone	Analgesic, antitussive
	Dilaudid (hydromorphone)	Analgesic
	Pholocodine	Analgesic
Synthetic substitutes	Meperidine	Analgesic
	Methadone	Analgesic, antitussive, treat morphine or heroin withdrawal and maintenance therapy
	Cyclazocine	Narcotic antagonist, naroctic addiction therapy
	Anileridine	Analgesic
	Alphaprodine	Analgesic

Opium is a milky exudate of the unripe seed pod of the opium poppy *(Papaver somniferum)*. It is harvested by cutting the seed pod and allowing the exudate to form in beads, which are allowed to dry into a brownish, gummy mass. This is called *crude opium*. The medicinal use of opium is recorded in the "Ebers Papyrus" with further allusions to its use in other early civilizations such as Greek, Arabic, and Chinese. Many of the great, early physicians, such as Hippocrates (460–357 B.C.), Galen (129–200 A.D.), and Paracelsus (1493–1541) freely prescribed opium for a number of medical conditions.

The earliest example of the development of a patent medicine containing opium was laudanum concocted by Paracelsus in the early part of the sixteenth century. Thomas Sydenham is also credited with its development, but his compound differed somewhat from Paracelsus' formula. In 1732, Thomas Dover prepared a more powerful concoction, "Dover's Powder," which was prescribed as a cure for gout. These and many other patent medicines were widely used in the United States, especially by middleaged homemakers and, as we have seen, contributed to the first federal legislation, the Harrison Narcotics Act of 1914, placing controls on the use of opiates in patent medicines.

Morphine sulfate was crystallized from opium by Frederick Serturner in 1803. It is the addicting chemical in opium and is about ten times more potent than raw opium. Morphine derived its name after the Greek god of dreams, Morpheus. Since its earliest development, morphine has been widely used as one of the most effective pain relievers and has been used in the treatment of dysentery. Morphine was so extensively used during the American Civil War that many soldiers became addicted to it. As a result, morphine addiction became known as the "soldiers' disease." Since opium addiction was epidemic in Hong Kong during the nineteenth century, morphine was used as a cure, and thousands of Chinese became addicted to morphine. Later, with the synthesis of heroin, morphine addiction was treated with this drug, which in turn created thousands of heroin addicts.

Heroin is the most addicting of the opiates, being approximately three times more potent than morphine. However, its pharmacology in the body is identical to morphine. Heroin was first synthesized by the Bayer Laboratories in 1874 and marketed as a nonaddictive cure for morphine addiction. It was not until 1905 that authorities began to recognize the addicting potentials of heroin. This led to the enactment by the Congress of the Pure Food and Drugs Act of 1906 and eventually to the passage of the Harrison Narcotics Act of 1914. Although the manufacture of heroin in the United States was prohibited in 1924, it was not until 1956 that its possession and use became illegal.

As with the other narcotics, heroin is an excellent analgesic (pain killer). However, its use in medicine has been banned because of its addicting potential and because other, less dangerous drugs are available. In the United States heroin is limited to illegal use. One of the real dangers is that an addict has no way of knowing the *potency* of the heroin purchased on the street. This makes the possibility of an overdose an ever-present danger. In addition, the addict has no way of knowing the *purity* of the drug, which opens the way for the possibility of injecting unknown substances along with the heroin. Other hazards associated with heroin addiction are the possibility of contracting serum hepatitis and tetanus from the use of unclean instruments for injections.

Estimates indicate that the death rate of heroin addicts is approximately double that of the nonaddict population within similar socioeconomic, age, and other demographic factors. The opiates tend to dull the appetite resulting in malnutrition, and to depress the cough reflex resulting in chronic bronchitis. During the early part of the 1970s, there was an outbreak of malaria, primarily in California. This was caused by Vietnam veterans addicted to heroin who shared their syringes with nonveterans. Many of the veterans had contracted malaria in Vietnam. The malaria parasite was thus injected into others.[9] These, along with the other hazards mentioned above, increase the death rate of heroin addicts considerably.

Codeine was first extracted from morphine sulfate in 1832. It is used as an active ingredient in a number of cough medicine preparations. As an analgesic, it is only about one-sixth as potent as morphine. Consequently, its addictive potential is much less than that of morphine or heroin.

Methadone is a synthetic opiate whose pharmacologic properties resemble those of morphine but is slightly more potent. Although methadone is addicting, it is used in maintenance treatment of morphine or heroin addicts. It has the advantage of being administered orally, warding off the craving for heroin or morphine. Methadone is prescribed in daily maintenance doses, which makes the addict more amenable to rehabilitation efforts. While under maintenance, the addict is able to function quite normally, and, most important, is removed from the daily ritual of seeking a heroin supply through illegal channels. However, it continues to be controversial for a number of reasons, with one of the major ones being that some believe this treatment merely substitutes one addicting drug for another. Since methadone maintenance has only been used on a relatively large scale since the early 1970s, much more information is needed to objectively evaluate its effectiveness as a treatment for drug addiction.

In contrast to methadone maintenance, is the use of cyclazocine in the treatment of heroin addicts. *Cyclazocine* is a synthetic substitute for heroin which reduces the pharmocological effects of heroin. It functions in the body as a narcotic antagonist, and although it produces a dependence, withdrawal from cyclazocine produces no further craving for it. The treatment of heroin addiction with cyclazocine consists of two basic steps: (1) the use of cyclazocine to reduce the craving for heroin which results in withdrawal from heroin. Daily injections of cyclazocine obstruct the euphoric action of heroin, which makes the use of heroin meaningless. (2) The final step in treatment with cyclazocine is to withdraw the addict from this drug. Since cyclazocine produces few, if any, of the effects of heroin, withdrawal from it is relatively simple.

In conclusion, the opiates (alkaloids, derivatives, and synthetic substitutes) produce the same basic effects. Dosage and mode of administration, as well as the pharmacologic nature, determine the speed with which the effects are felt. The opiates are addicting, resulting in a build up of tolerance, dependence, and the withdrawal syndrome. The immediate effects include euphoria (with some exceptions), relief of pain, decrease in respiration rate, contraction of the pupils of the eyes, nausea, constipation, decrease in body temperature, and depression of peristaltic contractions.

The Hallucinogens

The hallucinogens occur naturally or are synthesized. According to Ray, "These plants and the psychoactive chemicals they contain are classed as hallucinogens because their distinguishing characteristic, to our society, is the ability to induce bizarre alterations in perception and states of consciousness."[10] Generally, very small amounts of the psychoactive chemical of the hallucinogens are all that is needed to create its psychedelic effects. Specifically, a *psychedelic* is a chemical that is purported to expand the consciousness. Further, it is described as a chemical that creates altered perceptions of reality, illusions, hallucinations, and strange visions. *LSD* (d-lysergic acid diethylamide tartrate 25) is the most potent of the hallucinogens known and is responsible for the creation of the psychedelic subcultures that first attained notoriety during the 1960s. Let's examine some of the chief hallucinogenic drugs being used today.

LSD   The discovery of the hallucinogenic properties of LSD in 1943 by Albert Hofmann began a series of episodes that have had significant impact upon the American and other societies. LSD is a semisynthetic derivative of lysergic acid, an alkaloid found in the fungus *claviceps purpurea*. Hofmann first synthesized this alkaloid in 1938, but it wasn't until about 5 years later that he discovered its hallucinogenic potentials when he accidentally ingested some of it. In 1953, the Sandoz Pharmaceutical Company obtained permission from the Food and Drug Administration to conduct research studies into possible medical uses of LSD. In 1966, the National Institute of Mental Health and the Food and Drug Administration became the sole sponsors of legal distribution of LSD for research purposes.

Because LSD was found to create symptoms of schizophrenia, it was thought that the biochemistry of this mental illness had been found. Early research along these lines consisted partially of some psychiatrists using the drug to mimic schizophrenia so that they could study the illness through personal experiences. Other therapeutic expectations of LSD are in the treatment of alcoholism and reducing pain associated with terminally ill cancer patients. Early enthusiasm about the therapeutic value of LSD has changed to conservative caution as adverse side effects were discovered.

There was a significant decline in the use of LSD beginning in 1967 when researchers reported a possible chromosomal damage in LSD users.[11] However, the chromosomal damage was in leukocytes of persons treated with LSD and not the germ cells. In 1970, these same researchers indicated that their discovery probably did not represent any serious medical problem.[12] Probably "the clearest danger from the use of LSD-type drugs is to borderline psychotic and depressed patients."[13] Other negative results have occurred in people who have been given relatively large amounts of LSD without their knowledge. This is an extremely dangerous practice since the psychological set, the nature of the environment, and the presence of others for support are important influencers of the reactions that take place.

The use of LSD by relatively large numbers of young people had its beginning in 1960 when Timothy Leary began research into the psychedelic effects of psilocybin, using college students as subjects at Harvard University. His research design rapidly deteriorated from controlled scientific procedures to uncontrolled and unscientific use of the drug. As a matter of fact, Leary as the "researcher" used the drug along with his subjects, which eliminated any possibility of objectivity. In 1963, Leary established the International Federation for Internal Freedom (IFIF) for the purpose of conducting research into the psychedelic effects of certain hallucinogens, chiefly LSD and psilocybin. The Federation was short-lived for lack of financial and professional support, but it did serve to arouse curiosity among the young about hallucinogens and to create widespread controversy. The psychedelic era was underway, and Timothy Leary was dismissed from Harvard University.

In 1966, Leary founded the League of Spiritual Discovery based upon the belief that a psychedelic drug could assist one in finding a religious revelation. The credo of the League, coined by Leary, was to "turn on, tune in and drop out" which influenced many young people to use LSD creating a turned on, tuned in, dropped out generation of youth that extended into the early part of the 1970s with Timothy Leary as its guru.

But what is there about the hallucinogens that gives them this mystical power? Since very little significant research on LSD has been conducted since the early part of the 1970s, its specific pharmocodynamics are still unclear. It is believed by some authorities that LSD interferes with the action of serotonin, one of the neurotransmitters. When the serotonin level is lowered, the normal transmission of sensory impulses is interfered with resulting in a disorganization of perception—characteristic of the LSD experience. Although a tolerance for LSD develops, there is no apparent physical dependence. Furthermore, a cross tolerance between LSD, mescaline, and psilocybin appears to exist.

Mescaline   *Mescaline* is the chief psychoactive chemical found in peyote, a small cactus found mainly in Mexico. There are, however, a number of alkaloids in peyote (Laphophora williamsii), first identified in 1886 by Louis Lewin. It was not until 1919 that mescaline was synthesized by Spath.

Historically, peyote has been used in religious ceremonies by Indians in Mexico and Southwestern United States for several centuries. In the United States, the Native American Church (originally called the First-born Church of Christ) was founded in Oklahoma in 1918, and is the only American church that is allowed to use peyote as a part of its religious rituals.

The active ingredient of peyote, mescaline, is contained within the buttons, which are dried slices of the crown of the cactus plant. In sufficient amounts, mescaline results in a disorganized mental state characterized by visual hallucinations, nausea, a rise in blood pressure and an increase in heart action, dilation of the pupils of the eyes, and an elevated body temperature. An overdose may result in respiratory arrest followed by death.

Psilocybin   *Psilocybin,* isolated in 1958 by Albert Hofmann, is the psychoactive ingredient found in the *Psilocybe mexicana* mushroom. It was this mushroom that was ingested by Timothy Leary that resulted in his later psychedelic crusade. The mushroom is used principally in religious ceremonies in Mexico; when ingested, it causes nausea, relaxation, dilation of the pupils of the eyes, and profound alteration of mood and behavior. These symptoms last from 2–5 hours depending upon the dosage and are followed by mental and physical depression.

Other hallucinogens   *DOM* is a synthetic hallucinogen that has achieved some prominence among certain segments of drug abusers. It also became known as *STP* (purportedly after Timothy Leary's serenity, tranquility, and peace). Its pharmacological effects are similar to those of mescaline but its potency is as much as 100 times greater. However, despite its hallucinogenic properties, it has not attained much widespread use among drug abusers.

DMT is a semisynthetic hallucinogen whose effects are rapidly felt when inhaled or injected but last only for about 30 minutes. Because of these characteristics, DMT became known as the *businessman's trip.* During the early part of the 1970s there was some concern that the use of DMT would become a drug of widespread use. To date, however, it is not a widely used drug in comparison to some of the other drugs that are commonly abused.

PCP (phencyclidine), also known as angel dust, became a popular drug during the 1970s. It is a synthetic hallucinogen originally used as a veterinary anesthetic. The effects sought are similar to those of LSD; however, it has been demonstrated to have profound psychological effects on some users, resulting in destructive, aggressive behavior. With the adverse publicity about PCP during the late 1970s, it appears that recreational use of the drug has diminished, although it still remains popular among some segments of the population.

Marijuana

Despite the accumulation over the past 40 years of much scientific knowledge about marijuana, a myriad of nonsense and misinformation continues to cloud the thinking of many people: users, nonusers, professionals, nonprofessionals, legislators, and law enforcement officials. Once the ghosts of marijuana were created, chiefly by Harry J. Anslinger in the 1930s, it became and is still almost impossible to exorcise them from the minds of people. In his powerful position as Commissioner of the Bureau of Narcotics, Anslinger was able to influence legislation and to convince people, even the medical profession, of the crime-provoking nature of marijuana and its direct link to the use of heroin. *Both of these assertions are incorrect and were known to be incorrect at the time they were made.*

In 1944, for example, the *LaGuardia Report* * was published. The research for this report was begun in 1940 by the New York Academy of Medicine at the request of the late New York City Mayor Fiorello LaGuardia. Among its many conclusions were: (1) marijuana does *not* cause a person to become violent or criminal; (2) marijuana does *not* result in any basic changes in a person's personality structure; (3) marijuana *does* adversely affect a person's intellectual ability; (4) marijuana *does* produce a sense of euphoria and well-being; (5) there is *no evidence* that marijuana use results in physical or mental deterioration, and (6) the use of marijuana does *not* lead to morphine or heroin or cocaine addiction.[14] Even though the research was conducted by a prestigious team of experts including internists, psychiatrists, pharmocologists, public health officials, and others, the report created violent criticism from the American Medical Association and was ordered ignored by the Bureau of Narcotics by its director, Harry J. Anslinger.

The near hysterical reaction of the American people to the increased and widespread use of marijuana among youth during the 1960s and 1970s resulted in the establishment of the National Commission on Marijuana and Drug Abuse. This Commission was chaired by Raymond P. Shafer and consisted of thirteen prestigious persons who represented medicine, education, government, and law enforcement. The first of two reports was transmitted to the President of the United States, Richard M. Nixon, on March 22, 1972.

The first report was titled, *Marijuana: A Signal of Misunderstanding.* In the face of great controversy over marijuana use, Shafer attempted to convey in his letter of transmission the message of the kinds of objectivity practiced by the committee. He stated, "Whatever the facts are we have reported them. Wherever the facts have logically led us, we have followed and used them in researching our recommendations. We hope this Report will be a foundation upon which credibility in this area can be restored and upon which a rational policy can be predicated."[15] Former President Nixon rejected, out-of-hand, the findings and recommendations of the prestigious commission.

In 1973, Bedworth and D'Elia wrote, "The significance, timeliness, comprehensiveness, integrity, and objectivity of this report must motivate and lay the foundation for renewed and rational action by the government and people of the United States, and eliminate from the past, the marijuana ghosts that cloud judgment."[16] The recommendations of the Commission (although rejected by the President of the United States), in the judgment of these writers, were insightful, practical, (however profound), and foundational for further research into the

---

*The title of this report was officially, *The Marijuana Problem In the City of New York.*

Table 8–4: Summary of the National Commission of Marijuana and Drug Abuse, 1972

Society	Legislation	Law Enforcement	Research and Treatment	Education
1. Establish a social policy for discouraging the use of marijuana and preventing its heavy use.	1. Amend the federal law allowing personal use, but making it an offense for possession in public.	1. Relieve law enforcement of attempting to enforce a questionable law.	1. Improve statistical reporting.	1. Improve training programs for law enforcement personnel.
2. Deemphasize marijuana as a social drug problem.	2. Casual distribution with little or no remuneration not involving profit should no longer be an offense.	2. Concentrate on the trafficking and crimes against persons and property.	2. Greater cooperation between governmental and private agencies.	2. Public health courses emphasizing the social aspects of drug use should be included in the curricula of training programs for health professionals.
3. Facilitate medical, educational, religious, and parental efforts to reduce irresponsible use.	3. A plea of marijuana intoxication would not be a defense for any criminal act committed.	3. Relieve the courts of the large volumes of marijuana possession cases.	3. Develop better methods for detecting the presence of marijuana in the blood, breath, or urine.	3. The established clearinghouse for Drug Abuse information should be the single agency for disseminating drug information.
4. Remove the criminal stigma.	4. Uniformity of states laws making cultivation, sale, distribution for profit, and possession with intent to sell should remain felonies.	4. Increase surveillance, tighten procedures, and so forth to prevent the influx of drugs and to reduce domestic production and distribution.	4. Improve funding for foreign research.	4. The special Action for Drug Abuse Prevention should be the coordinating body for all federally supported drug education materials and should evaluate all existing materials.
5. Make possible more flexible public responses as new research findings become available.	5. But possession for personal use should no longer be an offense and distribution of small amounts should no longer be an offense. Possession of one ounce or less in public should not be an offense, but subject to seizure. Other recommendations for a uniform states law would set penalties of fines of $100 to $1,000 and minimum jail sentences of from 60—180 days.		5. Increase support of research relative to the value of marijuana in the treatment of disease.	
6. States should redefine marijuana in accord with present knowledge.			6. Promote the use of existing community-based treatment centers.	
7. The voluntary sector of communities should be encouraged to support the Commission's recommendation of discouraging the use of marijuana.				

personal and social hazards (if any) that may be associated with marijuana use. These recommendations are summarized in Table 8–4 for your review and conclusions.

What is this mysteriously controversial drug called marijuana? According to historical records, marijuana has been used as far back as 2000 B.C. However, it was probably introduced into the American society not more than 100 years ago. Approximately one decade following the end of World War II, marijuana became a common household word.

Marijuana (Cannabis sativa) contains a psychoactive chemical called delta-9—tetrahydrocannabinol (THC). THC was first synthesized in 1966; this made it possible to conduct more precise scientific research into its pharmacology in the human body. Prior to this, it was not possible to control dosage from the cannabis plant and results of its reactions on people varied considerably.

We know that THC is metabolized in the liver, but we do not know for certain the specific pharmacodynamics that produce its characteristic psychic changes in a person. These psychic changes appear to follow a particular sequence with experienced users of marijuana. Briefly, these are (1) a feeling of stimulation; (2) a feeling of mild tension and anxiety; (3) a feeling of well-being; (4) tranquility and introspective moods; (5) a feeling of hilarity; and finally, (6) contemplative silence. Other reactions that have been reported include a feeling of giddiness, bizarre hallucinations, visual and spatial distortions, synesthesia (the sensation of "seeing sounds" and "hearing visual stimuli"; this is more pronounced with the use of LSD), and distortion of the passage of time.

A number of adverse reactions to the use of marijuana have been reported; some have been substantiated. These include flashbacks, psychosis (this is probably because the user was already prepsychotic, and does not appear to be likely with a person whose personality is well integrated), and possible chromosomal damage. So-called "potheads" have been identified and it is thought that their compulsive use of marijuana is similar to the alcoholic's compulsion for alcohol. Finally, there has been some evidence linking marijuana use to cancer. However, these and many others need much more research before definitive conclusions can be made.

The Deleriants

Since the deleriants are quite irritating to the mucous membranes, their use as chemicals of abuse has not become widespread. The *deleriants* are volatile substances that are inhaled and include: toluene in some glues, the spot removers, trichloroethane, gasoline, some fluorocarbons (used in some aerosol sprays), benzene, acetone, ether, chloroform, and carbon tetrachloride.

A relatively large number of deaths have been reported resulting chiefly from suffocation and asphyxiation. Some of the chemicals, such as carbon tetrachloride, can damage the liver and kidneys; gasoline can result in lead poisoning, cardiac disturbances, and damage to the bone marrow. The use of aerosols has resulted in some cases of cardiac arrest and there are reports of brain damage from the use of other chemicals.

There are many substances that are abused by large numbers of people. Some of these appear to be generally not extremely harmful, while others have short-term and long-term devastating effects. Some drugs are legal; others are illegal; but the establishment of either of these statuses is not necessarily the result of the harmfulness of the drug. For example, alcohol use is legal while marijuana use in most states is illegal. Many authorities feel that alcohol is much more harmful than marijuana.

In summary, there are certain basic concepts pertaining to drugs that we must understand if we are to grasp the significance of drug use:

1. The potency and effectiveness of a drug are mutually exclusive characteristics. That is, the effectiveness of a drug refers only to its ability to produce a given effect regardless of the dose. Its potency refers only to the amount of the drug needed to produce a given effect.

2. Most drugs, especially those that are psychoactive, act on nerve cells, either their membranes or on the neurotransmitters.

3. Drugs can only enhance or inhibit a cell's functioning. They cannot cause a cell to function in ways not possible without a drug. It is this alteration of functioning that causes changes in people's feelings and perceptions.

4. Drugs are here to stay. It may be safe to assume that drugs become an inherent part of the social fabric once they are used by a significant part of society, and any attempts to remove them forcibly will cause social disruption.

The motivational force for avoiding the harmful use of any drug, tobacco and alcohol included, must be greater than the conscious or unconscious desire or urge to use them. Motivation for using a drug can become more powerful or meaningful to a person when certain psychological, biological, or social conditions are present. For example, a person who is—or feels he/she is—under great stress may be more apt to use a drug if it is available than at a time when no stress is present. Other emotional factors may also precipitate drug use, such as need-feeling to escape, or to enhance a situation.

GLOSSARY

Analgesic: A drug that relieves pain.

Anesthetic: A drug used to induce sleep and to reduce sensitivity to pain.

Addiction: Characterized by physiological tolerance, psychological craving, and the presence of the withdrawal syndrome.

Additive effect: Combining two or more drugs resulting in an effect equal to that of the drugs when taken separately.

Brand name drug: One that is identified by its trade or patent name.

Depressant: A drug that slows down the activity of the central nervous system.

Drug: Any medicinal substance possessing qualities that will aid in diagnosing, treating, curing, or preventing disease, or maintaining health.

Drug abuse: The use of legal drugs in a manner or amount contrary to their intended dosage or purpose, and the use of illegal drugs for the purpose of bringing about a change in feelings, mood, and behavior.

Drug dependence: Habituation or addiction to a drug.

Generic drug: One that is identified by its chemical name.

Habituation: Characterized by a psychological craving for a drug with an absence of the withdrawal syndrome.

Hypnotic: A drug used to induce sleep.

Materia medica: That branch of medical science concerned with the sources, preparation, properties, and uses of the drugs used in preventing, diagnosing, treating, and controlling diseases.

Narcolepsy: A condition of uncontrollable sleepiness.

Narcotics: Drugs that produce sedation in small amounts, coma and death in large amounts, insensitivity to pain, and feelings of euphoria.

Over-the-counter drug: One that can be purchased without a prescription.

Pharmacognosy: The science concerned with the study of the composition, use, and history of drugs derived from plants and animals.

Pharmacology: The science concerned with the nature and action of drugs on biological functions.

Potentiation: The process of combining two or more drugs resulting in an enhanced reaction.

Proprietary drug: The same as the over-the-counter drug.

Psychedelic: A chemical that is supposed to produce an expansion of consciousness.

Psychoactive (psychotropic): A drug that affects the functioning of the central nervous system resulting in distortion of the perceptions of reality.

Sedative: A drug that calms a person without inducing sleep.

Side effect: A reaction of a drug that does not contribute to its intended purpose and may result in complications.

Stimulant: A drug that speeds up the activities of the central nervous system.

Synergist: A drug that, when combined with another, produces effects greater than those when the drugs are taken separately.

Synesthesia: The sensation created from the use of certain drugs that a person "sees sounds" and "hears visual stimuli."

Therapeutics: The science concerned with drugs that have curative potentials.

Tolerance: The adaptation of the body to a drug resulting in the need for a larger dosage to create the desired reaction.

Toxicology: The study of poisons.

Withdrawal syndrome: The combination of physical and psychological symptoms that appear when an addicting drug is denied.

SUMMARY

Drugs are beneficial to humanity but their improper use can result in devastation and death. Drugs are derived from plants, animals, and minerals and are synthesized in the laboratory.

Pharmaceutical industries are concerned with finding and producing drugs that can assist in the diagnosis, treatment, control, and prevention of disease. Several federal laws have been enacted to help to ensure the quality, safety, and effectiveness of drugs available to the consumer. Recently, pharmacists have been allowed to substitute therapeutically equivalent drugs when the physician's prescription so indicates.

Drug abuse has become a major social and personal health problem in the United States. The drugs that are most commonly abused are the stimulants, depressants, hallucinogens, and deleriants. Drug abuse in the United States has resulted in social and political controversies, which, in turn, have produced some social and political action to attempt to alleviate this serious health problem. Essentially, the ultimate solution to drug abuse problems rests with individuals and the ways in which they perceive the use of drugs.

PROBLEMS FOR DISCUSSION

1. Distinguish between drugs, medicines, and chemicals. What is the chief purpose of drugs?
2. Identify the sciences concerned with drugs. Describe the role of each.
3. What controls are placed upon the manufacture and marketing of legal drugs? How do these controls protect and aid the consumer?
4. Distinguish between a generic and brand name drug. What are the chief differences of each?
5. What is meant by therapeutically equivalent?
6. Describe ways in which drugs are valuable in promoting and maintaining health.
7. List the characteristics that constitute drug abuse.
8. Give at least three reasons why authorities believe that drug abuse is one of America's most serious personal and social health problems. Do you agree? Explain.
9. What is meant by the therapeutic level of a drug? What is its significance in treating illnesses?
10. Distinguish between potentiation, synergistic effect, and additive effect.
11. What is drug dependence? Distinguish between habituation and addiction.
12. List the major federal legislation that has been directed toward the control of drugs and their use. How effective have they been? What do you think needs to be done to reduce drug abuse?
13. Do you think there should be a national or international moratorium on the development of new drugs? Support your contention.
14. List the categories in which the major drugs of abuse are classified.
    a. Distinguish between the pharmacological effects of drugs in each category.
    b. Give two examples of drugs in each category.
    c. Describe the extent of harm of each drug listed in "b" based upon personal hazards and disruption to society.
15. Identify the major historical events related to the use and abuse of LSD.
16. The use of marijuana continues to be controversial. Identify the factors associated with the controversy and discuss the truth or fallacy of each.
17. Do you think that the recommendations of the National Commission on Marijuana and Drug Abuse are generally sound? Explain.

REFERENCES

1. *FDA Fact Sheet,* "Medicines: Prescription and Over-the-Counter," U.S. Department of Health, Education, and Welfare; Food and Drug Administration, Washington, Oct., 1966.

2. HECHT, ANNABEL, "Generic Drugs: How Good Are They?," *FDA Consumer,* U.S. Department of Health, Education, and Welfare; Public Health Service; Food and Drug Administration, HEW Publication No. (FDA) 78–3068, Washington.
3. LIPPERT, JOAN L., "The Better Way: Money-Saving News About Prescription Drugs," *Good Housekeeping,* June, 1978, p. 250.
4. ANSEL, HOWARD C., *Introduction to Pharmaceutical Dosage Forms,* 2nd ed. Lea and Febiger, Philadelphia, 1976, p. 10.
5. BEDWORTH, ALBERT E. and JOSEPH A. D'ELIA, *Basics of Drug Education,* Baywood Publishing Company, Farmingdale, N.Y., 1973, p. 130.
6. LARKIN, TIMOTHY J., "Mixing Medicines? Have a Care!" *FDA Consumer,* U.S. Department of Health, Education, and Welfare; Public Health Service; Food and Drug Administration, HEW Publication, No. (FDA) 76–3020, Washington.
7. RAY, OAKLEY S., *Drugs, Society, and Human Behavior,* The C. V. Mosby Company, St. Louis, 1972, pp. 20–21.
8. *HEW NEWS,* U.S. Department of Health, Education, and Welfare; Food and Drug Administration, July 16, 1979.
9. RAY, OAKLEY S., *op. cit.,* p. 195.
10. *Ibid.,* p. 214.
11. IRWIN, S. and J. EGOZCUE, "Chromosomal Abnormalities in Leukocytes From LSD-25 Users," *Science,* 1967, pp. 313–314.
12. ERGOZCUE, J. and S. ERWIN, "LSD-25 Effects on Chromosomes: A Review," *Journal of Psychedelic Drugs,* Vol. 3, No. 1, 1970, p. 11.
13. GIARMAN, NICHOLAS J., "The Pharmacology of LSD," *LSD, Man and Society,* Richard C. DeBald and Russell C. Leaf (eds.), Wesleyan University Press, Middletown, Conn., 1967, p. 156.
14. SALOMON, DANIEL (ed.), *The Marijuana Papers,* The New American Library, New York, 1966, p. 307.
15. SHAFER, RAYMOND P., *Marijuana: A Signal of Misunderstanding,* The New American Library, New York, 1972, (Letter of transmission).
16. BEDWORTH, ALBERT E. and JOSEPH A. D'ELIA, *op. cit.,* p. 160.

9

alcohol, drinking, and your health

ATTITUDES ABOUT ALCOHOL

Historical Foundations

In the early part of the twentieth century, it was reported that alcoholic heredity "the transmission of a special tendency to use spirits . . . is much more common than is supposed. In the line of direct heredity, or those inebriates whose parents or grandparents used spirits to excess, we find that about one in every three cases can be traced to inebriate ancestors." This classic publication of 1915 goes on to state that, "If the father is a moderate drinker, and the mother a nervous, consumptive woman, or one with a weak, nervous organization, inebriety very often follows in the children."[1] We have come a long way from this *erroneous* supposition as we will see in the following discussions.

We actually do not know the beginnings of alcohol use or of its abuse. It probably extends back to prehistoric times and its abuse most likely accompanied its use. For example, DeRopp states that "of all the drugs that affect the mind and emotions it has the longest history. It was known, we can surmise with reasonable certainty, to Neolithic man . . ."[2] The first recorded use of alcohol dates to approximately 3000 B.C. in documents from Mesopotamia.

Attitudes about the use of alcohol have undergone a variety of changes. However, drunkenness has always been frowned upon in nearly every culture and era of time. We find, for example, early records of wine use and its relation to religious rituals. In ancient Egypt, a temple was constructed in honor of the goddess Hathor, the goddess of love and laughter. The temple became known as the place of drunkenness. In this instance we must conclude that excessive use of alcohol was morally acceptable at least within the confines of the temple.

In Athens, *symposia* were held which were social affairs for intellectual discourse. However, the origin of symposia literally means a "drinking party."[3] Although many symposia today retain upon occasion the drinking portion, most are conducted for an interchange of ideas. We also note that many early civilizations were relatively dry and in some instances, excessive drinking was punishable by public beatings. This was true, for instance, in Sparta and during various periods in Rome. Also, in many cultures, drinking by women was strictly forbidden. For example, an ancient law of Romulus provided for the death penalty for women who drank, except on religious feast days when even slaves were allowed to get drunk.[4]

In early America, most of the original settlers, Spanish, Dutch, English, and so forth, "believed that beer and wine had health-giving qualities."[5] Rum was also drunk by early settlers in America, and was widely used during the late 1700s and early 1800s. In 1794, the Whiskey Rebellion, which took place in Pennsylvania, was a protest against an excise tax imposed by the Congress in 1791.

During the American Colonial Period, temperance and prohibition movements were beginning. However, it was not until the early part of the nineteenth century that temperance movements began to pick up momentum. For example, in 1826, the American Society for the Promotion of Temperance was formed in Boston. Soon, similar organizations sprang up all over the nation, and in 1833, the American Society for the Promotion of Temperance called a convention in Philadelphia. At this convention the United States Temperance Union was formed. The temperance and prohibition movement gained popularity through the remainder of the nineteenth century and the early part of the twentieth century until the ratification of the 18th Amendment to the United States Constitution in 1919. The 18th Amendment was passed by both houses of Congress in 1917 and became effective on January 16, 1920.

By 1919, 34 states had enacted legislation prohibiting the sale of alcoholic beverages. The obvious purpose was to reduce the incidence of alcohol abuse. However, although nearly two-thirds of the American population lived in areas where prohibition was in force and over 104,400 licensed bars were closed, there was a *16 percent increase* in per capita consumption of distilled beverages— "to a level higher than it had been for over 45 years!"[6]

All experiments with legislative attempts at curbing the use of alcohol, beginning with the first national legislation in England in 1327 which limited the number of places where liquor could be sold, have failed. This failure was most exemplified by the 18th Amendment to the United States Constitution. So many Americans were outraged by this invasion upon their personal freedom and liberty to choose that many people who had never drank before did at this time. In addition, thousands of people began to make their own wine and beer. Many Americans openly defied the law, which was one that was impossible for many to respect, and enforcement of it was all but impossible. With this experience behind us, it is clear that responsible drinking is in the hands of each person, not some external group or government agent.

Facts and Myths About Alcohol

Despite the volumes of accurate information available about alcohol, many misconceptions that have evolved over the years persist today. Some have their roots in humanity's early experiences with alcohol when conclusions were drawn from unscientific findings, while others are associated with early religious or other beliefs, and still others evolved from medical beliefs of earlier centuries. The use of alcohol, for example, was an important factor in the settling of America. It was thought by some to provide strength for the hardship that had to be endured; it was used as a medicine for the common cold, snakebite, and other ailments, and it was used to endure the cold of the winter months.

The list of myths and truths provided in Table 9–1 contains many of the common ones. Actually, the kinds of inaccurate information about alcohol that can be found in American society is inexhaustible, and this list merely illustrates their scope.

THE NATURE OF ALCOHOL

Before we can appreciate fully the impact of alcohol abuse and alcoholism upon the American society, it is necessary for us to understand some of the fundamental factors related to the nature of alcohol, its chemical composition, pharmacodynamics, and relation to human health. We know, for example, that:

Table 9-1: Scope of Myths About Alcohol

Classification	Myth	Truth
Medical Use Myths	1. Alcohol will cure a cold.	We know of no cure for the common cold. Alcohol may help to relieve some of the symptoms of a cold because of its analgesic effects. The common cold will run its course, about 7 days, in spite of the drugs we take.
	2. Alcohol will cure snakebite.	Alcohol tends to increase circulation and causes dilation of the peripheral blood vessels. This will hasten the distribution of snake venom to the vital organs resulting in cardiac or pulmonary paralysis and possibly death. Alcohol should never be taken for snakebite.
	3. Alcohol increases body temperature and is, therefore, good to take in cold weather to keep the body warm.	Alcohol actually lowers body temperature. This results from dilation of the peripheral blood vessels and a loss of body heat through the skin. There may be a feeling of warmth that gives the false impression of a rise in body temperature.
	4. Wine is good for the blood.	This myth appears to extend back in history to very early civilizations when wine was used in religious ceremonies and at almost all gatherings. Wine was also drunk as a substitute for water. Whatever the origin, wine is no more beneficial to the blood than plain water.
	5. Whiskey will cure shock.	Since one of the physiological reactions to shock is a lowered body temperature, and the first aid measure is to keep the body warm, and since alcohol lowers body temperature, it should never be given for shock. Alcohol tends to increase the symptoms of shock.
Physiological Effects Myths	1. One's efficiency improves after a few drinks.	Very small amounts of alcohol adversely affect efficiency. One may think his/her efficiency has improved, but scientific research shows reaction time is greatly influenced by alcohol. For example, *professional drivers'* ability to drive diminishes significantly with alcohol blood levels as low as 0.03 percent— approximately one martini.
	2. Alcohol is a stimulant.	Alcohol has the same effect upon the central nervous system as other anesthetics such as ether. Alcohol is a depressant.
	3. Alcohol is an aphrodisiac since it stimulates sexual desire.	Alcohol releases one's sexual inhibition, which may increase the desire for sexual activity. However, it interferes with performance.
	4. Mixing drinks makes one drunk faster and/or will result in a hangover.	The blood level of alcohol is what causes drunkenness. And it doesn't matter in what form it is drunk. Alcohol also causes a hangover. Mixing drinks has no relation to either drunkenness or a hangover.
	5. Taking vitamin C before going to bed after drinking will prevent a hangover.	There is no evidence that anything will prevent a hangover except avoiding heavy drinking.

Table 9-1: (Continued)

Classification	Myth	Truth
Physiological Effects Myths (continued)	6. Alcohol makes one more intelligent and witty.	Alcohol affects judgment. One may think he/she is more intelligent and clever but the opposite is really true.
	7. Black coffee will sober a person up.	There is no relation between coffee and sobriety. The only thing that can sober one up is to stop drinking.
Alcoholism Myths	1. Alcoholism is inherited.	The relationship between heredity and alcoholism is still unclear. There may be a predisposition present in some people but most authorities agree that alcohol intake is the basic cause of alcoholism.
	2. It is a sign of masculinity to be able to hold your liquor.	"Holding your liquor" can be a danger signal. The body is building a tolerance for alcohol, which is an early sign of dependence.
	3. Most alcoholics are Skid Row bums.	It is estimated that only 3—5 percent of alcoholics are Skid Row bums; the remaining 95—98 percent are people in all walks of life. Many hold prominent positions in the community.
	4. Alcoholics are weak-willed.	Alcoholics are sick people. Willpower has nothing to do with alcoholism.
	5. Alcoholism is an illness of adults only.	Alcoholics can be found in all age groups including the very young. The highest incidence is among men in their twenties. The incidence is increasing among teenagers.
	6. Alcohol is simply a beverage and like other beverages is not associated with addiction.	Alcohol is a drug and like many others can be addicting to some people.

- alcohol abuse and alcoholism continues to rise in the United States;
- more adolescents are using alcohol than ever before;
- generally, there is widespread ignorance about alcohol;
- alcohol abuse and alcoholism is a multibillion dollar problem;
- alcohol excesses are associated with many human illnesses;
- more than 70 percent of the adult population uses alcohol;
- there is still much to be learned about intoxication and alcoholism;
- alcoholism can be successfully treated;
- there is a need for a national policy on responsible drinking;
- alcohol abuse and alcoholism is a major problem for American industry.

Kinds of Alcohol

Metheglin (mead), a fermented alcoholic drink made from water, honey, malt, and yeast, and usually containing spices, was probably the first form of an alcoholic beverage used by people. There is some evidence that it was used by people during the Paleolithic Age (Stone Age). Over the centuries, other forms of alcoholic beverages were made chiefly in the form of wines. These beverages are produced by a process known as *fermentation*. Alcohol is the end product of the action of yeast cells on the sugar (glucose) of the fruit and water. This form of alcohol is ethyl, also referred to as beverage alcohol, with a chemical formula of C_2H_5OH.

The alcoholic content of naturally fermented wines will reach a level of approximately 15 percent. The yeast cells cannot continue to live in this alcoholic environment and they die, stopping the fermentation process. However, since alcohol vaporizes at a much lower temperature than water ($172.5°F$ or $78°C$), it is a simple process to separate the alcohol from the water. It merely requires the heating of the wine to the vaporizing temperature of alcohol and condensing the alcohol by transmitting the vapor through a cooling tube. This is *distilling*. The result is pure or nearly pure alcohol, sometimes called *spirits*. Distilled or hard alcoholic beverages were produced around 800 A.D. in Arabia.[7] The alcohol content in distilled beverages is never full strength. The percentage of alcohol is measured, in the United States, in proof. The *proof* of gin, whiskey, vodka, and others is twice the alcoholic content. A gin, for example of 90 proof is 45 percent alcohol. Some countries do not use the proof as a measure of alcoholic content, but rather they use a degrees percent. For instance, absolute alcohol would be stated as $100°$ which is 100 percent alcohol.

Alcohols are found in a variety of forms. All of them are poisonous to the human body, but some are more devastating than others requiring very small amounts to result in damage to organs or death. Some of the common types of alcohol (besides ethyl) are *amyl* ($C_5H\ OH$), *butyl* ($C_4Hg\ OH$), *methyl* ($CH_3\ OH$), and *propyl* (C_5H_7OH). Only ethyl alcohol is fit for human consumption, but when consumed in large quantities, it too can be very devastating.

Ethyl alcohol that has been made unfit for human consumption is called *denatured alcohol*. This is achieved by the addition of one-ninth of its volume with methyl alcohol (wood alcohol) and a small amount of benzene. These chemical additions cannot be readily separated from the ethyl alcohol to make it fit once again as a beverage.

Pharmacodynamics of Alcohol

Ethyl alcohol is provided in a variety of beverage forms including beer, wine, whiskey, gin, and vodka. Wines are made through the fermentation process, beer through brewing, and the distilled beverages through distillation of malted grains. The quantity of alcohol, usually measured in percentage, for each of these beverages ranges from about 5 percent for beer to 50 percent for the distilled beverages. Table 9–2 provides the alcohol content for many commonly used beverages.

Ethyl alcohol, also called ethanol, dulls nervous impulses because of its sedative action on the central nervous system. Contrary to popular belief, alcohol

Table 9–2: Comparison of Alcohol Content of Common Beverages

Alcoholic Beverage	Percent of Alcohol by Volume	Size of Serving in Ounces	Quantity of Alcohol in Ounces*	Manufacturing Source
Beer	4–6	12	0.48–0.72	Fermentation of malted barley
Ale	6–8	12	0.72–0.96	Fermentation of malted barley
Wine (Natural)	9–12	5	0.45–0.69	Fermentation of fruit juices, mainly grape
Wine (Fortified)	20	5	1.00	Addition of spirits of alcohol to natural wines
Whiskey, gin, brandy, vodka	40–50	1	0.40–0.50	Fermentation of malted grains plus distillation
Cocktails				
Dry martini	40–50	3	1.20–1.50	Made with dry gin and a very small quantity of vermouth
Manhattan	40–50	3	0.77–0.92	Made with whiskey of 40 or 50 percent plus sweet vermouth of 18 percent
Highball	40–50	7	0.60–0.75	Made with 1.50 ounces of whiskey and 5.50 ounces of nonalcoholic mix

* Approximately 0.5 ounce of absolute alcohol is the amount that the body can oxidize in 1 hour.

is a depressant, not a stimulant. Because alcohol does not have to be digested, it is readily absorbed into the blood stream through the stomach lining and wall of the small intestine. The speed with which it is absorbed depends upon the contents of the stomach, how rapidly it is ingested, and how much the alcohol has been diluted with drink mix. Alcohol diluted with carbonated water, however, is absorbed more rapidly than that which is undiluted. The more rapidly alcohol is absorbed into the blood stream, the greater its sedative effects on the central nervous system. The effects of alcohol are increased as the blood alcohol percentage increases.

Since only a small amount of alcohol, up to about 15 percent, is eliminated through the skin (sweat), urine, and breath, the remainder must be oxidized by the liver. This means that the alcohol continues to be circulated by the blood until it is oxidized or eliminated. The alcohol that is absorbed is highly diluted by the blood and other body fluids, never reaching more than a fraction of 1 percent.

As the alcohol reaches the brain it affects the higher centers—the cerebrum—first, resulting in a lowering of inhibitions, euphoria, talkativeness, and so on. As the blood alcohol level rises, other centers of the brain are sedated until the inner brain is affected, resulting in stupor and unconsciousness. If sufficient quantities of alcohol have been ingested rapidly before unconsciousness or vomiting occurs, the blood alcohol level may continue to rise until the respiratory centers in the medulla are sedated resulting in death. This will occur when the blood alcohol level reaches 0.50 percent or more. Table 9–3 summarizes the effects on the central nervous system for selected blood alcohol levels.

The faster a person drinks, the faster the blood alcohol level will rise. If one drinks more than one-half ounce of absolute alcohol per hour, the alcohol will have a sedative effect on the central nervous system. This is because the body

233

Table 9–3: Effects of Blood Alcohol Levels on the Central Nervous System

Percentage of Blood Alcohol	Number of Servings	Area of the Brain Affected	Behavioral Response
0.00—0.05	0—2	Frontal lobe of the cerebrum	Slight to no response. The person is functionally sober.
0.06—0.10	2—3	Frontal lobe of the cerebrum	Reaction is slowed, lowered inhibitions, feelings of well-being and euphoria, judgment lowered, talkativeness. The person is high.
0.11—0.20	4—7	Parietal lobe of the cerebrum	Coordination is affected; slurred speech. The person is under the influence to being legally drunk.
0.20—0.30	7—10	Occipital lobe of the cerebrum	Vision is affected, depth and motion perception is impaired. The person is legally drunk.
0.15—0.35	5—12	Cerebellum	Equilibrium affected; staggering. The person is legally drunk.
0.25—0.40	9—14	Inner brain (diencephalon)	The person exhibits apathy. Surface blood vessels are dilated. A state of stupor and finally coma results. The person is dead drunk.
0.40—0.50	14—17	Medulla	Respiration depressed, subnormal body temperature. Death may result.

is capable of oxidizing only about one-half ounce of alcohol per hour. Generally, one serving of an alcoholic beverage, if absorbed immediately into the blood stream, will be equivalent to a blood alcohol level of about 0.03 percent. It can readily be seen that approximately five to six servings can result in legal intoxication (a blood alcohol level of 0.15 percent).

SOCIAL AND POLITICAL IMPLICATIONS OF ALCOHOL

Economics of Alcohol Use

It has been conservatively estimated that the misuse and abuse of alcohol results in an annual loss to the American society of over $26 billion. This loss is in terms of lost production (about $10 billion), health and medical expenditures (about $8 billion), motor vehicle accidents (about $7 billion), criminal acts (about $1 billion) and social welfare (about $0.5 billion).[8] The alcohol industry contributes to our economy approximately $23 billion each year in the form of salaries, goods, and services, and local, state, and federal taxes.

Productivity The estimate of loss of production and services is based upon the reduced productivity of male workers who have alcohol-related problems. It does not take into account the loss of female productivity. Another weakness in this estimate is that it is based only upon a comparison of incomes between families whose *male* head of the household is a problem drinker with *male* heads of families with no alcohol-related problems. Obviously, these figures are probably much lower than the actual production loss cost to industry and society. For example, we don't know the actual numbers of alcoholic women in the United States, but estimates run as high as 4.5 million, nearly one half the total estimated numbers of alcoholics.

Medical costs   In addition to loss of productivity, the medical costs for treating alcohol-related health problems is estimated at more than 12 percent of the annual health care costs in the United States. Most of this health care cost is for hospital expenditures, about 75 percent. About 12 percent is for physicians' fees, 4 percent for drugs, and about 9 percent for administration and facilities construction.

Motor vehicle accidents   More than half the motor vehicle fatalities (28,000), are alcohol-related. This is especially significant when viewed from the standpoint that the alcoholic and problem drinkers constitute only about 10 percent of the driving population and yet account for about two-thirds of the alcohol-related motor vehicle deaths. The remaining one-third of motor vehicle fatalities involves social drinkers and young drivers who drink.[9] (See Figure 9–1.)

Figure 9-1a & b:

Risks of Drinking and Driving

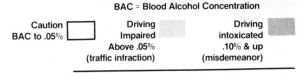

Body Weight	Drinks (Two Hour Period) 1 1/2 ozs. 80° Whiskey or 12 ozs. Beer
100	1 2 3 4 5 6 7 8 9 10 11 12
120	1 2 3 4 5 6 7 8 9 10 11 12
140	1 2 3 4 5 6 7 8 9 10 11 12
160	1 2 3 4 5 6 7 8 9 10 11 12
180	1 2 3 4 5 6 7 8 9 10 11 12
200	1 2 3 4 5 6 7 8 9 10 11 12
220	1 2 3 4 5 6 7 8 9 10 11 12
240	1 2 3 4 5 6 7 8 9 10 11 12

a

BAC = Blood Alcohol Concentration

Caution BAC to .05%	Driving Impaired Above .05% (traffic infraction)	Driving intoxicated .10% & up (misdemeanor)

How Much is Too Much?

Your chances of an accident increase

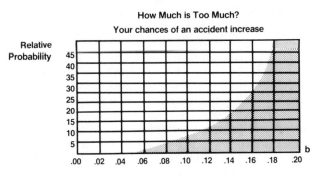

b

Source:
New York State Department of Motor Vehicles. Division of Safety Program Coordination. Albany. N.Y.

Criminal Behavior Irresponsible use of alcohol is significantly associated with such crimes as homicide, beatings, stabbings, shootings, sex crimes against children, suicides, deaths by fire, poisonings, drownings, and family assaults. Alcohol use is associated with at least 55 percent of all arrests that are made each year in the United States for all reasons. However, it is important to note that alcohol is *not* necessarily a *cause* of crimes. As the National Commission on Causes and Prevention of Violence has stated, "No drug, narcotic, or alcoholic beverage presently known will, by itself, lead to violence. Nevertheless, these substances may, through misuse or abuse, facilitate behavior which may result in violence to persons or property."[10]

Alcohol and Politics

In 1974, Morris E. Chafetz, Director of the National Institute on Alcohol Abuse and Alcoholism stated that "only 3½ years have passed since the Nation formally recognized alcoholism as a public health problem."[11] This recognition was exemplified by the establishment of the National Institute on Alcohol Abuse and Alcoholism within the structure of the National Institute of Mental Health in 1970. Later (1973) this became part of the newly created Alcoholism, Drug Abuse, and Mental Health Administration.

The purposes of the National Institute on Alcohol Abuse and Alcoholism were:

1. to develop and conduct broad programs to advance research on the nature of alcoholism;
2. to develop treatment and rehabilitation services for alcoholics;
3. to prevent alcohol abuse and alcoholism;
4. to provide grants to institutions to study the biological, behavioral, and sociocultural aspects of alcoholism.

As a result of the passage of the Comprehensive Alcohol Abuse and Alcoholism Prevention, Treatment, and Rehabilitation Act of 1970, a task force was established to study the problems associated with alcohol abuse and alcoholism. On February 18, 1972 the first report of the task force, *Alcohol and Health,* was issued. Although the report was reasonably complete and described numerous aspects of the alcohol abuse and alcoholism problems in American society, no recommendations for legislative action were given.[12] Some of the findings of this report are: (1) alcohol is the most abused drug in the United States and can impair health; (2) the abuse of alcohol can lead to alcoholism; (3) alcoholism is not a crime; it is an illness or disease and, therefore. the criminal law is not an appropriate device for preventing or controlling it.[13]

In June, 1974, the Task Force on Alcohol and Health issued its second report. In an introductory statement, the Task Force concluded that "most Americans drink. Drinking is learned mostly at home or from adolescent peers. Being a drinker—rather than an abstainer—is thus an American norm. But there is no universal American drinking pattern, and no common American attitude toward alcoholic beverages."[14] New findings were described in this second report. Probably one of the most important one was that heavy drinking during pregnancy can adversely affect the offspring of alcoholic mothers. When this occurs, it is called the *fetal alcohol syndrome.* A second important disclosure was that the proportion of American youth who drink has been increasing.

Unlike the first report, this one presented several rather profound recommendations. The one recommendation that has received positive action in some states is efforts to decriminalize public intoxication and alcoholism. Instead, provision for community care is being made.

Although the accessibility and quality of alcoholism treatment services are improving, a serious deficit of such services remains, and only a small portion of alcoholic people are receiving the care they require. Treatment programs supported by business and industry can be especially effective in earlier identification of employees with alcohol problems, and these programs report the highest rates of recovery.[15]

In June, 1978, the third report was issued. This report verified and expanded upon the findings in the first two reports. Special attention was given to an understanding of alcoholism and the complex relationships to physiological, psychological, cultural, and economic factors. It also emphasized that 11 percent of the 1.9 million deaths each year are alcohol related. The report stated that, "Although most people who drink do so without any noticeable detrimental effects, there are 10 million Americans whose excessive drinking endangers their own health, the happiness of their families, and the well-being of their fellow citizens."[16]

THE EFFECTS OF ALCOHOL ON THE BODY

Immediate Effects

Of all of the alcohols known, ethyl is the only one seemingly agreeable enough to the human body that it can be used as a beverage. Archeological records attest to the use of alcohol as an integral part of the diets of preliterate peoples. Because of the crude methods of fermentation, many of the nutrients of the fruits, grains, and even milk from which the wines were made remained. These undoubtedly added to the nutrient value of the beverage. However, today, little of these nutrients remain in the beers and wines and none is left in distilled beverages. Still, alcohol does provide one food value in the form of calories, which is an immediate source of heat and energy for the body. One fluid ounce of 100 proof distilled spirits yields 100 calories of heat energy.

Once ingested, alcohol is absorbed into the blood stream and carried to the liver to be metabolized. The enzyme *alcohol dehydrogenase* in the liver acts upon the alcohol, oxidizing it, resulting in the release of energy, carbon dioxide, and oxygen.

Small amounts of ingested alcohol tend to provide most people with feelings of pleasure and a release from fears, anxiety, and other emotional tensions. However, for some people, the same quantity of alcohol may result in increased anxiety, suspicion, distrust, confusion, disorientation, and hostility. The reason why many people drink is to achieve the pleasant psychological effects. As long as one does not drink quantities greater than can be oxidized and eliminated by the body, intoxication will not result. Intoxication occurs only when the alcohol blood level rises sufficiently to affect certain areas of the brain as described earlier.

Excessive Drinking

The drinking of alcohol in moderate amounts does not appear to be damaging to the body or central nervous system. Even excessive drinking on periodic occasions which results in drunkenness probably does not result in permanent damage to organs. One may, however, experience a hangover from such excessive drinking episodes. The symptoms of a hangover will vary somewhat from person to person and even at different occasions for the same person, but the general symptoms include headache, upset stomach, vomiting, thirst, and general weakness. Once the alcohol has been oxidized and eliminated from the body, these symptoms generally begin to disappear within a few hours. All the home cures for hangover, such as ingestion of vitamins, black coffee, raw eggs, milk, hot (or cold) shower, and so forth, have no truth in fact. The temporary damage to the body resulting from excessive intakes of alcohol will usually be repaired. Probably the best "cure" for a hangover is bed rest, fluids, and the ingestion of solid foods as soon as they can be tolerated.

Chronic, excessive alcohol consumption, however, affects the nervous system's sensitivity to the alcohol. As a result larger amounts of alcohol must be ingested to produce the same effects. This central nervous system adaptation is called *tolerance* and is an indication that the person is developing a dependence on alcohol.

There are several specific kinds of tolerance. *Acute tolerance* is characterized by a rapid adaptation to large quantities of alcohol over a very short period of time. *High tolerance* is characterized by the ability for the person to adapt to excessive quantities of alcohol without the usual effects. When, after several years of excessive chronic drinking, the person experiences intoxication with the ingestion of relatively small amounts of alcohol, it is called *loss of alcohol tolerance*. *Psychological alcohol tolerance* is characterized by an experienced drinker recognizing the symptoms of intoxication and consciously controlling them. It is thought by many authorities that high tolerance is the prealcoholic or early alcoholic stage, while loss of tolerance is the stage of alcoholism.

Diseases Associated With Alcohol Abuse

Excessive drinking and alcoholism have been implicated as primary or related causal factors in a number of pathological conditions. These are classified as gastrointestinal, cardiac, skin, neurologic, muscle, blood, nutrition, metabolic, and cancer. Among the most serious diseases associated with excessive alcohol consumption (alcoholism) are the *neurologic or encephalopathies*. The most important neurologic disorders are Korsakoff's psychosis, Wernicke's syndrome, and delerium tremens.

Korsakoff's psychosis is characterized by disorientation, failure of memory, and substituting imagined episodes for the loss of memory. It was first described by S. S. Korsakoff in 1887 and is apparently caused by a combination of excessive alcohol intake over a long period of time and a deficiency of niacin. Symptoms of neuropathy associated with Korsakoff's syndrome include impairment of reflex actions such as the ankle and knee jerk, and in later stages, loss of sensation to pain, progressive muscular weakness, and difficulty in walking.

Wernicke's syndrome was first described in 1881 by Carl Wernicke. The symptoms include eye muscle paralysis, clouding of consciousness, poor coordination, and indifference. It is associated with abnormal metabolic action in cells, chronic alcohol use, and a severe deficiency of thiamin. Wernicke's syndrome responds well to prompt treatment with thiamine and alcohol abstinence.

Delirium tremens (or the DTs) was first named by Dr. Thomas Sutton in 1813. This condition occurs in about 5 percent of chronic drinkers with symptoms appearing about 48 hours after total alcohol abstinence. Delirium tremens is sometimes referred to as the alcohol withdrawal syndrome and is characterized by nausea, vomiting, the shakes, weakness, hallucinations, and possibly collapse. These symptoms may last from 2–6 days and stop rather abruptly. Delirium tremens may result in death unless promptly treated.

Somewhat associated with delirium tremens is *alcoholic hallucinosis.* Its chief symptom is auditory hallucinations being manifest by some chronic alcoholics. It is distinguishable from delirium tremens in that it is a more chronic condition but without the disorientation and panic associated with the DTs.

Most of the chronic and progressive diseases are largely due to nutritional deficiencies and defects that usually accompany alcoholism as well as the direct effects of the alcohol itself. A noteworthy example are the conditions affecting the liver—namely, fatty liver, alcoholic hepatitis, and cirrhosis.

Fatty liver is the result of the liver metabolizing alcohol instead of fat. When alcohol is oxidized in the liver, there is a release of excess amounts of hydrogen. The cells make use of this hydrogen instead of oxidizing the fatty acids. Since the fat is not oxidized it is deposited in the liver. However, fatty liver is reversible, once alcohol abuse is terminated.

Alcoholic hepatitis usually does not occur until after several years of excessive alcohol abuse. This condition is a forerunner of cirrhosis, providing that hepatic failure does not occur first. Alcoholic hepatitis is an inflammatory liver disorder characterized by fever, abdominal pain, and jaundice. It usually subsides if alcohol intake is discontinued.

Cirrhosis of the liver is potentially fatal and always disabling to some degree. It is estimated that approximately 10 percent of alcoholics suffer from cirrhosis. Complications such as hemorrhage and cancer are always a threat. Liver cancer may result even after years of total abstinence from alcohol. Some authorities feel that liver disease is one of the most serious consequences of alcohol abuse.

Other diseases associated with alcohol abuse are summarized in Table 9–4. Some of these are due directly to the effects of alcohol while others are related to nutritional consequences.

Table 9–4: Diseases Associated with Alcohol Abuse

Disease	Characteristics
Cancers	There is a strong relationship between alcohol abuse and cancers of the hypopharynx, larynx, esophagus, oral cavity, and tongue.
Alcohol cardiomyopathy	Occurs mainly in men who have a long history of alcohol abuse. It is characterized by either a slow or sudden onset of left- and right-sided congestive heart failure. Symptoms are a large heart, distended neck veins, narrow pulse pressure, elevated diastolic blood pressure, and peripheral edema.
Liver disease	Progressively manifested as fatty liver, alcoholic hepatitis, and cirrhosis. Cirrhosis is characterized by damaged tissue replaced by scar tissue. It occurs 8 to 10 times more frequently in alcoholics then nonalcoholics.
Vitamin deficiency diseases	
1. Beriberi	A disease of the central nervous system and of the circulatory system. Symptoms include weakness, enlarged heart, irritability, poor memory, abdominal complaints, and constipation. Because circulation is affected, edema results. Caused by a deficiency of thiamine.
2. Pellagra	This is a disease characterized by mental, neurologic, cutaneous, mucous membrane, and gastrointestinal symptoms. It is caused by a severe and prolonged deficiency of niacin.
Delirium tremens	This is frequently manifested as alcohol withdrawal syndrome. Usually occurs after 10–20 years of excessive drinking and 48–72 hours following abstinence. The syndrome was named by Thomas Sutton in 1813. The symptoms include nausea, vomiting, shakes, weakness, hallucinations, and collapse. As with most withdrawal syndromes, the symptoms are self-limiting, usually subsiding within 2–6 days after the onset. The symptoms disappear abruptly if death does not occur, which is likely in about 15 percent of the cases. This is also called Saunders/Sutton syndrome.
Korsakoff's psychosis	This was first described by S. S. Korsakoff in 1887. It is characterized by loss of memory, disorientation, sudden delirium, or insidious stupor. It is frequently accompanied by peripheral neuropathy. This disease is more common in women than men. Recovery, if it occurs, usually results in 6–8 weeks with only slight impairment of memory.
Wernicke's syndrome	This is characterized by abnormal cell metabolism as a result of chronic alcoholism and severe deficiency of thiamin. It is frequently associated with polyneuropathy. The areas that become pathological are usually the paramedian and periventricular nuclei of the thalamus and hypothalamus.
Wet brain	Symptoms include coma, delirium, purposeless hand movements. It is an edematous condition of the brain. The prognosis is poor.
Marchiafava's syndrome	First described by Marchiafava and Bignami in 1897. It is characterized by degeneration of the corpus callosum. It probably has a nutritional basis associated with excessive alcohol intake over a long period of time.
Alcoholic hallucinosis	This is also known as acute hallucinosis. Since the hallucinations are usually accusatory and threatening, the person may attempt suicide as a result of panic. Sometimes, schizophrenia remains following recovery.

ALCOHOLISM

What Is Alcholism?

Unlike many of the diseases afflicting people, alcoholism is not clearly defined. There is a lack of agreement as to its cause, symptoms, and other characteristics, and conflict among authorities relative to its treatment. Probably one of the first attempts at defining and characterizing alcoholism was in 1849 when Magnus Huss gave the name *alcoholismus chronicus* to a condition associated with the chronic use of alcohol. He recognized that a group of symptoms, especially those found in alterations of the nervous system, resulted from drinking excessive quantities of alcohol over a long period of time.

Alcoholism generally develops slowly and insidiously; it is progressive, until the alcoholic is incapacitated by both the alcohol and the physiological damage that results from many years, usually, of excessive alcohol intake.

In the 1940s, E. M. Jellinek adopted the term "alcoholism with complication" to replace the one used by Huss. Jellinek went further to establish a classification of alcoholism as follows:

- *Alpha alcoholism,* characterized by the person drinking amounts beyond the social norms resulting in an interference with personal relations. The purpose of drinking is based upon the psychological need for relief from emotional tension with no further dependence or body damage.
- *Beta alcoholism,* characterized by excessive intake of alcohol sufficiently to cause polyneuritis, gastritis, and cirrhosis of the liver, but without dependence or the appearance of the withdrawal syndrome.
- *Delta alcoholism,* characterized by excessive drinking, increased tolerance, withdrawal symptoms, craving, but with the ability to limit the amount within social standards while drinking.
- *Epsilon alcoholism,* characterized chiefly by periods of extreme excessive intake alternating with long periods of abstinence. This has also been termed *dipsomania.*
- *Gamma alcoholism,* characterized by excessive drinking, development of tolerance, withdrawal symptoms, craving, and inability to stop drinking once it has begun. (This is the stereotyped alcoholic that most people associate with alcoholism).[17]

Briefly, then, alcoholism is a disease of some drinkers that is manifested in a variety of ways depending upon their genetic, psychological, and biological qualities. It has little relationship to the form in which alcohol is drunk or the amount that is drunk or when it is drunk. Alcoholism is related to the way in which the person responds to drinking and the way in which alcohol affects the behavior of the drinker. Alcoholism is a true addiction in terms of the person's inability to control whether to drink and how much, the development of tolerance (psychological and physiological), and the appearance of withdrawal symptoms when alcohol levels in the body are reduced or eliminated. Alcoholism is more closely related to why a person drinks than to the quantities of intake.

The first task force report on alcoholism stated: "The causes of alcoholism are unknown, although the number of theories that have been advanced are as numerous as the professions and scientific disciplines concerned with the problem."[18] These theories can generally be placed into three categories: physiological, psychological, and sociocultural.

The *physiological theories* include the genetotrophic, genetic, and endocrine theories. The *genetotrophic theory,* first suggested by R. J. Williams, basically combines a genetic trait and a nutritional deficiency. Essentially, this theory advances the concept that some people inherit an abnormal need for some vitamins. Since a normal diet cannot supply these—and if the person drinks alcohol—an abnormal craving for alcohol becomes established manifested as alcoholism.

The *genetic theory* advances the concept that alcoholism is the result of heredity. Since alcoholism appears to run in families, it has been suggested that some individuals inherit a predisposition or susceptibility to the adverse effects of alcohol ingestion. There is some evidence, for example, that there is an association between color blindness and cirrhosis of the liver, and between color blindness and alcoholism. Studies to explain why alcoholism seems to run in families are inconclusive. It is not known what effect of being exposed to alcoholic parents (environment) has on future development of alcoholism of the children. So far, studies of possible genetic basis for alcoholism are unsatisfactory. However, "the possibility that humans may inherit a predisposition for alcoholism or an immunity to it . . . has not been ruled out."[19]

The *endocrine theory* suggests that alcoholism may be caused by a dysfunction of the endocrine system. However, studies along these lines have not demonstrated a relationship between hypohormonal concentration and alcoholism. It is thought by some that the endocrine dysfunction may be the result of alcoholism rather than its cause.

The *psychological theories* of alcoholism, some of which have been popular for some time, suggest that alcoholism is a symptom of some personality or emotional disorder. There has evolved three major personality theories: psychoanalytic, learning, and personality trait theories.

The *psychoanalytic theory* has been further expressed by three schools of psychology: Freudian, Adlerian, and inner conflict. The *Freudian view* suggests that alcoholism is caused by unconscious tendencies toward self-destruction, oral fixation, and latent homosexuality. In contrast, the *Adlerian theory* advances the concept that alcoholism is a symptom of the individual's need and struggle for power. The *inner conflict view* is simply that alcoholism is a manifestation of a conflict between the drive for dependency and aggressive impulses. Although the application of psychoanalytic treatment techniques are reportedly successful with some alcoholics, conclusive scientific evidence that alcoholism has a psychoanalytic cause is lacking.

The *learning theory* is explained by application of the approach-avoidance reaction. Since people are generally attracted to pleasant situations and repelled by unpleasant situations, the alcoholic drinks to reduce the tensions and anxiety associated with feelings of unpleasantness. The alcohol, in other words, establishes a state of euphoria. This would seem to result in a cyclical reaction where the person drinks to avoid the unpleasant situation that results in guilt feelings, family, and other social problems, which act as the motivators to start to drink again. The learning theory is associated with reward and punishment, and there is considerable experimental evidence that the ingestion of excessive amounts of alcohol can be induced by reward and punishment techniques. However, this theory is not universally accepted.

The *personality trait theory* suggests that the alcoholic possesses certain traits that are indicative of alcoholism. Some of these traits are feelings of inferiority, low frustration tolerance levels, dependency and emotional immaturity, and fearfulness. Although many attempts have been made to identify a personality trait profile for predicting alcoholism, no satisfactory profile has been advanced.

Since different sociocultural groups have different rates of alcoholism, sociologists have attempted to find an explanation of these differences. This has resulted in the advancement of the *sociological theories* of alcoholism, which are chiefly concerned with variations in cultural attitudes and values. Two sociological theories are noteworthy: the cultural theory and the deviant behavior theory.

Since the ingestion of alcohol reduces anxiety and tensions produced by a society, it is proposed that cultural factors that create these may be responsible for the development of alcoholism. This is called the *cultural theory*. In contrast, the *deviant behavior theory* is based upon the way in which the society labels alcoholism. When the society labels excessive use of alcohol as deviant behavior, the person is forced into playing a deviant role. However, the deviant behavior may be *primary* resulting from social norms that label one to be deviant, and *secondary*, which is the behavior resulting from being labeled deviant.

In conclusion, there are a number of different, but not necessarily unrelated, theories that attempt to explain why alcoholism is caused in some people, while others apparently escape this disease. It is possible that with more concentrated research, evidence will begin to point toward partial truth in several or all of these theories that will eventually result in combining aspects of each as a multiple causation. Regardless of the specific cause of alcoholism, however, we know that ingesting alcohol itself is a primary factor. Finding the cause and eliminating it is an important and vital priority of the scientific community since there is no evidence that alcohol use will ever be eliminated as a beverage and the potential for and actual abuse is greater than for any other drug of abuse.

Treatment and Rehabilitation

Approximately 70 percent of all adults drink alcohol and there are an estimated 9–11 million alcoholics in the United States. The estimated number of alcoholics does not include the large numbers of problem drinkers, who may be borderline alcoholics, and the heavy to moderate drinkers who contribute enormously to many of America's social problems, such as crimes and automobile accidents. Although the most cost-effective procedure for dealing with alcoholism is prevention, we can not ignore the necessity to provide adequate treatment for those already afflicted. The various forms of treatment in existence have varying degrees of success. These treatment modalities may be placed into the three categories of social, psychological, and medical approaches.

The *social approaches* to the treatment and rehabilitation of the alcoholic include small and large group interactions and, sometimes, a transition between the two. Generally, these are represented by the halfway house, the day or night hospital, and Alcoholics Anonymous. The *halfway house* is essentially a place for the alcoholic to receive support and is provided with a retreat to dry out. Many alcoholics have lost contact with family and have no other place in which to receive help.

The *day hospital* is chiefly a treatment center that may be described as somewhere between the halfway house and a hospital. Many alcoholics do have a place to return to, such as a family, but are not ready to return. The day hospital fills this gap. The *night hospital* is the same as the day hospital except the alcoholic goes there to spend the night. For example, some alcoholics maintain employment during the day but are not ready to spend their nights alone or in their former family setting.

One of the most successful approaches to alcoholism is the program of rehabilitation of *Alcoholics Anonymous*. Founded in 1935 in Akron, Ohio by a businessman from New York City and a physician, Alcoholics Anonymous is a fellowship of alcoholics who have recognized their problem with alcohol and who have the desire and determination to stay sober. Although this organization is a closeknit group of men and women who are alcoholics, it has no officers and there are no dues or other requirements for membership except the desire to live a productive life without alcohol. Alcoholics Anonymous has no constitution or bylaws, but it does have the "Twelve Steps" to sobriety and is based upon its "Twelve Traditions."

The *psychological approaches* to the treatment and rehabilitation of the alcoholic may be further classified into intrapsychic and interpersonal techniques. The *intrapsychic* methods are based upon the controversial assumption that alcoholism stems from emotional or unconsciously motivated factors. The advocates of these approaches believe that the alcoholic needs the guidance and counseling of professionally trained psychotherapists, although they recognize the value of the volunteer in the total rehabilitative process. Generally, the techniques used in intrapsychic therapy include role-playing, psychodrama, and group therapy as well as one-to-one interaction with the therapist.

Interpersonal therapy concentrates chiefly upon the alcoholic's marital and family disorders in regard to their relationship to alcoholism. It gives attention to the kinds of relationships that exist between the alcoholic and his/her significant others. Again, there is recognition of the value that volunteer organizations such as Al-Anon, Al-Ateen, and most recently, Al-Atot can make in the alcoholics rehabilitation.

Al-Anon is an offshoot of Alcoholics Anonymous. It is an organization of spouses of alcoholics whose chief purpose is for the spouses to acquire insight into the problems associated with alcoholism as related to their alcoholic partners. It is important to note that the alcoholic husband or wife does *not* have to be a member of Alcoholics Anonymous for the spouse to join Al-Anon. *Al-Ateen* and *Al-Atot* are similar organizations, but their programs are designed for the teenagers and younger children respectively who have an alcoholic parent.

The *medical approaches* consist of intervention-emergency treatment and medical treatment based upon the metabolism of alcohol and its pharmacological effects on the body. The intervention-emergency procedures consist of detoxification and the use of anticonvulsive drugs and sedatives to reduce the mortality and morbidity rate of severe intoxication and postintoxication complications. These are associated chiefly with the withdrawal syndrome, especially, delerium tremens. In addition, complications for prolonged, excessive drinking, such as gastritis and liver disease are treated along with nutritional therapy.

Another medical approach, which is actually based upon learning theory, is *aversion therapy.* Disulfiram (antabuse) is a drug that interacts with alcohol causing distressing nausea. Disulfiram is an antioxidant which interferes with the metabolism of alcohol resulting in an accumulation of acetaldehyde which produces flushing, dizziness, heart palpitations, and fear. Aversion therapy is, therefore, a form of negative reinforcement.

In conclusion, "despite the number of alcoholism-related organizations and facilities, our response as a nation historically has been miniscule compared with the size of the problem. The result: very few men and women with drinking problems have received the best help available, and most have had no care at all."[20] The network of alcoholism-related organizations and facilities include a number of voluntary and governmental agencies, industrial programs, professional organizations, hospitals, community mental health centers, and private practitioners. None of these programs should be considered a complete treatment modality, but rather, as an adjunct to the various other forms of therapy.

GLOSSARY

Absolute alcohol: 100 percent alcohol; also called anhydrous alcohol

Alcohol: Compounds that contain a hydroxyl group (OH) that is attached to a carbon atom; a central nervous system depressant.

Alcoholism: An uncontrollable craving for alcohol, which may take a number of forms for satisfying the craving.

Denatured alcohol: Ethyl alcohol that has been made unfit for human consumption.

Distillation: Removing water from an alcohol liquid by evaporation and condensation.

Fermentation: The action of yeast on sugar resulting in the formation of alcohol and carbon dioxide.

Intoxication: Drunkenness as a result of the chemical action of alcohol on the central nervous system.

Prohibition: Laws forbidding the use of alcohol.

Tolerance: An adaptation to the effects of alcohol, requiring larger amounts to produce the effects.

SUMMARY

The use of alcohol extends to prehistoric times. The first *recorded* use of alcohol is in documents of Mesopotamia dating about 3000 B.C. There have been a variety of attitudes over the years about alcohol use—some related to religion, morals, benefit, and law. However, drunkenness has almost always been condemned.

Temperance movements began in earnest in the early part of the 1800s with the establishment of the American Society for the Promotion of Temperance. The movement was culminated in 1919 with the enactment of the 18th Amendment to the United States Constitution. However, in 1933 this Amendment was repealed by the ratification of the 21st Amendment.

There are several forms that alcohol can take, but only one is fit for human consumption: ethanol or ethyl alcohol. Ethyl alcohol is found in a variety of forms such as fermented wines, brews, and distilled beverages.

Alcohol is a central nervous system depressant, acting as a sedative. It is readily absorbed into the blood stream through the lining of the stomach and small intestine since it does not have to be digested. However, the speed of absorption depends upon a number of factors such as the contents of the stomach and the concentration of alcohol in the beverage. Small amounts of alcohol are eliminated through the skin, urine, and breath; the remainder must be oxidized by the liver.

The cost of alcohol abuse to the American society is enormous—about $26 billion annually. This cost is in terms of lost production, health and medical costs, motor vehicle accidents, criminal acts, and social welfare care.

The human body has the ability to adapt to excessive consumption of alcohol. This adaptation is called tolerance. Important neurologic disorders resulting from alcoholism are: Korsakoff's psychosis, Wernicke's syndrome and delerium tremens. These are associated with nutritional deficiencies as well as excessive use of alcohol. Damage to body organs may also result from chronic, excessive drinking. Some of the most important involve damage to the liver in the form of fatty liver, alcoholic hepatitis, and cirrhosis.

There is no universal agreement as to what constitutes alcoholism. Generally, the alcoholic is a person who cannot control the amount of alcohol intake or whether or not he/she shall drink. Alcoholism usually develops slowly over a period of years, is insidious, and progressive.

The cause or causes of alcoholism are unknown, although physiological, psychological, and social theories have been advanced.

Although the most cost effective approach to the problem of alcoholism is prevention, it is still necessary to find adequate treatment modalities for those already afflicted. Medical approaches and groups such as Alcoholics Anonymous are among the various types of treatments.

PROBLEMS FOR DISCUSSION

1. Describe some historical highlights of the use of alcohol and how attitudes developed and changed with time.
2. Describe the role of the use of alcoholic beverages during Colonial times in America.
3. Trace the temperance movements and explain their impact upon the use of alcohol and society in general.
4. List ten myths or misconceptions about alcohol use and explain why they are inaccurate.
5. Compare the forms alcoholic beverages take in terms of alcohol content, uses, production, and consequences when abused.
6. What is meant by blood alcohol content? What is its significance?
7. Describe the sedative action of alcohol on the various centers of the brain.

8. Explain how alcohol use in the United States is significantly associated with its economy. What is the cost of alcohol abuse to the American economy?

9. Describe the federal government's actions to deal with alcohol abuse and alcoholism, and explain their success. What do you think needs to be done on a national level to more adequately solve the alcohol problem? Support your proposal.

10. What are the immediate effects of drinking alcohol moderately? Excessively?

11. What are some of the chief consequences of excessive drinking over a period of several years?

12. Describe how the body develops tolerance to alcohol. What are the kinds of tolerances? What is the significance of tolerance?

13. Distinguish between Korsakoff's psychosis and Wernicke's syndrome. Distinguish between delirium tremens and alcoholic hallucinosis.

14. What is alcoholism? Describe its chief characteristics.

15. Using Jellinek's classification of alcoholism, distinguish between each type.

16. Describe the various causation theories of alcoholism. What can you conclude?

17. List the various forms of treatments for alcoholism and describe the success of each.

REFERENCES

1. TRUITT, W. J., *The Laws of Sex Life and Heredity, Or Eugenics,* S. A. Mulliken Company, Marietta, Ohio, 1915, pp. 229–232.
2. DeROPP, ROBERTS S., *Drugs and the Mind,* Grove Press, Inc., New York, 1957, p. 117.
3. *Webster's Third New International Dictionary,* G. & C. Merriam Company, Publishers, Springfield, Mass., 1976.
4. The University of the State of New York, The State Education Department, *Alcohol Education,* 1976, p. 43.
5. BEDWORTH, ALBERT E. and JOSEPH A. D'ELIA, *Basics of Drug Education,* Baywood Publishing Company, Farmingdale, N.Y., 1973, p. 104.
6. RAY, OAKLEY S., *Drugs, Society, and Human Behavior,* The C. V. Mosby Company, Saint Louis, 1972, p. 83.
7. RAY, OAKLEY, *op. cit.,* p. 79.
8. CHAFETZ, MORRIS E., *Second Special Report to the U.S. Congress on Alcohol and Health,* U.S. Department of Health, Education, and Welfare; Public Health Service; Alcohol, Drug Abuse, and Mental Health Administration; National Institute on Alcohol Abuse and Alcoholism, Rockville, Md., DHEW Publication No. (ADM) 75–212, 1975, p. 37.

9. U.S. Department of Transportation, National Highway Traffic Safety Administration, *The Problem Drinker and You* (Pamphlet), Washington, D.C. 1974.

10. CHAFETZ, MORRIS E., *op. cit.,* p. 41.

11. CHAFETZ, MORRIS E., *op. cit.,* p. 167.

12. CHAFETZ, MORRIS E., *First Special Report to the U.S. Congress on Alcohol and Health,* U.S. Department of Health, Education,and Welfare; Health Services and Mental Health Administration; National Institute of Mental Health; National Institute on Alcohol Abuse and Alcoholism, Rockville, Md., DHEW Publication No. (HSM) 72–9099, 1972.

13. *Ibid.,* p. viii.

14. CHAFETZ, MORRIS E., *Second Report, op. cit.,* p. xxii.

15. *Ibid.,* pp. x–xi.

16. *Alcohol and Health: Third Special Report to the U.S. Congress,* U.S. Department of Health, Education, and Welfare; Public Health Service; Alcohol, Drug Abuse and Mental Health Administration; National Institute on Alcohol Abuse and Alcoholism, Rockville, Md., June, 1978, p. vii.

17. KELLER, MARK and MAIRI McCORMICK, *A Dictionary of Words About Alcohol,* Rutgers Center of Alcohol Studies, New Brunswick, N.J., 1968, pp. 17–19.

18. CHAFETZ, MORRIS E., *First Report, op. cit.,* p. 61.

19. *Ibid.,* p. 63.

20. *Alcohol and Alcoholism: Problems, Programs and Progress,* Department of Health, Education, and Welfare; Health Services and Mental Health Administration; National Institute of Mental Health; National Institute on Alcohol Abuse and Alcoholism, DHEW Publication No. (HSM) 72–9127. Rockville, Md., 1972, p. 27.

10

your consumer
health choices

THE IMPORTANCE OF HEALTH CONSUMERISM

Health Information Evaluation

In 1967, Hollis S. Ingraham, former Commissioner of the New York State Department of Health stated that: "The pitchman of the frontier hawking Old Joe Crowfoot's snakebite remedy and Indian elixir from the back of a wagon has vanished from the American scene, but his place has been taken by television's great contribution to the mores of our times—the simulated doctor."[1] Besides TV, we are exposed to a variety of publications, books on health topics, magazine and newspaper articles, and pamphlets. How are we to know the accuracy of these publications, media advertising, and other sources of health information? To accept the challenge and responsibility, there are two steps that each of us can take to protect ourselves from being influenced by inaccurate health claims:

1. Become better informed in health affairs and establish criteria that we can use to evaluate objectively the health claims to which we are exposed on a day-to-day basis.
2. Become aware of reliable sources of health information.

Below are some suggestions that will help us to become wiser consumers of health products and services and to help us to evaluate the accuracy of health information disseminated through the various media.

Some suggested criteria to be used to evaluate health information:

- Who has written or is saying it? Is the author recognized by his/her colleagues?
- Does the author present *scientific* evidence to support the health claims being made?
- Does the publication (or other source) appeal to a person's emotions? (Be cautious.)
- Are health claims made that reputable health professionals cannot or do not make? Ask yourself why? (Be cautious.)
- Does the source of health information claim that he/she is the only one that knows this? (Be cautious. Reputable scientists are anxious to share their discoveries with their colleagues and to have their findings verified.)
- Do advertisers of health products make claims verbally that are not included on the label?
- If a drug, does the label include the initials USP or NF? (This means that the formula is standardized in the *United States Pharmacopeia* or *National Formulary* regardless of brand name.)

Reliable sources of health information include:

- Regional Office of the Food and Drug Administration
- County, city, or state health departments

- County, state, or national professional associations or societies (Such as American Medical Association, American Dental Association, American Association of Pharmacists, and so forth)
- Universities with health science departments or medical/dental colleges
- Your physician or dentist
- County mental health board
- Many voluntary health agencies (Be sure they are recognized and reputable. There are a few that are questionable.)

Being a wise health consumer means more than just purchasing health products and services. It also means knowing when *not* to purchase them—and when to self-medicate and when not to. There are a number of dangers associated with *self-medication* including an incorrect diagnosis and use of the wrong medication, a delay in proper treatment, and the possibility that medication used may mask important symptoms. Although certain precautionary measures should be taken, we should not see our physician or dentist every time something goes wrong. What is needed is the health wisdom to know when to consult a health professional and when it is not necessary.

Our Present Health Care

Approximately 75 percent of the American civilian, noninstitutionalized population consult a physician at least once every year. Physicians' assessment of these visits indicate that nearly half are for health problems they consider *not serious* and another third they consider *only slightly serious.* This means that only one-sixth of patient/physician contacts are absolutely *essential.* Since the American people spend approximately $27 billion for physicians' services each year, about $23 billion are for health problems considered not serious or only slightly serious.

Health care in the United States is big business accounting for approximately 9 percent of our Gross National Product (GNP). Some health care costs have shown a decrease in the percentage of the total health care costs since 1950, while others have shown a significant increase in the percentage of health care costs. The greatest increases in health care costs are in hospital and nursing home care, increasing from 31 percent and 2 percent respectively in 1950 to an estimated cost of 40 percent and 8 percent in 1980 respectively. Physicians' services have decreased from 22 percent in 1950 to an estimated 19 percent in 1980. Dentists' services have shown a decline from 8 percent in 1950 to an estimated 6 percent in 1980.[2]

Health care facilities and personnel are unequally distributed among the population of the United States. For example, in urban areas with one million or more persons, there are more than 17 physicians per 10,000 people, with about 15 per 10,000 being in a medical specialty. This is compared with rural areas having approximately 4 physicians per 10,000 people and only about 1 per 10,000 being in a medical specialty. There are more than 46 hospital beds per 10,000 persons in the large metropolitan areas as compared with only about 32 in rural areas.[3]

In 1977, the national average ratio of physicians to population was 175 to 100,000. New York City far exceeded this average with 311 non-federal physicians per 100,000 people, including 802 physicians per 100,000 in Manhattan. Despite what would seem to be an abundance of medical manpower, New York City trailed the rest of New York State in a variety of health indicators, including a 12 percent lag in the number of people protected from disease through immunization.[4]

The implications of this are clear. Other factors must be considered than merely the supply of health personnel or even the presence of a health problem. We must consider the (1) environmental factors, both physical and social; (2) the tolerance of people to the health problem; and (3) the motivation of the people to control or eliminate the health problem.

Our health care system, if indeed it is a system, has evolved over the years not as a result of careful long-range planning, but rather as a result of need, greed, politics, and accident. Intermingled within all of this has been some planning, cooperation, and interaction. Our health care system is composed of private health practitioners, health care facilities (hospitals and nursing homes), health departments at all levels, health care financers, voluntary health agencies, and most recently, the health systems agencies. In the past few years, efforts have been made to gradually bring these sometimes fragmented pieces together into a system. However, the people who are the users of the system are for all practical purposes left outside, frustrated by the complexities of it. Medicare, Medicaid, Workman's Compensation, Blue Cross, Blue Shield, Health Maintenance Organizations—all possess a complexity of language, process, red tape, forms, and directions that leaves the patient at the mercy of the administrators of the programs. What is needed is a health care system that is more concerned with the welfare of people than the glory of forms that no one understands and computers that do not care.

USING PUBLIC HEALTH SERVICES

Introduction

Public health practices make use of many of the basic biological, medical, social, and pure sciences in its efforts to prevent disease and promote health. The practices of public health are directed toward those health areas that are primarily a community responsibility and are carried out chiefly by governmental (official) and voluntary health agencies, but other agencies may also contribute to achieving public health goals. These agencies include the educational community, social services departments, law enforcement and safety services, and private practitioners. Public health is concerned with the quality of health of people within communities, either singly or in groups. The activities of public health, therefore, may be conducted by local health agencies, county health agencies, state health departments, or federal health agencies.

Since the beginning of the twentieth century, public health problems have evolved from those associated with communicable diseases toward those involving chronic and degenerative diseases and those associated with environmental pollutants. On the surface, it would seem that the decline in the importance of infectious diseases was a direct result of improvements in medical technology. However, this was not necessarily the case. In some instances, most of the decline had very little to do with advances in medical science and improved treatment. For example, the annual number of deaths from tuberculosis dropped by two-thirds before TB hospitals (sanitaria) and collapse therapy came into use in 1930. Even more surprisingly, the death rates had dropped to 15 percent of what they were at the turn of the century *before* antibiotics were introduced around 1950.

It is now apparent that the cause of the decline in the incidence of communicable diseases was not totally due to advances in medical care, but rather to fundamental changes in nutritional practices and living conditions that began to prevent these diseases on a wide scale. These changes in lifestyle altered the very conditions that caused the high rates of the disease.

Medical efforts also have had a limited impact upon many of the chronic and degenerative diseases. For instance, there is already strong evidence that the fantastic improvements in intensive care and emergency treatment for heart disease that have occurred in the past decade have had little impact on overall death rates from the disease. To offset the apparent inability of treatment efforts to reduce the diseases most prevalent in our society, massive efforts are currently being launched to *prevent* the diseases by changing the factors that place people at high risk for these diseases. One of these factors is the threat of environmental hazards. (See Figure 10–1.)

The chief environmental threats to health are pollutants:

1. *Air pollution* from industrial and automobile emissions;

Figure 10-1:

Major Environmental Pollutants and Their Interrelatedness

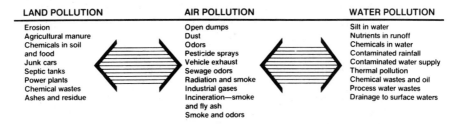

LAND POLLUTION	AIR POLLUTION	WATER POLLUTION
Erosion	Open dumps	Silt in water
Agricultural manure	Dust	Nutrients in runoff
Chemicals in soil and food	Odors	Chemicals in water
Junk cars	Pesticide sprays	Contaminated rainfall
Septic tanks	Vehicle exhaust	Contaminated water supply
Power plants	Sewage odors	Thermal pollution
Chemical wastes	Radiation and smoke	Chemical wastes and oil
Ashes and residue	Industrial gases	Process water wastes
	Incineration—smoke and fly ash	Drainage to surface waters
	Smoke and odors	

Adapted from: Environmental Circle. New York State Department of Health

2. *Water pollution,* to the extent that millions of Americans are exposed daily to mercury, PCBs, mirex and trichlorethylene, and other chemicals in drinking and recreational waters;

3. *Land pollution,* in the form of chemicals and solid wastes;

4. *Radiation,* in ever-increasing exposure levels from the sun, nuclear power, and the radiation used in medicine and dentistry.

Scope of Public Health Services

The purpose of community health activities is to promote and protect the health of the people equally and systematically. This means that programs that are planned and implemented must be available and accessible to all who need the services. The comprehensiveness of community health is reflected in the seven major program emphases: (1) *Environmental controls,* (2) *Prevention of disease, disability, and premature death,* (3) *Provision of medical and dental care,* (4) *Collection and analyses of vital records* (5) *Provision for formal public education,* (6) *Health planning and programs evaluation,* and (7) *Conducting continuous research into health matters.*[5]

Governmental health agencies are also known as *official health agencies.* They are established and function at local, state, national, and international levels. They are established by law for the purpose of protecting the health of people.

Direct health services are most often provided by city and/or county health departments. They are responsible for implementing laws enacted at the state level and for using funds allocated to them from local, state, and federal tax revenues. Local health departments also may use the services of private health practitioners. This is particularly true when the local health jurisdiction is relatively small or when qualified individuals are not available for employment for particular specialized health functions.

Health Systems Agencies

The most recent development in official health organization directly affecting localities has been the establishment of *health system agencies* (HSAs). HSAs are established on a regional basis, usually encompassing several counties. In states with a small population, the HSA boundaries may correspond to those of the state. Health systems agencies, which are governed by a majority of people who are considered to be consumers, plan the health activities and priorities of the region. Moreover, the HSAs control to a large extent the allocation of health resources for the region.

A health systems agency is either a private, nonprofit corporation or a public entity and is responsible for health planning and development in each health service area. They are responsible for preparing and implementing plans designed to improve health, increase accessibility to services, and restrain lost increases, among other things. However, in 1981, the federal government deferred to those who favor a "competitive" health care system; and significantly reduced funding for local health planning.

Federal Health Services

In 1979, as a result of a proposed cabinet reorganization by President Carter, a new Department of Education was established, leaving the health programs of the federal government in the newly reorganized Department of Health and Human Services. (Education and health formerly were a part of The Department of Health, Education, and Welfare.) The various offices and institutes responsible for federal health programs implement federal health legislation, setting regulations and providing monies to states, localities, and private health enterprises.

The chief federal agency concerned with the health of the nation is the United States Public Health Service (USPHS). The USPHS consists of six major subdivisions: Alcohol, Drug Abuse and Mental Health Administration; Center for Disease Control; Food and Drug Administration; Health Resources Administration; Health Services Administration; and the National Institutes of Health.

Voluntary Health Agencies

Voluntary health agencies differ from the official agencies in that they are supported by private, nontaxable funds and are directed by individuals who may not have any formal training in the area of public health (the volunteers.) In addition, the voluntary agencies tend to focus their efforts on a single major area of health concern. Because they are voluntary, they have no authority under the law for finding solutions to the health problems with which they are concerned. They do, however, tend to work closely with the official agencies and can facilitate focusing public attention on specific health issues.

There are literally thousands of voluntary health agencies in the United States, each one forming a special interest group attempting to educate the public, to influence health policy, and to fund research and demonstration activities concerned with the various health problems confronting society.

Because voluntary health agencies provide a means of positively directing funds that are tax deductible, they tend to be self-perpetuating. For instance, when tuberculosis became a controllable disease and was reduced in importance as a major health concern, the Tuberculosis and Respiratory Disease Association became the American Lung Association, being concerned with all diseases of the lungs. When polio was conquered, the National Foundation for Infantile Paralysis, Inc. became the National Foundation/March of Dimes, focusing its attention on birth defects.

Professional Societies

Although not strictly speaking public health agencies, we do need to make mention of the professional societies because they do have influence on public health practices, for example, an organization for physicians is the American Medical Association (AMA). The professional societies are made up of members of a particular health profession. These agencies are supported by the dues from membership. Professional societies, in addition to promoting the professions they represent, also attempt to educate the public and protect the health consumer from fraud.

HEALTH RESOURCES

Health Care Facilities

Health care facilities take a variety of forms depending upon the special health care needs, and include hospitals and nursing and related homes. Hospitals are classified as general medical and surgical and specialty hospitals. They may be government owned, nonprofit, or private. Nursing and related homes are those which provide (1) nursing care; (2) personal care and nursing; (3) personal care without nursing; and (4) domiciliary care. Other health care facilities include those for the mentally retarded, orphanages, and homes for the emotionally disturbed, unwed mothers, alcoholics, drug abusers, the deaf and/or blind, and the physically handicapped. In the United States there are more than 34,000 inpatient facilities with approximately 3.2 million beds and 2.7 million patients. This means that approximately one-half million beds remain empty at any given time.

The total estimated annual cost of hospital and nursing home care in the United States is about $66 billion. Physician and dentist fees cost an additional $35 billion. Approximately 43 percent of all health expenditures are paid for out of public funds. This amounts to an annual per capita cost of approximately $270.[6] Since there are approximately 374,000 physicians and dentists in the United States, the average annual gross income would be approximately $93,000.

The health care system in the United States has undergone marked changes in the past 40 years. Prior to the end of World War II, the health care system was dominated by the medical practitioner—the family physician—and the American Medical Association. However, according to Ehrenreich and Ehrenreich:

> . . . people are only beginning to discern the outlines of the new medical establishment, based in local networks of hospitals and medical schools, backed up by a highly technological and profitable health commodities industry, and represented nationally by the corporate voices of the American Hospital Association, Blue Cross and the American Association of Medical Schools. At the heart of the new system is no longer the free enterprise private practitioner, but the local, medical-school-centered medical empire.[7]

That was back in 1970, one year before Senator Edward Kennedy was chosen as chairman of the Senate Subcommittee on Health. At that time, Kennedy conducted hearings on the quality of health care in America. The results of those hearings brought to public and political attention the health care crisis that existed and still exists in America. The problems that people have encountered with attempts to obtain high quality health care at a cost they can afford, as presented in testimonials before the Senate Health Subcommittee, formed in part, the basis for Senator Kennedy's National Health Insurance Bill. By 1981, no such bill had been passed by the Congress.

Who are the health practitioners? A few decades ago, this would have been a relatively simple question to answer: physicians, dentists, and nurses. However, the kinds of health practitioners have increased in numbers and their titles, qualifications, and responsibilities have changed markedly since the end of World War II. For convenience, we are categorizing health practitioners into medical, nonmedical, and paramedical groups.

Medical health practitioners are those who have earned a doctor of medicine or similar degree. *Nonmedical* are those who do not possess a doctor of medicine or similar degree, and *paramedical* are those who assist the medical doctor in carrying out his/her responsibilities.

To become a medical practitioner, a person must complete at least 3 years of premedical school, 2 years of preclinical school, 2 years of medical school, and 1 year of internship. *Premedical* school consists chiefly of studies in biology, physics, chemistry, and the social sciences. *Preclinical* studies include biochemistry, histology, physiology, embryology, and genetics. *Clinical* studies involve practical application of previous training, consisting of patient care and participation in the "rounds" under the supervision of the attending physician. Following clinical studies, the medical student receives the Doctor of Medicine degree (M.D.), but must still prepare for state licensure. The *internship* provides this preparation and consists of practice within a hospital setting and under the supervision of a resident physician.

However, more than 90 percent of students who receive the Doctor of Medicine degree, which qualifies them for general medical practice, choose to specialize in one of the more than 30 medical specialties recognized by the American Medical Association. (See Table 10–1.) This requires from 2–5 additional years of training in residency in the chosen specialty. Upon completion, the medical student becomes Board Eligible, which simply means that the required additional training has been satisfactorily completed. Upon completion of a written and oral examination within the chosen specialty, the physician becomes Board Certified. Occasionally, a general practitioner may limit his/her practice to a specialty without having gone through the required and recognized training. These people are not recognized as specialists by the American Medical Association.

Nonmedical practitioners are those who diagnose and treat diseases within defined limitations. They include the following:

- *Audiologists,* who are trained to deal with the rehabilitation of persons with hearing problems.
- *Chiropractors,* who treat diseases through manipulation of the spinal column. (There are an estimated 17,000 chiropractors in the United States.)
- *Osteopathic physicians,* who have comparable education and training to that of medical general practitioners. In general, the osteopathic physician can diagnose and treat diseases in the same manner as the medical physician. These persons however, possess the degree of Doctor of Osteopathy (D.O.), rather than the Doctor of Medicine degree. There are approximately 12,000 in the United States.

Table 10–1: Some of the Major Medical Specialties and Subspecialties Recognized by the AMA

- *Anesthesiology* (Anesthesiologist). The study of anesthetics and anesthesia. A person who specializes in the administration of drugs necessary to produce anesthesia during surgery or for diagnosis of a medical condition. Approximately 13,000 in the United States.

- *Allergy* (Allergist). Concerned with the causes, diagnosis, and treatment of diseases resulting from a sensitivity to certain substances. Approximately 1,700 in the United States.

- *Cardiology* (Cardiologist). The subspecialty concerned with the health of the heart. Approximately 6,200 in the United States.

- *Dermatology* (Dermatologist). Concerned with diseases of the skin. Approximately 4,500 in the United States.

- *Gastroenterology* (Gastroenterologist). Concerned with health and diseases of the stomach and intestines. Approximately 2,000 in the United States.

- *Internal Medicine* (Internist). Concerned with diagnosis and treatment (including surgery) of diseases of the internal organs such as liver, lungs, and heart. Approximately 52,000 in the United States.

- *Pediatrics* (Pediatrician). Concerned with the health of children (usually under 13 years of age)——the prevention, diagnosis, and treatment of their diseases. Approximately 22,000 in the United States.

- *Colon and rectal surgery* (Proctologist). Concerned with the diagnosis and treatment of diseases of the colon and rectum. Approximately 700 in the United States.

- *General surgery* (Surgeon). Concerned with the operative treatment of diseases. Approximately 31,000 in the United States.

- *Neurological surgery* (Neurologist). Concerned with diagnosis and operative treatment of the brain, spinal cord, and disorders of the nerves. Approximately 2,900 in the United States.

- *Obstetrics and gynecology* (Obstetrician and gynecologist). Concerned with the health of women, especially diagnosis and treatment of diseases of the female reproductive organs and the care of pregnant women, delivery of the baby, and postnatal care. Approximately 21,000 in the United States.

- *Ophthalmology* (Ophthalmologist or Oculist). Concerned with the health of the eyes, diagnosis, treatment (including surgery) of diseases of the eyes. Approximately 11,000 in the United States.

- *Orthopedic surgery* (Orthopedist). Concerned with the diagnosis and treatment (including surgery) of diseases, injuries, and deformities of the bones, joints, and related structures. Approximately 11,000 in the United States.

- *Otolaryngology* (Otolaryngologist). Concerned with the diagnosis and treatment of diseases of the ear, nose, and throat. Approximately 6,000 in the United States.

- *Otology* (Otologist). Concerned with the diagnosis and treatment of diseases of the ear.

- *Otorhinolaryngology* (Otorhinolaryngologist). Concerned with the totality of the ear, nose, and throat.

- *Plastic surgery* (Plastic surgeon). Concerned with corrective or reparative surgery for restoring deformed or mutilated parts of the body or to improve body features, especially facial features. Approximately 2,000 in the United States.

- *Urology* (Urologist). Concerned with diagnosis and treatment of diseases and disorders of the kidneys, urinary bladder, and related structures, and the male reproductive organs. Approximately 7,000 in the United States.

- *Child psychiatry* (Child psychiatrist). Concerned with mental and emotional disorders of children. Approximately 2,500 in the United States.

- *Psychiatry* (Psychiatrist). Concerned with mental and emotional disorders. Approximately 24,000 in the United States.

- *Pathology* (Pathologist). Concerned with study of the changes in tissues, organs, and cells as a result of disease or other phenomena. Approximately 12,000 in the United States.

- *Radiology* (Radiologist). Concerned with the diagnosis and treatment of disease through the use of radiation. Approximately 16,000 in the United States.

- *General practice, including family practice* (General practitioner). Concerned with all health matters and diseases of people. Approximately 55,000 in the United States.

- *Dentists,* who possess the Doctor of Dental Surgery (DDS) degree and are concerned with the prevention of dental disorders and the diagnosis and treatment of dental and oral diseases and restoration of dental defects. There are approximately 107,000 in the United States. Dentistry like medicine has a number of specialties including:

  Oral surgeon. Specializes in dental extractions and surgery on related structures. The oral surgeon may specialize further in a specific area of oral surgery such as maxilofacial surgery.

  Endodontist. Specializes in dental pulp and root canal therapy. Many teeth that have involved infection of the dental pulp can be restored through root canal therapy.

  Orthodontist. Specializes in the correction of malocclusion.

  Pedodontist. Specializes in the diagnosis and treatment of oral and dental conditions of children.

  Periodontist. Specializes in diagnosis and treatment of conditions of the periodontium (the supporting structures of the teeth).

  Prosthodontist. Specializes in dental prosthetics such as provision of dentures and other oral appliances.

  Oral Pathologist. Specializes in the laboratory study of dental and oral diseases and their causes.

- *Opticians,* who specialize in the preparation of corrective lenses.

- *Optometrists,* who examine the eyes for refractory problems and fit eyeglasses. (The optometrist possesses the Doctor of Optometry (DO) degree. There are approximately 25,000 in the United States.)

The *paramedical practitioners* include a variety of persons whose training prepares them to assist the medical and/or nonmedical practitioner. Among the more common ones are nurses (2.3 million), dental hygienists (23,000), dental laboratory technicians (32,000), pharmacists (133,000), physical therapists (26,000), emergency medical technicians (260,000), electrocardiograph technicians (9,500), and many others.

Health Quackery

How would you define quackery? What are the characteristics of a quack: *Quackery* has traditionally been defined as fraudulent misrepresentation in matters concerned with health. This could take the form of services, such as diagnosis of disease, or the use of unproven or worthless products, such as drugs or devices. The *quack* is a person (or indeed, as we will see, an entire industry) who knowingly or not offers health services or products that are misrepresented, fraudulent, or are merely sold for profit. (See Figure 10–2.)

These kinds of definitions take us beyond the hard-core quack and quackery to the so-called legitimate practitioner who, for example, performs unnecessary surgery or prescribes unnecessary drugs or other forms of treatment. For instance, in 1973, according to the Journal of the American Medical Association,[8] one in four Americans received a shot of penicillin; 90 percent of these treatments were unnecessary.

Figure 10-2:
Some Patent Medicines from the Past

Consumer Reports has stated that, "The drug industry has been ranked as one of the two most profitable manufacturing industries in the country. (The other is soft drinks)."[9] The purchase of over-the-counter drugs, to say nothing of prescription drugs, has, in the past three decades, become an American tradition and ritual. This is chiefly the result of the skill of the pharmaceutical industry to manufacture "repeat drugs,"* the skill of the advertising industry to convince people they need or want the product, and the lack of health knowledge of people that makes them vulnerable.

Did you know, for example, that:

- There are about 600 different compounds in various forms from tablet to chewing gum sold for the purpose of curing or relieving heartburn, indigestion, bloating, cramps, and gas. This "stomach medicine" industry collects about $200 million annually from the American people.
- Sales of mouthwashes (which cure nothing, not even bad breath), amount to over $250 million annually. This is an expenditure that can safely be eliminated from the budget of any American family.
- Americans spend more than $460 million each year for antiperspirants and deodorants. This may be a desirable expenditure from an interpersonal relations viewpoint, but the profits involved are out of line with manufacturing and promotion costs.
- More than $400 million are spent each year for so-called arthritis cures.
- There are over 800 over-the-counter drugs and more than 100 prescription compounds for the relief of coughs grossing about $700 million annually.

*Repeat drugs are simply a drug with the same pharmaceutical properties as one already on the market, but is packaged differently.

These, along with a number of health devices that are either unnecessary or that are priced beyond a reasonable profit margin are what have become known as the "gray area" of quackery. For example, compare the complexities and price of a wheelchair with a ten-speed bicycle. You may be amazed!

Hard-core quackery, on the other hand, is quite a different story. This is characterized more by a deliberate—usually—effort by the quack to defraud the people. Most quacks are clever, offering a treatment or "cure" they know is worthless, and for a health condition that baffles medical science. Usually, their "cure" is a secret formula, known only to them. The quack may offer a form of treatment, such as "psychological surgery" that is completely fraudulent, but is attractive to people because it purports to avoid or eliminate the discomfort, pain, or inconvenience of legitimate medical treatments. The quack also claims to be able to "cure" those diseases that the medical practitioners are unable to cure. For example, the health conditions most exploited by the quack are in the areas of nutrition especially weight control, cancer, arthritis, health problems of the aged, mental and emotional health problems and beauty and attractiveness.

The methods used by the hard-core quack run the gamut from the use of fertilized dirt to complex electronic gadgets, from copper bracelets to vibrators, from bottled sea water to organic foods and herbs. It is estimated that the American people are duped into spending more than $2 billion each year for worthless quack remedies and devices.

CONSUMER PROTECTION

Although we are concerned chiefly with consumerism related to the promotion, maintenance, and restoration of health, it is important to mention that we are also consumers of many other products that enhance life. It is also important to point out that American industries are concerned with improving their products, developing new ones, and maintaining or increasing profits. Since there is ever-present the possibilities of industries becoming overly greedy, or careless, it is necessary for American consumers to be provided with protection from these and other unethical or fraudulent practices. As a result, the federal government has enacted legislation and created departments to provide this protection. Let us examine some of these.

The Food and Drug Administration

The Food and Drug Administration (FDA), the first consumer protection agency in the United States, has the most far-reaching responsibility of any federal regulatory agency. For example, the Food and Drug Administration can (1) prevent some products, such as unproven new drugs and harmful food additives, from ever being sold; (2) require products to be redesigned, formulated, relabeled, or packaged in a safer way; (3) initiate removal of products from the marketplace whenever new scientific data reveal risks that are not acceptable; (4) enforce product standards and take action against false or misleading labeling; and (5) take court action to seize illegal products, enjoin violative manufacturers or prosecute the manufacturer, packer, or shipper of adulterated or mislabeled products.

The FDA's authority and responsibility are governed by several acts of Congress beginning in 1906 with the passage of the original Food and Drugs Act, and the Meat Inspection Act.

The FDA has the power and authority to provide the American consumer with broad-ranged protection from fraud. However, there are a number of areas of protection in which the FDA does not have authority. For example, the FDA cannot guarantee the purity and safety of all of our food; the FDA does not have the authority to order the recall of unsafe or mislabeled products, nor does the FDA check on the safety of all products before they can be sold.[10] Our protection lies essentially with ourselves and in conjunction with the FDA and other government agencies.

The Federal Trade Commission

The Food and Drug Administration has no authority over the accuracy of advertising except those for prescription drugs, generally advertised in medical journals. However, the Federal Trade Commission has the authority to prevent the dissemination of false or misleading advertising of foods, cosmetics, and other health products. The Food and Drug Administration does control claims on the label of products. In general, if the FDA does not allow certain claims to be made on the label, the Federal Trade Commission will not allow them in advertising.

The Federal Trade Commission was created by an act of Congress in 1914. Its primary functions are to promote free and fair competition in interstate trade and to prevent unfair and deceptive practices. Its chief function is preventing the dissemination of false and misleading advertising in regard to foods, drugs, cosmetics, and medical and health devices. The Federal Trade Commission is an independent branch of the federal government whose members are appointed by the President with the approval of the Senate.

The U.S. Consumer Product Safety Commission

A relatively new agency of the federal government, the U.S. Consumer Product Safety Commission was created by the Consumer Product Safety Act of 1972. The Commission is primarily concerned with reducing injuries associated with consumer products used in the home, schools, and recreational areas. Its authority is expanded by the enactment of the Federal Hazardous Substances Act, Flammable Fabrics Act, Poison Prevention Packaging Act, and Refrigerator Safety Act. However, the Commission's jurisdiction does *not* include foods, drugs, cosmetics, medical devices, and several other product areas that come under the authority of other federal agencies.

Other Consumer Protection Agencies

There are a number of other federal agencies concerned with specialized areas of health and safety. These are summarized below:

- *National Highway Traffic Safety Administration* within the Department of Transportation. This agency develops and enforces safety standards for certain parts of motor vehicles.

- *Agriculture Department,* through its various subdivisions, inspects and grades meats, poultry, fruits, and vegetables.

- *U.S. Postal Service* protects the consumer from the use of the mails for fraudulent purposes.

- *The Bureau of Alcohol, Tobacco, and Firearms,* within the Treasury Department, is concerned with ingredient labeling of alcohol and safe storage and other precautions for explosives.

- *Office of Consumer Affairs,* within the Department of Health and Human Services, serves as a coordinating body for inquires and complaints on such subjects as prices, quality and safety of products.

PAYING FOR HEALTH CARE

Introduction

The U.S. Department of Health and Human Services estimates that by 1983, health care costs in the United States will constitute 9.7 percent of the Gross National Product, an increase of 3.2 percent from 1963 when it was 6.5 percent of the GNP. This is also reflected in increased health care costs for each American family. In 1963, a family of four had an average annual health care bill of about $530. This is expected to increase to $3,590 in 1983. There are a number of reasons for these increases besides just inflation. For example, *unnecessary* hospital and medical/surgical procedures cost an estimated $4 billion annually.[11]

During the Carter Administration, the Hospital Containment Act of 1979 was introduced into the Congress. In defense of the bill, the Administration indicated that its implementation would save the nation $59.6 billion annually in health care costs. This figure was arrived at by a savings to families of $27.5 billion through payment of insurance premiums, payroll and other taxes, and direct out-of-pocket expenditures. In addition, employers would reduce their contributions by $23.5 billion by savings on corporate income taxes, payroll taxes, and employee insurance premiums. State and local governments would realize over $8.6 billion savings through reduced costs for Medicaid and public hospital expenditures that would, in turn, reduce state and local taxes. These are extremely ambitious goals especially when placed within the context of one of the most powerful and profitable industries in American society.

The question is, even with the enactment of such a bill as the Hospital Containment Act, will the health care industry allow such enormous reductions in its profits? By the health care industry, we mean the entire conglomerate of health practitioners, providers of services, facilities, suppliers of equipment, and insurance companies. The second question is will the American people actively support government efforts to reduce health care costs? History tells us that the American people are willing to pay for health, longevity, and the fantasy of immortality. Let us examine the ways in which these payments can be made.

Direct Payment

Approximately 33 percent of annual health care expenditures are through direct payment by the health consumer. This is compared with about 40 percent by federal, state, and local governments, about 26 percent by private health insurances, and 1 percent by industry and philanthropy. In 1950, direct payment constituted 68 percent by government.[12] This represents a significant shift in the way that health expenditures are made and a shift in the controlling forces in health care in the United States.

Hospital care and physicians' fees constitute nearly 60 percent of the annual health care bill in the United States. The next largest expenditure is for drugs, about 8 percent. This means that the governments, insurance companies, and drug industries have the greatest financial interest in health care. As a consequence, the quality of health care is not directly in the hands of the consumer, but rather is controlled by governments, insurance companies, and the drug industry. These are also responsible for skyrocketing costs for health care. As more of the annual health care costs were assumed by third party payments and less through direct payment, the health care cost increased proportionately. (Figure 10-3 illustrates these relationships). The tragedy is that the quality and accessibility of health care has not kept pace with the increased costs.

Figure 10-3:

Comparison of Methods for Paying for Health Care with Increased Annual Health Care Expenditures.

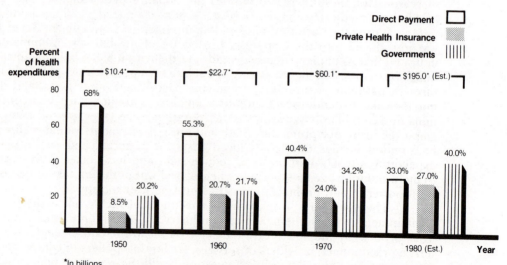

*In billions

Source of Data: **Health, United States, 1976-1977, Chartbook,** U.S. Department of Health, Education, and Welfare, p. 3.

264

Insurance companies have been reluctant, even resistant, to providing coverage for the promotion and maintenance of health and the prevention of disease and disability. They have also avoided coverage of physicians' fees unless services are rendered within a hospital seeting. One is impelled to ask why, especially when research has shown that it is less expensive to stay healthy than to restore health once it has failed. Perhaps a part of the answer is because insurance companies are in business for profit (even the so-called nonprofit insurance companies), and there is more profit in treatment than in prevention of health problems.

Voluntary health insurance coverage is usually categorized according to the kind of coverage: hospital expenses, surgical costs, regular medical, major medical, loss of income, and dental. Policies may be written for a single category or for a combination of coverages. In nearly all cases, there are also deductible and exclusion clauses. These are important for several reasons, one of which is that the cost of the policy is related to what is covered, the amount of deductibles and exclusions. The deductible clause simply means that, in the event of illness or accident, the consumer will pay the first "x number of dollars" before the insurance coverage actually goes into effect. Exclusions means that there are certain conditions or circumstances, as stated in the policy, that are not covered. (See Figure 10–4.)

Hospital insurance is basically a "room and board" coverage during a stay in a hospital. This may have some restrictions related to a private room, semiprivate, and so forth, as well as length of stay. Seldom do voluntary health insurance policies pay for all hospital expenses. Restrictions on coverages reduce the premiums accordingly. Although insurance policies are usually written in language that is difficult for most people to understand, it is important to read your prospective policy carefully and ask your insurance agent to interpret any clauses that are not clear to you.

Surgical coverage should be seriously considered in conjunction with hospital coverage. Since a common reason for going to the hospital is for surgery, one coverage without the other may prove financially burdensome. Again, look for deductible and exclusion clauses, since, for example, a surgical insurance policy may not cover elective surgery or certain kinds of surgery, such as openheart.

Regular medical expense coverage refers to health care that may or may not be associated with hospital or surgical coverage. These benefits may be physicians' fees (in the hospital or other setting), diagnostic procedures, such as x-rays, and so forth. Once again, however, there are usually exclusions and other clauses you need to be alert to.

Major medical expense coverage is essentially a supplement to the other basic coverages. It is primarily protection against a catastrophic illness or accident. Frequently, these policies provide some protection for expenses incurred for hospital, surgical, medical, diagnostic, unusual treatments (such as, use of dialysis machine), and so forth. Major medical coverage is designed to pick up health care

Figure 10-4:

How Our Health Dollar Is Spent

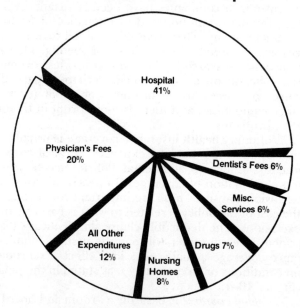

Hospital
41%

Physician's Fees
20%

Dentist's Fees 6%

Misc.
Services 6%

All Other
Expenditures
12%

Drugs 7%

Nursing
Homes
8%

Note: 49% of all health expenditures is for institutionalization

Source of Data: **Carter Administration National Health Plan Proposal,** Feb. 16, 1979, p. 25. (Draft transmitted to Governors for review.)

costs after the other basic policy coverages have been exhausted. Nearly all major medical policies have a deductible clause as well as a payment limitation. The payment limitations are expressed in precentage of costs. For example, the policy may cover only 80 percent of the major medical expenses; the policyholder must pay the other 20 percent.

Loss of income coverage is an insurance policy that pays an amount (usually on a monthly basis) directly to the policy-holder. The purpose of such policies is to provide the person with protection against loss of income as a result of illness. It is well to examine your employers sick leave regulations since many employers allow a number of sick days (sometimes accumulative) with pay. Also, these insurance policies usually have a clause that delays the time when the coverage begins. For example, there may be no coverage until after the person has been out of work because of illness for two or more weeks.

Dental coverage is an insurance policy or supplement to other health insurance that pays for dental care. These, as with other health insurances, usually have limitations, but generally they do provide for some coverage for preventive and maintenance care. This may include oral examinations and prophylaxes, as well as X-rays and restorative treatments. However, they also usually have limitations and deductible clauses.

GOVERNMENTAL HEALTH
INSURANCE

Protests, chiefly by the American Medical Association, American Dental Association, and the American Hospital Association, centered around the concept of "socialized medicine" have precluded the establishment of any comprehensive national health insurance program. Socialized medicine can be defined or interpreted in a variety of ways, but in this context it is primarily a health plan controlled, directed, and administered under government auspices. Historically, the concept of socialized medicine in the United States had its roots in the enactment by Congress of the Marine Hospital Service Act of 1798. This provided health care for merchant seamen and their families. Twenty cents a month was deducted from their pay to provide for this health care coverage. This act was the forerunner for the establishment of the United States Public Health Service. However, President Reagan in 1981, proposed eliminating health benefits for merchant seamen and their families. In recent times, the only other significant government health care insurance program is Medicare and its counterpart, Medicaid.

Medicare

One of the most restrictive insurance plans is Medicare, which came into being in 1966. Although many believe that Medicare is a "godsend" to the elderly, its restrictions and limitations make it one of the most inefficient health care insurance plans in existence. It consists of a Part A and a Part B. Part A provides a minimal coverage for hospital expenses, while Part B provides some coverage for medical expenses.

A person 65 years of age or over may apply for Medicare coverage. However, there are four conditions that must be present to receive benefits: (1) a licensed physician must prescribe hospital care for treatment of an illness or injury; (2) the treatment necessary can only be provided in a hospital; (3) the hospital must be participating in Medicare; and (4) the hospital care must be approved by the Utilization Review Committee of the hospital *or* by the Professional Standards Review Organization in the region.

There are a number of limitations to hospital coverage of Medicare. For example, there is a 90-day limitation, there is a deductible, and between the 61st and 90th day the patient is responsible for part of the payment. There are also several exclusions. However, Medicare does pay for the following, providing all conditions for eligibility are met:

- A semiprivate room, all meals and any necessary special diets
- Routine nursing services
- Special care units such as intensive or coronary care
- Drugs furnished by the hospital
- Operating and recovery room expenses
- Rehabilitation services such as physical therapy

267

- Radiological services for diagnosis and treatment
- Necessary laboratory tests.[13]

Medicaid

Unlike Medicare, Medicaid is a health insurance program co-sponsored by the federal and state governments. It is intended to provide adequate care for people who meet certain financial limitations. Medicaid programs vary from state to state, but several basic factors are common since these are directed by federal regulations. At this writing, all, but one state, Arizona, have a Medicaid plan. Medicaid, as with Medicare, is authorized by amendments to the Social Security Act (Title 19 and Title 18 respectively).

The purpose of medicaid is to provide health care protection for certain kinds of needy people and low income families. These include the aged (65 years of age or older), the blind and disabled, and the dependent children. For those who are eligible, Medicaid covers inpatient hospital care, outpatient hospital services, skilled nursing facility services (some kinds of nursing homes), physician's fees, screening and diagnosis and treatment of children under 21 years of age, home health care services (when available), and family planning services. Medicaid is also a supplement to Medicare, paying for services not covered by Medicare. For example, for those who are eligible, Medicaid will pay the deductible part of Medicare. In addition, many state Medicaid plans make provisions beyond those required by federal regulations, such as paying for prescribed drugs, dental care, and diagnostic services for adults.[14]

National Health Insurance

The first realistic proposal for national health insurance took place during the Truman Administration. As of 1980, there were nearly 25 national health insurance bills introduced into the congress. With the exception of two proposals, these bills failed to address the real issues surrounding our health care dilemma. Rather, they addressed or favored special interest groups—the medical profession, hospital industry, drug industry, and health insurance industry—not the real health needs of people.

On the other hand, the Health Security Act (Kennedy-Griffith Plan) claims to be comprehensive, administered by the federal government, and available to all U.S. citizens. No person would need to fear financial ruin because of illness and all would be able to receive adequate health care. The Carter Administration National Health Plan also addresses the health care needs of people.

The Carter Administration National Health Plan was designed as a phase-in of adequate health insurance for all Americans. It addressed the issues of the rising cost of health care, the persons who are uninsured or inadequately insured, the distribution of health resources, and the need to capitalize upon both governmental and private sources of funding.

At the time that *Health Care* was introduced, the plan called for a 5-year phase-in process. This would have meant that the plan would be fully operational by 1983. However, since there was a change in administrations from democrat to republican neither the Kennedy nor Carter plans are likely to be enacted in the near future.

GLOSSARY

Consumer: Any person who purchases health services and/or products.

Health Systems Agencies: Official health organizations, controlled by consumers, that plan health priorities, activities, and funding on a regional basis.

Medicaid: Federal and State government financed health insurance for individuals and families whose financial status is below the poverty level.

Medical practitioner: A person who provides health services and possesses the Doctor of Medicine degree (M.D.).

Medicare: Federally financed health insurance for persons 65 years of age and older and others who are in special categories.

National Health Insurance: Federally controlled health insurance available to all U.S. citizens.

Nonmedical practitioner: A person who provides health services but does not possess the Doctor of Medicine degree.

Official Health Agency: Organized at the local, county, state or national level and funded by tax revenues. Such agencies implement and enforce health laws.

Paramedical practitioner: A person who assists a physician in providing health services.

Quack: A person or group of persons who offer fraudulent health services or products for profit.

Voluntary Health Agencies: Organizations that are nonprofit, usually focusing their activities on a particular health problem, and funded through voluntary contributions.

SUMMARY

As health consumers each of us has the responsibility to become as informed about health affairs as possible. We also need to establish criteria for evaluating health claims and to make appropriate use of reliable sources of health information.

Our present health care system is one of the major industries in the United States. It consists of health care facilities, providers of health services, manufacturers of health products, and the insurance industry. Health care costs are increasing at astronomical rates; health care facilities and practitioners are unequally distributed; and many millions of Americans can not afford even minimal health care.

Health quackery is a multibillion dollar business in the United States. It is essentially the practice of offering fraudulent treatments for illnesses that are generally not completely understood by science. We need to be aware of the "gray areas" of quackery if we are to become wise health consumers.

There are a number of federal agencies that protect us from health products and services that are unsafe or ineffective. Since their authority is limited, health consumerism must be a partnership between government agencies and each individual.

There are a number of ways in which people pay for their health care: out-of-pocket payments, private health insurance, and government health insurance. To assist Americans to pay for health care costs, a number of national health insurance bills have been introduced into the Congress. However, except for Medicare and Medicaid there is no adequate national health insurance, leaving many Americans threatened by financial ruin if health should fail.

PROBLEMS FOR DISCUSSION

1. Give two reasons why each of us should learn how to evaluate the accuracy of health information and health claims.
2. What can you do to become a better health consumer? Why is it important for you to purchase health services and products wisely?
3. What are some reliable sources of health information?
4. Describe some of the limitations of our present health care system.
5. What is health quackery? Distinguish between hard core quackery and gray area quackery. What are the characteristics of a quack?
6. Describe the ways American people are protected from useless or harmful health products and services. How can you make effective use of these agencies?
7. Compare the functions of the Food and Drug Administration with the Federal Trade Commission in providing people with health protection.
8. Describe the adequacy of our health resources. In what ways does specialization in health services affect the adequacy of health care for people?
9. Distinguish between a medical and nonmedical practitioner.
10. List the ways health care bills are being met by the American people.
11. Distinguish between Medicare and Medicaid.
12. Do you believe the United States should have national health insurance for all Americans? Give reasons for your answer.

REFERENCES

1. INGRAHAM, HOLLIS S., M.D., "Quackery—Old and New," *Health News,* Vol. 44, No. 3, New York State Department of Health, Albany, 1967, p. 11.
2. *Health, United States, 1976–1977, Chartbook,* U.S. Dept. of Health, Education, and Welfare, DHEW Publication No. (HRA) 77–1233, 1977, p. 2.
3. *Ibid.,* pp. 24–26.
4. HERDMAN, ROGER, M. D., Keynote Address at the Annual New York State Health Education Conference, Cortland, N.Y., Oct. 21, 1977.
5. HANLON, JOHN J., *Principles of Public Health Administration,* 5th ed. The C. V. Mosby Co., Saint Louis, 1969, pp. 10–11.
6. *Health: United States: 1976–1977,* U.S. Dept. of Health, Education, and Welfare; Public Health Service; Health Resources Administration, DHEW Publication No. (HRA) 77–1232, Washington, 1977, pp. 345–346.
7. EHRENREICH, BARBARA and JOHN EHRENREICH, *The American Health Empire: Power, Profits, and Politics,* Vintage Book, New York, 1970, p. 29.
8. KAGAN, BENJAMIN M., SHIRLEY L. SANNIN, and FELIX BARDIE, "Spotlight on Antimicrobial Agents," 1973, *Journal of the American Medical Association,* Vol. 226, No. 3, p. 309.

9. Consumer Reports, *The Medicine Show,* Pantheon Books, New York, 1974, p. 314.
10. LARKIN, TIMOTHY, *Ten Fallacies About FDA,* U.S. Department of Health Education, and Welfare; Food and Drug Administration, HEW Publication No. (FDA) 76–1017.
11. WAXMAN, HENRY A., "Health Regulation: Who Gains?" *American Lung Association Bulletin,* The Association, New York, June 1979, p. 4.
12. *Health, United States, 1976–77, Chartbook, op. cit.,* p. 3.
13. U.S. Department of Health, Education, and Welfare; Social Security Administration, *How Medicare Helps During a Hospital Stay,* HEW Publication No. (SSA) 78–10039, Jan. 1978.
14. U.S. Department of Health, Education, and Welfare; Medical Services Administration; Health Care Financing Administration, *Medicaid-Medicare, Which is Which?* HEW Publication No. (HCFA) 77–24901.

11

the politics of health

INTRODUCTION

Ours is a government that has a distinct responsibility to lead the people, to protect their interests, and to protect and promote their health. Each state government has overlapping health responsibilities. Each of us has a responsibility to become involved in the political process as it relates to health promotion, which extends beyond our ability to vote. We must be prepared to deal effectively with politicians and civil servants alike, for it is they who formulate, enact, and enforce public health policy; and it is they who, in the final analysis, must ultimately respond to our demands.

The political process with which we have to deal is extremely complex, and sometimes frustrating, and threatening. It is, however, essential for uniform health promotional activities. This complexity was described eloquently by Theodore H. White:

> For some men, lawmaking is the most fascinating process of government. New laws call for the subtlest trickeries, the most brutal pressures, the most corrupt practices of American democracy—from the most bumbling city council wrestling with zoning ordinances, through state legislators wrestling with highway and labor legislation, to the Senate of the United States, which deals both with follies and with fate.[1]

There is no doubt that quality health care and health promotional activities are a right of the American people. It is the political arena that sets the stage for debate on how far this right extends.

HEALTH IN AMERICA: A HISTORICAL PERSPECTIVE

We begin our discussion of the politics of health in America with an overview of the health efforts of the Truman Administration. We then look at the efforts of the post-Truman administrations since federal health efforts tend to be significantly related to presidential policy and philosophy.

The Truman Years

President Truman assumed office immediately upon the death of President Roosevelt in 1945. Shortly thereafter, Mr. Truman began submitting proposals to Congress and the American people that would have vastly increased the federal government's role in the health care system. Although many of the Truman health proposals were defeated, his administration set the stage for massive increases in federal health expenditures over the succeeding 30 years.

The most controversial proposal submitted to the Congress by President Truman, beginning with his first health message to Congress in 1945 and repeated several times throughout the course of his administration, was a recommendation for *comprehensive national health insurance.* Each time the President submitted the proposal, it was defeated, largely because of a coalition of Republicans and conservative Democrats and the skillful lobbying of the American Medical Association.

President Truman's call for national health insurance was very similar to that made by modern-day politicians who support the concept. In his 1945 health message, Mr. Truman said:

> Millions of our citizens do not now have a full measure of opportunity to achieve and enjoy good health. Millions do not now have protection or security against the economic effects of sickness. The time has arrived for action to help them attain that opportunity and that protection ...
>
> People with low or moderate incomes do not get the same medical attention as those with high incomes. The poor have more sickness, but they get less medical care. People who live in rural areas do not get the same amount or quality of medical attention as those who live in our cities.[2]

In addition to President Truman's attempts to push a national health insurance bill through Congress, there were many other significant advances in the health field. On June 14, 1948, the President signed legislation providing for United States' membership in the World Health Organization.

The National Heart Act, establishing the National Heart Institute was signed into law on June 16, 1948. In addition to providing funds to states and localities for the establishment of programs to control heart and circulatory diseases, the bill also changed the name of the National Institute of Health to the National Institutes of Health (NIH). Eight days later the National Dental Research Institute was established within the NIH.

After the 1948 elections in which Democrats captured both houses of Congress, efforts for National Health Insurance intensified. The debate in Congress became extremely bitter with opponents, led by the American Medical Association (AMA), calling the proposal one of socialized medicine.

Although a national health insurance bill was never enacted, Congress did move, in 1950, by enacting amendments to the Social Security Act. These amendments established: Old Age Assistance (OAA), Aid to Dependent Children (ADC), Aid to the Blind (AB), and Aid to the Permanently and Totally Disabled (APTD).

Toward the end of his administration, President Truman established the President's Commission on the Health Needs of the Nation. It was his last major contribution to the federal government's role in the nation's health. It was the option of President Eisenhower to implement the Commission's recommendations.

The Commission put forth ten basic tenets upon which its report was based outlining a comprehensive national health policy.[3]

Whatever the success of the Truman administration in health legislation, there is no question that federal health policy was significantly influenced during this period. Of greater significance is the influence the Truman administration's policies had on both Republican and Democratic administrations into the 1980s.

Although the President's Commission on the Health Needs of the Nation set forth bold proposals, President Eisenhower did not respond. In his first State of the Union Message,[4] he made no specific reference to health other than a pledge to reorganize the administration's activities in the areas of health, education, and social security.

Very early in his administration, President Eisenhower set out to establish himself as being against national health insurance. On March 14, 1953, speaking to the members of the House of Delegates of the American Medical Association, the President said:

> I have found, in the past few years, that I have certain philosophical bonds with doctors. I don't like the word "compulsory." I am against the word "socialized." Everything about such words seems to me to be a step toward the thing that we are spending so many billions to prevent; that is, the overwhelming of this country by any force, power, or idea that leads us to forsake our traditional system of free enterprise.[5]

One of President Eisenhower's major health accomplishments occurred on April 11, 1953 when he established the Department of Health, Education, and Welfare (HEW). Essentially, the new department was created from a reorganization of the Federal Security Administration and the Public Health Service.

In July, 1953, the Congress extended the Hill-Burton Act of 1946. Enacted during the Truman administration, this act provided monies to the states for the construction of hospitals, to overcome the nation's severe deficit of hospital beds.

Mr. Eisenhower's second State of the Union Message was characterized by a continuance of his philosophy opposing national health insurance. Instead, he called for an increase in funds for medical research into cancer and heart disease, a broadening of the Hill-Burton Act, and a limited government reinsurance plan to allow private health insurance companies to offer broader coverage.[6] The President had only limited success in enacting these proposals.

Beginning in 1955 and continuing throughout the election year of 1956, President Eisenhower increased his efforts in the health area with a good deal of success. On July 14, 1955, the President signed the Air Pollution Act which he had called for in his health message of January 31. The law provided funds for air pollution studies through the Public Health Service and through grants to states, localities, and public and private institutions.

On July 28, the President signed the Mental Health Study Act of 1955. This bill, strongly supported by the President, established the Joint Commission on Mental Illness and Health which conducted a comprehensive study of the nation's mental health programs and resources.

One of the most significant bills passed by Congress from a humanistic viewpoint during the Eisenhower administration was the Poliomyelitis Vaccination Assistance Act of 1955. The bill authorized the Surgeon General to make grants to the states for free vaccinations to children under 20 years of age and pregnant women. The bill specified that the vaccinations would be made available to individuals regardless of ability to pay.

Eisenhower's second term was characterized primarily as one of expansion and continuation of existing federal health programs. In fact, the record shows that where existing programs were expanded it was quite often over presidential objection.

On September 2, 1958, President Eisenhower signed a bill that was to initiate the Kennedy administration's involvement in federal health affairs. This bill authorized the Department of HEW to conduct a White House Conference on the Aging during January, 1961, merely two weeks before President Kennedy assumed office.

The Kennedy Years

The White House Conference on the Aging focused on an issue of great controversy: national health insurance for the elderly. Proponents of such a program advocated its funding through Social Security. The leader of the opposition, as it had been in the past when debate centered on comprehensive national health insurance, was the American Medical Association. The AMA once again based its opposition on the issue of socialized medicine. The Conference, however, did endorse the concept of national health insurance for the elderly, a program now known as Medicare.

President Kennedy was quick to endorse the health insurance concept (he already had established a record in this regard as a Senator) and on February 9, 1961 in a Special Message to the Congress on Health and Hospital Care said:

> Those among us who are over 65—16 million in the United States—go to the hospital more often and stay longer than their younger neighbors. Their physical activity is limited by six times as much disability as the rest of the population. Their annual medical bill is twice that of persons under 65—but their annual income is only half as high.[7]

In his address, President Kennedy outlined many new health proposals. Several of these recommendations were enacted in the Community Health Services and Facilities Act of 1961.[8]

In his January 11, 1962 annual State of the Union Message, and again in a special message to the Congress on February 27, President Kennedy once again focused on the health needs of the nation.[9] In these messages he recommended that there be increased funding for medical and dental scholarships and a strengthening of the food and drug laws, among others. He had mixed success in persuading the Congress to enact his proposals. These proposals and their fate were as follows:

1. Compulsory national health insurance for the elderly—Defeated on the Senate floor.
2. A 10-year program of grants for the construction of medical and dental schools and a program of scholarships for medical and dental students —Defeated.

3. Federal aid for the immunization of children against the common child diseases—Passed.

4. Increase in funds for the National Institutes of Health—Passed.

5. Establishment of the National Institute of Child Health and General Medical Sciences—Passed.

6. Extension of the Health Research Facilities Act of 1956—Passed.

7. Increase in funds for the National Mental Health Institute—Passed.

8. Extension of the Air Pollution Act of 1955—Partially enacted.

9. Establishment of a National Environmental Health Center—Funds not appropriated.

10. Authorization of a 5-year program of loans for the construction and equipment of group practice medical and dental facilities—No action taken.

11. Encouragement of states to provide health services to migrant farm workers—Passed.

12. Reorganization of the Public Health Service—No action taken.

A White House Conference on Narcotic and Drug Abuse, called by President Kennedy, was held in 1962. The Conference focused its attention on identifying ways of stopping illegal drug traffic, with particular emphasis on rehabilitating the drug addict. Mr. Kennedy's interest in eliminating the problem of drug abuse was reiterated when he created the President's Advisory Commission on Narcotic and Drug Abuse in 1963. This Commission issued a variety of recommendations, many of which were incorporated into the Drug Abuse Control Amendments of 1965.

Later in 1963, President Kennedy once again called for national health insurance for the elderly. In addition, he urged appropriations for the training of health personnel, modernization of health facilities, and health research.

Legislation was enacted that dealt with mental health, designed to provide funds for the construction of mental health facilities. In addition, funds were appropriated for the training of teachers of mentally retarded and handicapped children, as well as for the improvement of education for the handicapped. The adoption of the Clean Air Act replaced the pollution control law, originally passed in 1955.

The year 1963 also saw the assassination of President Kennedy. Many of his proposals had not been acted upon and it was left to President Johnson to shepherd them through Congress.

The Johnson Years

President Johnson had a great deal of experience in the Congress. He entered the Presidency upon the death of President Kennedy with many "New Frontier" programs yet to be enacted and with an election year about to begin. He also had his own health agenda, which he rapidly incorporated into his "Great Society" philosophy.

In 1964 in a special health message to the Congress, President Johnson outlined a broad program.[10] He called for hospital insurance for the aged, an extension of the Hill-Burton Act, an increase in health manpower, an expansion of mental health activities, improved environmental health activities, the establishment of a Commission on Heart Disease, Cancer, and Stroke, an expansion of vocational rehabilitation, and increased efforts in international health.

President Johnson's belief in the ability of the federal government to significantly contribute to the elimination of disease in concert with the medical professions was undying. The faith was exemplified at the first meeting of the President's Commission on Heart Disease, Cancer, and Stroke:

> The point is, we must conquer heart disease, we must conquer cancer, we must conquer strokes. This nation and the whole world cries out for this victory. I am firmly convinced that the accumulated brains and determination of this Commission and of the scientific community of the world will, before the end of two decades, come forward with some answers and cures that we need so very much.[11]

The Johnson administration was involved in the enactment of more pieces of health legislation than had ever before been enacted. Contributing factors to this were the programs that had not been acted upon during the Kennedy administration, President Johnson's expertise in dealing with Congress, and the President's overwhelming victory in the 1964 election which also gave the Democrats substantial majorities in both houses of Congress.

This Congressional support led in 1964, after many years of controversy, to Senate passage of Medicare (national health insurance for the aged). After Senate passage of the Medicare bill, President Johnson said:

> In a free and prosperous society there is no need for any person, especially the elderly, to suffer personal economic disaster and become a tragic burden upon loved ones or the State through major illness when, by prudently setting aside the employers and employees contributions this can be avoided.[12]

This bill was later signed into law, and became the first national health insurance law ever enacted by the Congress. President Johnson signed the measure in Independence, Missouri in honor of President Truman. In 1965 President Johnson called for stricter controls on barbiturates and amphetamines which led to the enactment of the Drug Abuse Control Amendments of 1965, and further strengthened in 1968. In 1967 the Senate ratified the 1961 Convention on Narcotic Drugs, designed to facilitate the control of the international flow of illicit drugs.

In 1965, as a result of the Surgeon General's Report on Smoking and Health, Congress enacted the Federal Cigarette Labeling and Advertising Act. This bill required that as of January 1, 1966, all cigarette packages and cartons sold in the United States bear the statement: "Caution: Cigarette Smoking May Be Hazardous to Your Health." This bill was considered by many to be a victory for the tobacco industry since the Federal Trade Commission had previously proposed much stricter regulations.

The Heart Disease, Cancer, and Stroke Amendments of 1965 authorized funds for the establishment of regional medical programs to deal with these and related diseases. The bill was intended to upgrade the preparation of medical personnel as well as to improve the quality of health facilities and equipment.

On November 3, 1966, President Johnson signed into law the Comprehensive Health Planning and Public Health Services Amendments of 1966. (The Partnership for Health Act) which began a new era in health planning in the United States. The bill authorized state and regional coordination of health services. Monies authorized in the bill were allocated to the states through *formula* grants taking into consideration population, extent of need and per capita income. Monies were also made available for *project* grants in the areas of cancer, chronic illness, mental retardation, neurological diseases, tuberculosis, and venereal diseases. The significance of the Partnership for Health Act was that it was a precursor to legislation establishing Health Maintenance Organizations and Health Systems Agencies during the succeeding decade.

The cost of health care in America was addressed in 1966 by the President's National Advisory Commission on Health Manpower. The report of the Commission, issued in 1967, was a stinging indictment of the nation's health care system. The report said that the major problems existing at the time were caused by a lack of leadership and willingness to change by the medical profession.

The Partnership for Health Amendments of 1967 was the most important law passed during the first session of the 90th Congress. The bill provided funds for comprehensive health planning and a survey of the extent of hunger and malnutrition in the United States.

There is no doubt that federal involvement in the health of the American people significantly increased during the Johnson years. While the government acted to help ensure an upgrading of the quality of health in America, it did so by vastly expanding the government bureaucracy designed to implement the laws enacted by Congress.

The Nixon and Ford Years

The Nixon administration was slow to develop its health policies and recommendations. With the exception of the areas of drug abuse and population growth, there were no health messages to the Congress during the first half of 1969.

During the early years of the Nixon administration, Congress focused its attention on extending existing health legislation. However, President Nixon sought to be fiscally conservative in health affairs. He vetoed the Medical Facilities Construction and Modernization Amendments of 1970, saying that the bill was "a long step down the road of fiscal irresponsibility . . ."[13] The bill, however, was enacted over his veto. This was the first time in 10 years that Congress had overridden a presidential veto.

Congress passed the Comprehensive Drug Abuse Prevention and Control Act of 1970 at the request of the Administration. The bill provided funds for rehabilitation, drug education, increased law enforcement, and revision of the penalty structure for violation of federal narcotic laws. As a result, the National

Institute on Alcohol Abuse and Alcoholism was established in 1970 in the National Institute of Mental Health as a part of Congressional efforts to deal with the problem of alcoholism.

One of the major legislative controversies of the Nixon administration occurred in 1970, when President Nixon pocket vetoed a bill designed to provide grants to hospitals and medical schools for the training of physicians in general practice. The President vetoed the bill on the grounds that other, existing programs could accomplish the same goal. The controversy arose because the pocket veto occurred during the six-day Christmas recess. Opponents of the President charged that he had misused the power of the pocket veto since, they claimed, such a veto could occur only upon the permanent adjournment of Congress and not during brief recesses.

Even during the Nixon administration there was public debate over the value of national health insurance. The concept of national health insurance was no longer criticized as socialized medicine by most influential groups. The debate in 1971 centered not on whether national health insurance was necessary, but on what form it should take. The growing acceptance of national health insurance stemmed from the rapidly increasing cost of medical care. Although it was viewed as necessary by most groups, no action was taken.

More than one billion dollars was authorized in February, 1972, through fiscal 1975 for the establishment of a Special Action Office for Drug Abuse Prevention in the Executive Office of the President. The bill gave the new director authority to coordinate all federal drug abuse programs except those dealing with law enforcement. In addition, the bill created a National Institute on Drug Abuse within the National Institute of Mental Health, a National Advisory Council for Drug Abuse Prevention, and a National Drug Abuse Training Center.

In 1972, the National Commission on Marihuana and Drug Abuse issued its first report, *Marihuana: A Signal of Misunderstanding.*[14] The report created a great deal of controversy because it advocated a rational look at marijuana; that rational look being decriminalization of marijuana use. This recommendation was so repugnant to the Nixon administration that the President rejected the entire report.

Another controversy arose in 1972 with the release of the report of The Commission on Population Growth and the American Future.[15] Also rejected by the President, the Commission recommended wide-scale sex education programs, an abortion policy patterned after the existing law in New York State (subsequently upheld by the United States Supreme Court), approval of the Equal Rights Amendment, and contraceptive supplies, information and procedures available on demand.

Another Commission report deserving of mention, released during the Nixon administration, was that of the President's Committee on Health Education.[16] This was the first such committee ever established to study health education. It recommended that a National Center for Health Education be established in the private sector. This was accomplished. It was also recommended that a Bureau of Health Education be established within the Department of Health, Education, and Welfare. This Bureau was ultimately placed within the Center for Disease Control in Atlanta, Georgia.

For the remainder of President Nixon's term of office, he and his administration were preoccupied with other matters. Very little additional leadership was given in the health area. When President Ford took office, he continued the general pattern relative to health that was established by Nixon.

The Carter Years

When President Carter took office, he was extremely enthusiastic about the health proposals for which he had campaigned. Very early in his term of office, Carter proposed to refinance social security, to provide for preventive health care for low income children, and promised to develop a national health insurance plan by 1978. However, President Carter's success was limited and by the end of 1977, none of these proposals had been enacted. Instead, major federal health accomplishments were limited to an extension of ongoing federal health programs.

Throughout the Carter term, health care costs continued to skyrocket. As the 1980 presidential elections approached, the debate between the Kennedy and Carter supporters intensified. The Carter proposal was primarily limited to catastrophic coverage rather than being comprehensive as was the Kennedy plan.

In addition, beginning in 1979, a competitive or "free-market" approach to health care gained increasing support. This ultimately, became the prevailing philosophy during the early part of the Reagan administration.

THE IMPORTANCE OF POLITICAL INVOLVEMENT

Our Political Role

When considering the health of the nation or the health of communities, there is very little that is not either directly or indirectly related to the political process. If we choose to use any health service in the community, we are in a sense being affected by politics—from the quality of aspirin we may buy in the drug store, to the quality of health education programs in the schools, to the validity of the license of our personal physician.

For these reasons, none of us should choose to isolate ourselves from politics. We cannot escape it. We must learn to use the process to our benefit. If we do not, the rights of all of us will not be protected, but will be exploited for the benefit of a few.

We, the consumers, are the most powerful special interest group. We elect politicians to office. We purchase health products from manufacturers who are their own special interest group. We purchase and receive medical care and we must rely upon the political system to ensure high quality service. The health care system must ultimately be accountable to us. The political system is so complex and threatening to the average American that many of us choose to not even consider becoming involved.

Although bold leadership is desirable in health promotional activities, *we can make a difference.* Each of us can move institutions and politicians ever so slightly, which together can significantly improve our health. The late Senator Robert F. Kennedy illustrated this concept best when he said:

> It is from numberless diverse sets of courage and belief that human history is shaped. Each time a man stands up for an ideal, or acts to improve the lot of others, or strikes out against injustice, he sends a tiny ripple of hope, and crossing each other from a million different centers of energy and daring those ripples build a current which can sweep down the mightiest walls of oppression and resistance.[17]

What kind of a ripple can you make?

The Legislative Process (The Federal Level)

Authorizations and appropriations   There are two types of legislation —*authorizations* and *appropriations.* Authorizing legislation contains the basic substantive program authority; although dollar figures are usually stipulated in such legislation, it does not carry with it any guarantee of actual funding. Appropriation measures, on the other hand, deal strictly with the allocation of government funds and do not generally (with certain exceptions) deal with substantive program authorities.

The path of legislation   Figure 11–1 outlines the path of legislation (assuming the bill is introduced in the House of Representatives). The stages in this process are as follows:

1. *Introduction:* Upon introduction, a measure is assigned a bill number and referred to the full committee with jurisdiction over the subject matter of the bill.
2. *Committee Passage:* The full committee refers the measure to one of its subcommittees with more specialized subject matter jurisdiction. Hearings are scheduled and held within the subcommittee.

   After hearings, a *mark-up* session is held to consider amendments. After mark-up, a "clean" bill is "reported out" to the full committee, and may or may not be given a "clean" number. Once the measure has cleared these hurdles, it is placed on the "calendar" and assigned a "calendar number." On the appropriate date, it is taken up by the full chamber of either house or both houses, at which time it may be subject to amendment.

   When the bill is passed by one house, it may be sent to the other house for action where the procedure is begun again. In many cases, however, the other chamber will have been deliberating its own version of the measure. If both measures are identical, one bill will be voted upon by

Figure 11-1
The Path of Legislation

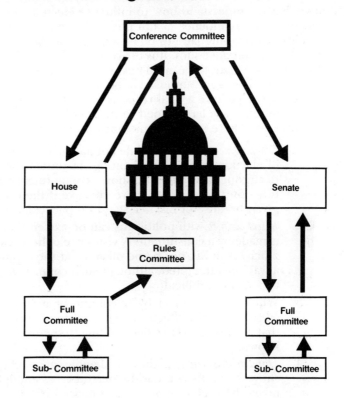

both bodies, emerging with a House or Senate number, and will be sent to the President for his signature. If the measures are different, however, a *conference* will be called between the House and Senate to resolve the differences. Conference members are usually the members of the relevant subcommittees that originally considered the measure. Upon agree-·ment, the measure will be sent to both chambers for approval, after which it will go to the President.

3. *The President:* Once the President receives the bill, he has four options:

- Sign the bill into law;
- Veto the bill within 10 days (Sundays not included); if he takes this course, he is required to send Congress a statement of his objections to the measure;
- Do nothing—if Congress is in session the measure will automatically become law after ten days;
- "Pocket-veto" the bill; this may occur when Congress adjourns before ten days have elapsed after passage, thus preventing the President from returning the bill.[18]

Because we often do not have lobbyists at our disposal, it becomes imperative that we understand how to influence elected and nonelected officials alike and then act to influence health policy. Of course, the most basic and essential political act is voting; and to be meaningful, it should be based upon the candidates' stands on the issues. It is the responsibility of the voter, therefore, to study the issues, evaluate the candidates' positions, and vote accordingly.

Politicians are supposed to be responsive to the demands of their constituents. They also have a dual responsibility in acting for the public good. Their actions in office are largely tied to the communications they receive from their constituents. There are many methods of influencing politicians:

1. *Campaign contributions,* while not having the impact they once had because of election reform laws limiting the amount individuals may contribute to any one candidate, still show a commitment on the part of the contributor. Contributions are more effective if the candidate knows that it was given because of his/her stand on particular issues.

2. *Direct contact* with politicians can be extremely effective, particularly if it is made by a constituent. A visit or telephone call can be made when the official is in his/her home office or at the capitol. Direct contact should always be attempted, although such contact with Congressmen or Senators is often difficult.

3. When direct contact by telephone or a visit is not possible, *sending a telegram* is quite effective. Its effect is enhanced because the official sees that constituents have been willing to spend money to make their feelings known.

4. *Handwritten letters,* if they are legible, are highly effective, because they show the politician that the person cares enough about an issue to have taken the time to write a personalized letter.

5. *Typed letters* are most effective when they are typed by the person who is addressing the elected official. Letters typed by one's secretary can be effective, however, especially if they provide the official with pertinent information about the issue.

6. Of the methods discussed here, the use of *petitions* is usually the least effective means of influencing an elected official. It takes little thought and even less time to sign one's name on a sheet of paper. Moreover, petitions do not produce volume. It is much more effective to produce individual responses rather than one response with scores of names attached to it.

Dealing with nonelected officials is more difficult in many respects than dealing with elected officials because they are not dependent on election for employment. Their basic function is to implement and enforce statutes and to recommend revisions in existing statutes to the legislative branch of government. Because of the lack of direct accountability to the public, bureaucratic institutions often enforce laws as they see fit and can change their methodology of enforcement without impeaching their obligations under the law, though the spirit of the law may be assaulted from time to time.

When influencing bureaucratic officials the same "rules" apply as were discussed above concerning elected officials. However, some additional suggestions are also appropriate. When a letter or telegram is sent to an official it is best not to send a copy to an official *lower* in the bureaucratic structure. If this is done, the response is more likely to come from the official with lesser power. Correspondence should nearly always be sent to officials higher in the bureaucratic structure to inform them of the issue at hand.

It is always helpful that when we communicate with an official, we represent other people. Those of us who sometimes must act alone must work much harder to influence the political process. Whatever the case, we must learn to weather the frustrations and be vigorous in our attempts to make an impact on the political system.

The Social Impact of Health Legislation

Whenever governmental involvement in health affairs is considered, the question always arises as to when statutes and regulations designed to protect our health infringe upon our freedom of choice; our freedom to behave as we wish even if we are risking our health. Each of us demands, expects and deserves governmental actions to protect the general welfare as it relates to health. However, legislation designed to control human behavior is always subject to debate. No one has yet defined when health legislation, designed to control human behavior for the public good, infringes upon our right to choose. Should we be able to consume saccharine if we choose? Should we be able to choose laetrile treatments in our misinformed attempts to cure cancer? Should 9–12 million Americans be able to elect alcoholism despite the efforts of modern-day temperance advocates? Indeed, should we be allowed to smoke to our heart's content, or at least to our heart's arrest?

When we allow our Senators and Congressmen to enact legislation that controls our choice, then we are, in effect, allowing them to enact prohibition bills that will have little effect on promoting health. The priority of government, therefore, must be to protect us from institutional infringements on our health and not punish individuals for falling prey to those institutions and industries that the government welcomes within its jurisdiction with open arms. Each time personal behavior is regulated by law without a corresponding statute regulating industrial or institutional infringements, the same organizations can claim victory and continue to exploit the public.

The effectiveness of legislation and other governmental regulations is, therefore, limited. It has been demonstrated that the most effective type of health legislation deals with the promotion of health, providing funding for programs that will reach large numbers of people, or to improve or create needed facilities. In addition, legislation that sets minimal standards for health programs helps to ensure uniform quality of services.

While it is true that government is and should be limited in its ability to regulate the lives of people, it is still a necessity with which we must learn to deal. It is imperative that if the health of Americans is to be properly promoted, each of us must contribute to the political process. It is we who are ultimately responsible for the success of this process. We have a responsibility not only for ourselves but to society as a whole.

· GLOSSARY

Commission: A governmental body directed and authorized to carry out a particular task.

Politics: The process of maneuvering to establish public policy.

Political process: The procedures used to initiate and pass legislation.

Socialized medicine: A health policy and program for the people or certain segments of the population, directed, authorized, and administered by the government.

Pocket veto: The act of the executive using veto power by having a bill unsigned beyond the adjournment of the legislative body.

SUMMARY

Each of us has a responsibility to become involved in the political process to ensure the promotion of society's health. Such action will help secure high quality health care and health promotional activities that are a right of the American people.

The health initiatives of the federal government can be conveniently categorized by Presidential administration. The Truman administration marked the beginning of massive increases in federal health expenditures. It was also characterized by significant efforts to enact compulsory national health insurance. In addition, the Truman administration was responsible for U.S. membership in the World Health Organization and creating the National Institutes of Health.

President Eisenhower's administration was quite conservative in the health field. The President was opposed to the concept of national health insurance, and most of his administration was characterized by extension and expansion of existing programs.

The Kennedy administration began with the President endorsing the recommendation of the White House Conference on the Aging, calling for national health insurance for the elderly. The President also submitted many new proposals to Congress with mixed success. The White House Conference on Narcotic and Drug Abuse resulted in many recommendations being incorporated into the Drug Abuse Control Amendments of 1965. There were also significant strides taken in the area of mental health services.

There was more health legislation enacted during the Johnson administration than had previously been enacted in the history of the country. Not only were existing programs extended and expanded, but new programs were also proposed in health planning, drug abuse control, chronic disease control, and national health insurance for the elderly.

Like President Eisenhower, President Nixon was a conservative in health affairs. Many existing programs were extended, but few new programs were proposed. National health insurance also became an acceptable concept although no program was enacted.

President Carter favored such programs as preventive health services, expansion of mental health programs, and national health insurance. However, exorbitant health costs prevented him from successfully enacting most of his major health proposals. Most recently, a free-market approach to health care is the prevailing administrative philosophy.

Nearly every aspect of health is either directly or indirectly related to politics. We must, therefore, learn to use the political process for our benefit. This includes not only influencing elected officials, but nonelected officials as well. If we do not use the political process effectively, we stand a good chance of being exploited.

It appears that the most effective health legislation provides funding for programs and facilities that promote health. In addition, legislation that sets minimal programmatic standards helps to ensure quality of service. Legislation, however, that mandates a control of individual behavior often is difficult to enforce and may threaten our freedom to act as we see fit.

PROBLEMS FOR DISCUSSION

1. Analyze the health responsibilities of government, state, and national.
2. Discuss the history of national health insurance in the United States. Is such a program necessary? Will such a program improve the health of the people?
3. Analyze the role of the American Medical Association in the area of politics. How has the AMA contributed to the nation's health? How has it detracted from the nation's health?
4. Do national health commissions make a significant contribution to the nation's health? Why? Why not?
5. Why was so much attention given to drug legislation during the 1960's?
6. Why was the Cigarette Labeling and Advertising Act of 1966 a victory for the tobacco industry?
7. Why should each of us become involved in the political process?
8. Discuss the pros and cons of lobbying.
9. Discuss the implications of health legislation designed to control individual behavior.
10. Compare and contrast the ability of people to influence politicians vis-à-vis bureaucrats.

REFERENCES

1. WHITE, THEODORE H., *The Making of the President: 1964,* Atheneum Publishers, New York, 1965, p. 182.
2. TRUMAN, HARRY S., "Health Message to Congress," November 19, 1945.
3. The President's Commission on the Health Needs of the Nation, *Building America's Health,* U.S. Government Printing Office, 1953, p. 3.
4. EISENHOWER, DWIGHT D., "1st Annual State of the Union Message," Feb. 5, 1953.
5. EISENHOWER, DWIGHT D., "Remarks to the Members of the House of Delegates of the American Medical Association," March 14, 1953.

6. EISENHOWER, DWIGHT D., "2nd Annual State of the Union Message," January 7, 1954.
7. KENNEDY, JOHN F., "Special Message to the Congress on Health and Hospital Care," Feb. 9, 1961.
8. *Ibid.*
9. KENNEDY, JOHN F., "Annual Message to the Congress on the State of the Union," January 11, 1962.
10. JOHNSON, LYNDON B., "Special Message to the Congress on the Nation's Health," February 10, 1964.
11. JOHNSON, LYNDON B., "Remarks at the First Meeting of the President's Commission on Heart Disease, Cancer and Stroke," April 17, 1964.
12. JOHNSON, LYNDON B., "Statement by the President Following Senate Passage of the Medicare Bill," Sept. 2, 1964.
13. NIXON, RICHARD M., "Veto of the Medical Facilities Construction and Modernization Amendments of 1970," June 22, 1970.
14. National Commission on Marihuana and Drug Abuse, *Marihuana: A Signal of Misunderstanding,* The New American Library, Inc., U.S., 1972.
15. The Commission on Population Growth and the American Future, *Population and the American Future,* The New American Library, Inc., U.S., 1972.
16. The President's Committee on Health Education, *The Report of the President's Committee on Health Education,* Department of Health, Education, and Welfare, PHS, 1973.
17. WORTMAN, ARTHUR and RICHARD RHODES (eds.), *Robert F. Kennedy: Promises to Keep.* Hallmark Editions, Kansas City, Mo., 1969, p. 25.
18. "Effective Intervention In the Governmental Process," American College of Preventive Medicine, Nov. 4, 1970.

PART

IV

personal
health
decisions

12

our nutrition behavior

NUTRIENTS

Introduction

The important chemical components of foods necessary for growth, energy, and regulation of body functions are called *nutrients.* The nutrients known to be present in foods are carbohydrates, proteins, lipids (fats), vitamins, and minerals. Although water, strictly speaking, is not considered a nutrient, it is essential for all of life's processes and for proper use by the body of the nutrients in the foods we eat.

Carbohydrates, lipids, and proteins are *macronutrients,* while vitamins and minerals are *micronutrients.* These terms are used to describe the relative quantities needed to maintain nutritional health. The chief function of the macronutrients is to provide the body with the energy it needs to carry on all of the activities of life: work, exercise, and the continuation of the vital processes, such as respiration, glandular functioning, and heart action. Although protein can be used by the body as a source of energy, its primary purpose is to provide the essential amino acids necessary for growth and the repair of worn out cells and tissues. The micronutrients are necessary for regulating body functions, and for becoming integral components of various body structures (bone) and fluids (hormones).

Protein

Protein is an integral component of all known living substances. It consists chemically of carbon, hydrogen, oxygen, and nitrogen; however, some proteins also contain sulfur, phosphorus, iron, and iodine. Protein contains the nutrient essentials called *amino acids* that are changed into body protein within the cell. However, before the amino acids can be absorbed by the body and carried to the cells for synthesis into body protein, the food protein must be digested; that is, the protein molecules must be broken down into their amino acid components. Protein digestion begins in the stomach with the action of the enzyme, *pepsin.* The partially digested protein passes into the small intestine where alkaline inactivates the pepsin, while other enzymes from the pancreas and small intestine complete the digestive process.

The amino acids are absorbed into the blood stream. Precisely how amino acids are absorbed is still unclear. Some investigators believe it is accomplished through simple diffusion while others believe that there may be a unique mechanism in operation for amino acid absorption. The amino acids are then transported to the liver where they become a part of the amino acid pool. Amino acids needed by the cells for synthesis into cell proteins are transported by the blood to the cell where protein synthesis takes place. Before proteins can be synthesized in the cells, all of the essential and nonessential amino acids must be present.

The amino acids that must be supplied by the food we eat are called the *essential amino acids.* Some of the amino acids needed for protein synthesis can be formed by the body and are called *nonessential amino acids.* The protein foods we eat that contain all of the essential amino acids are called *complete protein foods.* Rich sources of complete proteins include lean meats, fish, poultry, and milk; plant protein sources are usually incomplete, lacking one or more of the essential amino acids.

The chief functions of proteins are for growth and maintenance of tissues; the formation of hormones, enzymes, and antibodies; the maintenance of body fluid balance; and providing a source of energy. Protein is vital for growth of infants, children, and adolescents. If an adequate supply of protein is *not* present in the foods they eat, growth will be impeded. In adults, protein is necessary for replacing cells and tissues that are broken down. Inadequate protein intake in adults will result in a wasting away of body tissues.

Hormones are essential for regulating specific body functions. *Enzymes* are essential for such processes as digestion and protein synthesis. *Antibodies* protect the body from invasion of foreign substances, such as disease-producing microorganisms. Proteins in the blood, such as plasma proteins, facilitate the removal of fluids from the cells, thus maintaining the fluid balance. When this is interrupted, edema results. Protein contains approximately 4 kilocalories per gram if metabolized for energy. This is equivalent to that of carbohydrate. If carbohydrate intake is insufficient to provide the energy needed, protein becomes that source of energy.

Carbohydrates

Carbohydrates are compounds consisting of carbon, hydrogen, and oxygen, and are present in the food we eat as starch or sugar. The carbohydrates are classified a number of ways, including the categories of monosaccharides, disaccharides, and polysaccharides.

Monosaccharides are glucose, fructose, and galactose. They are found in fruits, corn syrup, and honey. The monosaccharides can be absorbed through the intestinal wall without further digestion. The *disaccharides* are sucrose, lactose, and maltose. Sucrose is familiar to everyone as ordinary table sugar derived from sugar cane or sugar beet. It is also present in molasses and maple syrup. Lactose is present only in milk and milk products. The disaccharides are digested in the stomach and small intestine to form fructose, glucose, and galactose for absorption.

The *polysaccharides* are the starches, dextrins, and cellulose. They are found in foods from plants. The digestion of polysaccharides begins in the mouth, continues in the stomach, and is completed in the small intestine.

The *starches* begin their digestion in the mouth where they are broken down into dextrin and maltose. This continues in the stomach. Enzymes in the small intestine break the starches down further into glucose, which is eventually absorbed through the villi into the blood stream.

Dextrins also begin to be digested in the mouth and are broken into maltose. Like the starches, dextrins are further digested in the small intestine and digested into glucose, which is absorbed into the blood stream.

Cellulose is not digested. It is carried into the large intestine for evacuation. Cellulose is important for promoting intestinal movement and affecting the intestinal flora. In essence, cellulose adds fiber or bulk to the feces and helps to prevent constipation.

Fats

Lipids are fats found in foods of both animal and plant origin. Fats consist of fatty acids of varying carbon chain lengths. Generally, short-chain fatty acids are liquid at room temperature while long-chain fatty acids are solid. The fats that are usually solid at room temperature are called *saturated fatty acids* because their carbon atoms contain all of the hydrogen possible. The *unsaturated fatty acids* are usually liquid at room temperature and lack two or more hydrogen atoms. Generally fats from animal sources are saturated and high in cholesterol while vegetable fats are generally unsaturated cholesterol free. There are, of course, a few exceptions. Fats are important in the diet as:

- a concentrated source of energy (fats contain about twice as many kilocalories per gram as carbohydrate or protein);
- a vehicle for satiety value of foods we eat (fats give us a sense of satisfaction);
- a source of linoleic acid, which the body cannot synthesize, and which is essential for growth;
- a vehicle for fat soluble vitamins A,D,E, and K.

The digestion of fats actually begins to take place in the mouth where they are warmed to become more fluid. This process is hastened by mastication (chewing). In the stomach, fats are acted upon by the enzyme lipase which begins to break off some fatty acids. The fat is acted upon in the small intestine by bile, which emulsifies the fat molecules. Enzymes break the fat molecules into diglycerides and monoglycerides, free fatty acids, and glycerol. Some of these products of fat digestion are absorbed through the intestinal wall into the blood stream while others enter the lymphatic ducts and are carried to the neck region where they enter the blood. The fat is carried by the blood to the tissues where it is used for energy or stored as adipose tissue for future energy use.

Vitamins

Vitamins are unrelated, organic compounds needed in very small amounts for promoting growth and maintaining life and are abundantly present in the foods we eat. Vitamins act as catalysts as they interact with each other and with other nutrients. They are categorized according to their solubility in either fat or water.

The *fat soluble* vitamins are vitamins A, D, E, and K. *Vitamin A* is essential (1) for preventing night blindness (the inability to see in dim light); (2) for promoting growth in children; (3) for maintaining the normal mucus secretions of mucous membranes; (4) for healthy skin tissues; and (5) for adequate tear secretions of the eyes. Rich sources of vitamin A are leafy green and yellow vegetables, such as sweet potato, squash, and carrots, as well as dairy products, eggs, and meats. The recommended daily allowance of vitamin A is from 2000 international units (IU) for infants to 6000 IU for lactating women.

Excessive amounts of vitamin A intake can result in serious health problems. As much as 50,000 IU of vitamin A ingested daily can result in hypervitaminosis in adults; less than one-half this amount will produce a toxic effect in children. This danger exists only when one consumes vitamin supplements; it is very unlikely when vitamin consumption is limited to the amounts contained in the foods we eat each day.

Vitamin D was discovered in 1922. It occurs in the body and in foods as complete vitamin D or as a provitamin. The provitamin is actually a form of cholesterol occurring in animals and ergosterol in plants and is changed into vitamin D upon exposure to ultraviolet light. The chief function of vitamin D in the body is for the efficient use of calcium and phosphorus. This vitamin facilitates the absorption of calcium and phosphorus through the intestinal membrane. These two minerals are essential for the proper development of bones and teeth and obviously are most important during prenatal, infancy, childhood, and adolescence. If vitamin D deficiency is severe and prolonged, the bones and teeth cannot develop properly, which results in a condition known as *rickets.*

In adults, subnormal levels of calcium, either from a lack in the diet or poor absorption in the intestines as a result of vitamin D deficiency, can produce osteomalacia. *Osteomalacia* is the result of resorption of calcium from the bones. Closely associated with osteomalacia is *osteoporosis,* which is characterized by a reduction in the bone size as calcium levels are depleted.

In the adult, adequate dietary intake of vitamin D and calcium can be assured if one or two glasses of fortified milk are consumed each day. Excessive consumption of vitamin D, however, can result in hypervitaminosis. This may occur if one consumes high-potency vitamin D synthetic preparations. In infants, the diet needs to be carefully regulated to prevent excessive intakes since many infants are given vitamin D supplements along with vitamin D fortified milk and cereals, for example. Excessive consumption of vitamin D can result in excessive thirst, nausea, and vomiting, high calcium blood levels, irritability, along with other symptoms. Obviously, the treatment is a reduction of vitamin D intake, usually the elimination of vitamin D supplements. The recommended daily allowance of vitamin D is 400 IU for people up to 18 years of age.

Vitamin E has, in recent years, been the subject of some controversy. There have been claims of its ability to grow hair, clear up skin problems, relieve arthritis, cure and prevent ulcers, and to improve sexual performance. Actually, there is no scientific evidence that vitamin E can do any of these things.

Adequate amounts of vitamin E are supplied in a normal diet and additional supplements are not needed according to latest research findings. The recommended daily allowances, depending upon sex, age and physiologic conditions is from 5–30 IU. Adequate amounts are supplied in such foods as vegetable oils, many vegetables, whole grain cereals, meats, fish, poultry, eggs, fruits, and nuts. However, vitamin E supplements are indicated for babies born prematurely where inadequate placental transfer of the vitamin may have occurred, and for persons with intestinal disorders in which fats are inadequately absorbed.[1] Otherwise, no vitamin E deficiency conditions have been observed in humans.

The fourth and only other known fat soluble vitamin is *vitamin K,* which is sometimes known as the "antihemorrhage vitamin." Its chief function is to aid in the coagulation of blood by promoting the formation of prothrombin. A deficiency of vitamin K results in hemorrhaging, especially in infants born prematurely. However, since vitamin K is plentiful in normal diets, no recommended daily allowance has been suggested. Excessive amounts of vitamin K have been shown to increase the breakdown of red-blood cells in infants. Table 12–1 pro-

Table 12–1: Sources of Water Soluble and Fat Soluble Vitamins

Water Soluble Vitamins	Sources
Thiamine	breads and cereals, pork, veal, beef, lamb, chicken breast, calf liver, eggs, nuts, beans, green vegetables, potatoes, milk
Riboflavin	dairy products, beef, veal, pork, lamb, chicken breast, calf liver, fish, eggs, nuts, beans, breads and cereals, green and yellow vegetables
Niacin	beef, veal, pork, lamb, chicken breast, turkey, calf liver, fish, eggs, beans, nuts, breads and cereals, green vegetables, potatoes
B_6	meats, bananas, grains, lima beans, cabbage, potatoes, spinach, milk
Pantothenic Acid	organ meats, grains, (most foods contain this vitamin, including fruits and vegetables)
Biotin	egg yolk, milk, organ meats, cereals, legumes and nuts; synthesized in the human intestines
Folacin	dark green leafy vegetables, liver, kidney
B_{12}	foods from animal sources, meat, eggs, dairy products
Ascorbic acid	citrus fruits, strawberries, broccoli, cabbage, tomatoes, potatoes
Fat Soluble Vitamins	
A	liver, egg yolk, dairy products, sweet potatoes, winter squash, greens, carrots, cantaloupe
D	fortified milk, eggs, cheese, butter, fish
E	vegetable oils, greens
K	greens, liver, egg yolk

vides a summary of vitamins and their sources; Table 12–2 shows the Recommended Daily Dietary Allowances (RDA) for fat soluble vitamins.

The *water soluble* vitamins are the B vitamins and vitamin C. The B vitamins include thiamin, riboflavin, niacin, vitamin B_6, pantothenic acid, biotin, folacin, and cobalamin.

Thiamine was isolated in 1926. It is essential for carbohydrate metabolism. Under conditions of severe deficiency, beriberi will result. *Beriberi* is a dietary deficiency disease that affects the nervous system and is characterized by degeneration of nervous tissue. Its symptoms include muscle weakness, especially in the arms and legs. If the disease is not properly treated it will eventually lead to heart disease, edema, and paralysis. The disease is almost unknown in the United States, but it is found in those areas of the world where the people subsist chiefly on polished white rice.

Riboflavin was synthesized in 1935. It aids in converting energy nutrients into the energy needed by the body, and it contributes to a healthy skin. A deficiency of riboflavin in children will affect growth, result in the eyes becoming overly sensitive to light, and possibly impair vision.

Niacin was discovered in 1937 when it was found to cure "black tongue" in dogs. It also aids in the release of energy during metabolism. A severe deficiency of niacin results in the disease known as pellagra. *Pellagra* is characterized by symptoms of diarrhea, dermatitis, dementia, and finally, death. Historically, the incidence of pellagra has been highest among peoples whose diet consists

Table 12–2: Recommended Daily Dietary Allowances (RDA)*

	Age (Years)	FAT SOLUBLE VITAMINS			
		A		D	E
		(RE)[a]	(IU)	(CH)[b]	(TE)[c]
Infants	0—0.5	420	1400	10.0	3
	0.5—1	400	2000	10.0	4
Children	1—3	400	2000	10.0	5
	4—6	500	2500	10.0	6
	7—10	700	3300	10.0	7
Males	11—14	1000	5000	10.0	8
	15—18	1000	5000	10.0	10
	19—22	1000	5000	7.5	10
	23—50	1000	5000	5.0	10
	51+	1000	5000	5.0	10
Females	11—14	800	4000	10.0	8
	15—18	800	4000	10.0	8
	19—22	800	4000	7.5	8
	23—50	800	4000	5.0	8
	51+	800	4000	5.0	8

[a] Retinol equivalents
[b] As cholicalciferal   } These are the units of measurement used for these vitamins.
[c] Tocopherol equivalents

*Source of Data: Food and Nutrition Board, National Academy of Sciences, National Research Council, 1980.

chiefly of corn, molasses, and salt pork. Pellagra has been effectively controlled by enrichment of corn in many of the southern states.

Vitamin B₆ is actually three chemical compounds, pyridoxine, pyridoxal and pyridoxamine. Pyridoxine was synthesized in 1939. It is particularly important for protein metabolism. Symptoms of severe deficiency, although very rare, include convulsions, loss of weight, irritability, depression, and anemia. It has also been found that *women who use oral contraceptives may need to increase their intake of vitamin B₆ since the metabolism of the essential amino acid tryptophan is impaired.*

Pantothenic acid is a component of coenzyme A, which is essential for the metabolism of carbohydrates, fats, and protein to produce energy. Since this vitamin is so plentiful in the foods we eat, deficiency symptoms have not been observed in humans.

Biotin was synthesized in 1943. It is necessary for metabolism of carbohydrates and the synthesis and oxidation of fatty acids. Since biotin is widespread in the foods we eat and can also be synthesized in the intestine, a deficiency is almost impossible.

Folacin is necessary for cell growth and reproduction. A deficiency can result in *megaloblastic anemia,* which is characterized by the enlargement of the red blood cells and failure of them to mature. However, this condition is not at all common among Americans, but it may appear in individuals suffering from other diseases, such as leukemia.

Cobalamin is important for normal functioning of cells, especially those of the nervous system, bone marrow, and digestive tract. A deficiency of cobalamin will result in pernicious anemia. *Pernicious anemia* generally occurs in later adult life resulting from the reduced ability for the intestine to absorb the vitamin. The symptoms of anemia are usually insidious at first and do not appear until the anemia is well advanced. At this time the individual will experience weakness, shortness of breath, and palpitation. In addition, there may be gastrointestinal symptoms, such as nausea, vomiting, diarrhea, and abdominal pain. Today, unless serious complications are present, chronic macrocytic anemia can be effectively treated and the prognosis is excellent.

Ascorbic acid (vitamin C) has a long history dating back to the first controlled, clinical therapeutic trial ever recorded (1747). This was conducted by James Lind who showed that sailors who were given citrus fruit on long sea voyages would not develop scurvy. *Scurvy* is a vitamin C deficiency disease that is characterized by general weakness, loss of appetite, rough and scaly skin with a brown color, spongy gums, and hemorrhages. Although scurvy is relatively rare in the United States, there are a number of people who manifest some of the symptoms which authorities attribute to moderate deficiencies of ascorbic acid. If the deficiency is allowed to continue, death may result. However, the disease is relatively easily reversed when adequate amounts of ascorbic acid are administered.

Vitamin C was isolated in 1933 by Linus Pauling. It is essential for the formation of collagen, the substance that binds the body cells together. It facilitates the healing of wounds and assists in the metabolism of some amino acids. Table 12–3 provides the RDA for water soluble vitamins.

Table 12–3: Recommended Daily Dietary Allowances (RDA)*

		WATER SOLUBLE VITAMINS						
	Age (Years)	*Ascorbic Acid (mg)*	*Folacin (ug)*	*Niacin (mg)*	*Riboflavin (mg)*	*Thiamin (mg)*	*B_6 (mg)*	*B_{12} (mg)*
Infants	0—0.5	35	30	6	0.4	0.3	0.3	0.5
	0.5—1	35	45	8	0.6	0.5	0.6	1.5
Children	1—3	45	100	9	0.8	0.7	0.9	2.0
	4—6	45	200	11	1.0	0.9	1.9	2.5
	7—10	45	300	16	1.4	1.2	1.6	3.0
Males	11—14	50	400	18	1.6	1.4	1.8	3.0
	15—18	60	400	18	1.7	1.4	2.0	3.0
	19—22	60	400	19	1.7	1.5	2.2	3.0
	23—25	60	400	18	1.6	1.4	2.2	3.0
	51+	60	400	16	1.4	1.2	2.2	3.0
Females	11—14	50	400	15	1.3	1.1	1.8	3.0
	15—18	60	400	14	1.3	1.1	2.0	3.0
	19—22	60	400	14	1.3	1.1	2.0	3.0
	23—50	60	400	13	1.2	1.0	2.0	3.0
	50+	60	400	13	1.2	1.0	2.0	3.0

*Source of Data: Food and Nutrition Board, National Academy of Sciences, National Research Council, 1980.

Minerals

Minerals are inorganic, crystalline chemicals that perform vital functions in the body, such as (1) controlling water balance; (2) regulating acid/base balance; (3) acting as catalysts for a number of body reactions; and (4) becoming integral components of body structures, including bones, enzymes, and hormones. Some minerals are needed in relatively large amounts and include calcium, phosphorus, sodium, potassium, chlorine, magnesium, and sulfur. Minerals that are needed in only trace amounts are zinc, cobalt, fluorine, aluminum, boron, molybdenum, selenium, cadmium, and chromium. Table 12–4 provides the sources of minerals and their functions in the body; Table 12–5 shows the Recommended Daily Dietary Allowances.

The acid/base balance of the body must be held within the limits of slight alkalinity with a pH between 7.2–7.4 for blood. In the cells and tissues this pH can fall to slightly lower levels and still maintain the vital levels of homeostasis. In terms of percentages, the human body is mostly water. Water levels of the body must be maintained if life is to continue. Water is necessary for all the chemical reactions that take place within the body. If water balance is not maintained, one of two conditions may result: (1) edema which is an accumulation of water in the tissues; or (2) dehydration, which results from a lack of water or the inability for water to pass to tissues and cells that need it. For example, if the sodium level of the body drops significantly, as may happen in heat exhaustion, water is withdrawn from the cells resulting in dehydration.

The catalytic action of minerals is exemplified in the formation of hemoglobin, for example. Copper is necessary for this formation to take place, but copper does not become a chemical component of the hemoglobin. However, iron is also necessary for hemoglobin formation and actually becomes a chemical component of the hemoglobin. If either copper or iron is lacking in the diet and hence in the body, iron-deficiency anemia will result since copper is essential for the body to make use of the iron in hemoglobin formation. However, it is important to recognize that a deficiency of copper in the American diet is quite rare since only about 2 milligrams per day are necessary in the healthy adult's diet. This is usually readily available in a daily, varied diet that includes meats. It will be noted that copper is *not* included in the RDA table for this reason. A final example that exemplifies minerals becoming an integral component of body structure is calcium, which is essential for bone and teeth formation. Calcium is also vital for proper blood coagulation (blood clot formation), metabolism of fat, and the transmission of nerve impulses across the nerve synapses.

THE PROCESS OF DIGESTION

Action of Enzymes

Proper digestion of the foods we eat is necessary before the nutrients can be used by the body. The process of digestion can be thought of in terms of mechanical and chemical actions required to reduce foods into absorbable substances to be assimilated by the body. Mechanical action begins in the mouth with the chewing of food and continues throughout the digestive process by the churning action of the gastrointestinal organs. Chemical digestion also begins in

Table 12-4: Summary of Information on Minerals

Mineral	Food Sources	Use in the Body
Calcium	milk, dairy products, cheese, some dark green leafy vegetables	Normal development and maintenance of bones and teeth, clotting of blood, nerve irritability, normal heart action, normal muscle activity.
Phosphorus	milk and cheese, egg yolk, meat, poultry, fish, whole grain cereals, legumes, nuts	Normal development and maintenance of bones and teeth, cell activity, maintenance of normal acid-base balance of the blood, normal muscle activity, metabolism of carbohydrates and fats.
Sodium	salt, meat, poultry, fish, eggs, milk	Maintenance of body neutrality and water balance, osmosis, regulates muscle and nerve irritability.
Potassium	meat, poultry, fish, cereals, fruits, vegetables	Osmosis, maintenance of body neutrality and water balance, regular heart rhythm, regulation of nerve and muscle irritability.
Chlorine	Same as sodium	Osmosis, maintenance of body neutrality and water balance.
Magnesium	dry beans, nuts, peanut butter, wheat germ and bran; seeds: sunflower, pumpkin, sesame, oatmeal, corn and cornmeal; fresh green vegetables	Constituent of bones, necessary for healthy muscles, nerves, organs, metabolism.
Sulfur	protein foods	For growth and health of hair, bones, and soft tissues.
Trace Minerals		
Iodine	salt water fish, foods grown in soil bordering salt water, iodized salt	Formation of hormones in thyroid gland.
Iron	liver and other organ meats, muscle meats, legumes, dried fruits, egg yolk, whole grain or enriched breads and cereals, dark green and leafy vegetables	Essential for formation of hemoglobin as a chemical component.
Copper	liver, muscle meats, nuts, legumes	Essential for formation of hemoglobin.
Manganese	blueberries, wheat germ, nuts	Essential for blood formation; endocrine glands.
Zinc	seafood, oysters, liver, wheat germ, yeast	Component of insulin and an enzyme.
Cobalt	supplied in vitamin B_{12}	A component of vitamin B_{12} necessary for formation of the red blood cells.
Fluorine	fluoridated water	Increases resistance to tooth decay.

Other trace minerals are aluminum, boron, molybdenum, selenium, cadmium, and chromium.

the mouth and continues in the stomach and finally in the small intestines. No chemical digestion of proteins takes place in the mouth, but are acted upon in the stomach and the small intestine by enzymes. *Enzymes* are substances that are capable of bringing about the chemical breakdown of foods.

Once carbohydrates, fats, and proteins are broken down through the process of digestion, they are absorbed into the vascular system. Undigested

Table 12-5: Recommended Daily Dietary Allowances (RDA)*

		MINERALS					
	Age (Years)	Calcium (mg)	Phosphorous (mg)	Iodine (mg)	Iron (mg)	Magnesium (mg)	Zinc (ug)
Infants	0—0.5	360	240	40	10	50	3
	0.5—1	540	360	50	15	70	5
Children	1—3	800	800	70	15	150	10
	4—6	800	800	90	10	200	10
	7—10	800	800	120	10	250	10
Males	11—14	1200	1200	150	18	350	15
	15—18	1200	1200	150	18	400	15
	19—22	800	800	150	10	350	15
	23—50	800	800	150	10	350	15
	51+	800	800	150	10	350	15
Females	11—14	1200	1200	150	18	300	15
	15—18	1200	1200	150	18	300	15
	19—22	800	800	150	18	300	15
	23—50	800	800	150	18	300	15
	51+	800	800	150	10	300	15

*Source of Data: Food and Nutrition Board, National Academy of Sciences, National Research Council, 1980.

portions of the foods are carried to the large intestines where they are prepared for evacuation. Another important function of the large intestine is to reabsorb water.

The Metabolic Process

Metabolism is the chemical change involved in the body's use of nutrients and the functioning of the body. Metabolism involves two processes called anabolism and catabolism. *Anabolism* is the synthesis of nutrients into new compounds within the body. *Catabolism* is the breakdown of various compounds into simpler ones within the body.

Energy is measured in kilocalories. A *kilocalorie* is the amount of heat necessary to raise the temperature of one kilogram of water one degree Celsius. A kilocalorie is frequently called a Calorie (spelled with a capital C) as opposed to a calorie (spelled with a lower case c). A calorie is the heat necessary to raise the temperature of 1 gram of water one degree Celsius.

Basal metabolism is the amount of energy required to maintain cellular activity and vital functions of respiration and circulation in a resting, fasting body. When we take in foods containing more calories than are used for the body's processes and activities, the surplus is stored as glycogen or fat. If this excess intake continues over a period of time, body weight will be increased. If however, we take in foods containing fewer calories than the body needs for its activities, the stored glycogen and finally body fat will be used for the energy needed. If this continues over a period of time, there will be a weight reduction.

Each pound of body fat is equivalent to 3500 calories. Therefore, to lose one pound of body fat, it will be necessary to reduce caloric intake below the level needed for daily activities. For example, if an adult male needs 2700 calories per day to maintain the energy levels necessary for him to conduct his daily activities, and he wishes to lose one pound of fat per week, it will be necessary for him to reduce his daily caloric intake by about 500 calories. Seven days times 500 calories per day equals 3500 calories or one pound of fat.

NUTRITION AND THE ECONOMY

Food Production

As of the late 1970s, only about one in 14 nations of the world was able to produce enough food for its people. For example, in 1975, only Australia and North America were exporting significant quantities of wheat and other grains. Generally, the nations with the greatest population densities are also those that are in the transition of technological development and are still using obsolete methods of agriculture and inferior seeds. Their agricultural lands are also depleted resulting in low yields per acre.

World Population Changes

In spite of the improved methods of agriculture, improved breeding techniques, and improved seeds, there is a critical need to increase food production to feed the world. By 1970, the world's population reached a 3.5 billion level. At this same rate of increase, it is estimated that by the year 2000, the world's population will have reached over 10 billion people. Of these, more than 8 billion will be in the developing areas of the world and less than 1.5 billion in the developed areas. To compound the problem further, more than 50 percent of the people in the developing nations will be under 15 years of age—consumers of food rather than producers.

Can We Feed Our New Generations?

Because of the ever-increasing size of the world's population without a corresponding increase in the amount of land able to produce additional food, we must consider the possible consequences of such a predicament. Can and should the United States increase its assistance to developing countries? Do we have a moral obligation to feed the world's poor?

The reality is that without assistance from the developed countries, millions of people in the developing nations are dying each year from starvation. In 1979, the Presidential Commission on World Hunger emphasized that hunger may be a more serious problem for the world than energy by the year 2000. It called on the United States to make the elimination of hunger the major focus of its relationships with developing countries during the 1980s. In addition, the Commission called for less attention to arming the world and more to increasing food production.

We are also faced with the problem of whether it is justifiable to use food as a political weapon. Should we cease providing food to the poor in countries whose politics run contrary to ours? Whatever the answer, the fact remains that our ability to produce food is ultimately limited by the amount of land and water available for its cultivation. Although many countries are attempting to limit population growth, the world's population will continue to increase for the forseeable future. How much will we be willing to sacrifice so that others will not starve? In the final analysis, the ultimate quality of life of the world may be raised while those of us in the United States may suffer a net reduction in the availability of those goods and services that we now consider necessities. The level of the health of the world may roughly be determined by the average health of all people of the world, for an unhealthy nation feeds on the health of others, lowering the health of all people.

Search for New Food Sources

The sciences associated with food production and the development of new food sources have for many years been working to find ways of adequately feeding the increasing numbers of people inhabiting the earth. Besides increasing productivity through greater control of crops and animals, making the most out of the nutrients available, and improving fertilizers, science has been diligently pursuing possible new sources of foods. For example, fish protein concentrate has been developed. High quality protein foods are also being made from soybeans, peanuts, and sunflower seeds, among others. Experiments are underway to grow various seafoods, such as oysters, in artificial "sea farms," and vegetables, such as tomatoes are being grown in greenhouses in a liquid nutrient rather than in soil. This makes tomatoes available the year around.

Food Waste and Energy Expenditure

It has been only in very recent years, that certain segments of the American people have become concerned about food waste, its impact upon the economy, and most importantly, its effects upon the waste of energy. As Martha Mapes and Barbara Stewart, both of Cornell University, have stated: "Wasting food, at the best, wastes fertilizer, energy, land, and both public and private money, not to mention the vitally important food itself.'.[2]

The United States has approximately 6 percent of the world's population, but generates 70 percent of the world's solid waste. It costs the American society an expenditure of about 12 percent of its total energy use just to dispose of our solid waste; much of this is food—edible food that is discarded needlessly. According to Mapes and Stewart, "In the United States, 16.5 percent of our total energy is consumed in the food system (field to table)."[3] They go on to emphasize that the United States spends nearly $5 billion annually for disposal of urban waste. This includes the cost for storage, collection, processing, transportation, and final disposal.

With the ever-increasing cost of food during the past two decades, its continuance into this decade, and the critical shortage of energy sources, it has become imperative that we become aware of the need for each of us to assume new responsibilities in regard to purchasing, storing, and wasting food. It is past time for us to evaluate our style of life, and begin to bring about changes in living patterns more consistent with a nation that no longer possesses unlimited resources that can be squandered as our first 200 years as a nation. The days of luxury, of waste, of self-indulgence, are over; the time is now for each of us to begin to accept personal responsibility for the next generation.

ENSURING AN ADEQUATE DIET

We in the United States consume about one-third of the available animal protein and about four times more grain than all of the developing countries combined. On the average, we eat from 2 to 4 times more protein each day than that recommended by the Food and Nutrition Board, National Academy of Sciences, National Research Council. They recommend a daily intake of protein of 23–34 grams for children (1–10 years), 45 to 56 grams for males (11–51+ years), and 44–46 grams for females (11–51+ years). They also recommend an additional 30 grams for pregnant females and an additional 20 grams for lactating females. It is important to recognize that these recommendations are deliberately set at levels higher than is needed for maintaining health, and the RDA tables for energy, protein, vitamins, and minerals are "designed for the maintenance of good nutrition of practically all healthy people in the U.S.A." To assist people in selecting foods that will provide all the known essential nutrients, several methods have been developed that include the four basic food groups, and calculating nutrient density of foods.

The Four Basic Food Groups

The basic four food groups were designed at Harvard University's Department of Nutrition as a guide to ensure a nutritional variety of foods in the individual's daily diet. The success of this guide was based upon the premise that eating a variety of foods from each of the four food groups each day would provide a person with all the nutrients needed for nutritional health. Essentially, the "Basic Four" consists of grouping foods commonly found in the diets of Americans on the basis of their similarity in nutrient content. These groups are: (1) dairy products; (2) meat or meat substitutes; (3) cereal and grains; and (4) vegetables and fruits.

Nutrient Density of Foods

In recent years, nutritionists have proposed another method for planning diets based upon the nutrient density of food. *Nutrient density* is based upon the nutrient/calorie ratio of foods. Since most Americans' calorie needs is not a significant problem and are usually met, nutritionists suggest selecting foods with a low calorie content but a high yield of other essential nutrients.

In selecting foods we merely need to consult reliable food tables, such as those published by the United States Department of Agriculture, to find those that are rich sources of nutrients and low in calories. Such a food would be considered high in nutrient density. For instance, one medium stalk of broccoli provides more than seven times the daily requirement for calcium and phosphorus, over 8 percent of the daily iron requirement, nearly all the vitamin A, and nearly three times the vitamin C requirement, and less than one percent of the caloric needs. *Broccoli, therefore, is a high nutrient density food.*

If we compare this with one slice of enriched white bread we will find that the bread contains approximately 30 more kilocalories of energy than the broccoli, and it is significantly lower in the other nutrients. The bread, in this comparison, has a low nutrient density. This approach to food selection can be important for those who are trying to reduce their daily caloric intake without sacrificing the other essential nutrients.

DIETARY GOALS FOR THE UNITED STATES*

Rationale

The Senate Select Committee on Nutrition and Human Needs identified several risk factors associated with cardiovascular disease, most of which are related to our dietary practices. Eating and drinking too much and not enough exercise lead to overweight. High consumption of total fat, saturated fat, and cholesterol, and a low polyunsaturated and saturated fat ratio leads to elevated blood cholesterol. High salt consumption and overweight leads to elevated blood pressure; and the presence of diabetes and cigarette smoking leads to an acceleration of the atherosclerotic process. The Select Committee also concluded that "In all, six of the ten leading causes of death in the United States have been linked to our diet." These causes of death are heart disease, some cancers, stroke and hypertension, arteriosclerosis, diabetes, and cirrhosis of the liver.

Dietary Goals

In 1977, the Senate Select Committee on Nutrition and Human needs released its report on the dietary goals for the United States. The report stated that "the value of dietary change remains controversial and that science cannot at this time insure that an altered diet will provide improved protection from certain killer diseases such as heart diseases and cancer." However, later on in the report, Dr. D. M. Hegsted, Professor of Nutrition, Harvard School of Public Health, stated that "There will undoubtedly be many people who will say we have not proven our point; we have not demonstrated that the dietary modifications we recommend will yield the dividends expected. We would point out to those people that the diet we eat today was not planned or developed for any particular purpose. It is a happenstance related to our affluence, the productivity of our farmers and the activities of our food industry. The risks associated with eating this diet are demonstrably large. The question to be asked, therefore, is not why should we change our diet but why not?"

The dietary goals are related to specific levels in terms of percentage of consumption of the macronutrients, salt, and cholesterol. It is recommended that

*See *Dietary Goals for the United States,* 2nd ed. Select Committee on Nutrition and Human Needs, United States Senate, U.S. Government Printing Office, Washington, D.C., 1977.

daily intake of energy foods should consist of 55–61 percent in carbohydrates with 45–51 percent being in the form of complex carbohydrate and naturally occurring sugars and only 8–12 percent in the form of processed sugars; 27–37 percent in the form of fat with 8–12 percent as polyunsaturated; 8–12 percent as monounsaturated and 8–12 percent saturated; and 10–14 percent in the form of protein. In addition, it is recommended that cholesterol intake be limited to a daily consumption of 250–350 milligrams, and salt intake be limited to 4–6 grams.

Since the establishment of these goals, there has been some debate among nutritionists. We anticipate that the controversy will result in revisions of the goals in the near future.

NUTRITION, GROWTH, AND DEVELOPMENT

Maternal Needs

Nutritional preparation for motherhood begins in infancy and continues throughout life. Adequate nourishment from infancy through the period of pregnancy is essential for the health of the mother and to ensure the birth of a healthy baby. Although adequate nutrition is important for the woman throughout her life cycle, it is especially important before becoming pregnant and during pregnancy. Both of these are important times to assess nutritional status and to make certain that nutritional needs are being met. This is important, not only for the woman, but also for the fetus.

The nutritional status of a woman reflects the many influences to which she has been exposed for many years prior to becoming pregnant. This includes such things as long-term use of alcohol, tobacco, and other drugs, all of which can have an effect upon her health as well as upon the health of the fetus and, finally, the newborn. Nutritional practices between pregnancies are important to the mother for several reasons: (1) nutrition depletions of the previous pregnancy can be restored; (2) nutritional status can be returned to prepregnancy levels; and (3) weight can be brought back to its ideal level. For these, and many other reasons, family planning practices to space pregnancies far enough apart may be desirable.

There are adverse reactions to some contraceptive methods that should be considered. The use of oral contraceptives and intrauterine devices are among the most convenient and effective forms of birth control. However, oral contraceptives that contain estrogen can affect metabolism. Oral contraceptives can also result in a deficiency of folate, one of the B vitamins. Carbohydrate metabolism may be affected in some women resulting in a decrease in plasma glucose tolerance and for plasma insulin levels to increase, resulting in the development of a pseudodiabetic condition. Finally, lipid metabolism may be affected by oral contraceptives resulting in an increase in the levels of triglycerides and cholesterol.

Those women who use the intrauterine devices as a birth control measure may experience frequent increases in menstrual blood loss. Women who use this method of birth control should have their iron status assessed periodically and should include iron-rich foods in their diets.

It is generally agreed that the total weight gain of the mother during pregnancy should be approximately 25 pounds. Of this, about one-third will be the weight of the fetus at maturity. Physicians usually emphasize an adequate gain in weight rather than an over-restriction of caloric intake. Weight gain over 25 pounds will probably represent additional deposits of fat that will need to be lost after the birth of the child if the woman is to regain her prepregnancy weight.

According to the Recommended Daily Dietary Allowances it is recommended that a pregnant woman increase her daily caloric intake by about 300 calories. This increase should constitute a balance comprised of about 20 percent protein, and 40 percent each of carbohydrate and fat. This increase in caloric intake should result from a selection of high nutrient density foods; not from foods that contribute little more than calories. *Under no circumstances should the pregnant woman undertake a reducing dieting regimen during gestation.* It is vital for the health of the mother and that of the fetus for the pregnant woman to be under the care of a physician throughout the period of pregnancy.

Besides protein, carbohydrate, and fat and the increase caloric needs during pregnancy, a woman will also need to increase her intake of iron, calcium, and several other minerals, and vitamins. Iron and calcium are particularly important. There is a greater need for iron as a result of the increase in the mother's blood volume and the development of the fetal blood supply. Calcium is needed in greater amounts during pregnancy for the building of fetal bones and teeth. Vitamins such as folic acid, B_{12}, and B_6 are needed in greater amounts at this time. Since these along with some of the minerals may be difficult to obtain in the pregnant woman's normal diet, the physician may prescribe multivitamin and mineral supplements. These should be taken only under the supervision of the physician since large doses of vitamins may result in adverse reactions affecting the health of the mother and/or fetus.[4]

Nutrition and the Growth of the Fetus

To a great extent, the health of the fetus depends upon the kinds of things the mother ingests during pregnancy. The nutrients, drugs, or other substances that the mother ingests during pregnancy, enter her bloodstream and are carried to the placenta where they pass from the mother's blood into the blood of the fetus. Waste products of the fetus are eliminated in the same way passing from the fetus through the placenta into the mother's bloodstream. It is important for a pregnant woman to recognize that some drugs, as well as nutrients, can pass through the placental wall and adversely affect the growth and development of the fetus.

It was only during the early part of the 1970s that it was recognized that the consumption of alcohol by the mother during pregnancy, could affect the growth and development of the fetus. Apparently, the alcohol consumed by the mother adversely affects fetal development and may result in what has become known as the *fetal alcohol syndrome.* The characteristics of babies born with the fetal alcohol syndrome include underdevelopment in height and weight, small head circumference, facial abnormalities, and dysfunctions of the nervous system. It has also been found that about 40 percent of fetal alcohol syndrome infants have cardiac malformations.[5] The syndrome is most prevalent among women who are chronic alcoholics. The National Council on Alcoholism has recommended that women who are pregnant should not consume more than 2 ounces of alcohol in any 24 hour period.

When mothers are well-nourished, babies are generally healthier at the time of birth and there is a lower incidence of birth complications. The greatest cause of infant mortality is premature birth. This is significantly lower among healthy mothers than those whose nutriture is below desirable levels. Undernutriture of mothers before and during pregnancy can result in retardation of fetal growth and development.

Lactation and the Infant

Lactation is the process of producing milk by a woman who has given birth to a baby. Only about 1 percent of women fail to lactate following childbirth. For the first few days after childbirth, a mother will produce a rather thick, yellowish milk called *colostrum*. The nutrient content of colostrum is somewhat different from mature human milk containing more protein, sodium, potassium, and vitamin A. It is also lower in energy value and fat. Colostrum provides the infant with certain antibodies for temporary immunity to diphtheria, tetanus, pertussis, typhoid, dysentery, and possibly other diseases. After about the tenth day the mother will produce mature milk.

It is not only important for a mother to lactate, but also to be able to sustain lactation and provide the nutrients in her milk that will result in a weight-gain in the infant. Therefore, the diet of a mother during the time of lactation and breast feeding is extremely important to ensure adequate nutrition for the nursing infant. Table 12–6 provides the Recommended Dietary Allowances (RDA) for pregnant and lactating women. If a mother is unable or chooses not to breast feed her infant, there are commercial formulas available that simulate human milk and that can provide the infant with adequate nutrients. However, if this decision is made, the formula selected should be based upon recommendations from the attending physician, usually a pediatrician.

Effects of Nutrition on Growth and Development

Energy is constantly needed for protein synthesis. This need is greatest during the periods of rapid growth. Additional energy is also needed at times the body is experiencing stress, such as during an illness. Table 12–7 provides the Recommended Dietary Allowances for infants, children, males, and females at various ages.

The extent to which a child grows and the rate at which growth takes place is predetermined by heredity. However, the quality of nutrition, along with other factors, influences this genetic plan. It is probably much more important to determine whether a child is growing properly by comparing his/her growth rate as well as size with previous measures, rather than comparing the child with standardized tables of height and weight. These tables merely provide averages of growth of large populations and since each person's heredity is different, a particular child may not compare with the averages. The important factor is whether or not the child is showing an adequate growth progress.

Table 12–6: Nutrient Needs of Pregnant and Lactating Women*

		Pregnant	Lactating
	Energy (Kcal)	+300	+500
	Protein (gm)	+30	+20
Vitamins	A (RE)[a]	+200	+400
	D (UG)[b]	+5	+5
	E (TE)[c]	+2	+3
	Ascorbic Acid (mg)	+20	+40
	Folacin (mg)	+400	+100
	Niacin (mg)	+2.0	+5.0
	Riboflavin (mg)	+0.3	+0.5
	Thiamin (mg)	+0.4	+0.5
	B_6 (mg)	+0.6	+0.5
	B_{12} (mg)	+1.0	+1.0
Minerals	Calcium (mg)	+400	+400
	Phosphorus (mg)	+400	+400
	Iodine (mg)	+25	+50
	Iron (mg)	30—60 in supplements	30—60 in supplements
	Magnesium (mg)	+150	+150

[a] Retinol equivalents
[b] Cholecalciferal   } These are the units of measurement used for these vitamins.
[c] Tocopheral equivalents

*Source of Data: Food and Nutrition Board, National Academy of Sciences, National Research Council, 1980.

Table 12–7: Recommended Daily Dietary Allowances (RDA)*

	Age (Years)	Weight (Kg)	(lbs)	Height (cm)	(in)	Energy (K cal)	Protein (g)
				ENERGY AND PROTEIN			
Infants	0—0.5	6	13	60	24	kg × 115	kg × 22
	0.5—1	9	20	71	28	kg × 105	kg × 2.0
Children	1—3	13	29	90	35	1300	23
	4—6	20	44	112	44	1700	30
	7—10	28	62	132	52	2400	34
Males	11—14	45	99	157	62	2700	45
	15—18	66	145	176	69	2800	56
	19—22	70	154	177	70	2800	56
	23—50	70	154	178	70	2700	56
	51+	70	154	178	70	2400	56
Females	11—14	46	101	157	62	2200	46
	15—18	55	120	163	64	2100	46
	19—22	55	120	163	64	2100	44
	23—50	55	120	163	64	2000	44
	51+	55	120	163	64	1800	44

*Source of Data: Food and Nutrition Board, National Academy of Sciences, National Research Council, 1980.

Growth failures exist in some children in many of the developing nations of the world. These are exemplified by extreme protein/calorie deficiencies that result in marasmus or kwashiorkor. *Marasmus* is a condition that results from a diet inadequate in both protein and calories. This results in extreme emaciation and growth failure. Marasmus is actually the result of starvation characterized by abnormal growth rate, extreme thinness, wasted tissues, and apathy to life.

Kwashiorkor develops when the infant's protein intake is inadequate but caloric intake is adequate. The child consumes a diet consisting of a starchy gruel that supplies the needed calories but not the essential protein for growth. Kwashiorkor is characterized by edema, changes in the health of the hair and skin, growth failure, and apathy.

EFFECTS OF FOOD ADDITIVES

Kinds of Additives

Additives in some of our foods are essential for the protection of our health and, ironically, some have the potential for destroying our health. For example, sodium nitrates and sodium nitrites are added to meats and inhibit the growth of *Clostridium botulinum* organisms. These organisms are responsible for producing botulism in humans, the most toxic form of food poisoning. Nitrates and nitrites also enhance the color of meats. However, in 1975, the United States Department of Agriculture proposed the elimination of nitrates and nitrites as a preservative because there is some evidence that they may combine with the amines of the protein in the meat producing nitrosamines. *Nitrosamines* have been shown to produce cancer in test animals. However, since nitrates and nitrites have been used for more than 30 years as a preservative in foods such as smoked poultry, hot dogs, and sausages, their continued use has been permitted since they are temporarily excluded from the 1958 Food Additives Amendment to the Food, Drug and Cosmetic Act.[6]

Although nitrates exist naturally in many of the foods we eat, such as spinach and other leafy vegetables, the results of studies at the Massachusetts Institute of Technology have increased the concern of government officials. The question appears to be whether or not the deliberate addition of nitrates and nitrites in foods should be continued. Is the risk of cancer from these chemicals greater than the risk of botulism if they are not used?[7]

Definition

The 1958 Food Additives Amendment states that a food additive is "any substance the intended use of which results or may reasonably be expected to result directly or indirectly in its becoming a component or otherwise affecting the characteristics of any food." In this respect, a food additive may be intentionally added to foods or it may have unintentionally become an integral part of the food. Unintentional additives may be the result of chemicals from the packaging, processing, or growing of the food. For example, in March, 1977, the Food and Drug Administration suspended approval of the use of beverage containers made from the plastic, acrylonitrite. Studies conducted by the Manufacturing Chemists Association found that test animals fed large amounts of acrylonitrite had significantly lowered body weight, growths in the ear ducts, and lesions of the central nervous system.[8]

Purposes

Additives not only enhance our foods and make them safer, they also help to lower the costs of foods. Without food additives, many of the foods we enjoy today would not exist and many we enjoy the year around would not be available out-of-season. Food additives are used as preservatives, antioxidants, emulsifiers, stabilizers, and thickeners, to maintain acid/base balance, add or restore nutrients, such as vitamins or minerals, to add color and enhance flavor, and a variety of other purposes.

DIETARY DEFICIENCIES

Causes of Deficiencies

Clinical manifestations of nutrient deficiencies are *not* common among Americans. These manifestations usually occur only after prolonged deprivation of the specific nutrient. Extreme deficiency of some nutrients may result in clinical symptoms much sooner than for others. For example, scurvy, the result of severe and prolonged deprivation of vitamin C, will manifest itself much sooner than Bitot's spot, a lesion on the conjunctiva of the eye, caused by a severe deficiency of vitamin A. This is because vitamin A is stored in the liver and deficiency symptoms will not occur until after this supply is depleted. Vitamin C is water soluble and excess amounts are excreted with very little storage.

Conditions that impose demands on the body other than those necessary for proper functioning, increase the need for additional nutrients. Stress may be physiological or psychological. Disease, for example, increases biological stress while emotional tension increases psychological stress. In either case, there is a need to increase nutrient intake, especially if the stress is prolonged, for the body to deal adequately with the stress demands.

Nutrient deficiency symptoms may also result from diets that are severely restrictive. Although those on strict vegetarian diets, for instance, can obtain an adequate diet, they will find it more difficult to ensure an adequate supply of some nutrients than those on a partial vegetarian or unrestricted diet. Some of the reducing diet fads that have become temporarily popular over the years may also deprive one of certain nutrients that can result in deficiency symptoms if strictly practiced. For example, in March, 1977, the Food and Drug Administration warned of possible hazardous consequences from adherence to the so-called liquid protein diet. The Administration stated at this time that "We have 16 reports of deaths and a number of severe illnesses that may be associated with the use of the predigested liquid protein diet. We expect to find others. All of the cases thus far involve people who subsisted on this type of diet without other nourishment for weeks or months."[9] It was reported that 10 of the 16 deaths resulted from heart irregularities. Although this is not strictly speaking the result of nutrient deficiency disease, it does point up the need for an adequate diet to take care of all of the nutrient needs of the body. Without it additional, and sometimes, fatal stress is placed on the body.

A more relevant fad diet that reached heights of populaity during the 1970s was the Zen Macrobiotic Diets. These diets have resulted in severe malnutrition in those who strictly followed the dictates of them.

Strictly speaking according to Deutsch, "A true *nutritional deficiency* is a state in which a physical disorder (deficiency symptoms) appears for lack of a particular nutrient."[10] However, as alluded to earlier, the common dietary deficiency diseases such as "scurvy, pellagra, beri-beri and other nutritional-deficiency diseases are almost unknown in the United States."[11] So for our purposes, we can conclude that there are no *common* types of dietary deficiency diseases in the United States today. Our problem is more one of nutritional excesses and abuses than deficiencies.

NUTRITIONAL ABUSES

Obesity

Nutritional problems among Americans are associated chiefly with excesses and abuses. Excess intake of calories has resulted in many Americans becoming overweight. This is compounded by a general decrease in physical activity. Our present-day caloric needs are not as great today as they were some 50 to 75 years ago. Although the caloric intake has decreased in quantity, the fact that our daily life styles require much fewer calories results in fat storage in the body resulting in obesity. In 1975, the Center for Science in the Public Interest estimated that approximately 40 percent of Americans are obese.[12]

What is obesity? How is it different from overweight? Body weight is the total weight of all the components of the body including muscles, bone, body fluids, and stored fat. Overweight is generally measured in terms of one's ideal weight. *Ideal weight* is considered by some nutritionists to be the amount one weighed during the ages of 22–25 years. *Desirable weight* refers to a range of weights for a particular height as compiled by life insurance companies. If we are approximately 10 percent above ideal weight, we are considered overweight, while 20 percent or more above ideal weight is considered obesity. *Obesity* is an excess of fat characterized by too many fat cells or too much stored fat in existing fat cells.

It has been concluded by some authorities that overfeeding in infancy and childhood can result in the development of a greater number of fat cells, which can be the forerunner of weight problems in later life. There are other factors that may also contribute to obesity besides eating too much. The nature of obesity, and its etiology, is very complex and needs further investigation. For example, Jean Mayer concluded that obesity seems to "run in families." A person whose parents are not obese has only about a 10 percent chance of being obese; when one parent is obese, the risk is about 40 percent, and when both parents are obese, the risk is 80 percent.[13]

Obesity may be either transient or persistent. *Transient* obesity may occur during preadolescence. Once full growth is reached, the obesity disappears and the person achieves ideal adult weight. *Persistent* obesity begins in childhood and persists after the adolescent growth spurt. It was once thought that fat babies were healthy babies, but in recent years, nutritionists have been reevaluating this concept and some believe that fatness in infancy could be a warning of later weight problems.

The health implications of obesity have been well documented. The obese person is more likely to develop cardiovascular diseases, diabetes, and high blood pressure. The person who is severely obese has a much lower life expectancy than the person of average or desirable weight. In addition, the obese person is more apt to be confronted with social and emotional problems.

Food Faddism

We shall begin our discussions of food faddism with the year 1794, when Sylvester Graham was born. At the age of 32, Graham was ordained by the Presbyterian Church in spite of the fact he lacked the necessary theological education. As an effective orator, he was able to convince large numbers of people that the cause of many of their ills was the kind of foods they ate, especially meats. Graham's most notorious exhortations revolved around putting the bran back into the flour. Whole meal bread, he preached, was natural. His influence survives him today in Graham food products, especially the graham cracker. Of significant importance is the fact that, even though he had no nutrition background, the supposed health-giving qualities of the graham cracker live on to this very day. This is evidenced in any hospital or nursing home at snack time—juice and a graham cracker! Sylvester Graham died in 1851 at the age of 57 years attempting to regain his health with an ice bath every morning, eating his dark bread, and a diet consisting of rice.[14]

Modern food quackery can be seen in the large numbers of books that are published each year by the quack. Many of these proclaim easy cures for illness, weight control, attractiveness, ever-lasting health, youth, vigor, and sexual satisfaction. Although the techniques of individual faddists may vary slightly, they all seem to have certain qualities that are similar to those of medical quacks. These were described in Chapter 10.

Let us examine one form of food quackery—those associated with losing weight. Most of these claim to provide a diet that will "melt" fat away, or remove fat only in the areas you want it removed. We have already seen that the storage of body fat is the result of excess caloric intake. The food faddist who claims his or her diet will result in a loss of one pound per day (or some claim, 10 pounds per week) would have to be a diet completely void of any calories whatsoever. Or to put it another way, the person would have to starve for that week.

Some food fads are harmless physiologically speaking. Some are dangerous. All are a waste of time and money. Two examples of fad diets that are dangerous are the Zen Macrobiotic diet and deliberate starvation resulting in anorexia nervosa. The macrobiotic diet is one that has been fabricated, while anorexia nervosa is associated with complex psychological motivations.

The *Zen Macrobiotic diets* were introduced into American culture, chiefly on college campuses in the early 1960s by George Ohsawa. He claimed that human diseases were unnecessary and could be prevented by a diet consisting of unpolished brown rice—"the only perfect support of life."[15] Some of the diets of Ohsawa include some kinds of vegetables. However, anyone adhering strictly to the macrobiotic diets will suffer severe malnutrition in the forms of scurvy, anemia, hypoproteinemia, and emaciation resulting from starvation amongst others.

Anorexia nervosa is a psychiatric disorder that is characterized by obsessive self-starvation that, when carried to extremes, results in death. Anorexia nervosa sufferers are generally white females between the ages of 13 and 30 years. Less than 6 percent are males and no cases have been reported among blacks. Although anorexia nervosa was once thought to be quite rare, recent figures indicate that it is on the increase in the United States, Britain, Sweden, and Italy, occurring in one of every 100,000 girls from middle to upper socioeconomic groups.

The profile of girls suffering from anorexia nervosa includes the following: (1) they are high achievers; (2) they are physically hyperactive; and (3) they are extremely well-behaved. It appears that these girls are attracted to (or motivated) anorexia nervosa by a desire to achieve prestige and acceptance in a society that places great emphasis upon appearance. Anorexia nervosa is characterized by overt efforts at starvation. The anorexic frequently recognizes what she is doing and the harm that will eventually result, but the compulsion for overthinness prevails. These girls need psychiatric assistance in addition to reversing their starvation behavior.

The Use of Food Supplements

Nutritionists and the medical community generally agree that the ingestion of vitamin and mineral supplements on a routine basis, "to make sure" that daily intakes are adequate is unnecessary and a waste of money. Most Americans receive enough of the important nutrients through their normal dietary patterns.

As with any drug, the consumption of vitamin and mineral supplements in large amounts could be dangerous. For example, the Food and Drug Administration National Clearinghouse for Poison Control Centers has indicated they record more than 4000 vitamin poisonings in the United States each year. Of these, more than 3200 cases involve children.[16] Leaving vitamin supplements on the dining room table or other places accessible to children is a dangerous practice. *If vitamin and mineral supplements are present in the household, they should be treated with the same precautions as any other dangerous drug.*

The Pill Doctors

The relatively high incidence of obesity in American society in the past three or four decades and the difficulties the obese person encounters in attempts to control weight has produced a new sort of "gray area quack"; the pill doctor. These are for all practical purposes legitimate, licensed physicians who limit their practice of medicine to treating obesity. Although most of these provide their patients with diets that can result in a loss of weight, they have also prescribed amphetamines to reduce the appetite. Studies have shown that amphetamine dosage must be increased only after a few weeks of treatment to maintain their appetite reducing effect. Amphetamines can also be dangerous for some people and they have a high potential for abuse.

According to an expert advisory group to FDA, amphetamines make only a trivial contribution to weight reduction programs, in spite of the fact that many physicians made them an important component of their weight reduction regimen. In July, 1979, the FDA announced the removal of amphetamines for use as an appetite suppressant in weight control programs. This probably will not put the pill doctors out of business since there are alternative drugs that can be used. However, some of these alternatives have less potential for abuse than the amphetamines.

Health Foods

Health foods and organically grown foods are, for all practical purposes, myths. There really is no such thing as a health food. What the body needs for health are the nutrients contained in the foods we eat. Some nutrients are more important for the health of some tissues, such as iron for red blood cells and calcium for bones and teeth, but no one food is more beneficial for general health than any other. To reiterate, we need a variety of foods each day to provide us with all of the nutrients necessary for the maintenance of health. Diets limited to only a few foods can be dangerous because they may be severely lacking in some of the known nutrients needed by the body. In addition, there may be essential nutrients yet to be discovered that are provided through a varied daily dietary intake.

Fruits, vegetables, and grains grown "organically" contain no nutrients that are not also present in those grown with the aid of artificial fertilizers. Artificial fertilizers provide the nutrients for plant growth more economically and in less time than those grown organically. The use of natural fertilizers requires the conversion of the organic matter into the minerals needed for plant growth. The end result is the same whether the nitrogen is provided through the use of artificial fertilizers or through the conversion of the organic matter through bacterial action. The plant cannot tell the difference and the quality of the food produced will be the same. The use of artificial fertilizers, however, is more likely to result in a greater yield per acre than with the use of organic matter.

If one is concerned about the residue of pesticides on the food, the amount that is allowed to remain at the time of marketing is very closely controlled. These incidental additives are safe as far as present knowledge is able to determine. Since pesticides are widely used in today's agriculture, even organic farms may be exposed to them. An organic farm adjacent to a non-organic farm is very likely to be exposed to the pesticides being used.

Food and Dietary Advertising

Food advertising in the United States is big business. The competition between food producers, packers, and distributors has led to the necessity for more intensified promotional programs. The use of the media, especially television, has made it possible to institute advertising techniques that are directed toward suggesting that certain food products or a particular brand of food will satisfy a basic need. These needs may be physical, such as related to weight control, social as related to appearance, or psychological as related to self-esteem. Many advertisements incorporate several of these need areas such as suggesting greater energy, improved appearance, and so on. Through advertising, claims are sometimes made that are questionable. For example, some food products are advertised to possess certain health-giving qualities or nutrients that may or may not be reality. However, the consumer does have some protection against false and misleading advertising since, regardless of advertising claims, the label on the product must be accurate and must follow certain standards.

How does food labeling help the consumer to purchase more wisely? In 1973, the Food and Drug Administration issued regulations for nutrition labeling and later that year established common name procedure, and a beginning toward establishing nutrition guidelines. In August, 1973, the Administration established new requirements for the labeling and promotion of vitamin/mineral products. Today, food labels provide a wealth of information to assist consumers to make comparisons between similar food products in regard to price and nutrient value. For example, all food labels must contain the name of the product, the net contents or net weight, and the name and place of business of the manufacturer, packer, or distributor.

On nearly all foods, the ingredients must be on the label. There are certain so-called standard foods whose ingredients do not have to be on the label. In these cases, the Food and Drug Administration has established *standards of identity* that require that foods called by a certain name, such as mayonnaise, must contain certain mandatory ingredients. These mandatory ingredients do not have to be listed on the label. If optional ingredients are added to the product, however, they must be listed on the label. For other standard foods, the ingredients must be listed on the label with the ingredient present in the largest amount by weight, listed first following in descending order of weight by the other ingredients. All additives to the food must be listed; however, colors and flavors added may be listed simply as "artificial color" or "artificial flavor" or "natural flavor" added.

Any food to which a nutrient has been added, or any food for which a nutritional claim is made, must have the nutritional content listed on the label. In addition, nutrition labels contain the amount of calories, protein, carbohydrate, and fat present in the product. They also include the U.S. Recommended Daily Allowances of protein and seven important vitamins and minerals that each serving of the product contains.* The listing of 12 other vitamins and minerals, cholesterol, fatty acid, and sodium content is optional.[17] See Table 12–8.

To prevent deception of consumers for products that appear from the label to be one thing when they actually are something else, FDA has ruled that these foods must have a common or usual name that conveys accurate information. For example, a beverage that looks like orange juice but actually contains little orange juice, must use a name such as "diluted orange juice drink."[18]

Labels may also contain a grade, such as "Grade A," and open dating,

*Nutrients which must be on the label are protein, vitamin A, vitamin C, thiamin, riboflavin, niacin, calcium, and iron.

Table 12–8: U.S. Recommended Daily Allowances (U.S. RDA)*

Protein	65 grams** (g)
Vitamin A	5000 International Units (IU)
Vitamin C	60 milligrams (mg)
Thiamin	1.5 milligrams (mg)
Riboflavin	1.7 milligrams (mg)
Niacin	20 milligrams (mg)
Calcium	1 gram (g)
Iron	18 milligrams (mg)
Vitamin D	400 International Units (IU)
Vitamin E	30 International Units (IU)
Vitamin B_6	2 milligrams (mg)
Folacin	0.4 milligrams (mg)
Vitamin B_{12}	6 micrograms (mcg)
Phosphorus	1 gram (g)
Iodine	150 micrograms (mcg)
Magnesium	400 milligrams (mg)
Zinc	15 milligrams (mg)
Copper	2 milligrams (mg)
Biotin	0.3 milligrams (mg)
Pantothenic acid	10 milligrams (mg)

*For healthy adults and children over 4 years of age.

**45 grams are recommended if the protein quality is equal to or greater than milk protein (casein).

which may be one or more of four kinds: (1) the date the product was packed; (2) the date the product should be sold or pulled from the shelf; (3) the expiration date, that is, when the product should be eaten; and (4) freshness date.

With the amount and quality of nutrition information found on most food products today, we can easily evaluate the accuracy of advertising claims. Familiarity with labeling information and how to use it can result in better nutrition at a lowered cost.

GLOSSARY

Anabolism: A phase of metabolism characterized by a chemical synthesis within the body.

Catabolism: A phase of metabolism characterized by a chemical breakdown within the body.

Food additive: Any substance added intentionally or accidentally that becomes an integral part of the food.

Hypervitaminosis: Symptoms of ill health resulting from the ingestion of large amounts of a vitamin.

Ideal weight: This is the weight a person achieved at age 22–25 years.

Metabolism: The sum of the chemical processes within the body necessary for building protoplasm, breaking down chemical substances, and producing energy for maintenance of the vital processes.

Nutrient: The chemical substances in foods necessary for maintaining life.

Nutrient density: The ratio of calories to other nutrients.

Obesity: A condition characterized by being 20 percent or more above one's ideal weight.

Overweight: A condition characterized by being 10 percent above one's ideal weight.

Persistent obesity: This stems from childhood and continues beyond adolescence as obesity.

Transient obesity: This is obesity that occurs during preadolescence but disappears following maturity.

SUMMARY

The science of nutrition is concerned with the application of nutrition knowledge as gleaned from scientific investigation of the eating behavior of people. It acquires its knowledge of nutrition from the investigations of several sciences: the physical and chemical, biological, and psychosocial sciences.

Foods contain the nutrients needed for nutritional health. These nutrients are classified as macronutrients which include carbohydrate, protein, and lipids, and the micronutrients which are the vitamins and minerals. Water is also a vital substance which is essential for all of life's processes.

The process of digestion involves mechanical and chemical actions. The purpose of digestion is to break foods into simpler chemical substances that can be absorbed into the vascular system and used by the cells for their vital processes.

All of the activities related to supplying enough food for people have significant impact upon our economy. Food production has progressed from that which involved raising only enough to take care of the needs of one's family, to that of supplying enormous quantities for those who cannot raise their own. With the rapid growth of the world's population, agriculture and other food production industries are faced with the challenge of increasing food production and finding new sources of foods.

There are several ways in which people can ensure themselves of an adequate diet. Using, for example, the basic four food groups as criteria for food selection, and selecting foods with high nutrient densities. The Senate Select Committee on Nutrition and Human Needs has developed recommended changes in the dietary practices of the American people.

Although many factors affect human growth, development and health, maternal nutritional health is a significant contributor. Adequate nutrition during pregnancy ensures adequate nutrition for the fetus. It is important for the pregnant woman to take care in the kinds of things she ingests during pregnancy. Drugs, such as alcohol, pass from the mother's blood stream through the placenta into the blood stream of the fetus. This can result in the fetal alcohol syndrome.

Food additives are necessary to ensure an adequate food supply, to enhance flavor in certain foods, to make them more attractive, and for other purposes. However, some additives have been found to be a risk to health.

Nutrition deficiencies resulting in clinical symptoms are relatively rare in the United States. America's nutritional problems are associated with nutritional abuses that result in overweight and obesity. This results from eating foods which contain excess calories and from our general sedentary life-styles.

Food faddism is a multimillion dollar business in the United States. Some of the diets promoted are very dangerous while others are harmless.

Essentially, the proponents of health foods promote the concept that certain foods are necessary for health. Others promote the concept of organic foods for better health. Nutritionists have found no evidence to support the concept that certain foods are more healthful than others.

The food advertising industry is instrumental in promoting certain kinds of foods. However, one who has minimal knowledge of nutrition is capable of evaluating the accuracy of advertising claims. In addition, the Food and Drug

Administration has established regulations for food labeling. The information required on the label can assist consumers in purchasing foods more wisely, both from an economic viewpoint and from a nutritional viewpoint.

PROBLEMS FOR DISCUSSION

1. What are nutrients? What are macronutrients? Micronutrients?
2. What nutrients are our chief source of energy (calories)?
3. Give three functions of protein foods in the diet. What are important sources?
4. Explain: Vitamin deficiency diseases are rare in the United States.
5. What are the truths or fallacies associated with vitamin E claims?
6. Describe how nutrition affects our economy.
7. Discuss the importance of reducing our food waste.
8. Describe how finding new food sources can affect the nutritional health of the people of the world.
9. What is meant by the nutrient density of foods?
10. Develop a daily diet consisting of nutrient dense foods containing all of the nutrients one needs within a 2000 calorie restriction.
11. Discuss the feasibility of the recommended Dietary Goals for the United States.
12. Describe why it is important for a woman to be concerned about her nutritional status long before she becomes pregnant.
13. Family planning through the use of oral contraceptives can produce some nutritional concerns. Explain.
14. What nutrient intakes should be increased during pregnancy? Explain why.
15. Describe why a pregnant woman should not take any drugs unless prescribed by her physician. What is the fetal alcohol syndrome?
16. Should mothers breast feed their infants? Explain.
17. Show how an inadequate diet during the growing years can affect the growth and development of the child.
18. What are additives? Why are they added to foods? How would our foods be effected if all additives were banned? Do you think that all additives should be banned? Explain.
19. What causes a deficiency disease? How prevalent are these in the United States?
20. Describe why fad diets can be dangerous. Give examples.
21. What is America's chief nutritional problem? Explain why.
22. What is obesity? How is it determined? How can overweight and obesity best be controlled?
23. What are the health implications of obesity?
24. What is anorexia nervosa? What causes it? Why is it important for the anorexic to receive proper treatment?

25. Discuss the value of using food supplements. What are some dangers?
26. What is a "pill doctor"? Why has the Food and Drug Administration removed the use of amphetamines as a treatment for obesity?
27. Explain: There is no such thing as a health food.
28. Describe how the food labeling regulations can help consumers.

REFERENCES

1. "Myths of Vitamins," *FDA Consumer,* March, 1974, U.S. Department of Health, Education, and Welfare; Public Health Service; Food and Drug Administration, HEW Publication No. (FDA) 77–2047.
2. MAPES, MARTHA C. and BARBARA P. STEWART, *Food Waste as an Individual Concern.* Division of Nutrition Sciences, College of Human Ecology, Cornell University, Ithaca, N.Y., 1979.
3. *Ibid.*
4. BEDWORTH, ALBERT E., (ed.), *Health Education, Physical Dimension of Health: Nutrition Education, Manual for Teachers.* The University of the State of New York, The State Education Department, Albany, 1979, pp. 71–73.
5. *The Nation's Health,* The Official Newspaper of the American Public Health Association, March, 1979, The Association, Washington, p. 16.
6. *HEW News,* U.S. Department of Health, Education, and Welfare, Food and Drug Administration, August 31, 1977.
7. *HEW News,* U.S. Department of Health, Education, and Welfare, Food and Drug Administration, August 11, 1978.
8. *HEW News,* U.S. Department of Health, Education, and Welfare, Food and Drug Administration, March 7, 1977.
9. *HEW News,* U.S. Department of Health, Education, and Welfare, Food and Drug Administration, November 9, 1977.
10. DEUTSCH, RONALD M., *Realities of Nutrition,* Bull Publishing Co., Palo Alto, Cal., 1976, p. 24.
11. JACOBSON, MICHAEL, "Our Diets Have Changed But Not For the Best," *The Feeding Web: Issues In Nutritional Ecology,* Joan Dye Gussow (ed.), Bull Publishing Co., Palo Alto, Cal., 1978, p. 183.
12. *Food Day,* Center for Science in the Public Interest, Washington, 1975 (Brochure).
13. MAYER, J., "Genetic Factors—Human Obesity," *Annals of the New York Academy of Sciences,* Vol. 131, Oct. 8, 1965, p. 412.
14. DEUTSCH, RONALD M., *The New Nuts Among the Berries,* Bull Publishing Co., Palo Alto, Cal., 1977, pp. 34–35.
15. DEUTSCH, RONALD M., *Realities of Nutrition. op cit.,* p. 26.
16. U.S. Department of Health, Education, and Welfare, "Myths of Vitamins," *FDA Consumer,* HEW Publication No. (FDA) 77–2047, 1974.
17. Morrison, Margaret, "A Consumer's Guide to Food Labels," *FDA Consumer,* Vol. 11, No. 5, U.S. Department of Health, Education, and Welfare, Food and Drug Administration, Rockville, Md., June, 1977.
18. *Ibid.*

13

perspectives on fitness

KINDS OF FITNESS

Total Fitness

The ancient Greeks recognized that human fitness consisted of a "sound mind in a sound body." However, since about the middle 1950s, the major focus has been on physical fitness. This is probably because it is more concrete and measurable than psychological or social fitness. Research has shown that those who are engaged in a planned program of physical fitness also tend to feel better mentally, emotionally, and socially.

Living adequately in today's world requires that we be totally fit—and physical fitness is basic. We are totally fit when all the organs and systems of the body are functioning to their optimal level; when we are able to deal with most of our mental and emotional problems; and when we function well within our social settings. For our purposes, we define fitness as a level of total health that makes it possible for us to function effectively and efficiently each day. Therefore, total fitness can be measured in terms of the following criteria:

- How well our body's tissues, organs, and systems function *together*.
- How well our body can *resist* disease.
- How *integrated* our personality is.
- How well we can *deal* with emotional and social stress.
- How well we can make appropriate *decisions* regarding most of our life situations.
- How well we can *sustain motivation* and *achieve* personal and social goals.
- How well we generally get along with family and friends.

In summary, we are totally fit to the extent that we can deal with life's situations whether they are chiefly physical, emotional, social, intellectual, or spiritual.

Physical Fitness

Each of us, however, needs to evaluate our health practices to determine which ones may be constraints to improving our fitness. It is important to consider the following questions about our health practices:

- *Do you smoke?* If so, it is important to stop before undertaking a physical fitness program.
- *Is your daily intake of food adequate in terms of nutrients?* Any physical fitness program should include an analysis of your personal nutrition and any changes needed as an integral part of your regimen.
- *Do you drink alcohol to excess?* Excessive drinking is difficult to define, but if you drink on a daily basis or drink excessively more than once a month, a rigorous physical fitness program could be dangerous.
- *Do you have planned times for resting, relaxing, and sleeping?* Although many physical activities can result in emotional relaxation, it is also important to receive adequate sleep or to engage in activities that are relaxing:

reading, listening to music, watching television, or talking with another person.

- *Do you have any significant health problems?* A physician's evaluation of your health status should be made prior to undertaking a physical fitness regimen. It may be necessary to tailor your exercise program to your specific needs.

Your level of physical fitness should be measured in terms of your personal physical qualities, sex, and age. Physical fitness, as with other aspects of health, is a matter of degrees. Probably all of us can improve our physical fitness by changes in our physical activities, the amount of time we devote to them, changes in our eating and other health related practices, and receiving periodic medical evaluation of our health. For example, although many of us have designed our own physical fitness program, we may improve our fitness if we become engaged in a physical fitness program under the supervision of a professional physical educator. To do otherwise may be dangerous for some of us, since a good physical fitness program takes into account one's present health status, one's health practices, and the kinds of activities that will be most effective in achieving physical fitness safely.

Physical fitness is achieved when we have improved the efficiency of energy expenditure to a level that permits us to endure sustained physical activities. Physical fitness is much more than the development of musculature. It includes the development of strong and efficient cardiovascular and respiratory systems resulting in efficient use of energy.

HEALTH AND OUR LIFESTYLES

Personal Behavior

According to the United States Public Health Service (USPHS), "specific individual behaviors, presumably subject to individual control, have been indicated as leading to disease and early death."[1] However, other personal behaviors under the control of the individual have been promoted as improving healthful living, preventing disease, and increasing longevity. The two most important examples are better nutritional practices and regular exercise. The USPHS report stated:

> For more than a generation, American living has become increasingly sedentary. Most of us drive or ride to work and most other places. Work itself, for much of the labor force, involves relatively little, if any, vigorous physical activity. Even in recreation, people commonly have tended to be spectators, not participants. The relative lack of physical activity has led to a decline in physical fitness among youth and adults alike.[2]

Fitness and Health Status

Despite the fact we are living increasingly sedentary lives, Americans are healthier today than ever before in our history according to most measures of health status. Many of our serious health problems, such as cardiovascular diseases, are declining and our life expectancy has increased. For example, our death rate has declined from 17 per 1,000 persons in 1900 to fewer than 9 per 1,000 persons today.[3] Nearly 800,000 people could expect to die each year from tuberculosis, gastroenteritis, diphtheria, and poliomyelitis if conditions were the same today as they were in 1900. However, today, less than 10,000 Americans will die of these diseases. Instead, the major threat to our lives today is cardiovascular diseases. But we can do something to reduce our risk from these by becoming involved in physical activities that strengthen our cardiovascular system and eliminating other risk factors.

Popular Physical Exercises

One of the more popular forms of physical exercises is running or jogging, even though only a relatively small number of us participate in this activity. According to the National Center for Health Statistics, only about 5 percent of Americans over age 20 years run or jog. However, latest figures indicate that approximately 50 percent of Americans are engaged in some form of regular physical exercise. The kinds of exercises vary somewhat and are different for different age groups. For example: one in three walk, one in seven are involved with calisthenics, one in eight swim, one in nine bicycle, one in twenty jog, and one in thirty lift weights.

More young adults report involvement in regular exercise programs than older adults. Swimming, bowling, and competitive sports, such as tennis, are the activities most reported. The percent of people between the ages of 12 and 74 years reporting that they were inactive or had little daily exercise is very low: 5.3 percent for males and 6.8 percent for females. (See Tables 13–1 and 13–2.)

In contrast, 63.6 percent of males and 50.9 percent of females report that they were very active, engaged in much exercise. Another 31.1 percent of males and 42.3 percent of females report that they were somewhat active. Contrary to popular belief, according to the Health Interview Survey of 1975, it appears that Americans' lifestyles do include physical activity.

Table 13–1: People Who Report They Are Inactive by Ages

Age in Years	Percent
12—17	1.5
18—24	4.2
25—34	5.1
35—44	6.9
45—54	8.1
55—64	8.4
65—74	12.5
Total, All Ages	
Male	5.3
Female	6.8

Source of Data: *Health: United States*, U.S. Department of Health, Education, and Welfare, Public Health Service, DHEW Publication No. (PHS) 78–1232, Dec. 1978, p. 217.

Table 13-2: People Who Report Being Engaged in Physical Activity by Ages

Age in Years	Percent Very Active	Percent Modestly Active
12—17	78.8	19.7
18—24	57.9	37.9
25—34	59.3	35.6
35—44	54.1	39.0
45—54	51.1	40.8
55—64	50.4	41.2
65—74	33.8	53.7
Total, All Ages		
Male	63.6	31.1
Female	50.6	42.3

Source of Data: *Health: United States*, U.S. Department of Health, Education, and Welfare, 1978.

STRESS AND FITNESS

Cause of Stress

All of us experience stress. It is a normal part of living and is inevitable. We experience it in relation to our families, college pressures, work, finances, sexual relations—in every aspect of our lives. Generally, we have developed ways of dealing with our everyday stress situations. Some of our means of coping are beneficial, others can be destructive. For example, the use of alcohol or other drugs may temporarily relieve stress, but the original cause is likely to remain. Also, we may develop guilt feelings from excessive use of alcohol or other drugs or behave inappropriately which can lead to greater stress. This new stress compounds the original cause and must also be dealt with in some beneficial or destructive way. We need to develop coping skills that reduce stress beneficially or the result may be a revolving door effect.

Results of Stress

Stress is associated with cardiovascular diseases, gastrointestinal disturbances, other diseases, and mental and emotional illnesses. When stress, or our reaction to it, is excessive, physiologic changes may take place resulting in serious physical and emotional consequences. According to a Surgeon General's Report: "People under stress experience measurable changes in body functions; a rise in blood pressure and secretion of adrenaline and other hormones at higher levels. The changes are basically defensive, mobilizing body energies to meet a threat."[4]

Coping With Stress

Many of the stress-producing situations we encounter almost daily can be reduced or eliminated. Such factors as improved working conditions and reduced college pressures can do much to prevent stress. There are also many things we can do for ourselves that will reduce stress: develop more effective coping skills, become involved in interesting recreational activities, and improve our physical fitness.

When we are physically fit we are better able to deal with stress situations. Stress is a drain on the body and a physically fit person is less likely to experience serious health problems. People who are engaged in a regular physical fitness program claim that during exercise, stress is reduced and, in many instances, disappears.

BENEFITS OF BEING FIT

General Benefits

Although studies are incomplete, there is evidence that a planned physical fitness program provides a variety of benefits. These include improved general health; decrease in emotional stress; feelings of achievement; improved self-confidence and attitudes toward the self, others, and occupation; and the ability to sleep more soundly and relaxed. Many people also claim that they eat better and are able to maintain their ideal weight with less difficulty. Contrary to popular belief, many people actually eat less once they have engaged in a well-planned physical fitness program.

The Muscular System

Some exercise programs are intended chiefly to increase the size, strength, and endurance of the voluntary muscles. Also called skeletal or striated, the *voluntary muscles* are those that are responsible for most of our movements such as walking, chewing, or grasping objects. Isometric and isotonic exercises affect primarily the voluntary muscles. *Isometric* exercises are those characterized by pushing or pulling against an immovable object or against other muscles. *Isotonic* exercises are characterized by placing resistance on a muscle or group of muscles but gradually allowing the muscle to move through its full range of motion.

Exercises such as jogging, walking, and swimming affect the fitness of the involuntary or smooth muscles and the *cardiac* or heart muscle, as well as the voluntary muscles. The *involuntary muscles* are those that make up the blood vessels and other organs such as the stomach. Obviously, the health of the cardiac and involuntary muscles is associated with cardiovascular diseases.

Conditioning

Body conditioning and physical fitness should not be confused. Although body conditioning exercises may affect total fitness, often they do not. Body conditioning is essentially the process of training particular muscle groups to perform efficiently for a given situation. For example, weight lifting will develop certain muscle groups but is not considered adequate for physical fitness. Another example is the professional baseball pitcher. The pitcher conditions his arm for accuracy and endurance, but little total fitness results.

On the other hand, physical fitness includes a broad exercise program resulting in cardiovascular, respiratory, and muscular efficiency. The result of physical fitness affects other body systems as well, such as the digestive and nervous systems, according to some studies.

The Cardiovascular System

The recent declines in death rates from cardiovascular diseases has raised several rather interesting questions. Is the decline the result of medical care and technology or is it due to improved personal health behavior? Since hypertensive disease death rates have been declining more rapidly than other cardiovascular diseases, investigations into such areas as relaxation therapy and personal human behaviors are being made. There is also evidence that four of the important risk factors related to coronary heart disease have declined. These are uncontrolled hypertension, cigarette smoking, consumption of saturated fats, and *physical inactivity.* According to the United States Public Health Service, "exercise and sports participation are recognized as a means of maintaining good health, especially of the cardiovascular system."[5]

Studies that have been conducted since the early 1950s indicate that those of us whose lifestyles include daily physical activity are less prone to cardiovascular diseases than those of us whose lifestyles are sedentary. However, to produce the *cardiovascular training effect* our exercise program should involve rhythmic repetitive, regular movements that result in increased blood flow throughout the body. This also requires that the exercises be sustained for prolonged periods of time without exhaustion. Examples of these exercises are brisk walking, jogging, running, bicycling, swimming, a number of competitive sports, and some forms of dancing.

There is substantial evidence to support the relationship between cardiovascular diseases and a sedentary lifestyle. However, the incidence of coronary disease is significantly greater among smokers than among physically active or nonactive people. This is also true for hypertensive and nonhypertensive people. Physical fitness programs are only one way to reduce the risk of coronary disease and may not be the most important one.

A good physical fitness program designed to improve the efficiency of the cardiovascular system must take into consideration these other factors. If you smoke, stop; if you have hypertension, seek professional advice; if you are obese, improve your diet. Select physical exercises that are appropriate for you as a part of a broad physical fitness program.

What happens to the cardiovascular system of a person who is engaged in an effective physical fitness program? The resting pulse rate of a person who is not physically fit is 70 or more beats per minute. Usually, a person who is physically fit will have a pulse rate below 60 beats per minute. The person who engages in a regular exercise program has increased blood volume and heart size and efficiency. As a result, it is not necessary for the heart to beat as often, which places less strain on the heart. The physicially fit person's pulse rate also returns to normal much faster than a person who is not physically fit. This is called the *recovery pulse rate.*

Studies indicate that those who do not exercise have twice as many heart attacks as those who do exercise. For example, people who expend less than 500 calories per week through exercise experience about twice as many heart conditions as those who expend more than 2000 calories per week through exercise. We expend about 100 calories for each mile we run or walk. In addition, when a person has a heart attack who has been exercising, the changes of recovery are much greater than for the sedentary person.[6]

Although evidence is still incomplete, logic tells us that exercise will prevent heart disease. There is also evidence that the risk from heart disease is reduced through exercise independently of other heart disease risk factors.

The Respiratory System

Exercises that will improve the cardiovascular system's efficiency will also improve the efficiency of the respiratory system. This is essential since these two body systems work cooperatively. Vigorous and consistent exercises result in an increased lung capacity and greater efficiency in the exchange of oxygen and carbon dioxide in the lungs' oveoli. This is important because a primary factor in being fit is the efficiency with which the body burns oxygen in the cells and eliminates the carbon dioxide byproduct in the lungs. This increases our endurance and makes it possible for us to deal effectively with sudden exertion. (See Figure 13–1.)

UNDERTAKING A PHYSICAL FITNESS PROGRAM

Reasons for Being Fit

There are a number of valid reasons for each of us to become involved in a carefully planned physical fitness program. Scientific and anecdotal evidence indicate that those of us who are engaged in a good exercise program are healthier than those whose lifestyles do not include an exercise program. Our circulation improves, our respiration improves, and our endurance improves when we exercise regularly. Although risk factors such as obesity, diabetes mellitus, high blood pressure, high blood cholesterol levels, and cigarette smoking contribute to cardiovascular diseases, when we exercise we tend to lessen the effects of these factors. For example, many people who smoke indicate that when they began a program of regular exercise, they reduced their cigarette consumption and some claim they were able to stop smoking altogether.

Guidelines

When planning a physical fitness program, there are four factors we need to consider: (1) it will require a change in our lifestyles; (2) we should have a complete physical examination to ascertain any existing health problems; (3) our program of exercise should contain a degree of consistency but also flexibility to ward off boredom; and (4) we should select exercises most appropriate for us with a gradual increase in intensity over several weeks. Before attempting strenuous exercises, warm up with light exercises such as walking. Not warming up properly can result in injuries to muscles, joints, and bones. The environment for exercise

Figure 13-1:

Benefits of Fitness

Planned Physical Fitness Program

Bicycling
Tennis
Dancing
Running
Hiking
Walking
Jogging
Swimming

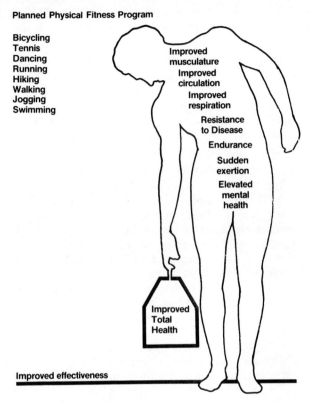

Improved
musculature

Improved
circulation

Improved
respiration

Resistance
to Disease

Endurance

Sudden
exertion

Elevated
mental
health

Improved
Total
Health

Improved effectiveness

should also be safe and free from hazards, For example, if you are a jogger, know the surface you will be jogging on and the nature of the flow of vehicular traffic.

Aerobics

Since the general awareness in the 1950s that a large number of young Americans were inadequately physically fit, many programs have developed in an attempt to rectify this situation. Physical fitness programs were given special impetus by both the Eisenhower and Kennedy Administrations. The President's Council on Physical Fitness and Sports was authorized. Programs to improve the fitness of youth were organized or improved in the physical education and athletic programs of schools and community agencies, such as the YMCA and YWCA; and individuals began personal regimens, such as jogging.

From the fad of jogging, there developed, among some segments, a near obsession with aerobics. Aerobics was popularized by Kenneth Cooper in 1968. Cooper points out that "aerobics refers to a variety of exercises that stimulate heart and lung activity for a time period sufficiently long to produce beneficial

329

changes in the body."[7] The exercises include running, swimming, and jogging— any form of exercise that will "increase the maximum amount of oxygen that the body can process within a given time."[8] This, Cooper refers to as the *aerobic capacity*. The aerobic capacity is dependent upon efficient and strong circulatory and respiratory systems that are developed through the exercise program.

It is generally believed that an active life is conducive to good health and that a low level of habitual physical activity leads to a deterioration in physical fitness and to increased liability to disease. There is some evidence to support this, particularly in relation to cardiovascular disease, but large population studies are needed to establish whether there is a well defined relationship between the degree and pattern of habitual physical activity and given health and disease criteria.[9]

What constitutes a beneficial physical fitness program? Authorities indicate that 15–30 minutes of aerobic exercise each day or at least three times a week will produce beneficial effects on the cardiovascular and respiration systems. These benefits are a reduction of blood pressure by as much as 10 points in hypertensive people, a lower serum cholesterol level, and a reduction in excess adipose tissue. For example, walking or running a mile a day will result in a loss of more than 10 pounds in a year.

According to the United States Public Health Service, "aerobic exercise, when carefully prescribed, has been found useful for patients with chest pain (angina pectoris) and those recovering from heart attacks . . ." In addition, "asthmatics and people with chronic obstructive lung disease often can improve their respiratory capacity. Diabetics can lower their blood sugar levels and insulin requirements, and overweight adults who have become diabetic often are freed of any indications of the disease when they achieve normal weight through exercise and diet."[10]

In recent years, increasing numbers of employee physical fitness programs have been initiated by business and government. In some instances, as many as 40 percent of the employees are involved in these programs. The result is that employees feel better, work better, and are absent from work fewer days.

EXERCISE TRAINING AND TESTING PROGRAM

Introduction

Formal training and testing programs may include a variety of activities that concentrate on improving muscle strength, coordination, physical skills, and cardiovascular fitness. The kinds of exercise programs you select are dependent upon what your goals are, your present status of health, age, and possibly, sex. As we have seen, some exercise regimens are directed more toward muscle development, such as weight lifting, while others, such as aerobic activities, will affect cardiovascular fitness.

Selecting a Program

The New York Heart Association has developed criteria for selecting formal exercise programs. Essentially, the Association suggests that you look for facilities that have:

1. aerobic exercises;
2. exercise sessions conducted three or more times each week;
3. qualified instructors;
4. exercise sessions that include a variety of activities to preclude boredom;
5. health education and other health programs related to nutrition, smoking, and so forth;
6. adequate dressing and storage facilities.[11]

In addition, the facility should have a policy to accept only participants who have undergone a physical examination including a stress test by a physician or other qualified person.

Cardiovascular Stress Testing

Cardiovascular problems sometimes are manifested only when we exert ourselves. Therefore, controlled exercise tests, such as the stationary bicycle or treadmill, are used to place graduated stress on the cardiovascular system. Instruments are attached to measure heartbeat, blood pressure, and electrocardiographic waves.

The test is conducted by gradually changing resistance on the treadmill or bicycle, or increasing walking or pedaling speed. The instruments that are attached to the person record cardiovascular changes as stress increases. Obviously, these tests should be conducted by a trained physical educator, physiologist, or physician. Any abnormal conditions that are revealed should be evaluated by a cardiologist.

Some cardiologists believe that the stress test is more reliable for males than females. Although the stress test can be used with young males, cardiologists recommend that it be done with all males over 35 years of age who contemplate a physical fitness regimen. Should the electrocardiogram indicate an abnormal heart condition, the physician may suggest further tests to determine its specific nature. An exercise program can then be tailored for maximum safe results.

GLOSSARY

Aerobics: A variety of exercises to increase heart and lung activity for a time period sufficiently long to produce beneficial changes in the body.

Aerobic capacity: The maximum amount of oxygen the body can process over a given period of time.

Fitness: A level of total health that makes it possible for us to function effectively and efficiently.

Recovery pulse rate: The time lapse between the pulse rate at the cessation of physical activity and its return to normal.

Stress: Physical or emotional tension caused by environmental forces, tending to produce a health problem if severe or chronic and not beneficially dealt with.

SUMMARY

Total fitness is the body and mind functioning at optimal levels. Physical fitness is basic to total fitness. There are certain basic criteria that can be used to generally ascertain our total fitness.

When planning a physical fitness program, it is important to take into account our personal health status, as well as the exercises for achieving fitness. Exercises should be tailored to meet our personal needs. A good physical fitness program consists of warm up periods and vigorous exercises that place an exertion on the cardiovascular and respiratory systems. Many forms of exercise, such as swimming and competitive sports, are engaged in, with jogging being the most popular.

There is evidence that fitness affects our health status, especially in terms of cardiovascular diseases. There are also other benefits from being physically fit including weight control and a reduction of stress.

Aerobic exercises appear to be most beneficial for achieving physical fitness. These exercises are especially important for improving the efficiency of the cardiovascular and respiratory systems. Aerobics is engagement in activities that increase the efficiency of these systems, especially in regards to the efficient use of oxygen by the body.

PROBLEMS FOR DISCUSSION

1. Describe the factors that constitute total fitness. Distinguish between total and physical fitness.
2. Analyze your physical fitness program. How well does it comply with the criteria for a well-planned effective program?
3. How many of the cardiovascular risk factors do you have? What can you do about them?
4. Describe the effects of aerobic exercises upon the cardiovascular and respiratory systems.
5. What can you do to reduce personal stress? Are you doing these? Explain.
6. In what ways does being physically fit affect your health status?
7. List five exercises that can be beneficial for achieving fitness.

REFERENCES

1. *Health: The United States,* U.S. Department of Health, Education, and Welfare; Public Health Service, DHEW Publication No. (PHS) 78–1232, Dec., 1978, p. 25.
2. *Ibid.,* p. 132.
3. *Ibid.,* p. 3.

4. *Healthy People: The Surgeon General's Report on Health Promotion and Disease Prevention,* U.S. Department of Health, Education, and Welfare; Public Health Service, DHEW (PHS) Publication No. 79–55071, 1979, p. 135.
5. *Health: The United States, op. cit.,* p. 202.
6. *Ibid.,* p. 133.
7. COOPER, KENNETH H., *The New Aerobics,* Bantam Books, New York, 1970, p. 15.
8. *Ibid.,* p. 16.
9. *WHO Chronicle,* Vol. 32, No. 9, Sept., 1978, World Health Organization, Geneva, p. 364.
10. *Healthy People, op. cit.,* p. 134.
11. *Exercising Your Right To Know: A Consumer Guide To Choosing and Using Exercise Training and Stress Testing Factilities.* Exercise Committee, New York Heart Association, Inc., New York, 1980, pp. 12–13.

14

preventing infectious diseases

INTRODUCTION

The importance of preventing or controlling a disease is dependent upon the degree to which it interferes with the functioning of the person and society—and its economic impact. Preventive medicine, a specialty of medical practice, has traditionally been given a low priority. It was not until the middle to late 1970s that preventive medicine was recognized as an essential and vital area of medicine that needed to be given greater emphasis than it had been given in the past.

Although it is not always necessary to understand the cause of a disease to effectively prevent it, prevention is less complicated when the cause is known. There are a number of diseases that have been effectively prevented, however, without knowledge of their cause. One notable example is the prevention of scurvy in 1753—its cause was not discovered until 1928! An understanding of the multicausal relationship that exists in most disease states improves the ability to prevent them. This relationship is referred to as the *epidemiologic model.*

THE EPIDEMIOLOGIC MODEL

The Disease Process

The science of *epidemiology* is concerned with the distribution and causes of disease, directed toward the establishment of effective preventive and control measures. Epidemiology emphasizes knowledge of the disease process recognizing the involvement of a multiplicity of influencing factors.[1] The disease process involves the interaction of the host (the person), agent (physical, chemical, or biological), and the environment (physical, biological, or social).

The disease process consists of four stages in the development and completion of the disease. The first is the *stage of susceptibility,* which includes our ability, under varying conditions, to resist the onset of disease. Some of these conditions may be under our control, such as lifestyles, while others cannot be controlled by us, such as age, sex, and genetic predispositions. The stage of susceptibility is essentially the time when a clinical disease has not yet appeared, but will when other factors become present. For example, a person experiencing a prolonged period of stress, anxiety, or depression is more susceptible to contracting tuberculosis.

The second is the *stage of presymptomatic disease* characterized by the onset of disease but with no clinical signs or symptoms as yet apparent.

The third is the *stage of clinical disease* characterized by overt and recognizable clinical signs and symptoms that can be analyzed resulting in a diagnosis.

The fourth is the *stage of disability* characterized by either residual defects leaving the person disabled to some extent or the onset of death. This stage may be manifest in obvious disabilities, such as paralysis of a part of the body (common in cerebrovascular accident or stroke), or the disease may become chronic and gradually progress until death results—for example, multiple sclerosis.

A composite of the four stages of the disease process is referred to as the *natural history* of the disease.[2] An understanding of the natural history of a disease is especially valuable in the prevention and control of the various chronic and degenerative diseases. By knowing the natural history of a disease, its onset may be precluded by eliminating the controllable risk factors associated with it.

Host Factors

The host in the epidemiologic model of the disease process is you. Whether or not you are a good host is dependent upon your genetic predispositions and how well you have succeeded in living unhealthfully. If you drink too much alcohol, worry too much, eat too much, smoke too much, expose yourself to health hazards, you are well on your way to becoming a good host for disease. These behaviors and many others are called *risk factors.* Some are under our control, others are not. Some are risk factors for specific diseases, while some are risk factors for several diseases. For example, cigarette smoking is a risk factor for lung cancer, cardiovascular disease, and emphysema among others.

The host factors related to the risk or prevention of disease may be placed into several epidemiological categories. There is no doubt that some people are healthier and able to resist certain diseases as a result of genetic endowments. Our heredity is not only associated with resisting disease or being predisposed to disease, but it is also associated with longevity. Barring unusual circumstances, such as accidental death or suicide, longevity seems to run in families. This is also true relative to certain diseases. For example, those of us from families with a history of diabetes or certain cardiovascular diseases are more at risk than those from families that do not have this history.

Other factors related to risk of disease or its prevention are our past experiences and living patterns, sex, age, type of personality, ethnic origin, and socioeconomic status. For example: a person may acquire immunity from previous exposure to a disease; some diseases are more prevalent in one sex than another—coronary heart attacks in males and diabetes in females, for example; certain types of cancers are more prevalent among older people; the "Type A" personality may be predisposed to coronary heart disease; some diseases are more common in certain races; and lead poisoning among children is more prevalent among those in lower socioeconomic groups.

In the above illustrations, we note that the host factors are interactional with the agent and environmental factors. We also note that the agent is in fact an environmental factor. In recent years, epidemiologists have altered the traditional epidemiologic model from host, agent, and environment to host and environment since the agent is a part of the environment. However, the agent is of sufficient importance in the disease process that it deserves special emphasis.

Agent Factors

An *agent* is a factor whose presence or absence contributes to the initiation of the disease process. The *presence* in the body of the tubercle bacillus is necessary for one to contract tuberculosis. The *absence* of vitamin C is necessary for one to develop scurvy. Agent factors in the disease process may be physical agents, chemical agents, or biological agents. Physical agents may be artificially imposed, such as air pollutants and x-ray radiation, or they may be natural, such as the sun's rays or variations in temperature. Examples of diseases associated with *physical agents* are skin cancer from over-exposure to the ultra violet rays of the sun, and liver cancer from breathing air polluted with asbestos fibers.

Chemical agents can take the various forms of liquid, gas or smoke, or solids, such as dust particles. Chemical agents may enter the body through inhalation, ingestion, absorption, or injection. Carbon monoxide poisoning results from inhalation; nutrients or chemicals are ingested (hypervitaminosis); mercury poisoning can result from absorption (or ingestion); and drug overdoses can result from injection, inhalation, ingestion, and absorption.

The agent most commonly associated with the infectious diseases are the *biological agents.* Disease producing biological agents are the viruses, associated with measles, mumps, and smallpox; rickettsiae, associated with Rocky Mountain spotted fever; bacteria, associated with syphilis and gonorrhea; the arthropods, associated with scabies; the helminths, associated with pinworms; protozoa, associated with malaria; and fungi, associated with athletes' foot.

The biological agents that contribute to the disease process are sometimes referred to as parasites. A *parasite* is a plant or animal that lives off the host but does not contribute anything to the welfare of the host. Ironically, from a philosophical viewpoint, the parasite that invades the human body with virulence sufficient to cause disease and finally, death of the person, represents a biological failure—a sort of survival for now, suicide later.

Environmental Factors

We have discussed in some detail the importance of the environment in the promotion and maintenance of health. Here we will learn that the environment is also a vital force in the disease process. In this context, the environment is the intrinsic and extrinsic. The *intrinsic* is that environment provided by the host while the *extrinsic* is that environment outside of the host. The extrinsic environment may be divided into the physical, psychological, social, and biological aspects.

As societies have advanced technologically, so have the hazards that accompany this advancement. The *physical environment* includes such factors as heat, cold, radiation, atmospheric conditions, water, and chemical agents. Although we have learned how to control many aspects of the physical environment, such as temperature for comfort and health, our technology has increased the risk factors for disease in relation to other physical aspects. For example, industrialization and increases in population have resulted in atmospheric pollution and increases of chemical agents that can contribute to some diseases. Today, most Americans are exposed to radiation levels far beyond those of people two or three generations ago. Even the unborn are exposed to pollutants, chemicals, and radiation that can affect their development and predispose them to diseases of various kinds.

The *psychological environment* cannot be separated from the physical environment because the physical environment has a direct impact upon our mental and emotional status. This is also true for the social environment, which is in constant interaction with the psychology of people. Essentially, the psychological environment is that aspect that influences the stressor factors affecting our behavior, or those factors that tend to create an atmosphere of security and contentment.

The *social environment* is related to socioeconomic factors, political and other social institutions associated with our social way of life. We know from epidemiological investigations that social factors are directly related to the onset and incidence of many diseased conditions.

The *biological environment* refers specifically to the plants and animals that act as agents in the disease process. They may be identified as the causative agent or an agent that contributes directly to the onset of disease. The *causative agent* is one that must be present for the disease to manifest itself. For example, infectious diseases cannot result unless the infectious (biological) agent is present. However, because the infectious agent is present does not necessarily mean that the disease is inevitable. As we have seen host, agent, and environment factors must also be right for disease to result.

PREVENTING DISEASE

How Disease Is Transmitted

The transmission of disease is applicable only to those that are communicable. Although all communicable diseases are infectious, not all infectious diseases are communicable. Some communicable diseases can be transmitted only through direct contact with the infected person, while others require an intermediate host. In addition, some communicable diseases can be transmitted through both contact with the infected person and through contact with fomites. A *fomite* is an inanimate contaminated object such as clothing, water, and food.

Direct transmission of a disease consists of the agent being directly transferred from the infected person to one who is not infected. If the agent has access to a portal of entry and the new host's environmental factors are favorable, it can establish itself resulting in the disease. *Indirect transmission* requires a vehicle for transferring the agent from the infected person to a noninfected person. The vehicle may be a fomite, vector, or the air. The *fomite* may be clothing, a surgical instrument, or an eating utensil. A *vector* may merely carry the agent or the agent may require the environment of the vector for its maturation before it is capable of causing disease. The *airborne* indirect transmission is usually by dust particles or droplets in the air.

Personal Responsibilities

Historically, the prevention and control of disease focused on the establishment of public health measures: sanitation, pure water supplies, and adequate sewage disposal. Most public health laws were aimed at the masses of people rather than at what individuals could do for themselves. These measures are still important, but it has been recognized during the past few decades that the prevention and control of many diseases rests with each of us.

Such personal health behavior as establishing daily living practices that are most likely to result in a promotion of our health potentials and seeking professional health care for the maintenance of health are responsibilities that only we can carry out. For example, many diseases are preventable through immunization. This is true of some of the communicable diseases, such as diphtheria, mumps, poliomyelitis, and rubella. However, vaccines available for these and other diseases are of no value in their prevention and control unless we take advantage of them.

As an incentive, therefore, it is sometimes necessary to legislate personal health actions. For instance, in July, 1979, the New York State Legislature strengthened its immunization laws in regards to the immunization of children.[3] The new amendments to the law require immunization of all children between the ages of 2 months and 18 years that attend public or nonpublic schools, day care centers, and institutions such as hospitals. The law requires immunization for poliomyelitis, mumps, measles, diphtheria, and rubella.*

Epidemiological Procedures

Fundamentally, epidemiology is concerned with discovering ways in which diseases can be prevented or controlled to raise the level of health of populations. Epidemiology may be placed into three areas of concentration: (1) descriptive epidemiology; (2) analytic epidemiology; and (3) experimental epidemiology.[4]

It is important to understand that the three areas of epidemiology are not mutually exclusive. *Descriptive epidemiology* deals with time, the place, and the people affected by the disease. Data relative to the time a disease occurs—year, season, month, day—can provide clues as to whether the disease follows a cyclical pattern. Data relative to place can provide information about the geography of the disease and whether there are peculiar environmental factors that contribute to the disease. A study of the people may reveal that the disease is more prevalent in certain nationalities, socioeconomic groups, sex, and so forth. Information gathered about these elements can result in an understanding of the disease process that can, in turn, result in the establishment of prevention and control measures.

Analytic epidemiology attempts to find significant relationships between the frequency, distribution, and other characteristics of the disease process. An analysis of data may show that a certain disease is more prevalent among people in a certain age group and sex, and in a particular geographic area, such as a nation. For example, it has been found that for lung cancer the rate is highest among men in ages 60–69 years who have smoked two or more packs of cigarettes a day and who began smoking before 15 years of age.

Experimental epidemiology is difficult to conduct because we cannot experiment directly on people. However, we can obtain valuable information through a variety of experimental techniques. These include prospective studies, which involve following a particular group of people over a period of time, and retro-

*The law, however, does not apply to children whose parents or guardians are bona fide members of a recognized religious organization whose teachings are contrary to the practices outlined in the law.

spective studies, which are primarily a historical analysis of two groups of people. Both of these methods were used in the late 1950s and early 1960s in regards to the association between cigarette smoking and lung cancer.

CONTROLLING DISEASES

Limitations of Control

Despite our efforts, and those of public health services and other social institutions, some diseases cannot be prevented. When disease does occur, procedures must be taken to control the progress of the disease in the person and to control its transmission to others if it is communicable. If the disease is a noncommunicable disease, control consists chiefly of reducing the risk factors associated with it and preventing complications from taking place.

However, the real and significant limitations of control measures, lie in the fact that they are instituted only after the disease has occurred. In the case of *immunization,* control consists of immunizing others that are susceptible to the disease; *isolation and quarantine* consist of protecting the well from the sick; and *medical procedures* involve the treatment of the sick. The most effective control measure is *prevention*—for through the use of effective preventive procedures, the disease will remain under control.

Immunization

Immunization is a process of rendering a person resistant to a particular disease. This may occur naturally or artificially. *Natural immunity* may result when a person has a disease, builds antibodies against the disease, and recovers from it. However, not all communicable diseases result in natural immunity. This is true, for example, with some sexually transmitted diseases. *Artificial immunity* is the process of rendering a person immune to a disease by introducing an antigen that stimulates the body to build antibodies to the disease. Although the person may have some reaction to the antigen, a clinical disease does not result. There are two kinds of artificial immunizations in use:

1. *Passive immunization* is the process of introducing an immune substance into the body of people who are susceptible to a disease or likely to contract it because of unavoidable exposure to infected persons. For example, immune globulin is an immune substance that can render a person resistant to infectious hepatitis; and gamma globulin can reduce the likelihood of chicken pox infection. Passive immunization usually remains effective for a limited period of time and a person may need to be reinoculated if the threat of the disease persists.

2. *Active immunization* consists of introducing specific antigens into the body that in turn stimulate the body's immune response. The *immune response* consists of the development of antibodies specific for the disease. The

antigens may be living, attenuated, or dead. In all cases, the specific antigen is not destroyed and is capable of stimulating the specific immune response in the person.

The smallpox vaccination was the first effective immunization developed by Edward Jenner in 1798. He noticed that people exposed to cowpox did not contract smallpox. Inoculation with the cowpox virus was capable of immunizing people against smallpox. However, it took nearly 80 years before its use became widespread. In 1979, the World Health Organization announced the probable complete worldwide eradication of smallpox since no diagnosed case had been found for over two years. *This is the first disease ever eradicated on a worldwide basis through human effort.* Smallpox vaccination is no longer required in the United States since the risks from complications from the vaccine far outweigh the risks of contracting the disease.

Quarantine and Isolation

Quarantine and isolation measures were used quite freely until about the 1930s when studies indicated that they were not as effective for the control of disease as previously thought. Prior to this time, it was common practice to placard (put a quarantine sign on the front door of the house), the official procedure used to warn others of the presence of a communicable disease. This practice is now, generally obsolete.

Quarantine is essentially an attempt at restricting the freedom of one who has a contagious disease and those who are well but suspected of transmitting it to others. *Isolation,* on the other hand, is removing the sick person from others. For the most part, strict quarantine has been replaced by the personal surveillance measures as more practical and less costly.

COMMUNICABLE DISEASES

Characteristics

The major characteristics of a communicable disease are its incubation period, the period of communicability, and the signs and symptoms that indicate a disease has been established. However, before the disease process can begin, certain preliminary events must take place. The microorganisms present in the infected or well person who is a carrier must find an exit from this host. After the exit, the microorganism must be transported in some way to a susceptible, healthy host. Once the microorganism finds a healthy, susceptible host, it must gain entry and if this new environment is right, it must multiply in sufficient numbers to cause an illness that is recognized by the signs and symptoms it produces.

Most biological agents that cause disease have limited adaptive abilities. The spirochete that causes syphilis, for example, cannot adapt to a dry environment outside of the host. Therefore, it must exit the infected host and enter the new host directly. Some infectious agents, however, can be transmitted through vectors or fomites; others need an intermediate host for maturing. For instance, typhoid fever bacteria can be transmitted through a fomite, Rocky Mountain Spotted Fever rickettsia through a vector; the malaria protozoa must have an intermediate host, the female Anopheles mosquito.

Generally speaking, the means by which the infectious agent must leave its host is the same means by which it gains entry into the new host. This means of entry is called the *portal of entry*. For example, the malaria protozoa leave the host by the mosquito puncturing skin and removing blood, and enter the new host by an injection (puncture) made by the carrier mosquito. The transmission of communicable diseases is illustrated in Figure 14–1.

The Incubation Period

The time it takes from the moment of entry until signs and symptoms appear is called the *incubation period*. Some disease producing microorganisms have a fairly constant and predictable incubation period, while others will vary. The factors associated with the variability of the incubation period include the amount and virility of microorganisms and the resistance of the host. Knowing the length of the incubation period is important in controlling some diseases since many are not communicable during this period. Once signs and symptoms appear, most infectious diseases are communicable to others. This stage of the disease process is called the *prodrome period*. It is manifest in some general symptoms of the presence of disease, such as a headache, fever, and other feelings of discomfort. If, however, no symptoms appear, the disease is said to be *subclinical*.

When the disease process reaches its peak, with general and specific symptoms that make its diagnosis possible, it is called the *clinical stage*. Next comes

Figure 14-1:

How diseases are transmitted

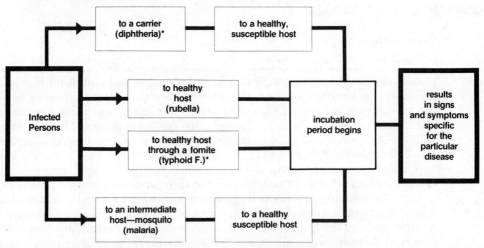

*May also be transmitted directly from infected person to well host.

the climax (fastigium) of the disease. The *climax* is the peak of the disease when signs and symptoms are most intense. When symptoms begin to disappear and the person feels better but is still sick, it is called the *decline stage.* Following the decline stage, and when symptoms are generally over, the person enters the *convalescent stage.* For all practical purposes, the body has succeeded in overcoming the infectious agent and is in a *period of recovery.* It is characterized by the person returning to the preinfectious condition. Some diseases are communicable during the convalescent stage of the disease.

SEXUALLY TRANSMITTED
DISEASES

The sexually transmitted diseases (venereal diseases) are those that are transmitted only through sexual contact with a person who is infected with the disease in its communicable period. An exception to this is that the fetus may contract a venereal disease from its infected mother prior to birth or at the time of birth.

Gonorrhea

Also called clap (and other slang expressions), gonorrhea is caused by a gram-negative diplococcus bacteria *(Neisseria gonorrhea).* It is transmitted from an infected person to a healthy person during sexual intercourse. Sexual intercourse in this case includes any sexual activity: kissing, penile/vaginal penetration, oral/ vaginal/penile, and anal contact. There are approximately one million cases of gonorrhea reported in the United States each year. The incidence of reported cases has steadily increased in the past 40 years from nearly 200,000 cases in 1941 to over a million cases in 1980. Figure 14–2 illustrates this increase. It will be noted that there was a significant increase in the incidence in the period from 1943 to 1947, during the peak years of World War II. This was followed by a rather steady decline until the middle to late 1960s with the inauguration and general social acceptance of "sexual freedom."

The symptoms of gonorrhea are usually explicitly manifest in the male, but may be asymptomatic in the female. In the male, the first symptoms to generally appear are a slight milky discharge from the urethra and a burning sensation during urination. Later, symptoms include a redness and swelling at the meatus of the penis, and an increase in the discharge, sometimes containing blood. The symptoms in the female may be absent or so insignificant that they go unnoticed.

Diagnosis of gonorrhea is by microscopic examination that reveals the presence of the gonococcus bacteria. A more accurate diagnosis is obtained by cultures. When diagnosed as positive, the treatment is a massive injection of penicillin intramuscularly. For persons sensitive to penicillin, other antibiotic drugs can be used. If left untreated, gonorrhea can result in serious complications in both the male and female, terminating in sterility and possibly meningitis and endocarditis, among others.

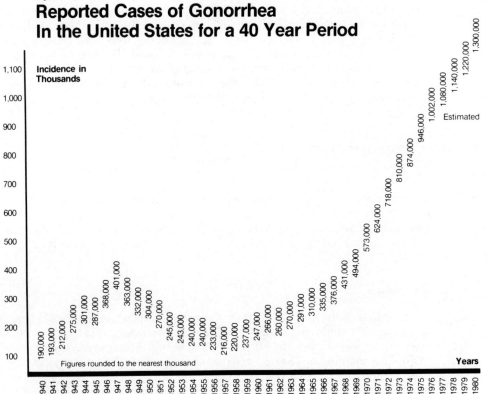

Figure 14-2:

Reported Cases of Gonorrhea
In the United States for a 40 Year Period

Incidence in Thousands

1,100

1,000

900

800

700

600

500

400

300

200

100

Estimated

190,000
193,000
212,000
275,000
301,000
287,000
368,000
401,000
363,000
332,000
304,000
270,000
245,000
243,000
240,000
240,000
233,000
216,000
220,000
237,000
247,000
266,000
260,000
270,000
291,000
310,000
335,000
376,000
431,000
494,000
573,000
624,000
718,000
810,000
874,000
946,000
1,002,000
1,080,000
1,140,000
1,220,000
1,300,000

Figures rounded to the nearest thousand

Years

1940 1941 1942 1943 1944 1945 1946 1947 1948 1949 1950 1951 1952 1953 1954 1955 1956 1957 1958 1959 1960 1961 1962 1963 1964 1965 1966 1967 1968 1969 1970 1971 1972 1973 1974 1975 1976 1977 1978 1979 1980

Source of Data: United States Department of Health, Education, and Welfare

Syphilis

The most serious of the venereal diseases is syphilis which is caused by *Treponema pallidum,* a spirochete. Syphilis is a chronic venereal disease that can attack any organ or tissue of the body if left untreated. Since the spirochete is extremely sensitive to drying and temperature variations, its transmission must almost always be by direct contact through sexual intercourse. However, syphilis can be transmitted by an infected mother to her unborn fetus resulting in congenital syphilis in the infant. Transmission of the syphilis spirochete is also possible through transfusion of infected blood or plasma. Diagnosis of syphilis is through microscopic examination, blood serologic tests, and spinal fluid examination.

The clinical course for untreated syphilis can be divided into three stages: (1) the primary or acute stage; (2) the secondary stage; and (3) the tertiary stage. The *primary stage* in the male is characterized by the appearance of a lesion called a *chancre* at the site of contact. This usually appears within 10–40 days after exposure to the infected person. The chancre is painless and will gradually disappear.

The *secondary stage* is characterized by fever, skin eruptions, and headache. These symptoms usually appear within 6–12 weeks following exposure. The secondary stage lasts several weeks. There then is a period, sometimes referred to as the *latency stage,* in which all symptoms disappear and can last as long as 30 years. During this time the disease is invading the muscle and nerve tissue throughout the body.

The *tertiary stage* is characterized by a variety of symptoms depending upon the organs or tissues involved. If the brain is infected, an organic mental illness, general paresis, results. The treatment of choice during all three stages of syphilis is penicillin. In the primary stage, a cure can readily be affected; in the secondary stage, cure is usually but more difficult. Cure is also possible in the tertiary stage, but damage to organs from the infection, especially the nervous system, is irreversible.

The incidence of syphilis in the United States has shown a rather steady decrease over the past 40 years. This is illustrated in Figure 14–3.

Granuloma Inguinale

In the United States, granuloma inguinale, a relatively rare disease, occurs chiefly among blacks. It is caused by a bacteria, the *Donovania granulomatis.* It is only mildly communicable. Generally, it involves the skin and sometimes the lymphatics. The first symptom is the appearance of a painless vesicle or papule.

Figure 14-3:
Reported Cases of all Stages of Syphilis in the United States for a 40 Year Period.

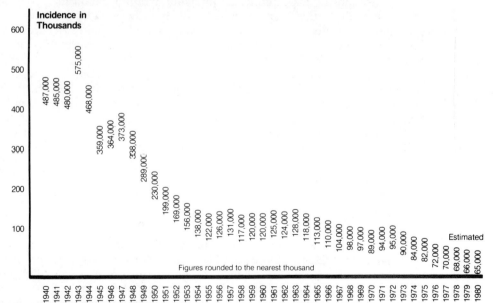

Source of data: United States Department of Health, Education, and Welfare.

If left untreated, granuloma inguinale will spread, involving the lower abdomen, buttocks, and thighs. Eventually, the victim will become anemic, weak, and finally die from the infection. In its early stages, granuloma inguinale is curable by the administration of streptomycin and other antibiotics.

Chancroid

Soft chancre, another name for chancroid, is characterized by an acute, localized and painful ulceration at the point of entry of the infectious agent. The infectious agent is a bacterium, *Hemophilus ducreyi*. Although the mode of transmission is through sexual intercourse, there have been reported cases of accidental transmission to persons who care for chancroid patients.

Chancroid is self-limiting, but it may persist for months, and complications may result. The disease can be successfully treated by the use of sulfonamides.

Chancroid is most prevalent in tropical and subtropical regions of the world with highest incidences occurring at seaports. Epidemiologically, there appears to be no natural resistance to the disease or any differences in incidence among ages, sexes, or races. In the United States, chancroid is relatively rare with less than one thousand reported cases annually. It is interesting to note that in the past 40 years the incidence of chancroid reached its peak in the United States with slightly more than 9,000 reported cases in 1947, immediately following the end of World War II.

Lymphogranuloma Venereum

As might be expected from the name, lymphogranuloma venereum is a disease that affects the lymph nodes. It is generally thought that this disease is much more prevalent than reported figures would indicate. According to the American Public Health Association, lymphogranuloma venereum is endemic in the southern United States.[5]

Lymphogranuloma venereum is transmitted by sexual intercourse with an infected person. It is caused by a filterable virus and is characterized by ulcerative lesions on the genitalia spreading to the lymph channels and lymph nodes, becoming systemic. The primary genital lesion usually appears between 5 and 21 days following contact with the infected person. The disease may spread to the urethra, anus, and rectum. Tetracycline antibiotics are effective treatments for the disease at all stages of development. Because of its self-limiting feature, it is seldom fatal but it may persist for years causing extreme debilitation and invalidism.

Herpes

There are two major types of herpes virus that are transmitted through close personal contact. Herpes simplex type 1 produces infections commonly known as cold sores or fever blisters. Of most concern, however, is herpes simplex type 2 that is often transmitted through sexual contact.

Herpes simplex type 2 is characterized by painful blisters on the genitals, thighs, and buttocks. It can also cause a central nervous system infection in infants born to infected mothers. It has become so common that some authorities estimate that the vast majority of the American public will contract it at least once in their lives. An interesting aspect of this disease is that once a person contracts it the virus remains in the body for the life of the person and symptoms may develop from time to time.

Herpes simplex type 2 has also been linked to the development of cervical cancer. This link has resulted in some authorities describing cervical cancer as a sexually transmitted disease. This is especially true of women who have had a variety of sex partners and began engaging in sexual intercourse at an early age.

Other Sexually Transmitted Diseases

The other sexually transmitted diseases, although not generally as serious as those mentioned above, deserve consideration. These are candidiasis, also known as moniliasis and thrush; trichomoniasis; and the crab louse. Rather than being an infection as the other diseases previously discussed, the crab louse is an infestation.

Candidiasis is caused by a yeast-like fungus called *Candida albicans.* This disease is found throughout the world and is characterized by a thrush containing white plaques when the site is in the oral cavity. Vulvovaginitis with inflammation and white plaques with a discharge are the symptoms when the site is the vagina. The disease usually responds to proper treatment but there may be recurrences.

Trichomoniasis is a relatively common and chronic disease of the female characterized by vaginitis and a rather profuse yellowish discharge. In the male, the disease usually infects the prostate, seminal vesicles, and urethra. The agent that is responsible for trichomoniasis is a protozoan called *Trichomonas vaginalis,* which responds to treatment. To control the disease, it is important that all sex partners undergo treatment concurrently.

There are three kinds of *pediculosis,* each resulting from a specific species of louse: (1) the head louse, the *Pediculus humanus capitis;* (2) the body louse, the *Pediculus humanus corporis;* and (3) the crab louse, the *Phthirus pubis.* We will limit our discussion of pediculosis to the crab louse which is usually transmitted by sexual intercourse, but can also be acquired from toilet seats, beds, and clothing from an infested person. It is characterized by itching in the genital area with resulting dermatitis. The crab louse can be destroyed by the application of a pediculicidal powder or solution. However, clothing, beds, and toilet seats should also be cleaned with an antiseptic.

DISEASES OF THE EAR

Introduction

The complex process of hearing may be interrupted at any point through adverse environmental conditions, injury, or disease. Hearing loss and impairment constitute a major health problem in the United States. It is estimated that approximately 15 million Americans suffer hearing impairment and of these, more than 10 million have never had medical evaluation of their condition.[6]

However, when considering hearing impairment to the point of limitation of activity, we find that over 700,000 Americans fall into this category.[7] According to the Department of Health, Education, and Welfare, about 1.8 million Americans may be so deaf that they cannot understand speech.

Deafness

There are two major types of deafness. *Conductive deafness* results from an accumulation of excess ear wax (cerumen) which becomes impacted in the external ear preventing sound waves from reaching the ear drum (tympanic membrane). Conductive deafness can also be caused by foreign bodies lodged in the external auditory canal. For example, inflammation may result from the insertion into the ear of such objects as toothpicks, hairpins, and cotton swabs.

Perceptive deafness involves the auditory nerve, cerebral pathways, or the auditory center of the brain. This type of deafness may result from infectious diseases such as meningitis, syphilis, typhoid fever, mumps, and measles. In addition, perceptive deafness may be caused by tumors that affect the nerval pathways; trauma, such as skull fracture; and chemicals, such as quinine, arsenic, alcohol, salicylates, or mercury.

Infections

The common infections of the ear are caused by bacteria, fungi, and viruses. For example, *acute external otitis,* which frequently follows swimming in fresh water, is caused by a bacterial infection of the ear canal. Its symptoms include an inflammation of the skin lining the ear canal. It is treated most successfully with antibiotics and rest. *Furunculosis* is also caused by a bacteria and is characterized by a feeling of fullness in the ear, and a pain when chewing. The tissue may swell, nearly closing the ear canal, resulting in hearing impairment. It is treated by heat applications and antibacterial agents.

An example of a fungus infection of the external ear is *otomycosis.* The fungus may cause itching or pain. It is treated by antibiotic drugs. A viral infection of the ear is *aural herpes zoster.* This infection results in pain, impaired hearing, and is accompanied by possible vertigo, and vomiting. Temporary facial paralysis is also possible. There is no specific treatment for this disease, except to relieve its symptoms.

DISEASES OF THE EYE

There are many diseases of the eye that can impair vision or result in blindness. Some are caused by infection, others are chronic or degenerative, and others may result from trauma.

Sty

A relatively common eye disease is *sty.* Most often a sty is caused by a staphylococcal infection. It is characterized by a swelling at the base of an eyelash and is quite painful. Usually the ulceration ruptures, discharging pus and reliev-

ing the pain. The infection can spread to neighboring structures unless an antimicrobial agent is applied.

Pink Eye

An infection of the eye that is highly contagious is *pink eye,* which is usually
caused by staphylococci or pneumococci bacteria. Vision is sometimes impaired
because of the adherence of a discharge to the cornea. Pink eye can be treated
with antibiotics and recurrences prevented by avoiding exposure to known irri-
tants and removing inverted eyelashes.

Trachoma

A leading cause of blindness in the world is *trachoma,* a contagious disease
of the conjunctivis. It is highly prevalent in Egypt, southern and central Europe,
and the Far East. It is related to psittacosis and lymphogranuloma venereum.
Both eyes are usually affected, characterized by conjunctival congestion, swelling
of the eyelids along with other symptoms that may involve the entire cornea. Scar
tissue can develop causing impaired vision and blindness.

Conjunctivitis neonatorum

Conjunctivitis neonatorum is acquired by infants during birth from a birth
canal infected with gonococcal, staphylococcal, streptococcal, or pneumono-
coccal bacteria. Silver nitrate solution is used to prevent the infection from gonococcal bacteria and antimicrobial drugs to prevent infection from other
microorganisms.

ORAL DISEASES

Tooth Decay

Although much is still to be learned about the specific mechanisms associated with dental caries (tooth decay), we do know that the three factors of the
epidemiologic model must be present: host, agent, and environment. More specifically, dental caries result from the formation of dental plaque on a susceptible
tooth. The dental plaque, which is a sticky transparent film on the surface of the
tooth (or other oral structures), consists of colonies of bacteria and sugar as a
nutrient for the bacteria. As the bacteria grow and reproduce into large numbers,
they produce an acid that attacks the tooth enamel, decalcifying it. This results
in the beginning of a dental carie.

Dental decay always begins on the external surfaces of a tooth. No single
bacteria has been implicated in the etiology of dental caries. Rather, several
bacteria are believed to be responsible including *Lactobacillus acidophilus* and
streptococcal bacteria. Dental decay is hastened when developmental defects are
present in the tooth known as *fissures.* Through a process called prophylactic
odontotomy, these fissures can be removed and the likelihood of caries developing reduced. (See Figure 14–4.)

Figure 14-4:

How Dental Caries Develop

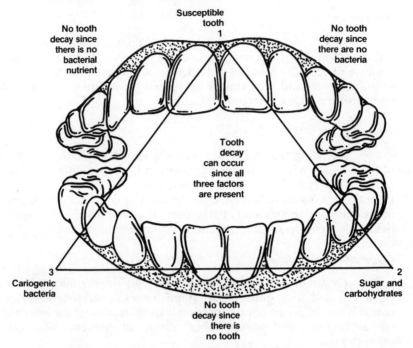

All Three Factors Must Be Present Before Dental Caries Can Develop

In the early 1970s, the National Institute of Dental Research developed an adhesive sealant that can be applied to the surfaces of teeth to fill in the fissues that are very susceptible to decay. The procedure is simple and relatively inexpensive. The sealant is merely brushed onto the teeth surface after they have been thoroughly cleaned and dried. The sealant may act as a protection from a few months to several years. If it should wear off, it can be reapplied. The sealant is also used to repair teeth that have been chipped.[8]

Pulpitis

The most frequent cause of pulpitis is secondary to dental caries. Other causes are thermal, chemical, and trauma to the dental pulp. Pulpitis is characterized by odontalgia (toothache), necrosis of the pulp, and inflammation of the periodontal membrane, and if allowed to progress, the formation of an abscess. Treatment usually involves root canal therapy and possibly removal of the abscess. Frequently, the tooth is needlessly extracted as the simplest alternative.

Periodontal Diseases

Periodontal diseases are characterized by inflammation and degeneration of any of the structures of the periodontium, the tissues supporting the teeth. The most common form is *periodontitis* whose symptoms include inflammation of the

350

periodontal tissues. This generally results from localized irritation from deposits of calculus or tartar. Other possible causes are malocclusion, restorations that were poorly applied, and improperly fitting prosthetics. Any bleeding of the gums at any time, but especially while brushing the teeth is a symptom of periodontitis. *Bleeding of the gums is never normal and should receive competent dental attention.*

Gingivitis is an inflammation of the gingivae (gums) due to infection, malocclusion, accumulation of dental calculus, impaction of food, and faulty fillings. The characteristic symptoms are red gums, lack of pain, and bleeding of the gums with only slight pressure. Treatment, obviously, consists of the elimination of the cause, topical application of certain drugs, and possibly surgery.

Also known as trench mouth or necrotizing ulcerative gingivitis, *Vincent's disease* is an acute or chronic infection of the gingivae. Symptoms include redness, swelling, pain, and ulceration of the gums. Vincent's disease may also involve other tissues of the mouth and throat. It is important to note that this disease is not contagious. Proper oral hygiene is the most effective prevention.

Halitosis

Bad breath or halitosis is never normal. When chronic, it is a symptom of an oral, digestive, or pulmonary disorder. Contrary to claims of producers and advertisers of mouth washes, these products cannot eliminate chronic halitosis. They may merely provide temporary relief of the condition. Halitosis can be eliminated only through identifying the underlying cause and correcting it. For example, one of the manifestations of trench mouth is foul breath. The trench mouth must be cured to eliminate the bad breath.

GLOSSARY

Antigen: A protein substance that stimulates the body's immune system.

Asymptomatic: Without symptoms.

Epidemiologic model: Consists of a susceptible host, agent, and suitable environment.

Fomite: A contaminated object.

Immunization: Naturally or artificially induced resistance to disease.

Incidence: The number of new cases of a disease during a given period of time.

Natural history: The stages that a disease passes through.

Prevalence: The number of cases of a disease in existence at a given time and in a particular area.

Primary prevention: Maintenance of health.

Risk Factors: Conditions that increase the probability for contracting a disease.

Secondary prevention: Measures taken after a disease exists to prevent further complication or new cases from occurring.

Tertiary prevention: Controlling the progress of a disease and rehabilitating the person.

Vector: An organism which carries the disease agent.

SUMMARY

Prevention of disease consists of the actions we take to maintain personal health.

The epidemiologic model reflects the multiplicity of the influencing factors associated with the causation of disease. These factors are the host, agent, and environment. The model emphasizes the interdependent and interactional nature of these factors. The disease process consists of four stages called susceptibility, presymptomatic, clinical, and disability.

Some risk factors associated with some diseases can be controlled by the individual, others cannot. Risk factors include genetic predisposition, past experiences and living patterns, sex, age, personality type, ethnic origin, and socioeconomic status.

Infectious diseases may be transmitted from one person to another through direct contact with the infected person or indirect contact. Not all infectious diseases are communicable, however, but all communicable diseases are infectious. Disease prevention, whether infectious or noninfectious, is dependent largely upon the responsible behavior of each person.

A key force in the prevention and control of disease is the science of epidemiology. It is concerned with the frequency and distribution of diseases in populations of people.

Immunization renders a person (or population) resistant to the communicable disease.

The time it takes for an infectious agent from the time of entry into the new host to multiply in sufficient numbers to produce symptoms of disease is called the incubation period. The appearance of symptoms is called the prodromal period. Once the characteristic symptoms of the disease are noticeable, it is said to be clinical. When symptoms begin to disappear, the stage of decline is reached, followed by the convalescent stage. When the person has regained his/her former health status, the period of recovery has been achieved.

Sexually transmitted diseases are also known as the venereal diseases. The common venereal diseases include gonorrhea, syphilis, and herpes. Other sexually transmitted diseases are candidiasis, trichomoniasis, and pediculosis.

Hearing loss may be the result of faulty heredity, congenital disturbances, infection, or trauma. Visual impairment can also result from a variety of diseases.

There are a variety of diseases that can destroy the health of the oral and dental structures. These include dental caries, pulpitis, periodontal diseases, gingivitis, and trench mouth. In most instances, these conditions can be prevented or successfully treated.

PROBLEMS FOR DISCUSSION

1. Distinguish between the three basic phases of disease prevention.
2. Why is preventive medicine becoming more recognized than it was 20 years ago?
3. What is the epidemiologic model of disease? How are its components interrelated?
4. What are the stages of the disease process?
5. Why is a knowledge of the natural history of a disease important for its prevention and control?
6. How are infectious diseases transmitted?
7. What can each person do to prevent or control infectious diseases? Noninfectious diseases?
8. What are the epidemiologic procedures? How do they contribute to the prevention and control of disease?

9. Why are the methods for the control of disease limited? What are these methods? How effective is each?

10. Compare natural and artificial immunities.

11. List the characteristics of communicable diseases.

12. Describe the usual course that a communicable disease takes listing its various stages.

13. What are the major sexually transmitted diseases? What do they all have in common? How can they be prevented?

14. What are the three stages of syphilis? What is unique about the latent stage?

15. Describe the difference between conductive deafness and perceptual deafness.

16. Describe the causes of three types of oral and dental diseases. How can they be prevented?

REFERENCES

1. WILNER, DANIEL M., ROSABELLE PRICE WALKER, and LENOR S. GOERKE, *Introduction to Public Health,* 6th ed. MacMillan Publishing Co., Inc., New York, 1973, p. 287.

2. MAUSNER, JUDITH S. and ANITA K. BAHN, *Epidemiology: An Introductory Text,* W. B. Saunders Company, Philadelphia, 1974, pp. 6–9.

3. "An Act to Amend the Public Health Law and the Education Law, in Relation to the Immunization of Children," Chapter 443 of the Laws of 1979, State of New York.

4. WILNER, et al., *op. cit.,* pp. 292–299.

5. BENENSON, ABRAM S., editor, *Control of Communicable Diseases In Man.* The American Public Health Association, Washington, 12th ed., 1975, p. 186.

6. U.S. Department of Health, Education, and Welfare, *Health News,* August 25, 1977, p. 2.

7. National Center for Health Statistics, *Facts of Life and Death,* DHEW Number (PHS) 79–1222, 1979.

8. *Seal Out Dental Decay,* U.S. Department of Health, Education, and Welfare; Public Health Service; National Institutes of Health; National Institute of Dental Research, DHEW Publication No. (NIH), 76–1140.

15

preventing noncommunicable diseases

CHARACTERISTICS OF CHRONIC
AND DEGENERATIVE DISEASES

Introduction

A *chronic* disease is one that persists over a long period of time and generally progresses and worsens unless measures are taken to halt or reduce its progress. A *degenerative* disease is one that is characterized by a progressive deterioration of a tissue or tissues resulting in a reduced function-ability.

Many authorities do not attempt to distinguish between chronic and degenerative diseases since most chronic diseases are progressive and most degenerative diseases are chronic. Generally, degenerative and chronic diseases are more common in the elderly, but many of these diseases do occur in the young.

Cause

For many of the degenerative diseases the cause or causes are unclear; for others, personal life styles may be contributing factors, while for still others there may be a genetic cause or predisposition. Some diseases result from aging (senescence) and others may be the result of a variety of factors—genetic, environmental, and personal life styles.

Probably as a result of the prevention and control of infectious diseases and the increased life span of people, the incidence and types of chronic and degenerative diseases have become more prevalent. For example, in 1900 there were 3.1 million people in the United States 65 years of age and over. By 1940, there were 9.0 million; by 1965, 18.5 million; by 1975, 22.4 million, and it is estimated that by the year 2000, there will be 31.8 million, increasing to 55.0 million by 2030. Obviously, with greater numbers of people reaching 65 years of age and older will also come an increase in the numbers of chronic diseases associated with old age.[1]

Prevention and Control

Many of the chronic diseases have an onset that is insidious and progressive so that by the time clinical symptoms appear, the disease has already advanced to a stage that is difficult to reverse or control. In many instances there are no effective control measures.

Since there are a number of factors that precipitate chronic diseases, prevention lies in improving the conditions that can function as causative (etiologic) factors. As we acquire greater insight into the genetic predisposing factors, we may be able to control the genotypes of future generations. That leaves us with determining the environmental and personal factors that act synergistically with certain hereditary predispositions in causing disease.

Efforts, therefore, must be made to improve the environment accordingly and to improve the way we live. We know, for example, that people who work in certain industries (environment), such as asbestos workers, are exposed to etiologic factors related to the cause of lung cancer. If these same people also smoke cigarettes (personal), their likelihood of developing lung cancer increases significantly. The prevention of lung cancer in this illustration rests with improving working conditions to reduce exposure to asbestos (environmental), and teaching these people not to smoke cigarettes (a change in lifestyle).

We need to examine those chronic and degenerative diseases that impair full functioning ability of the greatest numbers of people. These are heart conditions, arthritis and rheumatism, impairment of the back or spine, impairments of the lower extremities and hips, visual impairments, hypertension, mental and nervous conditions, diabetes, allergies, renal (kidney) disorders, and chronic repiratory conditions. Table 15–1 provides the number of cases of disability from selected causes that are present in the United States in any year. In the United States, there are approximately 30 million people whose functioning ability is impaired as a result of some form of chronic condition.

Senility

Physical or mental symptoms resulting from senescence is called *senility*. Physically, the person may manifest symptoms of feebleness or weakness. When such symptoms as loss of memory, judgment, confusion, and irrational behavior are manifested, mental senility is present. When these symptoms are severe to the point of mental incapacitation, the person possesses senile psychosis.

Mental and personality changes are usually gradual and may vary markedly from individual to individual. These variations appear to be associated with a presenescent personality among other factors. Although senility cannot be reversed, the senile person can be helped through empathy, understanding, patience, and group activities.

Table 15–1: Number of Persons With Impairment as a Result of Selected Chronic Conditions*

Chronic Conditions Causing Impairment or Limitations of Functioning	Number of Persons[1]
Heart conditions	4,753,000
Arthritis and rheumatism	4,396,000
Impairment of the back or spine	2,051,000
Hypertension	1,976,000
Impairment of the lower extremities or hip	1,889,000
Visual impairment	1,724,000
Allergies	1,644,000
Mental and nervous conditions	1,504,000
Chronic respiratory conditions	793,000
Renal disorders	358,000
Diabetes	262,000
Total Number of Persons Impaired	21,350,000

*Source of Data: United States Department of Health, Education, and Welfare, National Center for Health Statistics, 1978.

[1] Figures are rounded to the nearest thousand.

CARDIOVASCULAR DISEASES

Diseases of the Blood

Normal blood   Human blood consists of (1) red blood cells, *erythrocytes;* (2) white blood cells, *leukocytes;* (3) plasma; and (4) platelets. The principal consitutent of *red blood cells* is hemoglobin, which carries oxygen to the cells. *White blood cells,* are important in protecting the body from invasion of foreign substances such as bacteria. *Plasma* is the liquid portion of the blood and consists of more than a hundred constituents including proteins, inorganic salts, gases, waste products, enzymes, and hormones. *Platelets* are essential for normal blood coagulation.

Anemias   The *anemias* may result from loss or destruction of blood, or malfunctioning of the blood formation tissues. *Loss of blood* may be acute or chronic. Blood can be *destroyed* from toxins or other foreign substances or from hereditary factors. Anemias resulting from faulty blood formation include iron deficiency anemia and inhibition or failure of the bone marrow to produce blood cells.

Erythroblastosis fetalis   This blood condition is associated with the Rh factor in the blood. (The Rh factor is a term for a type of antigen present in a person's blood. A person's blood may be Rh negative or Rh positive.) It is estimated that approximately 87 percent of the white population in the United States is Rh positive, while the remaining 13 percent is Rh negative. An Rh negative woman who becomes pregnant may become immunized to the Rh factor by the passage of Rh positive cells from the fetus into mother's blood stream. On subsequent pregnancies, the Rh antibodies pass through the placental wall into the fetal circulation, and if the fetus is Rh positive, a hemolytic action* on the fetal blood cells takes place.

Erythroblastosis fetalis is characterized by an enlarged liver and spleen which results in stillbirth or death of the infant shortly after birth. If the infant is born alive, blood transfusion is necessary to eliminate the high levels of bilirubin present in the circulation. *Bilirubin* is a reddish bile pigment, a product of degenerated hemoglobin, and must be eliminated from the body.

Diseases of the Blood Vessels

Aneurysm   An aneurysm is a localized, dilated blood vessel more commonly found in arteries. There are two forms that aneurysms may take: (1) *fusiform,* which is a bulging of the blood vessel due to a weakened wall; or (2) *sacculated,* which is the formation of a sac on the side of the blood vessel. These are illustrated in Figure 15–1.

*Hemolysis is the liberation of the hemoglobin from the red blood cells.

Figure 15-1

Aneurysms

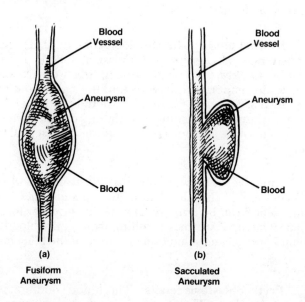

| (a) | (b) |
| Fusiform Aneurysm | Sacculated Aneurysm |

Aneurysms result from weakening of the blood vessel wall. Predisposing factors may be syphilis, arteriosclerosis, hypertension, infection, trauma, or congential. Treatment is dependent upon the etiology. In the case of syphilis, the disease must be treated first. Arterial grafting and bypass surgery are also successful in some cases.

Varicose veins   Abnormal lengthening of veins, dysfunction of the valves, and dilation are some of the characteristic symptoms of varicose veins. Varicose veins can have various degrees of debilitation depending upon the extent of varicosity, location, and whether or not ulceration is present. Varicose veins, generally, occur spontaneously with a hereditary factor being primarily responsible.

Treatment for varicose veins may include bed rest, support stockings (since varicose veins usually occur in the legs), and sometimes surgery. If surgery is used, portions of the dilated veins are removed and new circulatory pathways are formed.

Buerger's disease   The cause of Buerger's disease is unknown but is more frequent in smokers than nonsmokers and in males than females. Once the disease has been initiated, gangrene develops rather rapidly. The symptoms include coldness, numbness, and tingling in the feet. Phlebitis is common. Treatment consists of complete bed rest, control of room temperature, and medication to improve blood flow and reduce pain. Amputation may be necessary.

All forms of heart disease basically involve some malfunction or impairment in the heart that may affect its ability to pump blood. Heart disease may involve the valves, the inner or outer linings, the heart muscle, the coronary circulation, or a combination of these.

Congenital heart defects are malformations in heart structure that result from improper development of the fetal heart during the early months of gestation. It is estimated that about eight of every 1000 babies born in the United States have some kind of congenital heart problem. These defects vary in the specific part of the heart that they affect and in the degree to which they impair the heart's overall function.

The most common congenital defects involve holes in the muscular septum (wall) separating the right and left portions of the heart, and abnormalities of the valves which keep them from closing or opening as they should. Certain defects are known to be caused by influences on the fetus during pregnancy, such as German measles (rubella), exposure to too much radiation, or insufficient oxygen supplies to the fetus. A few defects may be inherited, although the role of inheritance in most congenital defects is unclear.

Prior to World War II, approximately one-third of all children with congenital heart problems failed to live past the age of 10 years. However, recent improvements in methods of diagnosis and treatment have greatly reduced the death rate from congenital disorders. More accurate x-ray and blood pressure measuring techniques make it far easier to identify the precise nature of congenital defects. Once identified, many congenital malformations can be corrected by open heart surgery.

One of the most significant advances in the treatment of such defects was the development of the heart-lung machine. The two veins that normally supply blood from the systemic circulation are attached directly to the machine. The machine removes carbon dioxide and oxygenates the blood, and pumps it just as the heart would. Blood returns from the machine directly into the aorta and on through the body. The machine thus assumes the functions of the heart and lungs. During this time, the heart is not actually pumping blood and, therefore, can be operated on, resulting in many congenital defects being corrected.

Rheumatic heart disease may result from rheumatic fever caused by a streptococcal infection (usually strep throat). Antibodies produced because of the disease can cause inflammation of many tissues in the body, among them, the inner lining of the heart. After the disease has passed, most parts of the body return to normal. However, in about one-half of the children with rheumatic fever, the heart valves are permanently affected, characterized by one or more of the heart's valves not opening or closing as they should. Rheumatic heart disease can also affect the conducting fibers in the heart that transmit impulses that make the heart beat.

Rheumatic heart disease can be largely prevented by identifying strep infections early and providing the appropriate antibiotic treatment. Largely through these measures, the numbers of deaths from rheumatic heart disease have significantly decreased in the U.S. since the 1940s.

Coronary heart disease (CHD) is a condition in which there is a deficient blood supply to the heart muscle. Specifically, the flow of blood to the heart muscle is reduced by a narrowing of one or more of the coronary arteries or their main branches. This narrowing is caused by *atherosclerosis,* a process that occurs gradually. Some evidence suggests that this process begins in childhood.[2] The narrowing of the artery is caused by the gradual formation of atherosclerotic *plaque.* This plaque consists of an accumulation of cholesterol and other fatty substances in the inner lining of the artery. As the plaque increases, the space in the artery becomes progressively narrowed, thereby obstructing the flow of blood. This reduced ability to carry adequate amounts of blood is called *ischemia.*

Some scientists believe that atherosclerosis begins when the cells of the inner lining of the artery become slightly separated from each other. The space between the cells allows substances in the blood, normally unable to enter the arterial wall, to penetrate the inner lining.*

The formation of atherosclerosis also requires that blood contain a relatively high amount of cholesterol. Given both preconditions, cholesterol and fats enter into the inner arterial lining. More or less simultaneously, some of the muscle cells from the middle layer begin to grow into the inner lining. These cells stop acting as normal muscle cells and begin to accumulate the cholesterol and fats. As this process occurs, the lining becomes thickened by the plaque, bulging into the space of the artery. The plaque may continue to accumulate, blocking off (occluding) more and more of the artery.

In the early stages of atherosclerosis, the plaque is soft and fatty. However, as the atherosclerosis becomes more advanced, the plaque becomes hard. The cholesterol turns into crystals very similar to crystals of table salt. Some of the plaque may pick up calcium from the blood and become as hard as bone. In its severe stages, the hardened plaque may reduce the size of the artery to 20 or 30 percent of what it was originally. The inner surface of the plaque also becomes rough, increasing the likelihood of clot formation.

Once atherosclerosis has progressed to the point of extensive narrowing of one or more coronary artery branches, the disease can affect an individual in several ways. In less severe stages of development, the deficiency in blood supply may cause transient pain, for example, during exercise (angina). In severe cases, a coronary artery may become totally blocked off resulting in the actual death of some of the heart muscle cells—the classic heart attack. In other cases, sudden acute lack of oxygen to the heart muscle can cause a person to die almost instantly.

Angina pectoris   Up to a certain degree of atherosclerotic narrowing, the coronary arteries can still provide enough blood to the cardiac muscle cells, even during heavy exercise. This is called *presymptomatic* atherosclerotic heart disease and is very difficult to detect. The disease is present, but there are no measurable symptoms.

---

*Arteriosclerosis is a general term that includes several conditions in which either the inner or middle layers of an artery undergo progressive, damaging changes resulting in decreased flexibility of the arterial wall. Atherosclerosis is one subset of arteriosclerosis, specifically involving the *inner* arterial lining.

When atherosclerosis progresses to a point where the heart muscle cannot get enough blood to meet its needs, however, symptoms appear. *Angina pectoris* refers to transient pain that occurs when the heart cells do not receive as much oxygen as they require.* This pain may result from exercise, anger, tension, or excitement. The lack of oxygen to the heart muscle cells produces pain, usually in the chest, but often radiating to the shoulders or arms.

Treatment of angina most commonly involves taking action to relieve the pain. These measures involve exercise programs, the use of nitroglycerine tablets, and attempts to help the person avoid situations that bring on the pain. None of these measures has been shown to have any affect on the atherosclerosis underlying the problem.

In recent years, coronary bypass surgery has been developed to treat severe cases of angina. This operation basically consists of hooking up a piece of vein from the patient's body into the coronary artery above and below the site of the atherosclerosis. This allows the blood to bypass the occlusion, frequently relieves the insufficient blood flow, and relieves the pain of angina. However, there is currently much dispute among medical scientists as to the value of the operation and many questions about its efficacy remain to be answered.

There are two kinds of angina: stable and unstable. *Stable angina* exists in persons when the pain comes only once in a while and as a result of a significant increase in the work of the heart. *Unstable angina* occurs when the occlusion of the vessel is more pronounced, and the pain is more severe and frequent. Patients with unstable angina are generally more likely to experience a subsequent myocardial infarction (heart attack).

Myocardial infarction is the death of cardiac muscles due to a severe lack of oxygen to the cells. An infarct is caused when a coronary artery or one of its branches becomes completely blocked off, thus eliminating blood flow to a specific area of the heart muscle.

There are several ways in which a coronary artery may become blocked. A common cause is the formation of a blood clot on the rough inner surface of the atherosclerotic plaque. Such clot formation is called *coronary thrombosis.* In other cases, part of the plaque may break off and be carried by the blood where it blocks a smaller artery; and in other cases, the plaque may simply "grow" to the point of obstructing the artery. A sudden occlusion of a coronary artery does not require a precipitating factor such as exercise or emotional tension. Heart attacks may occur at any time, and many occur while the person is asleep.

Between one-fourth and one-half of all persons with acute coronary attacks die within 24 hours after the appearance of symptoms. This situation is called *sudden death.* In cases other than sudden death, the heart continues to beat; however, the particular area of the heart muscle deprived of blood from the blocked artery becomes seriously damaged from the lack of oxygen. During the weeks following the attack, the dead cells are replaced by scar tissue.

The effect of a heart attack on the heart's pumping ability depends on the size and location of the damaged area. As a general rule, the smaller the occluded

*Chest pain, or angina pectoris, may also be functional with no signs of atherosclerosis. A functional angina pectoris is sometimes referred to as cardiac neurosis that results from prolonged anxiety or stress. It is not serious, but the pain is real.

artery, the smaller the area affected by the attack. Many heart attacks involve such small areas of muscle that the pumping ability of the heart is not seriously affected.

When the damaged area is moderately extensive, however, the pumping ability of the heart can be seriously affected. In such a situation, blood and fluid may begin to accumulate in different parts of the body, such as the lungs, liver, kidneys, and legs. This general syndrome is referred to as *congestive heart failure*. It is often treated with drugs (diuretics) to eliminate excess fluid or to increase the strength of the heart's contractions through the use, for example, of digitalis.

When the damage to the heart muscle is very extensive, an even greater failure in its ability to pump blood can occur. Extreme pumping failure leads to *cardiogenic shock.* This is usually caused by the death of at least 50 percent of the muscles in a ventricle. In these situations, the amount of blood pumped in each heart beat may be decreased by as much as two-thirds, resulting in the entire body being deprived of the quantity of blood it needs. The death rate from cardiogenic shock is very high and is one of the major causes of death among hospitalized myocardial infarction patients.

A second group of complications accompanying myocardial infarctions are called *arrhythmias.* In arrhythmias, the damage to the heart muscle somehow causes the transmission of electrical impulses through the heart to go haywire. Instead of producing normal contractions, the impulses occur irregularly so that the heart no longer beats as it should. In some cases, the electrical impulses may cease.

Some arrhythmias do not seriously affect the heart's pumping ability; however, there are several types of arrhythmias that are often fatal. The most important of these is *ventricular fibrillation,* in which the walls of the ventricle simply quiver rather than beating rhythmically. This causes an interruption of the flow of blood resulting in a lack of oxygen to the brain cells and, finally, in death within minutes.

Ventricular fibrillation and other serious arrhythmias can often be corrected by applying electrical shock with a *defibrillator.* This treatment basically overloads the heart with electricity, upsetting the abnormal impulse, and allowing normal impulses to begin once again. Cardiopulmonary resuscitation (CPR) can also be applied to artifically maintain circulation until necessary shock treatments can be provided. CPR, however, is very inefficient unless the person is hospitalized within a very few minutes.

It is estimated that about 50 percent of all persons with a first myocardial infarction die within a year after the attack. The actual cause of death varies, but in most cases, it is either cardiogenic shock or an arrhythmia. Furthermore, persons who have already had one or more myocardial infarctions have a significantly higher likelihood of dying from a subsequent attack than those experiencing their first.

Stroke

Stroke is the third leading cause of death for people of all ages in the United States accounting for about 200,000 deaths each year. Stroke results from a variety of conditions in which a lack of blood supply to a portion of the brain results in the death of brain cells. This often results in speech impairment, loss of memory and other mental disorientation, and impairment of motor functioning. If the damage is extremely extensive, death may be the result.

A clot in a cerebral artery is called a *cerebral thrombosis.* When this occurs, the brain cells normally dependent upon the blood supply from the artery die as a result of lack of oxygen. A stroke can also be caused by a blood clot that breaks loose in another part of the body and travels to the brain where it blocks a smaller artery. This is called *cerebral embolism.* In addition, if a diseased artery becomes weakened, it may burst, depriving the brain cells of sufficient oxygen. If blood comes in direct contact with brain cells, it will cause serious damage as well, because of the wastes present in the blood. This condition is known as a *cerebral hemorrhage.* All of these conditions can be precipitated by hypertension (high blood pressure), which speeds up the accumulation of atherosclerotic plaque and has a wearing effect upon the arterial walls.

Strokes are basically treated with physical and speech therapy, depending upon the parts of the body affected. Because nerve tissue cannot be regenerated, the severity of a stroke depends upon the extent of initial brain damage, the ability of other parts of the brain to compensate for the damaged area, and the ability of the circulatory system to compensate for the blood flow normally supplied by the damaged artery. Therefore, there may be some spontaneous recovery from a stroke over time. However, once a person has had one stroke, the likelihood of subsequent strokes is greatly increased.

Prevention of Cardiovascular Diseases

Many cardiovascular diseases, particularly coronary heart disease, are largely preventable. Such risk factors as smoking, saturated fat and cholesterol intake, obesity, hypertension, and lack of physical activity, have all been shown to be significant contributors to cardiovascular disease and can be significantly controlled by appropriate health behavior. The relationship of these factors to heart disease was graphically shown in the Framingham Study, which concluded that the more risk factors people were exposed to, the greater the likelihood that they would develop coronary heart disease.[3] It is hypothesized that the fewer the risk factors we are exposed to, the chances of developing cardiovascular disease become greatly reduced.

Cholesterol and Saturated Fats

There is substantial evidence linking excessive dietary intake of saturated fat and cholesterol to the development of atherosclerotic plaque. Cholesterol and saturated fats are found in greatest quantities in red meats and dairy products. Shellfish are also particularly high in cholesterol. It should be noted that while some vegetables contain saturated fats, no vegetable contains cholesterol.

Cholesterol is a fatty substance that is naturally present in the body. For example, it is an element in the construction of cell membranes. However, when we consume more cholesterol than the body needs, it becomes a major contributor to atherosclerosis. The cholesterol that accumulates in the atherosclerotic plaque appears to be primarily derived from circulating *lipoproteins.* Moreover, plaque contains 50 percent lipid by weight, and more than half of this lipid is cholesterol.

Lipoproteins are molecular structures comprised of proteins and cholesterol (a lipid). Two major lipoproteins have been identified: (1) high density lipoproteins (HDL), and (2) low density lipoproteins (LDL). Various studies indicate that it is LDL that has a tendency to accumulate in the inner lining of the artery, while HDL has a tendency to move away from the artery's inner lining. In addition, other saturated fats in the blood tend to be attracted to low density lipoproteins.

Levels of cholesterol and saturated fats in the blood seem to be related to diet and to genetic factors. People with excessive levels of serum cholesterol are said to have *hypercholesterolemia. Hyperlipidemia* is a general term referring to excessive levels of saturated fats in the blood.

As a general rule, we should limit our dietary intake of cholesterol and saturated fats. This can be more easily done through a reduction in the consumption of red meats, substituting fish (but not shellfish) and poultry, and limiting our intake of dairy products. For example, skim milk and low fat yogurt and low fat cottage cheese is to be preferred to whole milk, yogurt, and cottage cheese; (however, this is disputed by the dairy industry). Many of our dietary needs normally obtained from meat can also be obtained in vegetables. It is estimated that there would be a 25 percent reduction in coronary heart disease if the American people would make appropriate modifications in their diet.[4]

Hypertension

Blood pressure simply refers to the pressure the moving blood exerts on the arterial walls. When the ventricles contract, blood pressure in the arteries will rise slightly as a surge of blood rushes through them. This is the *systolic* blood pressure corresponding to the higher of the two numbers obtained during a blood pressure reading.

Between heart beats, the blood pressure is lower but does not disappear, partly because of the action of the arterial walls. Therefore, there is a relatively constant blood pressure between heart beats. This is measured as the lower of the two numbers obtained in a blood pressure reading and is called the *diastolic* pressure. Blood pressure is measured by a sphygmomanometer.

It has been estimated by the National High Blood Pressure Education Program that there are approximately 35 million Americans with high blood pressure, and that 40 percent of these are unaware of their condition. Of those who are aware of their condition, about one-third are receiving appropriate medical treatment, one-third are receiving inadequate medical treatment, and the remaining third are receiving no therapy despite the knowledge of their condition.

The evidence linking hypertension to coronary heart disease and other cardiovascular diseases is substantial.[5] For instance, the Framingham Study estimated a 1.5-fold increase in risk from coronary heart disease with a systolic blood pressure of 150 mmHg* or more, and more than a threefold increase in risk with

*Millimeters of mercury, the unit in which blood pressure is measured.

a systolic pressure of 180 mmHg. Other studies corroborate these findings. Hypertension is also a major cause of strokes and kidney failure.

Although the average blood pressure is usually considered to be 120/80 mmHg, it is influenced by a considerable number of variables, among them hereditary factors, race, emotional status, diet, and age. As a general rule, however, the lower the blood pressure the better as long as it does not threaten consciousness. A normal reading should not necessarily be considered ideal. For example, a reading of 110/75 mmHg should be considered healthier than a reading of 120/80 mmHg.

Hypertension is much more prevalent among blacks than among whites —more than twice as prevalent. Although socioeconomic conditions and educational levels modify the prevalence of hypertension, the discrepancy between the races persists.

There are two types of hypertension: essential and secondary. In most cases, *essential hypertension* can often be cured. This type of hypertension usually results from abnormal functioning of a particular part of the body; e.g. the kidneys. Once an abnormality is located and treated, the hypertension may be eliminated.

It is estimated that hypertension is the primary cause of more than 20,000 deaths in the United States each year in addition to contributing to thousands of deaths from heart attacks and strokes.[6] As with coronary heart disease, these deaths are largely preventable.

Quite often, hypertension can be adequately treated through weight reduction, dietary modification, and/or a reduction in salt intake. Many authorities advocate a substantial reduction in salt intake for the entire population as a major means of preventing hypertension. It is very difficult, however, to totally control the amount of salt ingested since many foods have salt added to them in their preparation. Mere reduction or elimination of table salt may not be enough.

If these measures are not adequate, chemotherapy is usually indicated, beginning with diuretics and progressing to other antihypertensive drugs. In general, all adults with a diastolic pressure of 120 mmHg or above should receive medical care immediately. All persons with a blood pressure of 160/95 or above should have their blood pressure confirmed within one month of the initial reading. All persons under 50 years of age with a blood pressure reading between 140/90 mmHg and 160/95 mmHg should be checked every six to nine months; and all adults with a diastolic pressure below 90 mmHg should be checked annually.[7]

Smoking and Cardiovascular Disease

In 1964, the initial report of the Surgeon General[8] indicated a distinct relationship between smoking and cardiovascular disease. This relationship has been strengthened in the intervening years. It is now possible to state that cigarette smoking is significantly related to coronary heart disease, augmenting the risk of heart attack by two- or three-fold.[9-10] It has been estimated that the abolition of heavy cigarette smoking would result in an approximately 30 percent reduction in coronary disease risk.[11]

The belief that smoking causes hypertension is a fallacy. In fact, there is some evidence that smokers have a slightly lower average blood pressure than nonsmokers. However, smoking has been shown to cause at least a temporary elevation in blood pressure during and immediately following the smoking experience.[12]

Although cigarette smoking is a significant risk factor of coronary heart disease, there is no evidence that smoking is related to the genesis of atherosclerosis. Smoking in combination with the presence of atherosclerotic plaque, however, provides a significant increased risk to the smoker.

CANCER AS A GROUP OF DISEASES*

Introduction

A paradox exists in regards to cancer. So much is known about it that volumes have been written, and yet so little is known that it remains our second leading cause of death, killing more than 420,000 people each year. Over 800,000 new cases of cancer are diagnosed annually and this does not include an additional 400,000 cases of nonmelanoma skin cancer and 45,000 carcinoma *in situ*** of the cervix, bringing the total to about 1.3 million new cases annually in the United States. However, of the more than 420,000 people who die each year from cancers, at least 134,000 do not have to. That is, we possess the skill and technology to prevent these deaths. However, people must be aware of *the absolute necessity for early diagnosis and adequate treatment.* Furthermore, many cancers are completely preventable; they do not even have to develop at all. For example, at least 80 percent of the lung cancers diagnosed each year could be prevented if people simply did not smoke cigarettes. Approximately 80–85 percent of the deaths from breast cancer are curable when detected and treated while they are still localized.

Characteristics of Cancers

When a cell reproduces in an unrestrained manner and more rapidly than is necessary to replace worn out cells (and to the extent that the cells accumulate into a new growth of tissue), a *neoplasm* or tumor is the result. A tumor is a mass of new tissue that persists and grows independently of its surrounding structures and that has no physiologic use to the body.[13] In contrast, normal cells have specific structures, rates of growth, and controlled division which enable them to contribute to a specific function for the tissues they compose. Cancer cells, on the other hand, do not follow an orderly sequence of division, but reproduce and spread out of control, interfering with the function of other cells and tissues rather than contributing to them. (See Figure 15–2.)

Neoplasms or tumors may be benign or malignant. A *benign* tumor is a neoplasm with similar characteristics to a cancer, but that reproduces much

---

*We are grateful to the American Cancer Society for granting permission to draw freely from its many publications about cancers.

**Cancers that are still in their site of origin are said to be *in situ.*

Figure 15-2:

Cancer—A Disease of the Cell

Normal

Cancer

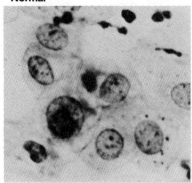 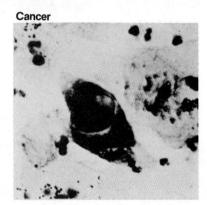

Normal cells appear to be uniform and are orderly in growth while cancer cells have enlarged nuclei, are disorganized, and vary greatly in size and shape.

U.S. Department of Health, Education, and Welfare Public Health Service National Cancer Institute

slower. Benign tumors seldom result in serious health problems unless they are located in tissues or organs whose function is interfered with because of their presence. A benign tumor is usually easily removed without further complications. A *malignant* tumor or cancer grows rapidly, crowding out normal tissues, and unless removed or destroyed will spread by metastasis to other areas of the body and eventually result in the death of the person. *Metastasis* is a spreading of cancer cells to other parts of the body by the blood or lymphatic systems.

Prevalence of Cancers

According to the American Cancer Society, approximately 105,000 people in the United States can expect to die from some form of cancer each year. This means that for all causes of death, one in five is the result of cancer. There has been a steady increase in cancer deaths due partly to the increase in the life span, changes in the way people live, introduction of environmental pollutants, and other factors. For example, in 1973, there were about 351,000 cancer deaths; in 1976, 377,000; and in 1980, 420,000.

There are over 3 million Americans who have a history of cancer. Each year, an additional 805,000 new cases will be diagnosed and approximately one-third of these new cases (268,000) will be cured. At least 25 percent more could be cured if their cancers were diagnosed and treated earlier. Table 15–2 summarizes the incidence of cancer according to site, sex, and deaths from each.

Table 15-2: Incidence and Deaths From Cancers by Site and Sex

Site	INCIDENCE		DEATHS	
	Male	Female	Male	Female
Skin	2%	2%	2%	1%
Oral	5%	2%	3%	1%
Breast	NA*	27%	NA*	19%
Lung	22%	8%	34%	15%
Colon and rectum	14%	15%	12%	15%
Pancreas	3%	3%	5%	5%
Prostate	17%	NA*	10%	NA*
Ovary	NA*	4%	NA*	6%
Uterus	NA*	13%	NA*	5%
Urinary	9%	4%	5%	3%
Leukemias and lymphomas	8%	7%	9%	9%
All others	20%	15%	20%	21%

Source of Data: *Cancer Facts and Figures:* 1981, American Cancer Society, 1980.

*Not applicable

Classification of Cancers

Cancers are classified according to the characteristics of the healthy cells that make up the tissue from which the cancer cells develop. There are three classifications of cancers:

1. *Sarcomas* arise from connective tissues, which are the muscles, bones, tendons, and ligaments.
2. *Leukemias and lymphomas* arise from the vascular forming organs—the blood and lymph.
3. *Carcinomas* arise from the epithelial cells that cover the external and internal surfaces of the body—the skin and membranes.

Cancers are also classified according to the specific location of the cancer. For example, if the site of the cancer is the lung, it is called lung cancer; if on the breast, breast cancer, and so on.

Cigarette Smoking

Besides the *causal* relationship between cigarette smoke and lung cancer, epidemiologic studies have also shown an association with cancers of the urinary bladder, larynx, esophagus, lips, mouth, pancreas, and kidneys. The incidence, as well as the number of deaths from lung cancer has shown a steady rise for both men and women over the past 50 years. (See Table 15-3.)

Although cigarette smoking is the chief factor associated with lung cancer and a number of others, more and more evidence is pointing to an association between pipe and cigar smoking. For example, pipe smoking has been *causally* connected with cancers of the lips and *associated* with other parts of the oral structures such as the esophagus, larynx, and pharynx. Evidence is continuously

Table 15–3: Number of Deaths from Lung Cancer Over a 50-Year Period

Year	Number of Deaths
1930	3,000
1940	9,000
1950	18,000
1960	36,000
1970	60,000
1980	101,000
1981	105,000

being compiled to indicate that tobacco smoke is one of the most lethal substances consumed by people in relation to cancers.

Environmental Pollutants

On a worldwide basis, approximately 85 percent of cancers are caused by exposure to environmental factors according to the World Health Organization.[14] Hundreds, perhaps as many as 1500, substances have been shown to be carcinogens or cocarcinogens. A *carcinogen* is an agent that causes cancer. A *cocarcinogen* is an agent that promotes cancer development but is not in itself a cause. These cancer causing substances may be present in the food we eat, the water we drink, the air we breathe, the clothes we wear, or the drugs we take. Let's look at a few important examples: vinyl chloride, asbestos, and diethylstilbestrol (DES), and radiation.

Vinyl Chloride In 1974, it was recognized that vinyl chloride, an ingredient in the manufacture of plastics, causes cancer of the liver. It has also been used as a propellant and solvent in some aerosol sprays. The numbers of people exposed to vinyl chloride is unknown but probably is in the hundreds of thousands.[15]

The rare liver cancer, angiosarcoma, is more prevalent in those who have worked in the vinyl chloride industry for more than 15 years (or had their first exposure to it at least 15 years ago.) The relationship of this occupational hazard to the cause of liver cancer was first discovered by a physician in the B.F. Goodrich Company who observed three cases of it among the workers. This was followed by an intensive study of those workers by the National Institute for Occupational Safety and Health (NIOSH) which established the relationship between vinyl chloride and liver cancer.

Asbestos The relationship between asbestos fibers and asbestosis and lung cancer has been known for nearly 50 years. In 1960, it was recognized that asbestos was the cause of mesothelioma, a very rare but always fatal cancer of the membranes surrounding the lungs and abdominal cavity.

Those who work in the asbestos industries and who also smoke cigarettes have a much greater risk of developing lung cancer than those who do not smoke. It is estimated that this increased risk is 90 times greater than for the average nonsmoker. Of the more than 1 million present and past asbestos workers, it is thought that approximately 400,000 will die from lung cancer, gastrointestinal cancer, or mesothelioma. Families of asbestos workers are also at greater risk since asbestos fibers are brought home on the clothes of the worker, exposing others in the family to this carcinogen.

Diethylstilbestrol (DES)   For more than 30 years, diethylstilbestrol was widely prescribed to women to prevent miscarriages. Many women who took this drug were able to carry the fetus to full term and gave birth to healthy babies. However, in 1971, medical scientists noticed that certain medical problems of children born from mothers who took DES were more prevalent than for those whose mothers did not take DES.

In daughters from mothers who took DES, there is a greater likelihood of developing vaginal adenosis (this is not cancerous) or a rare type of vaginal cancer, clear cell adenocarcinoma. These daughters should have a medical examination to determine whether any DES abnormalities exist. In sons of mothers who took DES, there is a greater likelihood of such genital abnormalities as undescended testicles, underdevelopment of the testicles, benign cysts, and low sperm count or abnormally shaped sperm.[16]

Radiation   There are two forms of radiation that can cause cancers if exposure is intense enough, or if at lower intensity, over a long enough period of time. These are the ultraviolet rays from the sun and radioactivity. The chief cause of skin cancer is overexposure to the sun's rays. Light skinned persons and those whose occupations require daily exposure to the sun are most susceptible to developing skin cancer.

Persons who are most likely to be exposed to excessive amounts of radioactivity are miners, persons who work with radioactive materials such as medical and paramedical personnel, and persons who work in nuclear power plants. Medical use of radiation includes radiotherapy and diagnostic x-rays. In recent years, there has developed considerable public concern about the safety associated with nuclear electrical energy. Several potentially dangerous "accidents" have occurred that have exposed large numbers of people to low doses of radioactivity. What the outcome of these, and probably others in the future, will be cannot be predicted. Unfortunately, we will have to wait, probably many years, before we can ascertain accurately what kinds of health problems are caused by these low doses of radiation on the people exposed and the unborn. There is no question but that certain dosages of radiation exposure cause cancers and malformation of the unborn—the extent is not known, however. In the meantime, it is important that citizen awareness of the potential health hazards from radiation is translated into political controls to reduce radiation exposure.

Viruses

There is some evidence that some viruses may cause cancers in humans. However, much more research is necessary to establish proof. Viruses have been implicated etiologically in a number of human cancers including leukemia, Burkitt's lymphoma, cervical cancer, breast cancer, and sarcomas. These conclusions, however, have been based upon animal experiments and much more research is required before definite conclusions can be drawn.

Common Forms of Cancers

Skin cancer   Skin cancer is the most common, but preventable, of all cancers, striking more than 400,000 Americans each year. Skin cancer is also very curable with only about 6,700 deaths each year. It is most common in geographic areas in which people are excessively exposed to the sun's rays. Skin cancer is easily prevented by avoiding overexposure to the sun's rays and by taking a few simple precautions when exposure is necessary. For example, the use of an effective sunscreen that contains para-aminobenzoic acid (PABA) when outdoor activity, such as swimming, is engaged in. *Ordinary suntan lotions offer no protection.* Overall, the concept that a heavy suntan is healthful is erroneous. Continuously achieving a suntan, although it may for the present improve one's appearance, may in a few years make the skin look old and may result in skin cancer.

However, the most serious type of skin cancer is malignant melanoma. This is not necessarily associated with overexposure to the sun's rays. Each year, approximately 14,000 new cases of malignant melanoma are diagnosed and approximately 5,000 people die from it.

Oral cancers   Nearly all of the approximate 9,000 deaths occurring each year from oral cancer are unnecessary. This is so because cancers in this site are easily detected. Each of us should conduct a self-oral examination periodically and report any abnormalities to our physician. Oral examinations for detecting cancer should also be a component of the annual dental checkup by the dentist or dental hygienist. This is especially important for those in the high risk group.

Each year, more than 26,000 oral cancers are diagnosed with slightly less than one-third being diagnosed too late for effective treatment and cure. According to the American Cancer Society, approximately 60 percent of oral cancers are diagnosed after metastasis has taken place, which represents only about a 25 percent cure rate. A cancer is considered cured if the patient is still alive with no sign of the disease after 5 years following its initial diagnoses. The cure rate for localized oral cancer is 67 percent.

People most susceptible to oral cancers are those with broken teeth or ill-fitting dentures that result in constant irritation in the mouth, and those who are heavy smokers, and drinkers. Prevention of oral cancers obviously lies in correcting these conditions that contribute to their development.

Breast cancer   Although breast cancer is the leading cause of cancer deaths among women in the United States, the bright side is that it is highly curable when detected in its early stage of development. When diagnosed in situ, there is a better than 85 percent cure rate. However, when the cancer has spread involving the lymph nodes, the cure rate may drop to 56 percent depending upon the extent of regional involvement.

According to the National Cancer Institute, there is no known cause of breast cancer. However, a number of risk factors have been identified: daughters or sisters of breast cancer patients are at higher risk than those with no familial history; an unmarried woman and those who have never borne children are at greater risk than other women. The etiology of breast cancer seems to be multifactorial rather than the result of a single factor. Some studies suggest that there may be a genetic predisposition; other studies have implicated viruses (in experimental animals) and possibly a lowering or loss of the woman's immunological mechanisms. There is no evidence that breast cancer is caused by a single blow to the breast.

Breast cancer can be detected early through monthly breast self-examination. Most breast cancers that are detected in their localized stage (about 90 percent) are detected by the woman herself. If each woman would consistently examine her breasts each month, the death rate for breast cancer would drop dramatically, providing the woman seeks competent medical attention when any irregularities are noted. Other diagnostic techniques that can be used, especially with women who are at high risk, are mammography, xeroradiography, and thermography. Generally, mammography or other forms of x-ray diagnosis should not be performed routinely for all women since the radiation could actually contribute to the development of breast cancer.

Surgical removal of the breast, often in conjunction with chemotherapy and radiotherapy, is the treatment of choice. Surgical removal of the breast is called *mastectomy*. When it involves the lymph nodes and underlying muscles it is called *radical mastectomy*. *Modified mastectomy* preserves the muscles of the chest, is less disfiguring, and allows for greater freedom of arm movement.

Lung cancer   Between 80 and 90 percent of all lung cancers occur among smokers. The incidence of lung cancer is three to four times more frequent in men than in women. However, in recent years, more women are smoking than ever before and the incidence among women is following the pattern as it has been for men over the past 50 years. Lung cancer is the leading cause of cancer deaths among men and the third leading cause of cancer deaths among women. The 5-year survival rate for men with diagnosed lung cancer is only about 8 percent while for women it is about 12 percent. Obviously, prevention of lung cancer lies chiefly with the elimination of cigarette smoking.

Colon and rectum cancers   Approximately 120,000 new cases of colon and rectum cancers are diagnosed each year in the United States. It is the most common of the internal cancers, accounting for about 55,000 deaths per year. It is slightly more prevalent in women than men.

The cause or causes of colon and rectum cancers are unknown but there is some evidence that American's high carbohydrate, low fiber diets may be associated with it. However, at present, there is no proof that there is a connection. Such factors as polyps and ulcerative colitis are predisposing factors. However, there is no evidence that hemorrhoids have any relationship to colon or rectal cancers.

When detected early, colon and rectum cancers are highly curable, over 70 percent. A proctoscopic examination should be a routine procedure for the regular annual physical examination of all persons over 40 years of age. When cancer is diagnosed, the treatment usually consists of surgical removal of the neoplasm and part of the colon. When an extensive amount of the colon must be removed, a *colostomy* is necessary. A colostomy is an artificial opening in the abdominal wall through which waste products are excreted.

Cancer of the pancreas   Pancreatic cancer is nearly always fatal with only about 1 percent survival rate. For reasons still unknown, the incidence of pancreatic cancer is rising significantly. Although the etiology of pancreatic cancer is unknown, there seems to be a higher incidence among those "with preexisting chronic pancreatitis than among the general population."[17] There is no known prevention for cancer of the pancreas which accounts for about 21,000 deaths each year in the United States.

Prostate cancer   Approximately 70,000 new cases of prostate cancer are diagnosed each year in the United States resulting in about 22,000 deaths. Prostate cancer is seldom fatal in men under 45 years of age, but by age 55 years, it is the third leading cause of cancer deaths among men. Also, the death rate from prostate cancer is significantly higher for married men than for single men. After age 75 years, prostate cancer is the leading cause of cancer death among men.[18]

Treatment for prostate cancer is surgical removal of the gland, or if advanced where surgery is countraindicated, radiation therapy is used. The 5-year survival rate in advanced cancer is from 50–70 percent. The cause of prostate cancer is unclear, but some authorities believe that a hormonal imbalance may be an important factor.

Ovarian cancer   Death rates for ovarian cancers have increased slightly during the past 30 years, but the 5-year survival rate has shown a gain from 25 percent in 1940 to 34 percent in 1979. However, of the 10 out of 1000 women over the age of 40 years who develop ovarian cancer, only about two will be cured. According to the American Cancer Society, "The remainder will suffer repeated bouts of intestinal obstruction as the tumor spreads over the surface of the bowel, develop inanition, malnutrition and literally vomit to death."[19]

Uterine cancer   The death rate from uterine cancer has declined more than 70 percent over the past 40 years. Much of this decline is due to more women receiving a Pap test on a regular basis. The *Pap test* was developed by George Papanicolaou and consists chiefly of obtaining cells from the cervix of the uterus, which are then microscopically examined for any abnormal conditions. This test makes it possible to detect abnormal cells before they develop into cancer. At this stage of development virtually all abnormal conditions are curable.

The American Cancer Society estimates that approximately 99,000 new cases of uterine cancer, including cervix carcinoma in situ, will be discovered each year. There are approximately 45,000 cervix carcinomas in situ diagnosed each year. Of the 54,000 uterine cancers annually diagnosed, approximately 16,000 are of the cervix and 38,000 are cancer of the endometrium with approximately 7,400 deaths from cervical cancer and 3,200 deaths from endometrial cancer.

Cervical cancer seldom appears before the age of 20 years. It is most common in women between the ages of 40 and 50 years, those who were sexually active at an early age with several sex partners, and those in the lower socioeconomic strata. Endometrial cancer is most common at the time of, or shortly after, menopause and especially if the onset of menopause comes late in life (after age 55 years). Uterine cancer is also more frequent in married rather than single women and in women who have borne children than those who never have borne a child.

Urinary cancer There are more than 54,000 new cases of urinary cancers diagnosed each year with approximately 18,000 deaths. More than 68 percent of urinary cancers are of the bladder with the remaining 32 percent being of the kidneys or other urinary structures. The overall 5-year survival rate for both men and women is approximately 62 percent. This is an improvement of about 20 percent over the past 25 years. This improvement is chiefly the result of the development of supervoltage radiation which makes it possible to administer radiotherapy to the deep seated tumors of the bladder with minimal damage to normal tissues. Advances in surgery are also contributing to an improved cure rate. For example, it is possible to completely remove a cancerous bladder (a cystectomy). This is accomplished by diverting the ureters from the kidneys so that the urine can drain directly into the large intestine.

The causes of bladder cancer are chiefly environmental. For example, it has been found that people who work in the aniline dye industry where betanophthylamine is used are more susceptible to bladder cancer. The relationship between cigarette smoking and bladder cancer is well established. In addition, it has been found that there is a higher incidence of bladder cancer in those parts of the world where large numbers of the people are infected with *schistosomiasis*. This is a parasitic worm that becomes imbedded in the bladder causing chronic irritation that may eventually result in cancer.

Leukemias and lymphomas There are two kinds of leukemias: (1) acute leukemia, which is most common in children; and (2) chronic leukemia, which is most common in adults over 40 years of age. Leukemias may be lymphocytic or granulocytic.* Death from leukemias usually results from increased susceptibility to infection and hemorrhage. Several factors have been identified as possible causes of leukemia. These are radiation, certain chemicals such as benzene, and viruses. Acute leukemia responds more readily to treatment than chronic leukemia. The treatment consists of chemotherapy and radiotherapy for the leukemia itself. However, since death is usually the result of complications from infection or hemorrhage, support therapy is an important part of the treatment regimen.

The chief forms of the lymphomas are Hodgkin's disease, lymphosarcoma, and reticulum cell sarcoma. Although *Hodgkin's disease* can occur at any age, it is most frequent in the 20–45 year age group.

*The granulocytes prevent infection by engulfing foreign substances while the lymphocytes are involved in the production of antibodies.

Hodgkin's disease is characterized by painless swelling of the lymph glands located in the neck, armpits, and groin. The etiology of Hodgkin's disease is unclear and much research is being conducted along these lines. We do know that biopsy of the lymph node indicates malignancy of the reticular cells and the Reed-Sternberg cells in all cases of the disease.

Treatment consists of high voltage radiation in the early stages and chemotherapy in patients who have advanced Hodgkin's disease. When diagnosed and treated in the early stages, Hodgkin's disease responds to treatment in most cases, either through cure or being controlled—in some cases up to 10 years.

Cancer Prevention and Control

It is clear that many cancers can be prevented, life prolonged through proper cancer management, and cures affected in many instances when the cancer is diagnosed early and treated properly. Although cancer is the second leading cause of death, most of these (about 90 percent), are of people over 45 years of age. Approximately 60 percent of cancer deaths occur in people 65 years and over. Although cancers are perplexing health problems, many more deaths (nearly three times as many) are the result of accidents in the under 45 year age group. (See Table 15–4 for a comparison of cancer and accidental deaths by age groups.) This is the period of life of most productivity and represents the greatest life-years lost.

Table 15–4: A Comparison of Deaths from Cancers and Accidents for Various Age Groups

a. Cancer Deaths

Age Groups by Years

1—4	5—15	15—24	25—44	45—64	65 and over
656	1,849	2,659	16,485	130,993	224,543
		21,649			355,536

b. Accidental Deaths

Age Groups by Years

1—4	5—15	15—24	25—44	45—64	65 and over
3,439	6,308	24,316	22,399	19,000	23,961
		56,462			42,961

Source of Data: *Facts of Life and Death*, U.S. Department of Health, Education, and Welfare, National Center for Health Statistics. Washington, DHEW Publication No. (PHS) 79–1222, 1979, pp. 33–38.

Safeguards for preventing cancers   Not all cancers can be prevented, but many deaths from some of the common cancers can be prevented through seven simple actions that each of us can take.

1. To prevent *lung* cancer, reduce and eventually stop smoking cigarettes.

2. To prevent *skin* cancer, avoid excessive and repeated exposure to the sun. If exposure is necessary, protect yourself from the sun's rays by using a chemical sun screen, wearing a hat, and wearing clothing that covers most of the body.

3. Since we do not know the specific etiology of *breast* cancer, preventive measures are also unknown. However, most deaths from breast cancer can be prevented through monthly breast self-examination and an annual medical examination. For women who are in the high risk group, mammography, thermography, or xeroradiography may be indicated. It is important to note that about 8 of every 10 lumps that are found are *not* cancerous.

4. To prevent *oral* cancers, reduce and eliminate cigarette smoking and drink alcoholic beverages in moderation. Most oral cancers are easily detected through self-examination and annual professional examination by a dentist or dental hygienist.

5. *Cervical* cancer deaths have decreased more than 50 percent over the past three decades. This is attributed to more women receiving the Pap test during their annual physical examination.

6. *Colon and rectal* cancers are the most common form of cancer in the United States with the exception of skin cancers. About 75 percent of colon and rectal cancers can be detected by a proctoscopic examination. Every adult over the age of 40 years should have a proctoscopic examination as a part of the annual physical checkup.

7. The general safeguard to the prevention of cancer deaths is early detection and prompt and competent treatment. This can best be assured through an annual physical examination for all adults.

Warning signals of cancer   Usually, the presence of one or more of the seven cancer warning signals does not turn out to be cancer. However, when a signal is detected, it is important to seek competent medical attention as soon as possible, for, as we have seen, many cancers are treatable when diagnosed early. The American Cancer Society and many other agencies have for many years urged people to become familiar with cancer's seven warning signals because such knowledge can save your life. These warning signals are:

1. Any change in bowel or bladder habits.
2. A sore that does not heal.
3. Unusual bleeding or discharge from any body opening.
4. Thickening or lump in the breast or elsewhere on the body.
5. Indigestion or difficulty in swallowing.
6. Obvious change in a wart or mole; color, size, and so forth.
7. A nagging cough or hoarseness.

Early detection programs In recent years, professional associations and governmental and voluntary health agencies have sponsored a number of screening programs to detect some cancers as early as possible. Some of these are directed toward the general population while others are directed only toward those who are in high risk groups. Most are simple tests that are generally inexpensive to perform. Examples of screening programs are pap test screening, breast self-examination workshops, colon-rectum hemoccult guaiac test, and oral examinations.

As a result of these programs, many cancers are detected early and successfully treated, lowering the death rate for these cancers. A simple self-applied test for colon-rectum cancer was developed in the mid 1970s. It consists of three slides. The person applies a small stool specimen on each of the three slides on three consecutive days which is then taken or mailed to a laboratory where a hemoccult developer is applied. The slide is then read by a physician for the presence of blood in the stool specimen. Incidentally, blood in the stools does not necessarily mean that cancer is present. It does mean that further tests are indicated.

Cancer Management

Treatment, control, and cure are the three chief elements that constitute cancer management. In addition to cancer management is the management of pain that frequently accompanies some forms of advanced cancers. Fortunately, there are a number of drugs available to the physician that can be used to control pain. These include aspirin, acetaminophen, propoxyphene, and the narcotics such as morphine and meperidine.

Recent advances in treatment modalities are resulting in the cure or control of many cancers that were formally usually fatal. There are four general acceptable forms of treating cancers: surgery, radiation therapy, chemotherapy, and immunotherapy.

Surgery *Surgery* is probably the first form of treatment for cancer and is certainly the oldest of the accepted methods. During the nineteenth century, surgery became the standard treatment. However, once a cancer has metastasized, other methods must also be used to destroy the metastasized cells. Some authorities believe that new surgical techniques beyond those being used will do little to improve the cure rate from cancers. Although it is still an effective method of treatment when the cancer is localized, more and more attention is being given to finding other methods that can seek out the cancer cells that have invaded other parts of the body.

Chemotherapy The use of drugs in the treatment of cancer is a relatively new approach, beginning in 1945 with the use of nitrogen mustard for treating lymphomas. In the ensuing years, more than 30 drugs have been found to have varying degrees of success in treating a variety of cancers.

Radiation therapy Since cancer cells are generally more sensitive to radiation than normal cells, this form of treatment can be used to destroy the cancer with less damage to the surrounding normal tissues. The forms that radiation treatment may take are x-rays, radium, and radioactive isotopes. Radiation therapy may be either external or internal. *External radiation* is given by x-ray machines or by radioisotope sources and may be used for curing the cancer or for palliation. *Internal radiation* is most often used in treating uterine cancer. This is accomplished by implanting a radioactive substance into the cancer. These implants may be removable or permanent.

Immunotherapy   One of the newer approaches to cancer treatment, immunotherapy, has shown promise of using the body's own defense mechanisms to combat cancer. It is based upon the theory that cancer is a foreign body that stimulates the body to reject it as it would other foreign bodies. The potential success of immunotherapy is based upon evidence resulting from the spontaneous remission of some cancers in some people, which suggests some sort of biologic equilibrium between the cancer and the host.

Experiments have been conducted through the use of microorganisms to raise the body's immune response. Although much more research is necessary, immunotherapy is being used in treating a limited number of human cancers with high future expectations.

Rehabilitation

Developing cancer, submitting to treatment, and finally recovering can be an extremely traumatic experience. Not only do some cancers leave us physically changed, but the total experience frequently has emotional and social after effects. The recovered cancer victim is in need of rehabilitative services, and today it is considered one of the four basic elements of cancer management; the other three are prevention, diagnosis, and treatment.

Goals   There are three chief goals of the cancer rehabilitation program, all of which are intended to achieve the aim of returning the cancer victim to a useful life as cured or as one whose life can be prolonged in spite of the cancer. These goals are:

1. *Restorative rehabilitation,* which is to return the person to his or her precancer condition with no handicap or at least an insignificant handicap as a result of the cancer.
2. *Supportive rehabilitation,* which is to return the person to a state of self-sufficiency even though a permanent disability has resulted from the cancer.
3. *Palliative rehabilitation,* which is to return the person to a state of self-sufficiency despite the presence of the cancer. This goal is achieved by significant reduction of pain that is accompanying the progression of an advanced cancer that cannot be cured but may be retarded in its progress.

The rehabilitation team   Depending upon the nature of the cancer one has developed and the extent of physical damage resulting from it, along with the social and emotional trauma, the rehabilitative team may include a variety of people and services. These services, which are available at all of the comprehensive cancer research centers and many large hospitals, include such assistance as: *medical services; physical therapy; occupational therapy; enterostomal therapy* (provided for patients who have undergone surgery for a colostomy, ileostomy, or artificial bladder); *maxillofacial therapy* (concerned with prosthetics for reconstructing damaged head and neck structures); *speech therapy; social services; vocational guidance services; mental health services;* and *patient health education.*

Unproven Methods

Since the beginning of humanity, there have been those who have claimed to have a "cure" for cancer. Over the years, cures have taken about every conceivable form from salves, poultices, diets, "natural" drugs, to a variety of mechanical, electrical, and inert gadgets. During the 1960s and 1970s, and it appears, through the 1980s, the most publicized unproven methods were (are) Krebiozen and Laetrile.

Krebiozen reached heights of popularity during the 1960s. Following scientific investigation of this substance, the National Cancer Institute announced that it consisted of horse plasma or horse meat and sometimes merely mineral oil. The NCI found no evidence that Krebiozen possessed any anticancer properties whatsoever.

Laetrile is manufactured from apricot kernels and contains a chemical substance known as amygdalin. Amygdalin is a poisonous compound that releases cyanide when acted upon by enzymes in the body. Initially, proponents of Laetrile claimed that since cancer cells were different from normal cells, they are unable to neutralize the cyanide released as can normal cells, and therefore were destroyed. Scientific investigation revealed that this is not true. Laetrile proponents then claimed that it was actually a vitamin (B-17) and acted as a cancer prevention.

Laetrile is forbidden in interstate commerce by the Food and Drug Administration but is available, and legal, in some states. Late in the 1970s, the National Cancer Institute agreed to scientific investigation of the drug to determine finally what, if any, anticancer properties it may contain. To date, there is no scientific evidence that Laetrile has any effects upon the prevention or treatment of cancer.

So widespread are unproven methods of cancer management resulting in delayed treatment by proven methods and the unnecessary deaths of thousands of Americans that the American Cancer Society has taken a stand against the promotion of these dangerous methods. The American Cancer Society has published a list of unproven methods and of publications and organizations that promote them as a warning to people.

Unfortunately, most of the unproven methods remain unproven because there has been little or no scientific research to determine their validity. This is chiefly because of the lack of funds and scientists to conduct thorough investigations into every theory that crops up from time to time. Instead, research is conducted into those areas which seem, at the time, to be most promising. In the meantime, we are left with the question, "Are any of the unproven methods really the panacea we have been seeking for centuries?"

OTHER MAJOR CHRONIC
DISEASES

Diabetes Mellitus

The National Commission on Diabetes states that *diabetes* is a metabolic disorder characterized by hyperglycemia, a relative or absolute insulin deficiency, and an accelerated probability of vascular disease. Diabetes is a complex, chronic, systemic disorder that interferes with the metabolism and body chemistry. Although the cause of diabetes is unknown, 25 percent of the cases have a familial history indicating that heredity may play an important part in its etiology.

Juvenile diabetes may make its appearance abruptly in children or young adults. It is estimated that more than 10 million Americans have diabetes. Approximately, 4 million diabetics are known. Of these, approximately 10 percent are juvenile diabetics. For those with juvenile diabetes, daily injections of insulin are required since there is a total, or substantial lack of insulin being secreted by the islet cells of Langerhans where insulin is naturally manufactured in the body. As time passes, cardiovascular complications often result, usually after about 15 years.

Maturity diabetes usually has its onset in those in their 50s or 60s. Frequently, these diabetics do not require insulin injections, if proper diet is maintained. It is thought that approximately 2 percent of the population of the United States are diabetics. Long-term complications of diabetes are common, usually affecting the vascular sytem. The risk of cardiovascular complications is significantly increased if the diabetic also has high blood pressure, high blood cholesterol levels, and smokes cigarettes. For example, diabetics are twice as prone to coronary heart disease and stroke as nondiabetics and five times more likely to develop arterial disease of the extremities. It is estimated that approximately 75 percent of diabetics die of cardiovascular disease. This is compared to about 50 percent for the general population.

The Arthritic Disorders

There are nearly 4.4 million Americans whose functioning ability is impaired as a result of arthritic disorders. However, it is estimated that as many as 20 million people suffer from one or more forms of arthritis. These include rheumatoid arthritis, degenerative arthritis, gout, and bursitis among others.

Rheumatoid arthritis is a chronic systemic disease that usually involves the joints. It takes the form of adult rheumatoid or juvenile rheumatoid arthritis. *Adult rheumatoid arthritis* is usually insidious and its cause is obscure. The *juvenile form* is very similar except that it occurs in the joints that are undergoing growth. Rheumatoid arthritis is characterized by swelling, pain, and tenderness. Symptoms are usually most severe in the morning and subside to some extent with activity providing fatigue does not occur. Generally, aspirin is the safest analgesic for long-term treatment. There is no cure for arthritis, but a variety of treatment regimens to relieve some of the symptoms are available. These include administration of hormones such as cortisone, diet, rest, controlled exercise, and the use of gold compounds.

Epilepsy

Epilepsy affects the functioning of the cerebrum. It is chronic, characterized by recurrent attacks whose onset is sudden and of short duration. The etiology of epilepsy is unclear, however, it is thought that if seizures occur before 2 years of age they are usually related to developmental defects or birth injuries, while those that occur after the age of 25 years are probably due to cerebral trauma, tumors, or other organic brain conditions.

Grand mal seizures may be accompanied by an aura. The *aura,* if present, provides evidence of the area of the brain that is the focal point of the attack. The aura may be manifested as a visual or olfactory hallucination, muscular movements of the mouth, numbness, tingling, or twitching of muscles. For example, if the aura is an olfactory hallucination, the posterior temporal lobe of the brain is the focal point of the attack. During a seizure, the person may cry, fall, lose consciousness, and have uncontrolled contractions of the muscles of the extremities. Following the seizure, the person may fall into a deep sleep, complain of headache and soreness in the muscles. The seizure usually lasts for up to about 5 minutes.

Petit mal seizures usually occur in childhood and may occur several times a day. They are characterized by a partial loss of consciousness, sometimes accompanied by muscular contractions lasting up to about 30 seconds. During the seizure the person suddenly stops whatever activity in going on, and following the attack, continues with the activity as though no seizure had occurred.

Psychomotor attacks are characterized by a loss of environmental contact manifested in staggering, purposeless movements, and unintelligible vocal sounds. Confusion accompanies the attack and may last for 2 or 3 minutes following it.

Epileptic equivalents are a group of disturbances that may take place in those individuals who experience epileptic seizures. They may take a number of forms, such as abdominal pain and mental confusion.

Treatment for epilepsy may be symptomatic for those forms where the cause is unknown, or, elimination of the cause when known. For example, if a tumor in the brain is responsible, it must be removed. Drug therapy is used to prevent the seizures from occurring. For grand mal, phenobarbital, among others, is effective in controlling the seizures. Petit mal is controlled by the use of trimethadione or paramethadione. Psychomotor seizures can also be controlled by these drugs, but the dosage must be larger in most cases.

Renal Disorders

The term *renal* refers to the kidneys. Each normal person has two kidneys, one located on each side of the spine and just below the rib cage. The kidney is a complex organ composed of about one million *nephrons,* or functioning units. Within each nephron is a group of tiny blood vessels called the *glomerulus* which connects with a sac called the pelvis of the kidney. The structure connecting the glomerulus with the pelvis is called the *tubule.* The pelvis is further connected with the urinary bladder by the ureter, a relatively large tube. From the urinary bladder is the urethra, the tube that carries the urine from the urinary bladder to be excreted. Figure 15–3 illustrates the structures which make up the excretory system.

The kidneys have three main functions: (1) They produce urine for excretion from the body. Generally, a healthy person will excrete from 1 to 2 quarts of urine each day. (2) They produce a hormone called renin which is important for regulating normal blood pressure. If too much urine is produced, hypertension may result. (3) They produce a hormone called erythropoietin which controls red blood cell production. If there is a significant reduction in erythropoietin in the body, anemia may result. When there is disease or injury to the kidneys, they cannot perform these functions; water balance is interfered with, resulting in an accumulation in the tissues causing swelling (edema). If there is a prolonged dysfunction and adequate treatment is not initiated, death will result.

There are a number of forms that kidney disease can take. Some of these are mild temporary dysfunctioning resulting in short-term illness. However, if a disease of the kidney results in severe impairment and is left untreated, uremia will set in which is characterized by the presence in the blood of constituents of urine. These produce a toxicity resulting in nausea, vomiting, headache, vision impairment, coma, and convulsions among other symptoms. If left untreated, death will result. It has been estimated that over 8 million people in the United States have diagnosed kidney disease while an additional 3.3 million have undiagnosed kidney diseases.[20] More than 54,000 people die each year in the United States from some form of kidney disease. Figure 15–4 summarizes the Six Warning Signs of Kidney Diseases.

Diseases of the kidney may be the result of certain infections or they may be noninfectious diseases. The diseases of the kidney are summarized in Table 15–5. Treatment for kidney disease depends upon the type of disease encountered. Some treatments affect a cure, some repress progress of the disease, and some act as substitutes for the diseased kidneys. Generally, treatment may involve the use of:

Figure 15-3:

The Excretory System

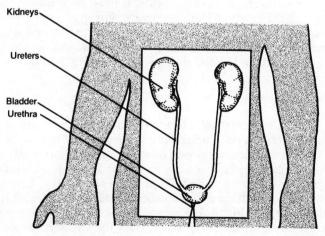

Kidneys

Ureters

Bladder
Urethra

Figure 15-4:

Six Warning Signs of Kidney Diseases

 Burning or
difficulty
during
urination

 More
frequent
urination,
particularly
at night

 Passage
of bloody-
appearing
urine

 Puffiness
around eyes,
swelling of
hands and feet,
especially in
children

 Pain in
small of back
just below
the ribs
(not aggravated
by movement)

 High Blood
Pressure

National Kidney
Foundation

- *diuretics,* which increase the flow of urine;
- *antibiotic drugs* which destroy microorganisms;
- *steroid drugs,* which suppress symptoms;
- *artificial kidneys,* which temporarily take over the functions of the kidney;
- *peritoneal dialysis,* which restores normal chemical composition of the blood;
- *kidney transplant,* which is the surgical replacement of a diseased kidney with a normal one from a kidney donor.

Allergic Disorders

When certain substances called *allergens* or *antigens* enter or come into contact with the body resulting in an altered reactionary state of tissues, it is called an *allergic reaction.* Probably everyone is allergic to something, but certain people have varying degrees of sensitivity to many common allergens usually found in a normal environment. Although these allergens may have profound effects on

Table 15–5: Summary of Diseases of the Kidney

Classification	Type	Characteristics
Infectious	Pyelonephritis	Inflammation of the kidney and its pelvis. Treated by the use of antibiotics.
Noninfectious	Nephrotic syndrome (Nephrosis)	Involves the glomerular membrane. Protein escapes from the blood into the urine. Cause is unknown. Steroid hormones can suppress the disease.
Noninfectious	Acute glomerulonephritis	Involves the glomeruli. May follow certain streptococcal infections. Usually is of short duration.
Noninfectious	Chronic glomerulonephritis	Frequently is asymptomatic. Results in uremia. Regulation of the diet and the use of antibiotics are the forms of treatment but there is no cure.
Noninfectious	Kidney stones	Calcium salts, uric acid, and other substances crystallize. Stones are removed by increased fluid intake, medication, and surgery.
Noninfectious	Acute kidney shutdown	Caused by hemorrhage from accidents resulting in a crushing of the kidney. Artificial kidney or peritoneal dialysis techniques may be necessary.
Noninfectious	Polycystic kidney	Results from structural defect and is present at birth. Kidney tissue contains cysts. It is an autosomal dominant hereditary disease.

some people, they are also innocuous to others. Some authorities believe there is a genetic factor or factors associated with most allergies.

The exact mechanisms involved in allergic reactions are still unclear, but there is evidence that they are associated with the histamine level in the body. The allergen responsible for an allergic reaction stimulates the body to produce antibodies which, in turn, interfere with the body's ability to control the level of histamine produced. When the histamine level rises, the tissues respond in the characteristic allergic syndrome. The specific symptoms depend upon the tissues affected. It is also believed by some authorities that other body chemistry may be involved, such as the acetylcholine, heparin, and epinephrine levels. The use of antihistamine drugs, which tend to reduce or eliminate allergy symptoms, strongly implicate histamine as the chief agent in allergic reactions.

The allergic syndrome may be manifested as hay fever symptoms, asthma, gastrointestinal disturbances, edema, and others. These are determined by the specific kind of allergens classified as (1) inhalants, which enter the body through the respiratory tract; pollens, for example; (2) foods, such as eggs, milk, and chocolate; (3) drugs, such as aspirin and some antibiotics; (4) infectious agents, such as bacteria or fungi; (5) contactants, such as poison ivy and animal fur; (6) physical agents, such as radiation; and (7) emotional stress.

Some individuals are allergic to only one agent, but the general rule is that they are more likely sensitive to several agents. There are more than 1.5 million people in the United States whose effectiveness is limited because of hay fever and asthma. Table 15–6 summarizes some of the common allergies.

Visual Disorders

Color blindness   It is estimated that about 4 percent of the American population suffer from some form of hereditary color blindness. This is called dichromatism. Since this is a sex-linked genetic trait, more males are color blind than females. Generally, the person will be able to perceive most colors, but will have difficulty with distinguishing between one or two specific colors—red and green, for example.

Errors of refraction   These are conditions in which the image does not fall clearly on the retina and causes sight to be distorted. Conditions of refractive error include hyperopia, myopia, and astigmatism.

Hyperopia, commonly referred to as farsightedness, is the most frequent of the refractive errors. In this condition, the image theoretically falls behind the retina either because the eyeball axis is too short or because the refraction of the light rays coming into the eye is too weak. The opposite condition is *myopia* or nearsightedness and is also quite common. In myopia, the image falls in front of the retina because the axis of the eye is too long or the refractive power of the eye is too strong. *Astigmatism* is characterized by unequal refraction through the various parts of the lens. This results in an image, part of which may be focused with other parts being perceived out of focus.

Cataract   A major cause of impaired vision and blindness in the United States is cataract, either developmental or degenerative. Developmental cataract occurs congenitally or early in life as a result of heredity, nutritional, or inflammatory disturbances. Degenerative cataract is characterized by a loss of transparency in a normally developed lens and is the result of changes due to aging, or the effects of heat, x-rays, trauma, disease, or drugs. The major symptom is a painless

Table 15–6: Some of the Common Allergies

Type	Characteristics
Hay fever (Allergic rhinitis)	Seasonal (generally); symptoms include sneezing, rhinorrhea, nasal congestion; and possibly conjunctivitis and pharyngitis
Bronchial asthma	Wheezing resulting from a narrowing of the bronchi and bronchioles. Difficulty in breathing.
Gastrointestinal allergy	Manifested by nausea, vomiting, abdominal pain, and diarrhea. Usually results from eating certain foods, but also from certain orally administered drugs.
Hives (Urticaria)	Manifested by the presence of edema of either the skin or subcutaneous structures or both.

loss of vision. In advanced cases, the lens must be extracted for restoring sight with the aid of prosthetics. Although surgery is not always indicated as a treatment, when it is performed, it is up to 95 percent successful. The actual operation usually takes only about 45 minutes.

Retinal detachment   This may be either partial or complete and results in blindness when the retina is separated from its pigment layer. A person who experiences a retinal detachment complains of flashes of light followed by the sensation that a curtain has been pulled across the eye. Surgery is often successful in reattaching the retina and preventing blindness, although some vision impairment may remain.

Glaucoma   A major cause of blindness in the United States is glaucoma. The National Society for the Prevention of Blindness estimates that there are about 1.8 million Americans over 35 years of age who have glaucoma. It is characterized by tension built up in the eye resulting from an imbalance between production and outflow of aqueous humor. Most cases of glaucoma can be successfully treated with drug therapy, although in severe instances, surgery may be required. Glaucoma can be detected and treated early. Tests for glaucoma are usually a routine part of the eye examination given by an ophthalmologist. Diagnosis consists of measuring the intraocular pressure by the use of a tonometer, an instrument with a tiny plunger that fits on a part of the eyeball.

Strabismus   This is a condition in which one eye is not parallel with the other because one or more of the ocular muscles is paralyzed. This limits the amount of eye movement possible. Strabismus also results in blurred vision, headache, and diplopia. Diplopia is the perception of two images from a single object. Strabismus is treated with corrective lenses, orthoptic training, and surgery. Strabismus in infants should be brought to the attention of the physician as soon as noticed. Parents should not think that the child will outgrow it. If left untreated, blindness in the weaker eye will result.

Amblyopia   This is also known as "lazy eye" and is the most frequent cause of visual impairment in the preschool child. It is estimated that up to 2 percent of children have amblyopia. If the condition is not diagnosed and treated early, usually before the child enters school, the lazy eye may have already lost its visual capability. The American Association of Ophthalmology recommends a medical eye examination of all infants and again by age 3 years.

Blindness   The incidence of blindness in the United States is greatest among people over 60 years of age accounting for more than 63 percent. The diseases of the eye that can result in blindness include conjuntivitis neonatorum, trachoma, cataract, and glaucoma. Blindness may also result as a complication of other, more systemic diseases, such as diabetes mellitus. Or, genetic or environmental factors may cause blindness.

GLOSSARY

Benign: A neoplasm that grows very slowly, not cancerous.

Blood pressure: Measured in millimeters of mercury, the amount of pressure exerted on the wall of an artery.

Carcinogen: An environmental agent capable of producing cancer.

Cocarcinogen: An environmental agent that will activate a carcinogen.

Coronary circulation: That part of the circulatory system that supplies the heart muscle with blood.

Embolism: Blockage of a blood vessel by a blood clot transported from some other area of the body.

Hemorrhage: The escape of large volumes of blood from a blood vessel.

In situ: Localized, confined to the site of origin.

Malignant: A neoplasm that is cancerous.

Metastasis: A cancer that has spread through the vascular system.

Neoplasm: Any new growth of tissue; a tumor.

Oncology: The science that studies tumors.

SUMMARY

The cause of degenerative diseases are unclear, but some are associated with personal lifestyles, genetic predispositions, or senescence. As the numbers of people reaching 65 years of age and older increases, we can expect an increase in the incidence of the chronic and degenerative diseases.

Chronic and degenerative diseases incapacitate large numbers of people and are leading causes of death, but many can be prevented or controlled.

Blood pressure refers to the pressure the moving blood exerts on the arterial walls. Blood pressure is influenced by diet, weight, heredity, and the like.

There are three categories of heart disease: (1) congenital heart defects; (2) rheumatic heart disease; and (3) coronary heart disease. Coronary heart disease results when there is a deficient blood supply to the heart muscle. This reduction in blood flow is caused by atherosclerosis.

A myocardial infarction is caused by a shutting off of a coronary artery due to plaque build-up, a coronary thrombosis, or when a piece of plaque breaks off and blocks a smaller artery further down stream. When heart muscle tissue is damaged, it can result in sudden death if the damage is extensive, or in congestive heart failure. Extreme pumping failure results in cardiogenic shock, often resulting in death.

Stroke is the third leading cause of death in the United States. It results from a variety of conditions in which a lack of blood supply to a portion of the brain results in the death of brain cells. A stroke can be caused by a cerebral thrombosis or a cerebral embolism, and is highly influenced by atherosclerosis and high blood pressure.

Cardiovascular diseases are influenced by a variety of controllable factors. Such risk factors as smoking, high levels of saturated fat and cholesterol intake, obesity, hypertension, and a lack of physical activity have all been shown to be significant contributors to cardiovascular disease.

Many of the deaths from cancers each year in the United States are unnecessary and many new cases that are diagnosed could be prevented if people would simply avoid behaviors that contribute to their development.

Cancer cells are unlike normal cells in several respects. They grow out of control and interfere with the functions of normal body tissues. They also migrate to other parts of the body where they grow causing further dysfunction of the tissues in the new site. Tumors or neoplasms may be benign or malignant. The prevalence of cancers is influenced by environment, type of population, race, sex, geography, and personal health behaviors.

Cancers are classified as sarcomas, leukemias and lymphomas, and carcinomas. These classifications imply the tissue from which the cancer arises. Cancers are also identified by the site in which they occur.

There are several factors that have been associated with the cause of cancer: cigarette smoking, environmental pollutants, radiation, and viruses. Many more cancers can be prevented than are through certain changes in our life styles. The American Cancer Society has developed the seven safeguards and the seven warning signals of cancer, for prevention and early detection and prompt treatment.

Treatment, control, and cure are the three chief elements of cancer management. The accepted methods of treating cancers are surgery, radiotherapy, chemotherapy, and immunotherapy.

As with many health areas, cancer quackery is ever-present. Over the years, a variety of quack cancer "cures" have sprung up. These may be in the form of drugs, vitamins, regimens, or devices. In addition, there are a number of treatments that claim to be effective against cancer but which lack any scientific evidence to support the claims.

There are a number of other chronic and degenerative diseases that are major health problems. Some incapacitate thousands of people, while others are leading causes of death. These diseases include diabetes mellitus, arthritis, epilepsy, kidney disorders, and allergic reactions.

PROBLEMS FOR DISCUSSION

1. What are four of the major degenerative diseases? Why are they important health concerns in the United States?
2. What is diastole? What is systole? Relate these to blood pressure.
3. What is blood pressure? How is it measured?
4. Identify three major types of cardiovascular diseases.
5. Describe congenital heart defects.
6. How is rheumatic fever related to rheumatic heart disease?
7. What is atherosclerosis? Distinguish it from arteriosclerosis.
8. Describe the nature of atherosclerotic plaque.
9. What is ischemia?
10. Describe angina pectoris. What is the difference between stable and unstable angina?
11. What is a myocardial infarction? How does it contribute to sudden death? To congestive heart failure?
12. Distinguish between a cerebral thrombosis and a cerebral embolism.
13. How are cholesterol and saturated fats related to heart disease?
14. Distinguish between HDL and LDL.

15. How is hypertension related to cardiovascular disease? Distinguish between essential and secondary hypertension.

16. List several diseases of the blood. Describe each.

17. What is cancer? Are all tumors cancer? Explain. Are all neoplasms tumors? Explain.

18. Describe the chief etiological factors associated with most cancers. Which ones does each person have personal control over?

19. List the eleven most common forms of cancers and state their incidence, treatment, and curability. State which ones should have a much lower death rate and why.

20. Describe the ways in which cancer can be prevented and ways in which the death rate can be reduced.

21. What are the accepted treatment modalities for cancers? How do these differ from the unproven methods?

22. What are the purposes of rehabilitation of the cancer victim? What does the rehabilitation team consist of?

23. What are the characteristics of the cancer quack? What are the chief dangers of being treated by a quack?

24. Discuss why some health problems, such as arthritis, are important even though they are not leading causes of death.

25. Summarize what you can do to prevent many of the chronic and degenerative diseases. Which ones are most preventable? Which ones are most treatable?

REFERENCES

1. *Health: United States: 1976–1977,* United States Department of Health, Education, and Welfare; The Public Health Service; Health Resources Administration, pp. 3–4.

2. ENOS, W. E., R. H. HOLMES and J. BEYER "Coronary Disease Among United States Soldiers Killed In Action In Korea," *Journal of the American Medical Association,* Vol. 152, 1953, p. 1090.

3. TRUELT, J., J. CORNFIELD, and W. KAUNEL, "A Multivariate Analysis of the Risk of Coronary Heart Disease," *Journal of the American Medical Association,* Vol. 235, 1967, p. 825–827.

4. *Dietary Goals for the United States,* Report of the U.S. Senate Select Committee on Human Nutrition.

5. KANNEL, W. B., M. J. SCHWARTZ, and P. M. MCNAMARA, "Blood Pressure and Risk of Coronary Heart Disease: The Framingham Study," *Diseases of the Chest,* Vol. 56, 1969, p. 43–52.

6. National High Blood Pressure Education Program, *Handbook for Improving High Blood Pressure Control in the Community,* National Heart, Lung and Blood Institute, US DHEW, p. 7.

7. U.S. Department of Health, Education, and Welfare, *Report of the Joint National Committee on Detection, Evaluation, and Treatment of High Blood Pressure,* National Heart, Lung and Blood Institute, DHEW Publication No. (NIH) 78–1088, p. 6.

8. U.S. Department of Health, Education, and Welfare, *Smoking and Health,* Report of the Advisory Committee to the Surgeon General of the Public Health Service, 1964.

9. JENKINS, C. D., R. H. ROSENMANN, and S. J. SYZANDKI, "Cigarette Smoking—Its Relationship to Coronary Heart Disease and Related Risk Factors in the Western Collaborative Group Study," *Circulation,* Vol. 38, 1968, p. 1140–1155.

10. HAMMOND, E. C., "Smoking in Relation to the Death Rates of One Million Men and Women," *National Cancer Institute Monography,* Vol. 19, 1966, p. 127–204.

11. PAFFENBARGER, R. S., "Physical Activity and Fatal Attack: Protection or Selection?," *Exercise in Cardiovascular Health and Disease.* Amsterdam, E. A. (Ed.), Yorke Medical Books, 1977, p. 35.

12. U.S. Department of Health, Education, and Welfare, *1978 Surgeon General's Report.*

13. *Health Education: Cancer Prevention and Control, Teacher's Training Manual,* The University of the State of New York, The Education Department, Albany, 1976, p. 8.

14. *Cancer and the Worker,* The New York Academy of Sciences, New York, 1977, p. 1.

15. *Ibid.,* p. 5.

16. *DES. The Wonder Drug Women Should Wonder About,* New York State Department of Health, 1979 (pamphlet).

17. BOWDEN, LEMUEL, *Cancer of the Pancreas,* Professional Education Publication, The American Cancer Society, 1972, p. 1.

18. *Progress Against Cancer of the Prostate,* National Cancer Institute, DHEW Publication No. (NIH) 75–528.

19. BARBER, HUGH R. K., EDWARD A. GRABER, and TAE HAE KWON, *Ovarian Cancer,* American Cancer Society, Inc., 1975, p. 2.

20. *Your Kidneys: Master Chemists of the Body* (Pamphlet), National Kidney Foundation, New York, 1976, p. 10.

16

genetic health:
being born healthy

THE SCIENCE OF GENETICS

Being born healthy is sometimes determined by chance, sometimes determined by science, sometimes determined by the courts. Sometimes it is not determined at all, since fetal death may occur instead.

Historical Perspectives

Genetics is the science that strives to discover the truth about the development of life, its perpetuation and alterations as directed by the mechanisms contained within the genes. A generally accepted definition of genetics is "the science that studies the transmission of hereditary factors and the way by which they express themselves during the development and life of an individual."[1] *Genetic health,* therefore, is a matter of life, living, or death. As we will see, our health before birth, after birth, and all through life depends to a great extent upon our genetic potentials determined at the moment of conception.

Although there has always been speculation about the reasons for differences and similarities of people, even in the same family, it was not until the mid-1800s that the basic principles of heredity were discovered to provide some of the answers. Johann (Gregor) Mendel in 1843 began his work in a small garden in a Moravian monastery. Through careful experimentation with a variety of plants, he soon discovered certain hereditary patterns always resulted from the same cross-pollinations. These observations are known as Mendel's laws and were derived chiefly from his experiments with peas between 1856 and 1863. Although Mendel published the results of his experiments in 1866, it was not until 1900 that his work became generally recognized.

Principles of Genetics

The ovum from the mother and the sperm cells from the father contain the hereditary characteristics that determine the genetic make-up of the child. These hereditary characteristics from the ovum and the sperm cells are called the *genetic code.* Each ovum and sperm cell possesses 23 chromosomes and each chromosome possesses more than 1000 genes. The genes from each parent and the ways in which they combine determine the design of the new life being formed. Essentially, they determine physical features, such as sex, hair, and eye color, and potentials including body size and intelligence.

The prenatal and postnatal environments play significant roles in regards to which of certain potentials *shall* develop and the degree to which they *do* develop. For example, a child inheriting a high level of intellectual potential will more likely realize this potential if the environment during life is intellectually stimulating. A child inheriting the potential for tallness will develop more of this potential when certain environmental conditions exist—for example, proper nutrition, rest, exercise, and so forth during infancy and childhood.

The genetic potentials of each of us are determined by the way genes combine. The specific genetic make-up is called our *genotype;* it consists of the actual genes that we have acquired from each parent gamete, which pair up shortly after conception. The pairing of the genes is called an *allele.* Alleles may be homozygous or heterozygous. A *homozygous* allele is one that contains two identical dominant or two identical recessive genes. A *heterozygous* allele is one that contains one dominant and one recessive gene.

The expression of genes is called the *phenotype.* Homozygous alleles can be expressed in only one way. However, heterozygous alleles are expressed according to the presence of the dominant gene. For example, suppose a child has received a brown-eyed gene from the female gamete and a brown-eyed gene from the male gamete; the genotype is two brown-eyed genes and since no other genes are present for eye color, the phenotype will be a brown-eyed child. However, suppose a child receives a brown-eyed gene from the female gamete and a blue-eyed gene from the male gamete. The genotype is one brown-eyed gene and one blue-eyed gene. The phenotype will be a brown-eyed child since the gene for brown eyes is dominant over the blue-eyed gene. The dominant gene always masks the expression of the recessive gene. However, either the brown-eyed or blue-eyed gene can be passed on to the following generation.

The total genotype of a person is called the *genetic pool.* The genetic pool includes all of the genes that can be transmitted to our offspring. Reproduction guarantees the survival of the genetic pool and influences evolution of the species however so slightly.

Genetic equilibrium ensures the stability of the species—that is, the particular genotypes will remain constant for generations. *Evolution* takes place when the genetic equilibrium is interrupted. The forces of evolution are chiefly gene mutation, natural selection, and genetic drift.

Gene mutation is the appearance of new alleles through spontaneous change. It is an error that is made during cell division when the deoxyribonucleic acid (DNA) is being duplicated. (DNA is discussed later.) These errors may be due to either internal or external forces, such as, radiation and certain chemicals. *Natural selection* is determined by environmental factors that favor the reproduction of certain alleles or gene combinations over others. Natural selection results from the constant interplay between the organism and the environment. According to Rosenthal, "natural selection refers to the processes whereby some organisms perpetuate their kind by reproducing themselves while others fail to do so."[2] However, natural selection does not produce new genes or gene combinations. *Genetic drift* is the random fluctuations in the frequencies of certain alleles or gene combinations occurring in small populations.[3]

DNA is composed of the genes which, in turn, make up the *chromosomes.* Chromosomes are located within the nucleus of the cell. The gametes, or sex cells (ovum and sperm), contain 23 chromosomes each as a result of reduction division (meiosis). Other body cells retain the original 46 chromosomes by the process of mitosis, a form of cell division where the daughter cells are identical to the mother cells. (See Figure 16-1.)

DNA is a self-replicating molecule. This replication takes place before cell division and the DNA present is shared equally between the daughter chromosomes.[4] There are four kinds of nitrogenous bases in a single DNA molecule. They are adenine, cystosine, guanine, and thymine (which are represented by a, c, g, and t respectively on the DNA helix.) A DNA molecule is composed of hundreds of genes. The genes ultimately determine all hereditary characteristics. (See Figure 16-2.)

Figure 16-1
Mitosis in Animal Cells

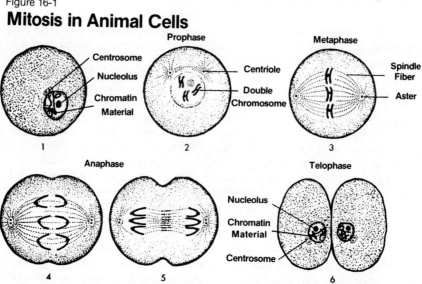

Figure 16-2:
Helix

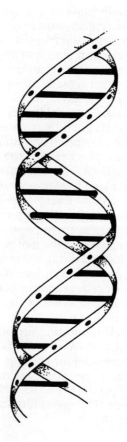

Since DNA is not capable of producing proteins directly, it orders their production through a series of ribonucleic acid (RNA) molecules. Each gene forms a polypeptide* chain that is regulated through the production of RNA. RNA is similar in its molecular structure to DNA with three nitrogenous bases: adenine, cystosine, and guanine; but RNA contains a fourth, uracil, which is complimentary to adenine. RNA functions as messenger RNA, transfer RNA, or ribosomal RNA. *Messenger RNA* embodies the basic plan and order of amino acid molecules for the synthesis of a protein molecule. The *transfer RNA* passes out into the cell and, depending upon its nitrogenous base series, will pick up an amino acid molecule. Finally, the *ribosomal RNA* combines with proteins to form the ribosomes of the cell. This is the site of protein synthesis.[5]

WHAT IS GENETIC HEALTH?

Introduction

Genetic health and genetic disease are frequently perceived as being opposites. Functionally, this is not necessarily true. Much depends upon the nature of the genetic disorder, its extent, and the part of the body involved. A genetically healthy person is one who has inherited genetic potentials that allow or assist in effective functioning. A genetically diseased person is one who has inherited a potential that manifests itself to the extent that it interferes with or precludes the ability to contribute significantly to self and society.

However, this is not to be construed to mean that an identified genetic defect is any less a defect if it seemingly does not alter one's ability to function. As we have seen, health and disease run a range from total disability to maximum, efficient ability to function. The significance of a genetic defect is the degree to which it interferes with this functioning ability, while the significance of healthy inheritance is the extent to which it contributes to functioning ability. Therefore, the chief distinction between genetic health and genetic disease lies in the extent of manifestation of the favorable or unfavorable traits. Some genetic defects manifest themselves fully but without significant interference with one's ability to function. For example, color blindness, a genetic defect, is is not important as either a health or disease factor. It may cause some inconvenience, but will not greatly alter how well one can get along as a human being.

A further example is one who inherits the sickle-cell *trait.* Although this is not manifested as a genetic defect, the person could pass the defective gene to his or her children who may inherit sickle-cell anemia which *is* a serious genetic defect. However, those who possess the sickle-cell trait may actually find it to be an advantage if they live in a malaria zone. Those with the sickle-cell trait are resistant to the malaria parasite and will not suffer the symptoms of malaria.

Inherited Potentials: The Genotypes

Most babies are born essentially healthy. This can be attributed to a number of factors, such as the very nature of heredity, prenatal care, improved

*A polypeptide chain is the union of three or more amino acids.

methods of monitoring the development of the fetus, and improved delivery techniques at the time of birth. However, the most critical period in life is from the twelfth week of pregnancy through the first month following birth. This period of life is exceeded in mortality rate only after age 70 years.

Generally, nature provides the fetus with two conditions for ensuring genetic health and being born healthy. These are the genotypes necessary for proper development and a prenatal environment to guarantee this proper development. If either of these is sufficiently altered, the fetus may not develop the qualities associated with health. Control of these factors therefore, becomes imperative to increase the likelihood that defective genes are not present in either parent; if they are, it is important to determine probability of them being transmitted to the new life and for the mother to take the proper precautions during pregnancy so as not to adversely change the prenatal environment.

Many genetic defects can be predicted even before conception takes place. For example, certain ethnic groups are more susceptible to certain genetic defects than are others. Sickle-cell anemia is most common among people of Mediterranean origin. The sickle-cell trait can be detected by use of the Sickledex test. It is a simple test requiring a drop of blood from a finger prick which is placed in a test tube containing several chemicals. If the fluid turns cloudy within 5–10 minutes, sickle-cells are present. The test, however, does not distinguish between the trait and sickle-cell anemia. If a positive reaction occurs, the prospective parents should receive genetic counseling to determine the probability of sickle-cell anemia being transmitted to their offspring.[6]

Similar to sickle-cell anemia, Cooley's anemia may manifest itself genotypically as the trait or as the disease. Those with Cooley's anemia *trait* are healthy and will live a normal life. Those with the disease are unable to produce hemoglobin and will require blood transfusions to control, but not cure, the anemia. As with sickle-cell anemia, Cooley's anemia can be detected by a simple blood test. However, to confirm the presence of the disease, a more complicated test called hemoglobin electrophoresis is required.

Developed Potentials: The Phenotypes

Although the genes establish the direction that development can take, an adverse prenatal environment can result in developmental defects. Smoking, drinking alcohol, and taking certain drugs during pregnancy, for example, can affect the course of fetal development. According to the National Foundation/ March of Dimes, a child is born with a defect every two minutes in the United States.[7]

About 50,000 American children died or were born with defects during the 1964–65 epidemic of rubella because their mothers contracted the disease while pregnant. Rubella is most dangerous during the first three months of pregnancy. It can cause miscarriage, stillbirth, or a birth defect. The tragedy is that the disease can be entirely prevented by inoculating girls before they reach childbearing age. Inoculation is also equally effective after reaching childbearing age, but *it must be done at least three months prior to becoming pregnant.*

Another dramatic example of how the prenatal environment can result in birth defects is the infamous thalidamide experience. More than 8000 babies were born with *phocomelia,* a condition characterized by stunted extremities. As a result, some physicians urge their pregnant patients to refrain from taking any drugs during the first trimester of their pregnancy.[8] The National Foundation/ March of Dimes recommends that *a pregnant woman should not use any drugs during pregnancy unless prescribed by her physician.* She should refrain from smoking, drinking alcohol, using over-the-counter drugs and the like, and seek early prenatal care from a competent physician.

How the Environment Impacts on Genetic Health

Any adverse factors present in the prenatal environment can interfere with the genetic code or with the full expression of the genetic potentials. The quality of the prenatal environment is determined by the quality of the mother's health before, during, and after pregnancy. Since the most critical prenatal period is the first six weeks of pregnancy, *it is extremely important that a woman prepare for pregnancy long before conception takes place.* This becomes even more crucial when we consider that many women are unaware of their pregnancy until after 6 weeks have passed. However, we need also to consider all of the environments that can impact on the fetus during the perinatal period. (The *perinatal period* is from conception to one month following the birth of the child.) The environments to consider are: (1) the direct maternal environment; (2) environmental factors acting on the mother during pregnancy; and (3) factors in the larger, external environment.

The *maternal factors* include any metabolic disorders of the mother, such as diabetes or thyroid disorders; the age of the mother; and the number and spacing of prior pregnancies that can affect maternal health. *Environmental factors acting on the mother* during pregnancy include viral diseases and other infections, such as rubella and venereal disease; the use of certain drugs (including tobacco and alcohol); and maternal diet. *External factors in the larger environment* include excessive exposure to radiation (x-rays), and environmental pollutants. For example, water polluted with mercury compounds can contaminate fish and when eaten by the mother may result in neurological defects of the fetus.

As important as the environments are in ensuring a healthy baby, and as important as the combinations of genes are, "less than half of all birth defects can be attributed to a single environmental or hereditary cause."[9] Most birth defects result from an interaction between heredity and environment. Some babies developing in an adverse prenatal environment, for example, are born void of any birth defects. This is probably due to the baby inheriting greater resistance to the adverse effects of the undesirable environment. However, birth defects can be significantly reduced in numbers if greater care is taken by the mother (and father) to provide the most healthful environments possible for the developing fetus.

THE NATURE OF GENETIC
HEALTH PROBLEMS

Manifestation of Genetic Health Problems

The *potential* for manifestation of a genetic defect may occur during any of six periods: (1) in the germ cell; (2) in the gamete; (3) in the zygote; (4) in the fetus; (5) in the newborn; or (6) during later life.[10] Some potentials for birth defects may be detected through laboratory techniques, such as detecting the trisomy of chromosomes related to Down's syndrome; studies of fetal blood or amniotic fluid through amniocentesis; or through overt signs of malformation or dysfunctioning of the fetus, neonate, child, or adult. Depending upon many factors, the birth defect may be manifested through fetal death, miscarriage, stillbirth, characteristic symptoms of a disease at birth, or sometime after birth.

For example, *phenylketonuria* (PKU) is manifested in mild to severe mental retardation shortly after birth. It is caused by a recessive gene that results in the inability of the infant to metabolize phenylalanine, an essential amino acid present in milk. This inherited condition is characterized by the absence of the enzyme, phenylalanine hydroxilase, normally found in the liver and necessary for metabolizing phenylalanine. As a result, phenylketone bodies are formed that damage brain cells resulting in mental retardation. However, the presence of this genetic potential can be detected shortly after birth by the use of the Guthrie blood test. When the test results are positive, the infant can be placed on a diet low in phenylalanine preventing the manifestation of mental retardation. Hospitals routinely administer the Guthrie blood test to all new-born infants; this has greatly reduced the incidence of this form of mental retardation.

Inherited and Congenital Defects

Initially, birth defects can be placed into two broad categories: those that are inherited (genetic), and those that are congenital. The *inherited defects* are directed basically by faulty genes while the congenital defects result from a faulty prenatal environment. The *congenital defects* are ones that exist before or at the time of birth. However, some authorities use the term congenital in a broader sense to include defects that are inherited or that develop during prenatal life. This concept implies a defect resulting from some fault in the reproductive cells of either or both parents (genetic), or the result of some injury to the fetus. The latter is considered a direct effect, such as radiation or chemicals present during prenatal life that alters the course of the developing fetus.

This confusion in the use of these terms has been somewhat clarified by the use of the term "birth defect" to mean either inherited or congenital. However, as we have seen, some genetic defects are not present at birth but manifest themselves some time later in life. The National Foundation/March of Dimes defines a birth defect as "an abnormality of body structure or function, whether genetically determined or the result of environmental influence on the unborn baby, or both."[11]

Birth defects are further classified according to the type of genetic transmission involved. For example, they may be referred to as dominant or recessive autosomal (caused by non-sex chromosomes), sex-linked (x-linked), and so on.

A useful classification that is used is to group birth defects by the way they affect the person: structural, functional, errors of metabolism, or blood diseases. The *structural defects* affect the body's parts, size and shape; for example, club foot or cleft palate. The *functional defects* affect the body's ability to perform certain normal tasks; for example, cystic fibrosis and color blindness. When the body is unable to convert certain chemicals into others, such as the inability to produce the enzyme phenylalanine hydroxilase, it is referred to as an *inborn error of metabolism.* Genetically determined *blood diseases* are characterized by the inability for the blood to carry out its specialized functions. Examples include sickle-cell anemia and hemophilia.[12]

Some Recent Advances

Generally, genetic research is directing its attention to the overall management of genetic disease, discovering new techniques for prevention, diagnosis, and treatment. This is necessary because "no genetic disease has yet been cured, in the strictest sense of the word, nor is any likely to be rendered curable very soon, for this would require actual repair of the genetic defect so that it would be neither expressed as disease nor transmitted to a subsequent generation."[13]

However, much research is being conducted on gene therapy and some dramatic results have been realized. Probably the area of basic research that received the most attention in recent years is *genetic cloning.* In the mid-1960s, John Gurdon, a biologist, succeeded in removing the nucleus of an egg cell from a frog and replaced it with the nucleus from a body cell. The egg cell behaved as a fertilized egg and produced a new frog identical to the one from which the body nucleus came.

It is important to reemphasize that living organisms are much more than their genetic traits. Human behavior is also influenced by the environment. Ausubel and associates state that "even if it becomes genetically possible to clone an Einstein, there is no guarantee that the products will have any of the behavioral qualities of the 'parent.' We still do not know the relative influence of environment and genetics in determining personality or behavioral traits."[14]

Research is also being conducted in other areas, such as cell biology and biochemical genetics. As a result of these areas of research, a whole new specialization called *genetic medicine* has emerged. It includes a new clinical discipline that is concentrating its efforts on detecting, diagnosing, preventing, and treating this puzzling group of diseases. This new field of genetic medicine has accomplished the following:

- detected more than 60 genetic disorders during prenatal development;
- established screening programs directed at high risk groups;
- provided genetic counseling of high risk groups with possibilities of intrauterine diagnosis, elective abortion, and occasionally treatment during prenatal development;
- developed therapeutic techniques, such as dietary control for PKU, and galactosemia, for example; and studied the administration of appropriate

substances, such as vitamin B_{12} for some forms of anemia, and growth hormones for dwarfism.

- investigated the removal of toxic substances, such as copper for those suffering Wilson's disease, characterized by modular cirrhosis of the liver.
- developed ways of enhancing enzyme production for such conditions as hereditary jaundice.
- developed ways of restoring the activity of certain genetically defective enzymes through vitamine therapy techniques.[15]

One of the most exciting and promising areas of research is related to recent developments in growing, storing, and distributing human cells in the laboratory. This is making it possible to map which genes belong on which chromosome and for researchers to investigate how individual genes can be "turned on" as well as how the body reacts to viral infection.[16] No longer will scientists need to wait the relatively long period of time from conception to birth to maturity to observe the results of human reproduction. Using these new techniques, it is possible, in many instances, to grow cells in the laboratory from a sample. As a result of experiments on human cells, many diseases not recognized as inherited have been found to be due to defective genes or chromosomes. Consequently, more than 2000 different genetic disorders have been identified. Because of the dramatic improvements in preventing and treating many genetic-related diseases, and because of new areas of research in human genetics, there is "a torrent of new ideas and techniques that are on the verge of revolutionizing medicine."[17]

In 1972, the National Institute of General Medical Sciences established the Institute for Medical Research in Camden, New Jersey. Scientists doing genetic research can usually obtain human cells for investigation through its national library of human cells. It is hoped that the "Human Mutant Cell Repository," as it is called, will eventually contain cell cultures for most of the important genetic diseases.[18]

Societal Attitudes About Genetic Health

Because of the explosive advances in genetic research over the past two decades, it has been nearly impossible for many of us to keep informed of what has been happening and to make appropriate interpretations about these advances. As a result, confusion is common. It is difficult for many of us to understand the implications of genetic research findings and to apply these. There are conflicting views about what certain genetic advances mean to our society. Will these advances be used for the good of our society? What are the probabilities that new techniques will be misused? Many of our attitudes about genetic health emanate from misinformation, emotionally charged propaganda, and ignorance.

Generally, societal misconceptions about genetic health fall within the following areas:

- understanding what constitutes genetic health, birth defects, and distinctions between these;
- confusion regarding the extent of genetic-related health problems, such

as the incidence of genetic deaths, disabilities caused by genetic-related defects, and the cost of genetic-related problems;
- understanding the causes of genetic-related problems;
- confusion relative to the prevention of many of the genetic-related defects;
- conflicting views and "old wives tales" about prenatal care;
- risks involved in prenatal diagnoses;
- benefits related to genetic counseling and screening programs;
- application of research findings to the lives of people;
- success of treatment and rehabilitation techniques.

Over the years, many social stigmas and inappropriate attitudes about genetic-related defects have evolved. As a result, individuals and families kept inherited problems a secret. However, with the educational efforts of the numerous voluntary health agencies, new public enlightenment of these defects is gradually coming about. With this, more inherited problems are being detected and treated early, often preventing permanent disability.

THE EXTENT OF GENETIC DISORDERS

Incidence and Prevalence

According to the National Foundation/March of Dimes approximately 250,000 babies are born each year in the United States with some form of genetic-related defect. This is approximately one baby born with a defect every 2 minutes. More than 60,000 children and adults die each year as a result of birth defects, and 500,000 babies die each year *prior* to birth as a result of defects. It is estimated that more than 15 million people in the United States suffer from some form of genetic-related defect that interferes with their ability to function adequately.[19] More than 1.2 million infants, children, and adults are hospitalized each year for treatment of birth defects.[20]

Some General Statistics

It is estimated that "12 million Americans carry true genetic diseases due wholly or partly to defective genes or chromosomes."[21] Approximately 3 million Americans have genetic defects that have resulted from fetal injury due to prenatal infection, drugs, radiation, and the like. According to the National Institute of General Medical Sciences, 36 percent of all spontaneous abortions are caused by gross chromosomal defects. This amounts to more than 100,000 spontaneous abortions per year in the United States. At least 40 percent of all infant mortality results from genetic factors. Approximately four-fifths of the 6 million people who are mentally retarded are believed to carry a genetic component. About one-third of all children admitted to hospital pediatric wards are admitted for genetic reasons. It is thought that each of us in the United States possesses between 5 and 8 recessive genes that can transmit a serious genetic defect to our children. The estimate is that 80 percent of all birth defects are genetic in nature.

Each year a couple stands a 3 percent chance of having a genetically defective child.

All of these statistics do not include the 10–12 percent of the population that possess enzyme abnormalities resulting in adverse reactions to one or more drugs that are commonly used. Genetic-related defects must be considered one of America's major health problems and be given personal, political, societal, and economic priority. (Table 16-1 lists some of the important genetic defects.)

Epidemiology of Genetic Disorders

There are four essential elements to the epidemiology of genetic disorders: (1) distribution; (2) causes; (3) prevention; and (4) treatment and control. Epidemiology of genetic disorders recognizes the multiplicity of influencing factors, such as the prevalence of genetic disorders according to ethnic groups, age, socioeconomic groups, and families. We know, for example, that certain genetic defects are more prevalent among certain ethnic groups, some more prevalent in certain socioeconomic groups, some manifest themselves at certain ages, while some seem to "run in families."

THE IMPACT OF GENETIC DISORDERS

The impact of genetic disorders is incalculable. It includes the anguish, pain, disability, and death of millions of Americans. It also includes the emotional anguish of parents and siblings of one born with a genetic defect. In addition, there are the social implications since many people born with a defect are in need

Table 16-1: Prevalence of Some Important Genetic Defects

Birth Defect	Number Afflicted
Congenital heart malformation	248,000
Muscular dystrophy	200,000
Polydactyly	184,000
Clubfoot	149,000
Diabetes mellitus	90,000
Cleft lip/palate	71,000
Spina bifida and hydrocephalus	53,000
Down's syndrome	44,000
Sickle-cell anemia	16,000
Hemophilia	12,400
Cystic fibrosis	10,000
PKU	3,100
Turner's syndrome	3,100
Thalassemia	1,000
Galactosemia	500
Tay-Sachs disease	100

Source of Data: The National Foundation/March of Dimes, *Birth Defects: The Tragedy and the Hope*, The Foundation, White Plains, N.Y., pp. 11–12.

of treatment, habilitation, and rehabilitation. The actual cost to families and to society can not even be estimated, but the economics are staggering.

Impact on Families

Birth defects are a leading cause of infant mortality. Infant mortality becomes especially important when viewed in terms of the number of life-years lost from this cause of death. For example, birth defects resulting in infant death account for 4.5 times as many life-years as heart disease and eight times as many as cancer.[22] This is important because birth defects frequently result in death in infancy while heart disease and cancer are more associated with death in later years, sometimes after the person has already made significant contributions to self and society.

Some genetic diseases manifest themselves in maturity rather than at birth; these diseases take on a particular significance because the presence of the disease may be unknown until after a new family has been formed. This is exemplified in the case of Huntington's disease, for example. Since Huntington's disease is autosomal dominant, each child from an affected parent has a 50 percent chance of developing the disease. The majority of cases are manifested at about 35 years of age, although symptoms may appear anywhere from 10 to 60 years of age. New families may already be established before it is known which of the children, if any, inherited Huntington's disease and the cycle starts all over again.

These kinds of genetic diseases are especially perplexing. Should children born of an affected parent be allowed to have children of their own? What about the children who have not inherited the disease? Should they be deprived of a normal family life as well as siblings who have inherited the disease? On the other hand, how can society hope to prevent further incidences if they are allowed to have children? (Examples of late appearing genetic disorders are presented in Figure 16-3.)

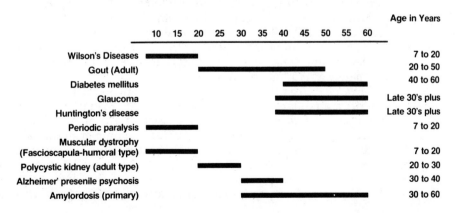

Figure 16-3:
Late Appearing Genetic Diseases

These and many other questions are exemplified in the case of spinal cerebral degeneration which attacks the central nervous system. Symptoms of the disease do not usually appear until the mid-20s. In 1970, with the assistance of the National Genetics Foundation, the Kenneth Swier family of South Dakota staged a family reunion. Of the 95 members of the family that attended, physicians found that twelve under the age of 12 years had early signs of the disease, and definite symptoms in eight adults were found. Since spinal cerebral degeneration is a dominant hereditary trait, the probability of transmitting the disease to children from those affected is 50 percent. Some of the members of this family have already decided not to have children, while others feel they are entitled to the same normal life as anyone else.[23]

Impact on Society

The impact of genetic disorders on society includes the loss of productivity of afflicted individuals, the provision for treatment and care, and the economic burden. For example, it is estimated that 36 million future life-years are lost as a result of birth defects, and about one-quarter of all hospital beds and places in institutions for the handicapped are occupied by those suffering from disorders due wholly or partially to genetic-related causes. In addition, 20 percent of all heart attacks occuring in men before the age of 60 years are caused by one of three genes that regulate the body's fat metabolism and another 5 percent is thought to be polygenic in nature. The single-gene that predisposes one to heart attack is estimated to occur in one in every 160 Americans.[24]

The responsibility for society to launch prevention programs is obvious. Unfortunately, we still do not have techniques for detecting many of the genetic defects so as to predict their probability in future generations. However, many can be detected before they result in irreversible damage to the person, and some can be diagnosed in utero and parents can elect to terminate the pregnancy.

Economic Significance

We have no way of estimating precisely the cost of genetic diseases. However, we do know, for example, that it costs approximately $250,000 to maintain a seriously defective person throughout his/her lifetime. Screening high risk pregnant women for Down's syndrome could prevent approximately 1000 cases of the disease each year. This would result in a lifetime care savings of approximately $250 million. There are about 5000 new cases of Down's syndrome each year in the United States. Using the $250,000 lifetime maintenance figure, the lifetime committed expenditure for *new* cases of Down's syndrome is approximately $1.25 billion each year.

Even the cost of *preventing* many of the genetic-related diseases is staggering, but prevention is much less an economic drain than treatment. For example, intensive care of a child with Tay-Sachs disease costs about $35,000 each year. There are an estimated 50 new cases each year resulting in an annual cost of about $1,750,000. Identifying carriers of Tay-Sachs using intrauterine diagnostic techniques and elective abortion could eliminate most annual new cases of the disease. The cost of the research to develop these new techniques was approximately equal to the cost of one year's care of children with Tay-Sachs disease.

THE CAUSES OF GENETIC
DISORDERS

We have discussed some of the general causes of genetic disorders, such as the maternal and environmental factors. Emphasis has been placed on the importance of healthful prenatal and postnatal environments. This importance needs to be reemphasized here since these environments can essentially be controlled by the mother and father who are able to provide the most suitable environment for ensuring the development of a healthy fetus and a healthy baby, child and adult. Besides the impact of the environment as a cause of genetic defects, scientists have identified three other genetic factors that can result in abnormalities. These are: (1) defective genes; (2) chromosomal aberrations; and (3) multifactorial or polygenic factors.

Defective Genes

This causation of genetic defects is sometimes referred to as single-gene causation. Essentially, these disorders are caused by a defective gene which may be recessive or dominant or sex-linked. It is estimated that about 2 percent of all genetic defects are caused by a single-gene. *Recessive single-gene* defects can occur only when *both* parents possess the gene and it is transmitted to the offspring through both the sperm and the egg. In the case where both parents possess the defective gene, there is a 25 percent chance that each child they have will be affected. There have been over 780 recessive single-gene disorders identified including sickle-cell anemia, Tay-Sachs disease, phenylketonuria, cystic fibrosis, and galactosemia.

Sickle-cell anemia and the sickle-cell trait are most prevalent among Afro-Americans. It is also found among peoples of Arabian, Greek, Maltese, Sicilian, Sardinian, Turkish and southern Asian ancestry.[25] Sickle-cell anemia is a recessive gene hereditary blood disease. It is characterized by sickle-shaped red blood cells instead of the normal round, donut-shaped cells. The disease "is complicated by the activities of the spleen, which quickly destroys the abnormal blood cells before the person can manufacture new ones to replace them."[26] This results in severe anemia.

Sickle-cell *trait* is present when the individual has inherited one recessive (defective) gene and one normal gene. One possessing the sickle-cell *trait* is normal, but mild symptoms may appear under severe environmental conditions, such as deprivation of sufficient oxygen which can result in the red blood cells sickling. This is rarely serious and those with the trait usually lead normal lives. Approximately 1 in 12 blacks possesses the sickle-cell trait while about 1 in 600 has the sickle-cell anemia.

Although the symptoms of sickle-cell anemia vary somewhat from one person to another, they can include paleness, listlessness and tiredness, shortness of breath, severe pain in arms, legs, back and, abdomen. Those with sickle-cell anemia are highly susceptible to infections which can result in intensification of symptoms and a sickle-cell crisis. Repeated crises can be fatal. (See Figure 16–4.)

Much research is being done related to finding effective drugs to treat those with sickle-cell anemia, finding anti-clotting drugs to prevent the sickled cells from blocking blood vessels, finding ways to transplant normal red blood cells, and finding safe ways to remove excess accumulations of iron in sickle-cell patients.

Tay-Sachs disease is an example of the group of diseases known as *inborn errors of metabolism.* It is a single-gene recessive hereditary defect. As with other recessive genetic defects, both parents carrying the trait have a 25 percent probability of transmitting the disease to *each* of their children.

Tay-Sachs disease is characterized by a lack of the enzyme hexosaminidase A (Hex A). Hex A is necessary for the body to properly use lipids (fats). These fatty substances therefore, accumulate in the cells, especially brain cells, resulting in destruction of the brain cells and eventually death of the child. The chief fatty substance that is present in brain cells is sphingolipids. These are necessary in certain amounts for proper functioning of the brain. Hex A ensures that the amount of sphingolipids remain at the necessary level. However, a child with Tay-Sachs disease does not produce Hex A which results in an accumulation of the sphingolipids causing symptoms of Tay-Sachs disease.

Approximately 82 percent of babies born with Tay-Sachs disease are born to parents who have no previous family history of the disease. It is, therefore, important for couples of Jewish ancestry to have a simple blood test that can detect the presence of the trait prior to the woman becoming pregnant. If both prospective parents have the trait, they should be counseled about the prospects of their children being born defective. If they decide to proceed with having children, the fetus can be monitored by amniocentesis. If this diagnostic test indicates that there is no Hex A in the amniotic fluid, the developing fetus has

Figure 16-4:

Sickle Cell Disease
Probabilities of Effects in Offspring

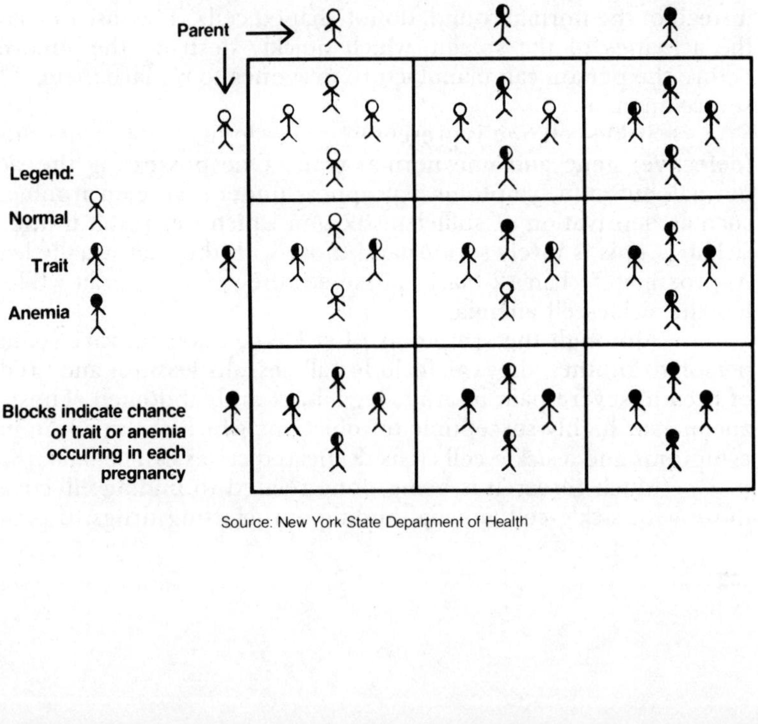

Legend:

Normal

Trait

Anemia

Blocks indicate chance
of trait or anemia
occurring in each
pregnancy

Source: New York State Department of Health

the disease and the parents may choose to terminate the pregnancy. (Amniocentesis is discussed in the section entitled "Diagnosing Genetic Defects" on page 412.)

Cystic fibrosis is a leading cause of death in white children. It is characterized by a thick, sticky mucus in the respiratory and digestive systems. In the lungs, the thick mucus interferes with breathing and results in susceptibility to respiratory diseases and finally lung damage. In the digestive system, the thick mucus interferes with the secretion of the pancreatic enzymes into the small intestine resulting in maladsorption of nutrients. It is estimated that cystic fibrosis occurs in 1 in every 1600 births. At present, there is no test to predict which prospective parents are carrying the recessive gene responsible for transmitting cystic fibrosis to the child. It is estimated that there are approximately 10 million people who possess the defective gene that causes cystic fibrosis. However, the disease can be detected by what is known as the "sweat test" in infants afflicted with cystic fibrosis. Since these infants have a high salt content in their sweat, this test can result in early diagnosis of the disease and appropriate treatment can be administered preventing much of the lung damage that would otherwise take place.

Generally, treatment for cystic fibrosis consists of postural drainage that assists the child to expectorate mucus from the lungs and the bronchial tubes; the use of aerosol inhalants that loosen the thick mucus; medications, such as antibiotics to prevent respiratory infections; diet supplements, such as vitamins; and administration of pancreatic enzymes. As a result, more cystic fibrosis children are living longer and more normal lives.[27]

Galactosemia is characterized by the inability for the child to metabolize the sugar galactose which is chiefly found in milk. Galactosemia is another one of the inborn errors of metabolism. The enzyme galactolinase is essential for metabolizing galactose. However, this enzyme is lacking in infants with galactosemia and as a result, galactose builds up in the lens of the eye causing genetic cataract. The toxic levels of galactose may also cause damage to the liver and brain. In the latter case, mental retardation results.

Galactosemia can be detected by blood and urine tests in the infant and by amniocentesis during prenatal life. The disease is treated by special maternal diets during pregnancy and special diets for the infant after birth. In many cases, the manifestations of the disease can be prevented.

Dominant, single-gene defects, unlike the recessive, single-gene defects, can be transmitted to the offspring by only one parent who possesses the defective gene. If one parent possesses the dominant, defective gene, the risk of *each* child being afflicted with the defect is 50 percent. If both parents carry the gene, the risk is 75 percent. Scientists have identified 940 dominant, single-gene defects with Huntington's disease being one of the most dramatic.

Huntington's disease was first described in 1872 by Dr. George Huntington. He named the disease hereditary chorea because of the characteristic symptoms resulting from degeneration of the nervous system. These symptoms include uncontrollable jerky, twisting muscular movements, and mental abnormalities.

There are no laboratory tests available to detect Huntington's disease. At present, we must wait for specific symptoms to appear before a diagnosis can be made. There is no cure for Huntington's disease although drugs are available to lessen some of the severe symptoms. Those with the disease frequently die of such complications as heart failure or pneumonia.

It especially is important for research in this area to direct its attention to identifying those who carry the defective gene *before* they have children. In this way new cases can be prevented. It is estimated that approximately 14,000 Americans have Huntington's disease.

The *sex-linked, single-gene* disorders result from a defective gene that is carried on the X-chromosome. At present, about 150 such defects have been identified. Female babies receive one X chromosome from their mothers and one X-chromosome from their fathers. Male babies always receive the Y-chromosome from their fathers and an X-chromosome from their mothers. Since female babies have two X-chromosomes one can be defective and will not manifest the disorder it controls because it is balanced by the other normal X-chromosome. Therefore, a female may carry the trait for a recessive sex-linked disorder but not the disease. However, if a male baby receives the defective X-chromosome from its mother, he will be affected by the disease. This risk of transmitting the defect to each male offspring is 50 percent if the defective gene is present. If a male with an x-linked disease marries a woman carrier of the disease, the female children may also be affected since the father will transmit the defective X-chromosome to his daughter and the mother *may* transmit her defective X-chromosome to the daughter. There are many examples of x-linked defects including hemophilia, one form of muscular dystrophy (the Duchenne type), and the Lesch-Nyhan syndrome.

Hemophilia is sometimes referred to as the "bleeder disease" because the person has a deficiency in one of several blood components that is necessary for clotting. It affects an estimated 12,000 to 13,000 Americans under the age of 20 years. There is an annual incidence of approximately 1,200. It can be detected by a blood test and is treated by blood transfusions to replace the antihemophilic globulin that is deficient, and by the use of certain medications. Hemophiliacs are in danger of excessive bleeding from injury and the complications resulting from this bleeding.

The Duchenne type muscular dystrophy is the most severe and common of the several forms of muscular dystrophies. The symptoms of the disease begin in the muscles of the pelvic girdle and progress to the shoulders and eventually to most of the body's voluntary musculature.

The symptoms of Duchenne muscular dystrophy usually appear between the ages of 2 and 6 years. It is sometimes apparent shortly after birth. The disease progresses rapidly with death occurring within 10 to 15 years after clinical symptoms appear. Antibiotic therapy has been effective in delaying death.

The *Lesch-Nyhan syndrome* is a rare disease that is characterized by mental retardation and compulsive self-mutilation and life-threatening uremia that results in kidney damage. It is caused by a defective enzyme that results in overproduction of uric acid. The use of the drug allopurinol has been found to be effective in inhibiting the formation of uric acid which lessens the likelihood of uremia developing. A test of prospective mothers can determine whether or not they are carrying the abnormal gene. Amniocentesis is also used to determine the genetic status of the fetus in utero.

Chromosomal defects can result from aberrations of whole chromosomes, as in trisomy 21, Down's syndrome; parts of chromosomes, as in translocation, Down's syndrome; or too many or too few chromosomes in a cell, as in mosaicism, Down's syndrome. "Significant chromosomal abnormalities occur in approximately one of every 250 live births, or an incidence of 0.4 percent."[28] (See Figure 16–5.)

Down's syndrome (mongolism) is a typical example of a genetic defect resulting from a chromosomal aberration. There are three genetic types of Down's syndrome: (1) trisomy 21; (2) translocation; and (3) mosaicism. (See Figure 16–6.) *Trisomy 21* is the result of three number 21 chromosomes instead of the normal two. It is thought to take place because of a phenomenon in either

Figure 16-5:

Formation of a Translocation Chromosome

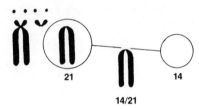

14/21

A translocation occurs when a piece of one chromosome breaks off and attaches to a different chromosome. This "translocation chromosome" has been formed by the breaking and rejoining of chromosomes 14 and 21 (with loss of the little pieces).

Source: United States Department of Health, Education, and Welfare, DHEW Publication No. (NIH) 74-538, p. 73.

Figure 16-6:

Genetic Types of Down's Syndrome

13 14 15	21 22 Sex	
𝕏𝕏 𝕏𝕏 𝕏 𝕏	𝕏 𝕏𝕏 𝕏𝕏	Normal female with 15:21 translocation
𝕏𝕏 𝕏𝕏 𝕏 𝕏	𝕏𝕏 𝕏𝕏 𝕏𝕏	Down's syndrome female with 15:21 translocation
𝕏𝕏 𝕏𝕏 𝕏𝕏	𝕏𝕏𝕏 𝕏𝕏 𝕏𝕏	Down's syndrome male with trisomy 21
𝕏𝕏 𝕏𝕏 𝕏𝕏	𝕏𝕏 𝕏𝕏 𝕏𝕏	Down's syndrome male with 21:21 isochromosome

Source: United States Department of Health, Education, and Welfare, DHEW Publication No. (NIH) 74-538, p. 7.

the maternal egg or paternal sperm. Since Down's syndrome is most prevalent in children born of women over 45 years of age, it is theorized that the older eggs in meiosis produces the extra chromosome. It is known, for example, that women possess all their eggs at birth and like the woman herself who is over 45 years of age, so are her eggs. Approximately 95 percent of all cases of Down's syndrome are due to trisomy 21.

Down's syndrome is characterized by mild to severe mental retardation accompanied by recognizable physical features. It is one of the most common forms of mental retardation. The presence of it during fetal life can be detected by amniocentesis. Incidentally, these children are more susceptible to heart defects, respiratory infections and leukemia than are normal children.

Down's syndrome resulting from *translocation* accounts for approximately 4 percent of all cases, while *mosaicism* is very rare. Translocation results from one of the D group of chromosomes (number 13, 14, and 15) translocating a portion of the chromosome, say 14, to, in effect, create a third number 21 chromosome. Mosaicism is, essentially, the presence of different chromosome numbers in different body cells; some cells contain 46 while others contain 47 chromosomes.

Scientists have identified five risk factors associated with Down's syndrome as follows:

- *Advanced maternal age.* The risk of having a baby with Down's syndrome increases significantly with age of the mother at the time of pregnancy. The risk for women between the ages of 40 and 45 years is about 1 in 100. Over the age of 45 years the risk increases to about 1 in 65 births. This is compared to women under age 35 years where the risk is about 1 in 1500 births. (See Figure 16–7.)

- *Mothers who have had a previous child with Down's syndrome.* Up to age 35 years of the mother, the risk for having a second child with Down's syndrome is about 1 percent.

- *Pregnancy of a woman with Down's syndrome.* Although pregnancies among women with mongolism are rare, the risk is about 50 percent.

- *Parental mosaicism.* Fathers or mothers with a trisomy 21 cell population have a high, but unpredictable risk of having a child with Down's syndrome.

- *Familial translocation.* The risk of having a child with Down's syndrome from a mother with a D/21 chromosomal translocation is about 20 percent. If the father possesses this translocation, the risk is only about 2 percent. However, if either parent carries a balanced 21/21 translocation, the risk is 100 percent.[29]

Multifactorial Inheritance

Multifactorial inheritance is less defined than either single-gene or chromosomal inheritance. Multifactorial or polygenic inheritance includes a rather large group of disorders that result from the interaction of several genes or the interaction of genetic material with the prenatal environment. The inci-

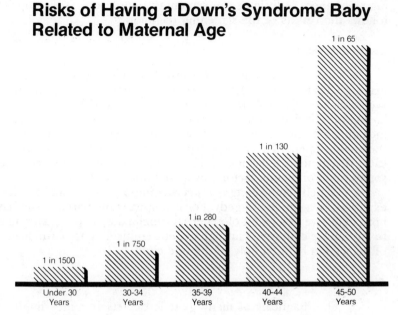

Figure 16-7

Risks of Having a Down's Syndrome Baby Related to Maternal Age

Source of Data: U.S.Dep't of Health, Education, and Welfare, Public Health Service DHEW Publication No (NIH) 74–536. p. 10.

dence of multifactorial diseases is somewhat obscure, but it has been placed somewhere between 1.7 to 2.6 percent of all live births.[30] It is possible that in some cases of multifactorial inheritance the individual actually inherits a greater susceptibility to environmental factors than do others which then leads to the disease. It is thought that this probably takes place in the case of allergy, atherosclerosis, hypertension, some forms of cancer and mental illnesses, along with many other diseases. Finally, authorities generally agree that even though a multifactorial disease occurs in a family, the chances of a repeat of the disease in future offspring is rare, probably about 5 percent.

PREVENTION OF GENETIC DISORDERS

Genetic Screening

Essentially, genetic screening consists of examining, usually high risk populations, to determine whether certain individuals are carriers of a specific genetic anomalie, or whether there are familial risks related to certain genetic defects. The importance of genetic screening rests with the detection of abnormal genetic potentials and preventing new cases of the defect from occurring. Although many genetic-related defects still allude scientists and defy detection, many others can be detected by rather simple laboratory tests.

Genetic screening cannot adequately be separated from genetic counseling since there is little use in screening people unless appropriate counseling follows the results of the screening techniques.

Genetic Counseling

Genetic counseling is a relatively new specialty of genetic medicine. Its major goal is to prevent the occurrence of genetic defects. The genetic counselor accomplishes this goal through determining the risks potential parents face in having a defective child. This can be achieved through a variety of techniques including genetic screening, and family histories. The family history necessitates the establishment of a family pedigree. The genetic counselor must determine the cause of a genetic defect in a family, whether it is due to defective genes, chromosomes, environmental factors, or a combination of these.

Genetic counseling is especially important for families that have already experienced a genetic tragedy. For example, some parents who have had a child born defective as a result of maternal rubella during pregnancy may be reluctant to have more children. Through genetic counseling they will learn that this kind of defect can happen only to the one child.

Diagnosing Genetic Defects

The diagnosis of many genetic defects is quite simple since they are obvious at birth; for example, cleft lip/palate or club foot. Some defects can be diagnosed between the sixteenth and twentieth weeks of pregnancy through amniocentesis. This involves the taking of a sample of amniotic fluid that surrounds the fetus. The procedure is relatively simple and safe when done by a competent physician. It basically is achieved by inserting a hypodermic needle through the mother's abdominal wall into the uterus and withdrawing some of the amniotic fluid. This fluid contains cells that were shed by the fetus during its growth. These are cultured in the laboratory and examined for biochemical and chromosomal defects. (See Figure 16–8.)

Other diagnostic techniques being used with a high level of success are chemical analysis of the amniotic fluid. This can be done in conjunction with examination of fetal cells withdrawn by amniocentesis. Some inborn errors of metabolism can be diagnosed in this manner. Fetal blood sampling is used to detect some blood defects; ultrasonics that take a "picture" of the fetus may detect structural or developmental deformities; and the use of x-ray late in pregnancy in sometimes helpful in detecting developmental problems.

TREATMENT OF GENETIC DISORDERS

Very few genetic disorders can be cured. Most of those that can are structural malformations, such as club foot and polydactyly. Many, however, can be treated by (1) chemical regulation; (2) corrective surgery; and (3) rehabilitation.

Figure 16-8
Amniocentesis

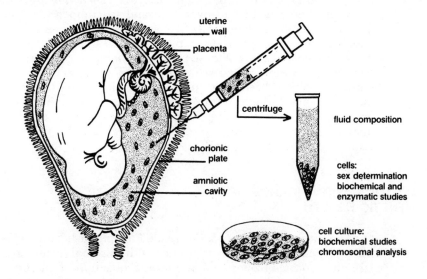

uterine wall
placenta
centrifuge
fluid composition
chorionic plate
cells:
sex determination
biochemical and
enzymatic studies
amniotic cavity
cell culture:
biochemical studies
chromosomal analysis

Chemical Regulation

This area of treatment includes medication for controlling symptoms, and special diets to effect metabolic disturbances resulting from inborn errors of metabolism. In many cases, the afflicted persons can lead fairly normal lives. In other cases, the symptoms can be alleviated and in others, further damage prevented. Some genetic defects require a combination of treatments while for others there is no treatment at all.

Corrective Surgery

Corrective surgery can cure some structural defects, but surgical techniques also are limited. Surgery for large structures of the body has nearly reached its peak and new advances will need to focus on organ transplants and cellular engineering. Some examples of genetic disorders that can be corrected or reduced by surgery are some heart malformations, organ transplants, and tissue grafts.

In addition, some exciting progress is being made in the whole area of genetic and molecular engineering. This may or may not be a form of surgery depending upon the nature of the engineering and how one wishes to interpret it. Certainly, genetic cloning is a form of surgery, at least in its initial stages.

Rehabilitation

Rehabilitation techniques are making it possible for many individuals to become more effective in many aspects of living. For example, some of the

413

mentally retarded can be taught to do many everyday tasks for themselves, and, in some cases, to make a living at certain kinds of occupations.

Other persons with genetic disorders, such as many of the physical handicaps, are being helped to overcome and to compensate for these handicaps. Recent federal legislation has brought about a revolution in the lives of the handicapped. There is a dramatic change in the attitudes associated with the handicapped and many of these people are beginning to become more productive members of society. Their self-sufficiency is the result chiefly of two factors: (1) improved physical environments that are eliminating barriers to their ability to function, and (2) the handicap's determination to be independent and contributing members of society. Depending upon the nature of the defect, rehabilitation may direct its attention toward the physical, intellectual, emotional, or social aspects of life, but frequently, it includes several of these areas.

POLITICAL SIGNIFICANCE OF GENETIC HEALTH

The political actions or inactions related to genetic health are frequently a reflection of the social attitudes associated with this vital health area. Social attitudes are often formed from total ignorance, acquisition of misconceptions, misinformation, and fear. Research into genetic health has made such enormous advances in the past two or three decades that the general public, legislators, and even members of the medical sciences have been unable to keep up with the flow of information. As a result, confusion, fear, and anxiety have permeated the American society. In spite of this, we need to recognize that certain realities exist: (1) discoveries in genetics can be, but need not be awesome; (2) there is a need for a national genetic health program (the numerous voluntary health agencies in genetic-related health problems have adequately demonstrated this need); (3) there is a need for a national genetic policy, especially related to further research into genetic engineering and molecular biology; and (4) legislators can no longer ignore the existence of the importance of genetic health to the survival of society —they must begin to be informed and to make some very difficult decisions.

National Genetic Health Program

A national genetic health program can take a variety of forms. However, there are several fundamental factors that must be considered, for instance, the whole complex area of scientific, political, and public ethics that surround any significant social issue. This was dramatically illustrated in July, 1978 when the first "test-tube" baby was born in England. Conception of the mother's egg took place in the laboratory and the embryo grown in a "test-tube" and later transplanted in the mother's uterus where it grew to maturity and was born by caesarean section. Definitions, limitations, freedoms, laws, and their interpretations, and new legislation need to be considered as bases for a national genetic health program.

We can not afford to allow policies governing genetic health to evolve "naturally." A national concerted effort is urgently needed to bring about, as rapidly as possible, appropriate application of research findings to the genetic health of people.

What constitutes our present national genetic program? At present, the program can be described as having four elements: (1) individual research scientists; (2) voluntary health agencies; (3) governmental agencies; and (4) a communications network. Generally, individual scientists are located at university settings or university medical colleges functioning as a result of grants from government, voluntary health agencies, or private foundations. Examples of government agencies concerned with genetic health research and application are the National Institute of General Medical Sciences and the National Institute of Neurological Diseases and Stroke. In addition, there are numerous voluntary health agencies concerned with specific genetic health issues. Some are concerned with a specific genetic defect or group of defects, while others are concerned more generally with genetic health.

It would appear that what is needed is a national genetic health council made up of individuals from both the private and public sectors. Among other things, this council would be responsible for monitoring research, making appropriate legislative recommendations, establishing a viable communications network and public education related to genetic health, and identifying areas of research need and funding sources. Such a council would make it possible for reducing duplication in services and research, coordination of efforts, establishing national genetic screening programs, reducing waste in terms of human resources and funds, and, most importantly, bringing about the application of new discoveries for improving the genetic health of people in the most rapid manner possible.

The legal, ethical, and moral issues raised by the whole area of genetic research, gene therapy, molecular biology, and genetic medicine dictate that a national genetic health policy is long over-due. As long ago as 1970, the proceedings of the Fogarty International Center raised many urgent concerns which could be the preliminary basis for establishing a national genetic health policy. For example the following questions were discussed:

- Who shall meet the ethical issues raised by prenatal diagnosis?
- When is abortion murder?
- What will prenatal diagnosis do to the rate of elimination of recessive genes with deleterious effects?
- How do we strike the balance between risks to mother and fetus, on the one hand, and disease prevention on the other?
- What is the significance of prenatal diagnosis for control of disease?[31]

Neel concluded during this conference that "it is an encouraging sign of our growing awareness of these problems that with the development of prenatal diagnosis the need to consider the ethical implications has been so early recognized."[32] However, more than a decade later no specific national genetic health policy has been established, but the urgency continues. Neel suggested that an expanded committee of the American Society of Human Genetics and the American College of Obstetrics and Gynecology could function to update a list of those genetic defects that would warrant termination of pregnancy, for example.[33] However, before any significant and comprehensive national genetic health policy can be formulated, there are numerous political decisions that must be made. These will necessarily result from urgings from the scientific community and from the electorate.

Political Decisions

Who will decide when a genetic defect is in fact a defect? How severe does the abnormality have to be before it is a defect? Should a carrier of a genetic defect be allowed to have children? Who will decide this? At what stage of fetal development does the fertilized egg become a person? These and many other questions have been grappled with by scientists, the courts, and others concerned with answers. It was in 1884 that Justice Oliver Wendell Holmes ruled that "the unborn child was a part of the mother at the time of injury," which meant that a child born defective or injured had no legal recourse against the mother or others who may have caused injury while the mother was pregnant. However, this position was reversed in 1946 in a case where a fetus was negligently injured during delivery. The court stated in this case that "the law is presumed to keep pace with the sciences and medical science certainly has made progress since 1884."[34] Thus, the courts have recognized, at least in these kinds of circumstances, the fetus as a person. However, there are instances of contradiction, as, for example, in legalized abortion.

Legislators will continue to be faced with decisions of enormous proportions as advances in genetic medicine are made. Moreover, the general citizenry will need to be kept informed of these advances since political decisions are greatly influenced by constituent support or opposition. For example, amniocentesis will become useless as a diagnostic technique if legislators should be influenced to pass laws that would forbid abortion under any circumstances. In 1869 the Roman Catholic Church equated abortion with murder.[35] If this concept should be revived and enacted into law, monitoring a fetus of high risk parents would be meaningless since it would be illegal to terminate the pregnancy even though it were certain the child would be deformed. It would further mean that larger numbers of babies with birth defects would be born, many doomed to die in agony within a few years. There would be increased cost to the family and society for care of these infants, and, of course, the anguish of the family during the baby's dying days, weeks, or years would be substantial.

Other political decisions are also necessary as a result of progress being made in gene therapy and genetic engineering. At a conference sponsored by the National Institute of Neurological Diseases and Stroke the following statement on the subject was made:

> With regard to potential misuse of research results concerning gene therapy, it was felt that all scientific developments can be used to benefit or harm mankind. The new techniques would not provide more dangerous possibilities for the abuse of human development or behavior than the already available methods including artificial insemination, hormones, drugs, or behavioral techniques. Society has to protect itself

against the misuse of any new findings, not by preventing their discovery (through curtailing research) but by establishing new reasonable laws and enforcing them properly. When the new techniques have actually developed to the stage at which abuses are feasible, scientists should inform the public and together with legal experts and concerned laymen plan the proper development of laws.[36]

Thus, humanity is once again at a crossroads—one path that signals the right to be born healthy, another path to continue the roulette of the "genes games," or another being the possibility of misapplication of new-founded genetic knowledge. Obviously, which route or routes we take cannot be decided by one person, a group of people, a political party—it is a decision that involves all of society.

GLOSSARY

Allele: The pairing of genes.

Chromosomes: Consist of the genes and are the determiners of genetic makeup.

Congenital: A condition occurring during fetal development or at the time of birth.

Gamete: Sperm or egg.

Gene mutation: An alteration in a gene affecting hereditary potential.

Genetic: Characteristics controlled by genes, hereditary.

Genetic code: The hereditary characteristics contained within the germ cells of both sexes.

Genetic drift: Random fluctuations in the frequencies of certain alleles occurring in small populations.

Genetic health: The potential level of functioning ability as determined by genetic makeup.

Genetic pool: The total genotype of a person.

Genotype: One's actual gene combinations as determined at the time of conception.

Heterozygous: A genetic characteristic containing a dominant and recessive gene.

Homozygous: A genetic characteristic containing two dominant or two recessive genes.

Meiosis: A form of cell division that takes place in the germ cells resulting in daughter cells containing one-half the chromosomes of the mother cell. Also called reduction division.

Perinatal period: The time from conception to one month following birth.

Ribosome: The site of protein synthesis within a cell.

Zygote: The fertilized egg.

SUMMARY

Genetic health is determined by the genes, the chromosomes, and the prenatal environment. The science of genetics strives to discover the truth about the development of life, its perpetuation, and alterations as directed by the mechanisms contained in the genes.

The genetic code is contained within the hereditary characteristics of the 23 chromosomes from the ovum and the 23 chromosomes from the sperm. This code, or genotype, is determined at the moment of conception. The genotypes and the action of the prenatal environment determine the phenotypes of the new life. The total genotype is called the genetic pool.

Genetic health is determined by the genes, chromosomes, and the maternal and greater environments. We are genetically healthy if our functioning ability is not significantly interfered with by a genetic defect.

The potential for the manifestation of a genetic defect may occur during any of six periods: in the germ cell, gamete, zygote, fetus, newborn, or later in life. Some potentials for genetic defects can be detected by screening techniques and laboratory tests either before pregnancy occurs or during fetal development.

An inherited trait is controlled by the genes, while a congenital defect occurs during fetal development or at the time of birth. Genetic research is generally concentrated on the overall management of genetic diseases. It includes discovering new techniques for prevention, diagnosis, and treatment of these conditions.

The causes of genetic disorders are from defective genes, chromosomal aberrations, or multifactorial. Defective genes may be recessive, single gene, dominant, single gene or sex-linked, single gene. Chromosomal aberrations may be associated with whole chromosomes, parts of chromosomes (translocation), or too few or too many chromosomes in body cells (mosaicism). Multifactorial inheritance results from the interaction of several genes or of genetic material with the prenatal environment.

The prevention of genetic disorders revolves around education of the public, improved genetic screening programs, genetic counseling of high risk groups, and improved diagnostic techniques. Treatment of genetic disorders can help to reduce or eliminate the devastating effects of some genetic disorders. What is needed is a national genetic health program and policy. This will necessitate some important and difficult political decisions.

PROBLEMS FOR DISCUSSION

1. Analyze the elements in a definition of genetic health: development of life, its perpetuation, and alterations. What determines genetic health?
2. Discuss the principles of genetics including the genetic code, phenotypes, and genotypes.
3. Describe the effects of genetic pools on evolutions. What is evolution? What factors are responsible for evolution?
4. What is DNA? What is its relation to heredity? To RNA? What are the forms of RNA? What are their functions? What is the DNA helix?
5. Distinguish between mitosis and meiosis.
6. What conditions does nature provide the fetus to ensure its genetic health? Why do genetic defects sometimes appear?
7. How important is the maternal environment to the developing fetus? What are some things that the mother should do to decrease the possibilities of an adverse prenatal environment?
8. List some factors in the external environment that can affect the developing fetus. What is society doing to reduce these factors?
9. What diagnostic techniques are available for detecting potential genetic defects?
10. Distinguish between inherited and congenital defects.
11. What are some recent advances in genetic research? What are their significances to society?

12. What is genetic cloning? Discuss the possible impact of genetic engineering on humanity. Include in the discussion the possibilities for misuse and the need for controls.
13. Discuss the evolution of genetic medicine and its importance to solving some of the genetic health problems.
14. In what ways has our ability to grow, store, and distribute human cells contributed to genetic research? What impact will this have on the future of genetic defects?
15. Discuss why societal attitudes about genetic health are important. List some of the areas genetic misconceptions are most prevalent. What needs to be done to eliminate these misconceptions?
16. Discuss the extent of genetic health problems in the United States. What are their impact on family, society, and economic drain?
17. List and describe the various causes of genetic health problems. Give at least one example for each cause.
18. What are the risk factors associated with Down's syndrome?
19. List the methods available for preventing genetic disorders. What is the effect of each?
20. How effective are the various treatments for genetic defects? Give examples of genetic defects that are treated by each method.
21. What are the political implications of genetic health problems?
22. Discuss the legal implications associated with genetic health.

REFERENCES

1. CRM Books, *Life and Health,* Del Mar, Cal., 1972, p. 266.
2. ROSENTHAL, DAVID, *Genetic Theory and Abnormal Behavior,* McGraw-Hill Book Company, New York, 1970, p. 2.
3. SAVAGE, JAY M., *Evolution,* 2nd ed. Holt, Rinehart and Winston, Inc., New York, 1969, pp. 50–51.
4. SULLIVAN, NAVIN, *The Message of the Genes.* Basic Books, Inc., New York, 1967, p. 122.
5. SAVAGE, *op. cit.,* pp. 9–11.
6. LINDE, SHIRLEY MOTTER, *Sickle Cell: A Complete Guide to Prevention and Treatment.* Pavilion Publishing Company, New York, 1972, pp. 64–65.
7. The National Foundation/March of Dimes, *Preventing Birth Defects Caused by Rubella,* The Foundation, White Plains, N.Y., (Undated).
8. *Essentials of Life and Health,* 2nd ed. CRM Books, Random House, Inc., New York, 1977, p. 149.
9. The National Foundation/March of Dimes, *Birth Defects: The Tragedy and the Hope.* The Foundation, White Plains, N.Y., 1975, p. 7.
10. MELLIN, GILBERT W., "The Frequency of Birth Defects," *Birth Defects.* Morris Fishbein (ed.), J. B. Lippincott, Co., Philadelphia, 1963, p. 3.
11. The National Foundation/March of Dimes, *Birth Defects, op. cit.,* p. 3.
12. *Ibid.,* p. 4.

13. The National Institute of General Medical Sciences, *What Are the Facts About Genetic Disease?* National Institutes of Health, DHEW Publication No. (NIH) 75-370, Bethesda, Md., 1975, p. 29.

14. AUSUBEL, FREDERICK, JON BECKWITH, and KAARE JENSSEN, "The Politics of Genetic Engineering: Who Decides Who's Defective?" *Psychology Today,* June, 1974, pp. 32–33.

15. The National Institute of General Medical Sciences, *op. cit.,* p. 23.

16. PINES, MAYA, *The New Human Genetics,* The National Institute of General Medical Sciences, DHEW Publication No. (NIH) 76–662, p. 3.

17. *Ibid.,* p. 21.

18. *Ibid.,* p. 23.

19. National Foundation/March of Dimes, *Questions and Answers on Birth Defects,* The Foundation, White Plains, N.Y. (undated).

20. *Birth Defects: The Tragedy and the Hope, op. cit.,* p. 2.

21. *What Are the Facts About Genetic Disease? op. cit.,* p. 6.

22. *What Are the Facts About Genetic Disease? op. cit.,* p. 8.

23. *Time: The Weekly Newsmagazine,* January 25, 1971.

24. *What Are the Facts About Genetic Disease? op. cit.,* p. 21.

25. The National Foundation/March of Dimes, *Fast Facts About Sickle-cell Anemia,* The Foundation, White Plains, N.Y. (undated).

26. CRM Books, *Life and Health, op. cit.,* p. 144.

27. Cystic Fibrosis Foundation, *Questions and Facts About Cystic Fibrosis,* The Foundation, Atlanta, Ga., (undated).

28. *What Are the Facts About Genetic Disease? op. cit.,* p. 10.

29. The National Institute of Child Health and Human Development, *Antenatal Diagnosis and Down's Syndrome,* DHEW Publication, No. (NIH) 74–538, pp. 5–6.

30. *What Are the Facts About Genetic Disease? op. cit.,* p. 11.

31. NEEL, JAMES V., "Ethical Issues Resulting From Prenatal Diagnosis," Maureen Harris (ed.), *Early Diagnosis of Human Genetics: Scientific and Ethical Considerations,* National Institutes of Health, HEW Publication No. (NIH) 72–25, Bethesda, Md., pp. 219–228.

32. *Ibid.,* p. 228.

33. *Ibid.,* p. 220.

34. SADLER, BLAIR L., "The Law and the Unborn Child: A Brief Review of Emerging Problems," Maureen Harris (ed.), *op. cit.,* p. 212.

35. *Ibid.,* p. 213.

36. FREESE, ERNST, (ed.), *The Prospects of Gene Therapy,* National Institutes of Health, DHEW, Publication No. (NIH) 72–61, Bethesda, Md., 1972, p. 15.

17

health through safe living

421

EPIDEMIOLOGY OF ACCIDENTS

Introduction

It has been said that preceding every accident there has been a careless act. The act may be by the person whose behavior in itself is hazardous, by the design of a product that failed to recognize faults in construction, by a worker who failed to follow specifications, or by a natural phenomenon that created a hazardous condition not recognized or heeded by people. Whatever the initial cause of an accident, most can be prevented through improved human behavior, design of products, and care in manufacture. With these thoughts in mind, it is necessary to reemphasize the importance of taking personal responsibility for health. Know what you are buying, how to use it, and take the necessary precautions to prevent accidents from occurring.

Who Has Accidents?

As we know, accidents are the fourth leading cause of death in the United States for all ages, claiming more than 103,000 lives each year. Accidents, however, are the *leading* cause of death for people in ages 1 to 44 years claiming approximately 55,800 lives each year. Table 17–1 shows the number of deaths from accidents for various age groups. It will be noted that the largest number of accidental deaths occur in the 15–24 year age group, tapering slightly in the 25–44 and 45–64 year age groups, rising again in the 65 years and over age group. It is also significant to note that in all age groups, male accidental deaths exceed females.

Although accidents claim only about one-tenth as many lives each year as cardiovascular diseases, they are important because most of these lives are lost during the productive years. Therefore, in terms of human effectiveness and productivity, many more life-years are lost as a result of accidents than the three leading causes of death combined.

These figures become even more significant when placed in the context of the total number of annual deaths for each age group. Table 17–2 places accidental deaths each year in perspective with total annual deaths. The percentage of annual accidental deaths is extremely significant in childhood and adolescence showing a marked decrease after age 25 years. Obviously, careless behavior is much more prevalent among the young. One could conclude that chronological

Table 17–1: Accidental Deaths Each Year in Selected Age Groups

	AGE GROUPS					
	1—4 years	*5—14 years*	*15—24 years*	*25—44 years*	*45—64 years*	*65 years and ove*
Total	3,500	6,300	24,300	22,400	19,000	24,000
Male	2,100	4,300	19,200	17,700	13,600	12,500
Female	1,400	2,000	5,100	4,700	5,400	11,500

Source of Data: *Facts of Life and Death*, U.S. Department of Health, Education, and Welfare, National Cente for Health Statistics, 1979.

and physical maturity are accompanied by psychosocial maturity. This would appear to result in greater concern for one's own safety and avoiding hazards that are likely to result in injury or death. (The ten leading causes of accidental deaths are shown in Table 17–3.)

Accidental Injuries

Statistics on accidental injuries can be quite misleading since many never come to the attention of medical personnel and are therefore not recorded. The three leading sources of accidental injuries are: (1) motor vehicles; (2) in and around the home; and (3) the workplace. There are approximately 5.2 million injuries each year from motor vehicle accidents; 9.9 million work-related; and over 31 million that occur in the home. Of all the annual *deaths* from all accidents,

Table 17–2: Annual Accidental Deaths in Relation to Total Deaths for Selected Age Groups

Age Groups	ANNUAL NO. OF DEATHS FROM ALL CAUSES			PERCENT OF DEATHS DUE TO ACCIDENTS		
	Total	Male	Female	Total	Male	Female
1—4 years	8,600	5,000	3,600	40.6	42.0	38.8
5—14 years	12,900	8,100	4,800	48.8	53.0	41.6
15—24 years	46,200	34,300	11,900	52.5	55.9	42.8
25—44 years	101,900	67,300	34,600	21.9	26.3	13.6
45—64 years	446,200	285,100	161,100	4.3	4.7	3.4
65 years +	1,245,200	624,800	620,400	1.9	2.0	1.9
Totals*	1,861,000	1,024,600	836,400	5.3	6.7	3.6

*There are an additional 48,300 infant deaths (under 1 year of age) not shown in the table.

Source of Data: *Facts of Life and Death*, U.S. Department of Health, Education, and Welfare, National Center for Health Statistics, 1979.

Table 17–3: The Ten Leading Causes of Accidental Deaths

Cause	Annual Number of Deaths*
1. Motor vehicle accidents	47,000
2. Accidental falls	14,100
3. Fires	6,300
4. Drowning	5,700
5. Poisoning by solid and liquid substances	4,200
6. Respiratory obstruction and suffocation	3,000
7. Surgical and medical complications and misadventures	3,000
8. Firearms	2,100
9. Projected and falling objects	1,900
10. Poisoning by gases and vapors	1,600

*Rounded to the nearest one hundred.

Source of Data: *Facts of Life and Death*, U.S. Department of Health, Education, and Welfare, National Center for Health Statistics, 1979.

nearly 47 percent result from motor vehicle accidents (more than 47,000). The next highest number of annual deaths results from falls, accounting for more than 14,000, followed by fires claiming more than 6,000 lives each year. Finally, the total number of accidental injuries in the United States each year is in excess of 75 million, many of which result from hazardous products as well as careless behavior.

Consumer Products and Injuries

According to the United States Consumer Product Safety Commission there are approximately 9.3 million injuries requiring hospital emergency room treatment in a given year, resulting from consumer products. The type of products resulting in high incidences of injuries varies depending upon the age of the person using it. For example, bicycles and equipment are the most frequently related consumer product hazard for those under 15 years of age. For those over 15 years of age, bicycles and equipment rank fourth as product related injuries.

The Consumer Product Safety Commission has established 18 consumer product categories in which accidents have been reported related to a product's use. The category in which the greatest number of accidents, requiring hospital emergency room treatment is "Home Structures and Fixtures, and Construction Material." This includes such items as nails, doors, architectural glass, flooring, and so forth. The second category with the most reported accidents is "Sports Ball and Related Equipment" which includes baseball, football, basketball, and others.[1] Table 17–4 lists seven categories and the subcategories with the highest number of accidents.

Established as an independent regulatory agency, the Consumer Product Safety Commission's primary responsibility is to reduce risks of injury associated with consumer products. Specifically, the Commission implements the Consumer Product Safety Act, the Federal Hazardous Substances Act, the Refrigerator Safety Act, the Poison Prevention Packaging Act, and the Flammable Fabrics Act. In this regard, the Commission's goals are:

- To protect the public from unreasonable risks from consumer products.
- To assist consumers to evaluate safety of products.
- To develop standards for consumer products.
- To promote research into causes and prevention of product-related deaths, illnesses and injuries.

BEING ACCIDENT PRONE

Definition

At the beginning of this chapter we stated that several factors appear to be responsible for accidents including the individual's unsafe behavior. However, apparently some people have more accidents than could reasonably be expected. These individuals are said to be *accident prone.* We know, for example, that the majority of motor vehicle accidents are experienced by a minority of drivers. This

Table 17–4: Categories and Subcategories with the Highest Consumer Product Accidents*

Categories and Subcategories	Number of Reported Accidents in Thousands
1. Home structures and fixtures, construction materials	2,098
a. Stairs, ramps, and landings	567
b. Nails, carpet tacks, screws, and thumbtacks	292
2. Miscellaneous	1,578
a. Motor vehicles	419
b. Glass	357
3. Sports ball and related equipment	1,373
a. Baseball	400
b. Football	399
c. Basketball	366
4. Riding or ride-on recreational equipment	770
a. Bicycles	491
b. Skates, skateboards, and scooters	224
5. Other sports and recreational equipment	697
a. Swings, slides, and playground equipment	164
6. Home furnishings	681
a. Nonglass tables	178
b. Chairs, sofas, and sofa beds	154
7. Kitchen appliances and unpowered housewares	604
a. Knives and cutlery	303

*Only seven categories and thirteen subcategories with the greatest number of reported accidents are given.

Source of Data: *U.S. Consumer Product Safety Commission Annual Report, Fiscal Year 1977, Jan. 1978, Washington, pp. 117–121.*

is reflected in automobile insurance premiums by some insurance companies that have "safe driver" clauses. Studies of workers also show that some have more accidents than other workers under the same working conditions. Some employers have used worker's accident records as a reason for dismissal.

Characteristics

Psychologists have long been interested in finding a common personality or other characteristics of the accident prone person. Although no specific personality profile has been developed, certain factors have been identified that suggest a relationship to accidents. For example, there is evidence to indicate that accident prone persons generally have low self-concepts and poor social adjustment. A third factor is preoccupation with the self, especially with personal emotional problems. It has also been suggested that accident proneness may be an unconscious urge for self-punishment, related to guilt feelings from past misdeeds. It is obvious that to effectively prevent accidents, more than improvement in the environment is necessary with the accident prone person. Some form of psychotherapy along with accident prevention education is essential.

425

PREVENTING ACCIDENTS

Causes of Accidents

Before we can effectively prevent accidents, we need to know what causes them and correct these causes. If, for instance, the cause is poorly designed equipment, this must be corrected. The U.S. Consumer Product Safety Commission is constantly inspecting and investigating products to ensure their safety. For example, under the Consumer Product Safety Act, the Commission placed a ban on the use of certain refuse bins. These bins were so designed that they could be tipped over quite easily. The Commission ruled that refuse bins must be able to withstand a horizontal force of 70 pounds and a vertical force of 191 pounds. "Refuse bins which cannot meet the test requirements may not be manufactured for sale, offered for sale, or otherwise distributed in commerce on or after June 13, 1978.[2] Another example is the recall of certain makes of hair driers that contained asbestos which could be a cancer hazard.

If the cause of accidents is a lack of knowledge or training in the use of equipment, the preventive measure is education. This has been conclusively demonstrated in regards to motor vehicle accidents. Those who have completed an adequate driver education program are safer drivers than those who have not. We have also been able to reduce highway accidents by improving highway construction and removing hazardous obstacles and other conditions.

Individual Responsibility

When all factors are considered, the most effective means of reducing accidents is through improved human behavior. Each of us needs to learn how to use products, to read the labels of medicines, household chemicals, and other products. Many accidents occur while the person is under the influence of drugs such as alcohol. Obviously, we should never attempt to operate power equipment under these circumstances. Further, we need to take the responsibility to remove hazardous conditions in and around the home, and the workplace. Accident prevention must be a concern of each of us.

In conclusion, accidents are caused by people in the way they behave and the way they design their products. Accidents can be prevented, or certainly reduced, by improving personal behavior, accepting responsibility for accident prevention, learning how to use products safely, and correcting unsafe conditions. However, accidents do occur, and it is important for us to know what to do in emergency situations.

FIRST-AID

Introduction

It is not possible, nor advisable, to present a detailed description of first aid procedures in a book of this nature. We do suggest that each of you pursue training in first aid from one of the recognized programs offered through some hospitals, voluntary health agencies such as the American National Red Cross, governmental agencies, and medical emergency corps. It is only through one or more of these concentrated training programs that you can become skilled in the numerous first aid procedures. We have, however, presented below some general areas in which you may become involved and general principles of first aid for each. These areas include first aid for asphyxiation and suffocation, controlling bleeding, first aid for fractures, burns, shock, poisoning, and childbirth.

General Principles

In most circumstances of sudden illness or injury, competent assistance is available within a few minutes. Exceptions to this may occur when you are isolated from a community such as when camping. Therefore, the first and most basic principle is to immediately seek help. This can be accomplished by calling your local emergency corps, the state police, sheriff, hospital, or the telephone operator if these other numbers are not readily available. Obviously, it is wise to have all emergency numbers near your telephones.

There are three general goals of first aid:

1. To prevent death of the victim.
2. To prevent further injury.
3. To prevent complications.

Preventing death   In the event of an accident or sudden illness, look first for signs that are threatening the life of the victim. These are stoppage of breathing, severe bleeding, shock, and poisoning. A person can live for only a few minutes without oxygen. If breathing has stopped, artificial resuscitation must begin immediately. If a person is bleeding severely, it must be stopped. Besides the loss of blood, which is life-threatening, bleeding will also contribute to intensifying shock. Poisoning, depending upon its chemical nature, can result in death within a matter of minutes. The poison must be diluted and removed from the body. Do only what you are skilled in doing to prevent the death of the victim.

Preventing further injury   A victim of an accident should not be moved unless it is necessary to prevent death or further injury. For example, a victim of an automobile accident may have to be removed from the car if there is a danger of it catching fire. First aid procedures should be used to prevent any injury from becoming worse. Fractures, for instance, should be splinted.

Preventing complications   Burns and wounds should be protected from infection. Cover with a sterile, dry compress and bandage.

Specific Principles

Asphyxiation   results from the inhalation of a poisonous gas. One of the most common is carbon monoxide. Remove the victim from the gas-filled area to fresh air. If the victim has stopped breathing, artificial resuscitation should be applied.

Suffocation results from a lack of oxygen. It may be caused by a blockage of the windpipe, or pressure on the chest. Remove the cause and give artificial resuscitation. Drowning is essentially a form of suffocation. Give artificial resuscitation. When a person is choking as a result of an object lodged in the windpipe (or throat), perform the Heimlich maneuver or procedure suggested by the American Red Cross. (See Figure 17–1 which illustrates the international choking sign and first aid for choking.)

Bleeding can usually be controlled by applying a compress directly over the wound *and* elevating the part of the body that is involved. Increase the pressure until the bleeding stops. Do not remove the compress even if it becomes saturated with blood. Apply another compress directly over the first. If no compress or other cloth is available, apply pressure with the hand directly on the wound. If bleeding continues, apply pressure on the appropriate pressure point:

Figure 17-1

First Aid for Choking

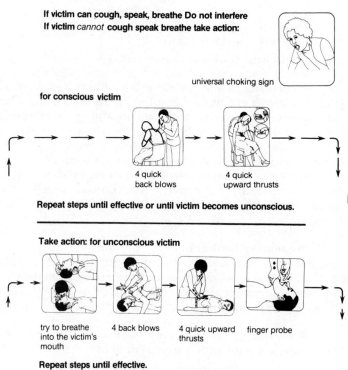

If victim can cough, speak, breathe Do not interfere
If victim *cannot* cough speak breathe take action:

universal choking sign

for conscious victim

4 quick back blows

4 quick upward thrusts

Repeat steps until effective or until victim becomes unconscious.

Take action: for unconscious victim

try to breathe into the victim's mouth

4 back blows

4 quick upward thrusts

finger probe

Repeat steps until effective.
Continue artificial ventilation or CPR, as indicated.

Everyone should learn how to perform the above steps for first aid for choking and how to give mouth-to-mouth and cardiopulmonary resuscitation. Call your local Red Cross chapter for information on these and other first aid techniques.

Caution: Abdominal thrusts may cause injury. Do not *practice* on people.
Source: New York State Department of Health.

carotid artery for head and neck bleeding; brachial artery for arm or hand bleeding; femoral artery for leg or foot bleeding. Use these pressure points in addition to direct pressure and elevation, not as a substitute.

If there is severe bleeding of the arm or leg that cannot be controlled by a compress, the use of a tourniquet may be necessary. *Use caution.* Improper use of a tourniquet can cause further damage. Use it only when other methods to control severe bleeding have failed.

Fractures can be painful and contribute to shock. Do not attempt to grind the bones together to diagnose a fracture. If the victim is conscious and unable to move the part, or is in pain upon attempting to, assume there is a fracture. The best policy is that whenever in doubt, treat as a fracture. *It is not necessary to be sure.* To treat a fracture, immobilize the limb by applying a splint that extends beyond the joints above and below the fracture.

Burns, depending upon the extent and severity, can be painful, contributing to shock, and can easily become infected. For third degree burns, cover with a clean (sterile preferred) *dry* compress or cloth, and treat for shock. For second degree burns, use cold water and cover with a cool compress or cloth. For first degree burns, use cold water or cold compresses.

Shock is a condition that results because the blood tends to "pool" in the blood vessels in the viscera. This deprives the brain of needed blood and oxygen. It is important to keep the victim lying down, maintain body temperature, and give liquids if the person is conscious. *Never try to force liquids into an unconscious or nauseous person.* Handle the person with care, give reassurance, and elevate the feet about 6 inches to help restore circulation to the brain.

Poisoning can present some problems, especially if the nature of the poison (acid or alkali or other) is unknown. The general principle is to dilute the poison with large quantities of water or milk. Vomiting may be induced unless the poison is acid or alkali. Do not attempt to dilute the poison if the person is unconscious. When the nature of the poison is unknown, dilute with water or milk; however, if the person becomes nauseous, stop immediately. Contact your local poison control center as quickly as possible. The specific steps are: (1) dilute; (2) contact the poison control center; (3) follow the directions of the poison control center; (4) save the container from which the poison was taken and save the vomitus.

Childbirth is a natural process. Most babies will be born without complications. Give support to the mother, call an ambulance or emergency squad. If the baby is born before help arrives, place the baby on the mother's abdomen, keep it warm, and keep the mother comfortable. It is not necessary to cut the umbilical cord if help is on the way. Never cut the umbilical cord until the afterbirth (placenta) has been expelled. Keep the afterbirth for the physician's examination.

Cardiopulmonary Resuscitation (CPR)

CPR is a first aid procedure that requires us to be thoroughly trained in its techniques. (See Figure 17–2.) It is usually effective for cardiovascular diseases resulting in a stoppage of heart action and breathing. CPR may have to be employed for long periods of time until medical attention is available; nevertheless, the death rate of cardiac arrest victims is exceedingly high unless hospitaliza-

Figure 17-2

When Breathing Stops

If a Victim Appears to be Unconscious

TAP VICTIM ON THE SHOULDER AND SHOUT, "ARE YOU OKAY?"

If There is No Response

TILT THE VICTIM'S HEAD, CHIN POINTING UP. Place one hand under the victim's neck and gently lift. At the same time, push with the other hand on the victim's forehead. This will move the tongue away from the back of the throat to open the airway. IMMEDIATELY LOOK, LISTEN, AND FEEL FOR AIR.

While maintaining the backward head tilt position, place your cheek and ear close to the victim's mouth and nose. Look for the chest to rise and fall while you listen and feel for the return of air. Check for about 5 seconds.

If the Victim is Not Breathing

GIVE FOUR QUICK BREATHS.

Maintain the backward head tilt, pinch the victim's nose with the hand that is on the victim's forehead to prevent leakage of air, open your mouth wide, take a deep breath, seal your mouth around the victim's mouth, and blow into the victim's mouth with four quick but full breaths just as fast as you can. When blowing, use only enough time between breaths to lift your head slightly for better inhalation. **For an infant**, give gentle puffs and blow through the mouth and nose and do not tilt the head back as far as for an adult.

If you do not get an air exchange when you blow, it may help to reposition the head and try again. AGAIN, LOOK, LISTEN, AND FEEL FOR AIR EXCHANGE.

If There is Still No Breathing

CHANGE RATE TO ONE BREATH EVERY 5 SECONDS **FOR AN ADULT.**
FOR AN INFANT, GIVE ONE GENTLE PUFF EVERY 3 SECONDS.

Mouth-to-Nose Method

The mouth-to-nose method can be used with the sequence described above instead of the mouth-to-mouth method. Maintain the backward head-tilt position with the hand on the victim's forehead. Remove the hand from under the neck and close the victim's mouth. Blow into the victim's nose. Open the victim's mouth for the look, listen, and feel step.

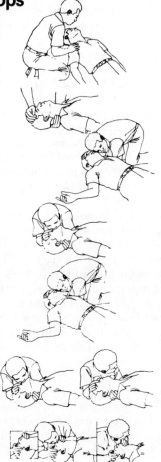

tion occurs within a very few minutes, or support equipment is available and applied. As we have seen, between one-fourth and one-half of all people with coronary attacks die within 24 hours after the appearance of symptoms. There are, however, dramatic cases of people who would not have survived if CPR had not been administered promptly.

CPR is a first aid measure that helps the victim's heart to pump blood to vital organs without adequate internal stimuli. This technique also includes artificial resuscitation which results in oxygen being forced into the lungs by the first aider. These two procedures must be properly coordinated for maximum effectiveness in preventing the death of the victim.

Several organizations have established and conduct programs to train people in CPR procedures. We should not attempt CPR unless we have been properly trained in its intricate techniques. All paramedic personnel who are associated with local emergency corps have undergone intensive CPR training and are usually competent to administer it in emergency situations. If you are concerned, you should contact your American National Red Cross, American Heart Association, American Lung Association, or emergency corps for information about training sessions.

GLOSSARY

Accident: An event that happens by chance, unforseen, or remote causes.

Accident prone: A person who experiences a greater number of accidents than would be expected under the circumstances.

Asphyxiation: Inhalation of a poisonous gas.

First aid: Immediate care given to a victim of accident or sudden illness to prevent death, further injury, or complications.

Injury: Damage to a part of the body; may be accidental or intentional.

Suffocation: Inability to breathe properly causing a lack of oxygen in the blood.

SUMMARY

There are a variety of causes of accidents, some of which could be prevented by improved behavior of people. Accidents are significant because of the large number of people injured, incapacitated, and killed each year. Accidents are the leading cause of death in the United States of people under 45 years of age. Motor vehicle accidents claim more lives each year than any other single accident. This is followed by accidental falls.

To help reduce risk factors associated with consumer products, the Consumer Product Safety Commission was established. This Commission is responsible for enforcing a number of federal laws related to safety of consumer products. Its overall goal is to protect consumers from unreasonable risks from the products they buy.

Some people are accident prone. Psychologists have been able to identify several personality characteristics associated with accident proneness. However, a specific personality profile has not been established.

There are several measures that can be taken to reduce the number of accidents. Prevention of accidents is primarily a personal responsibility, but other factors must also be considered.

Since all accidents and incidences of sudden illness can not be prevented, it is advisable for each person to become familiar with, at least, basic first aid principles. First aid is the immediate and necessary care given the victim of an accident or sudden illness. The goals of first aid are to prevent death, further injury, or complications.

PROBLEMS FOR DISCUSSION

1. List the probable causes of most accidents and describe how these causes can be reduced or eliminated.
2. Why do you think accidents should be considered a major health problem?

3. Analyze the figures associated with accidental deaths for various age groups as presented in Table 17–1. In terms of human productivity, why are these deaths important? Compare with the deaths from cardiovascular disease, cancer, and cerebrovascular accidents. What can you conclude?

4. Describe how the design of consumer products can contribute to accidents. What is being done to help to reduce unsafe consumer products?

5. What is accident proneness? Describe some of the major personality characteristics of one who is accident prone.

6. What can you do to reduce accidents?

7. What are the purposes of first aid?

8. What precautions should you take as a first aider?

REFERENCES

1. *U.S. Consumer Product Safety Commission, Annual Report, Fiscal Year 1977,* The Commission, Washington, Jan., 1978, pp. 117–121.
2. *Ibid.,* p. 18.

index